Sufism and American Literary Masters

SUNY series in Islam

Seyyed Hossein Nasr, editor

Sufism and American Literary Masters

Edited by

Mehdi Aminrazavi

Foreword by
Jacob Needleman

Cover art from Fotolia

Published by State University of New York Press, Albany

© 2014 State University of New York

All rights reserved

Printed in the United States of America

No part of this book may be used or reproduced in any manner whatsoever without written permission. No part of this book may be stored in a retrieval system or transmitted in any form or by any means including electronic, electrostatic, magnetic tape, mechanical, photocopying, recording, or otherwise without the prior permission in writing of the publisher.

For information, contact State University of New York Press, Albany, NY
www.sunypress.edu

Production, Diane Ganeles
Marketing, Michael Campochiaro

Library of Congress Cataloging-in-Publication Data

Sufism and American literary masters / edited by Mehdi Aminrazavi ; foreword by Jacob Needleman.
    pages cm. — (SUNY series in islam)
Includes bibliographical references and index.
   ISBN 978-1-4384-5353-8 (hc : alk. paper) 978-1-4384-5352-1 (pb : alk. paper)
  1. American poetry—Islamic influences. 2. Sufi poetry, American—History and criticism. 3. Sufism in literature. 4. Muslims in literature. 5. Islam in literature.
6. Mysticism in literature. I. Aminrazavi, Mehdi. II. Needleman, Jacob.

PS166.S85 2014
810.9'382974—dc23
                                   2014028931

10 9 8 7 6 5 4 3 2 1

To Mitra, my daughter for her resilience and courage in light of adversity

هر در که زنم ، صاحب آن خانه تویی تو   هر جا که روم ، پرتو کاشانه تویی تو

در میکده و دیر که جانانه تویی تو   مقصود من از کعبه و بتخانه تویی تو

مقصود تویی ، کعبه و بتخانه بهانه

Thou art the dweller of every house on whose door I knock,
Whereever I sojourn, Thou art the Light of the door way.
Be it tavern or monastery, Thou art its soul of souls.
In praying to the Ka'bah or the house of idols, I have Thee in mind,
The purpose is Thou, the Ka'bah and the idol house are but an excuse.

Baha' al-Din 'Amili

Contents

Foreword   xi
   Jacob Needleman

Introduction   1
   Mehdi Aminrazavi

The English Romantic Background

1. English Romantics and Persian Sufi Poets: A Wellspring of Inspiration for American Transcendentalists   15
   Leonard Lewisohn

The Master: Emerson and Sufism

2. The Chronological Development of Emerson's Interest in Persian Mysticism   55
   Mansur Ekhtiyar

3. Ralph Waldo Emerson and the Muslim Orient   75
   Marwan M. Obeidat

4. Emerson and Aspects of Sa'di's Reception in Nineteenth-Century America   91
   Parvin Loloi

5. Emerson on Hafiz and Sa'di: The Narrative of Love and Wine   117
   Farhang Jahanpour

The Disciple: Walt Whitman

6. Whitman and Hafiz: Expressions of Universal Love and Tolerance   153
   Mahnaz Ahmad

7. Walt Whitman and Sufism: Towards *"A Persian Lesson"* 163
   Massud Farzan

The Initiates: Other American Authors

8. Literary "Masters" in the Literature of Thomas Lake Harris, Lawrence Oliphant, and Paschal Beverly Randolph 175
   Arthur Versluis

9. American Transcendentalists' Interpretations of Sufism: Thoreau, Whitman, Longfellow, Lowell, Melville, and Lafcadio Hearn 191
   John D. Yohannan

10. The Persians of Concord 213
    Phillip N. Edmondson

11. Omarian Poets of America 221
    Mehdi Aminrazavi

12. "Bond Slave to FitzGerald's Omar": Mark Twain and *The Rubáiyát* 245
    Alan Gribben

13. *Mark Twain's Ruba'iyyat: AGE–A Rubáiyát* 253

Glossary 263

Bibliography 269

List of Contributors 279

Index 283

Foreword

The essays in this book offer fascinating revelations concerning the correspondences between Islamic mysticism and the work of such quintessentially American writers as Ralph Waldo Emerson, Henry David Thoreau, Walt Whitman, Herman Melville, and Mark Twain. As such, this book is likely to take an important place in the academic fields of American studies and comparative literature. But its significance transcends the limits of academia and touches on the deepest and most troubling questions of our present era. And in so doing, it reminds us of the noble purpose of literature in the development of the mind.

Our world its seems exists mainly under influences that inevitably lead to division and conflict, even as on the surface of events globalization and advancing technology often inspire dreams of a united human family. It has become clear that in our contemporary civilization, despite all hope to the contrary, fear, anger, and avarice, the ancient devils that set human beings against each other, remain the real "lords of life," to appropriate an Emersonian phrase. The essential question, which is now a literal matter of life and death, therefore remains: Where and what are the forces that can lead individuals, peoples, and nations toward an acceptance of each other in fact as well as in dreams, and inspire an awareness of the ultimate oneness and value of life? The themes of the following essays hold fundamental clues to the answer to this question.

Those clues reside in the juxtaposition of the words "Sufism" and the names of some of the most iconic American writers of the nineteenth century. Sufism is generally understood as both a doctrine and practice embedded in the religion of Islam. These essays taken as a whole posit that somewhere behind the historical, geopolitical, and philosophical incommensurabilities that now seem so harshly to separate Islam from the views of mainstream America, there remain significant traces of a philosophical convergence that resonates in some of the most "American" poetry in existence. A study of these traces not only opens a new avenue of mutual understanding between the Islamic and American souls, but will provide a springboard for a deeper understanding of the opportunities that literatures provides as a medium for reconciling seemingly intractable differences.

Ralph Waldo Emerson's 1844 essay "The Over-Soul" remains one of the most eloquent examples of nineteenth-century transcendentalism's explication of Indian spirituality. Of particular influence was the doctrine of Atman, or Higher Self, which forms the essence of the human Self and is inseparable from Brahman, which forms the corresponding essence of the universal Self. Part of Emerson's genius was his ability to reconsider such prototypical American values as the emphasis on pragmatism and individual agency in the light of spiritual, even esoteric reinterpretations of these values. Another case in point is "Self-Reliance" (1841), which opens with a dynamic characterization of the American ideal of individualism and self-determination and closes having reinterpreted such models as mere facets of the Higher Self within.

This kind of work constitutes philosophy, and indeed literature itself, at the height of their power: serving as reminders of humanity's higher identity, which is continually forgotten in the necessary life of action in the world. Through great ideas greatly expressed, literature enables readers to function, and even grow, in a cultural milieu that relies on a worldview and explanatory model that tend to reductionist absolutism, relativism, titillation, and the provocations of subjective morality.

Visionary works of philosophy and literature are among the cultural forces necessary to open our minds to the possibility of transforming human beings, by nature dangerously gifted animals, into instruments of conscience and compassion; yet open-mindedness is not in itself enough, and here the meaning of Sufism can perform an essential task. Sufism is indeed a system of ideas rooted in the great perennial vision of man and reality that lies at the heart of all the world's spiritual traditions, but the contemporary, albeit modest, awakening interest in Sufism is directed mainly to its status as a practice leading to a higher state of Being. In short, Sufism is a Way. What is meant by that term is a guided inner struggle, in which a man or woman strives to emerge from a state of egoism, submitting to a supreme Goodness that is both idea and energy.

When the influence of Indian spiritual tradition was first appearing in nineteenth-century America, any information was almost entirely limited to purely philosophical content, with only fragmentary and speculative practical applications. In general, the discipline, the full practice of the Way, was known haphazardly, if at all. Even Hinduism, which mainly influenced the transcendentalists and contains the idea of the practice of a Way at its heart, was seen as pure philosophy with no central place in the day-to-day lives or writings of the American Transcendentalists.

These days, the popularity of Zen and Tibetan Buddhism, as well as various forms of yoga, indicate that at least certain components of the practice and inner workings of Eastern religions have become a growing influence in America. Without such prevalent practical applications of Eastern spiritual traditions, including Sufism, the quest to reawaken and rediscover the Way within Western religious traditions would be vastly impaired, perhaps to a debilitating extent.

We ask the same questions today that occupied the minds of every nineteenth- and twentieth-century American transcendentalist, including one most relevant to our purposes: Can true literary masterworks reach beyond the worlds of inspiration and ideas to aid in the practical search for finding solutions to the universal problems of the human condition? In the light of the following essays, we may begin to think about the ways in which Sufism illuminated the writings and lives of the most influential American writers of the nineteenth century, and also extrapolate the answers to apply to our lives two centuries later.

Jacob Needleman

Introduction

For centuries, the Western fascination with the East has been the subject of countless books, plays, and movies, particularly after the economic and intellectual effects of colonialism in the early nineteenth century introduced "Oriental" cultures to a sophisticated drawing-room audience. However, Hafiz, Sa'di, Jami, Rumi, and other Sufi masters had a place, however obscure and inaccurately portrayed, in the corpus of English translations long before Oriental themes and settings became a popular characteristic of nineteenth-century poetry. In fact, Sufi poetry was available to a European audience as early as the sixteenth century: the earliest reference to Persian poetry occurred in English in 1589, when George Puttenham included four anonymous "Oriental" poems in translation in *The Arte of English Poesie;* translations of Sa'di's *Gulistan* were available in Latin as early as 1654's *Rosarium,* translated by the Dutch orientalist Georgius Gentius. From the early seventeenth century onward, Western interest in Persian and Sufi poetry steadily increased, though such interest most often took the form of general references to Persian language and culture and not to specific poets and their works. Such references were already a standard component of the medieval travel narrative, and almost always misidentified the names of Iranian and Arab poets, mystics, and philosophers, accompanied by equally creative spelling variations. Moreover, there was no literary value attached to literal translations, and no effort made to replicate the formal elements of the original poems. Instead, Sufi poetry entered Western literary circles as versified adaptations or imitations. Sa'di's *Gulistan,* Hafiz's *Divan,* Omar Khayyam's *Ruba'iyyat,* as well as Firdawsi's monumental work of Persian epic *Shah Nameh,* were all available to English audiences in some form by 1790. With their libertarian sentiments and didactic bent, Sufis appealed to an Enlightenment-era mentality that emphasized deism and an ethical rather than doctrinal conception of religion.

By the end of the seventeenth century, references to individual Sufi poets occurred with greater accuracy and specificity. *The Travels of Sir John Chardin* (1686) in particular was notable for its surprisingly accurate assessment of the basic tenets of Jalal al-Din Rumi's *Mathnawi* and Mahmud Shabistari's *Gulshan-i raz,* including Rumi's proofs of the existence of God *in* man and the emphasis on individual and social tranquility that lay at the heart of Sufism's esoteric teachings. As a result of personal experience with the Sufis of Isfahan and a detailed understanding of the Persian language, Chardin included an unprecedented amount of factual information about Sufism itself, such as an extensive etymology of the term and an explanation of the important differences between Sufism as a mystical order and Sufism as the political basis of the Safavid Dynasty.

Though themes such as the vanity of the world, the analogies between experience in Nature and in love, and the inability of human reason to explain or address the world's mysteries were not unique to Sufism, they found an eloquence of expression in the *ghazals* of Hafiz, for instance, that resonated with the nineteenth-century Western world even in translation. Though its traditional themes and images were often exploited for purely aesthetic purposes, Sufi poetry did in fact have a more significant effect on Romantic and Transcendental poetry than simply providing a storehouse of Oriental imagery. The image of "the East" as a place of great wisdom that possessed an esoteric knowledge lacking in the West gained popularity due to its compatibility with the spirit of Romanticism, which saw the essence of Eastern wisdom in the concept of *carpe diem*. The phrase, meaning "seize the day," was coined by the Roman lyric poet Horace, but emerged as a popular theme in sixteenth- and seventeenth-century love poetry, often as an incitement to a love affair. By the nineteenth century, *carpe diem* had become an axiom as well as a poetic motif, and invoked a sense profound spirituality intertwined with the very notion of daily existence that should not be confused with the present-day, self-serving connotation of the phrase.

What is remarkable is that the spiritual map of "the East" of nineteenth- and early twentieth-century Europe and America had no geographical location, and all Easterners were allegedly conveying the same message—that of living in the present, accompanied by a lack of concern for the material and a focus on goodness, peace, and love. The fact that there is no such thing as a monolithic East and that the Orient consists of diverse cultures was overshadowed by the interest of European and American literary masters and intellectuals in developing a utopian model inspired by the East. This fascination with the stereotypical image of Eastern cultures may have had something to do with the wounds of post-Civil War American society. As the extent of the inhumanity, cruelty, and tragedy of the Civil War was becoming more and more apparent, the perceived Eastern message of the temporality and fleeting nature of life and the idea of existence being closely connected with suffering was indeed therapeutic and soothing to the traumatized American society. Sufi beliefs in their most simplistic interpretations resonated on the level of the national consciousness. "Eastern wisdom," with its perceived message of brotherhood and love, transcended boundaries of education and sophistication. In fact, the spirit of universalism was so strong at the time that Islam itself was of little interest to American scholars; it simply served as the context within which Sufi poetry and prose were composed, not the true source of its message. This, of course, was the case for all Eastern spiritual traditions; the fact that they all were saying the same thing bore testament to the universality of the message and the irrelevance of the particularity of the religious doctrines that distributed them. Thus, the giants of American literature emphasized the intricacies of the message of Sa'di, Hafiz, and other Persian Sufi masters but paid little or no attention to the religious tradition to which they belonged. The search was for that which unifies, and the need to discover the common humanity and decency of man made it necessary to break the barriers that religious traditions had imposed upon society.

Exploring other religious and spiritual traditions therefore became the earliest attempt to establish a dialogue among civilizations and create a global village. The corpus of Sufi poetry available in the 1840s was dramatically increased from that available at the turn of the century, and would only increase further as the century continued. By the end of that decade, Persian Sufi poetry had reached Concord, where the Sufi poets found an audience that appreciated them on philosophical and religious as well as literary levels. As a community of writers and intellectuals, the New England writers drew from the same available sources to produce unique written reactions in the forms of poetry, essays, and letters, all manifesting a similar attraction to the Persian-inspired ideals of Sufism. The spiritual landscape of New England spread throughout the rest of America in the form of inspired movements such as Transcendentalism and Perennialism, which stated that the Muslim Sa'di, the Hindu Rabindranath Tagore, and the other masters of "Eastern" wisdom had access to the same Universal Wisdom as Emerson and Whitman.

Sufism became entrenched in the American literary and spiritual scenes in two ways: the scholarly in the late eighteenth and early nineteenth centuries and the popular in the twentieth century. It seems hardly necessary to mention and nearly impossible to overemphasize the importance of Sir William Jones in transmitting Oriental history and literature to the West over the course of his government service in Bengal and Calcutta (1783–1794). The sheer quantity of information that he communicated back to England and America in the records of the Asiatic Society of Bengal, the journals *Asiatic Researches* and *Asiatic Miscellany*, and in his posthumous collected *Works* is even more impressive with the knowledge that he was simultaneously serving as a puisne judge and diplomat in the service of the East India Company. Jones was well aware of the exhaustion of neo-Classical poetic themes, images, and forms, and he saw in the poetry of Hafiz a possible infusion of new passion and spiritual awareness, provided the lyrics were free from the beleaguered eighteenth-century diction that characterized previous translations of the *Divan*. One of Jones's most famous poetic translations was "A Persian Song," based on Hafiz's eighth *ghazal* and widely circulated in the *Annual Register*, *Gentleman's Magazine*, *Monthly Review*, and *Town and Country* between 1772 and 1786. He was not the only scholar to bring new translations of Sufi poetry to the West; he was, however, the most prolific and most passionate contributor to the corpus of Sufi materials that was available to poets seeking to represent the Orient at the turn of the nineteenth century. The German influence was gradual but immense, most notably the work of famed orientalist Joseph von Hammer-Purgstall. He translated Hafiz's complete *Divan* into German in 1812 and 1813 and sent a copy of these translations to Emerson, who translated them into English (sometimes with such literalness that they maintain the German word order) and distributed them among the Concordians who shared his interest in Sufi poetry.

The first popular American publication to include a poem by Hafiz was *The American Museum or Universal Magazine* in 1792, which printed, uncredited, "Ode Translated from the Persian of Hafez," one of the poems translated by John Nott in 1787. Though it was preceded by the "Tale of Hafez" included in the first volume of the *New York Magazine or Literary Repository* (1790), a story which starred two men named Hafez and Saadi, those characters were not intended to represent the poets of Shiraz; they were simply evidence of the name recognition attributed to symbolic Eastern figures in an imaginative landscape strongly shaped by the *Arabian Nights* and other popular Oriental materials. Additionally, the Oriental Translation Fund, founded in 1828 as an arm of the Royal Asiatic Society of Great Britain and Ireland, supplied scholarly information to American journals such as the *Knickerbocker* and the *American Monthly Magazine*. The society's most valued contributions were translations, though the fund also published memoirs, articles, and other materials of interest to American students of Persian poetry. Limited by different trade routes that bypassed India and the Near East and a complete unfamiliarity with the Persian or Arabic languages, American newspapers printed uncredited or pseudonymous translations, and occasionally complete fabrications, alongside British and French sources such as Sir William Jones and Sir William Ouseley. As in Britain, Hafiz and Sa'di proved to be the two most popular Persian poets, though Edward FitzGerald's 1868 second edition of *The Rubaiyat of Omar Khayyam* inspired the creation of the Omar Khayyam Club of London and America as well as a circle of "Omarian Poets," including Nathan Haskell Dole and Henry Harman Chamberlin. Also as in Britain, the popularity of Persian poetry inspired a wave of imitations produced by less notable poets who did little more than patch together Oriental tropes and Byronic sentiments.

The popular twentieth-century version of Sufism came through such spiritual masters as Inayat Khan, who came to America in the 1930s from India. From the 1930s to 1950, the Muslim immigration from Lebanon, Syria, and later Palestine further strengthened the Sufi presence in America. The spiritual emphasis of the anti-war movement against the Vietnam War created a market for gurus and spiritual masters to come to America; it is during this period that Sufi centers (*zawiyyah* in Arabic and *khanaqah* in Persian) were established in major American cities. In the aftermath of the 1978–79 Iranian revolution, there was a large migration of Iranians to the United States which helped to establish various orders of Persian Sufi tradition. A full survey of the journey of Sufism to America would be a very interesting work, which however goes beyond the scope of this volume.

The political dimension of the response to Eastern philosophy and poetry by the American literary masters of the nineteenth century is also one that must serve as a subject of future inquiry. However, it seems noteworthy that at a time when the spirit of colonialism in Europe and America was heavily characterized by a condescending and even cruel ethnocentrism that declared the "Other" had nothing to offer, distinguished American scholars called attention to the profundity of the spiritual fruits of these civilizations. Perhaps these attempts to revere and respect the wisdom of the so-called inferior races were in part a subtle method of spiritual protest against the colonialists' perspective, comparable to the way in which contrasting the themes of Rumi's poetry of love against Osama Bin Laden's theology of hate toward the West calls to attention the noble aspects of Islam in the present day.

This volume is divided into three parts. Following a chapter on the English Romantics as the background for the American literary master's interest in Sufism, the first section is devoted to a study of different aspects of Ralph Waldo Emerson's relationship with Sufism. The second section explores Walt Whitman's mystical writings and his influences, touching on Emerson and Sufism in the process. Finally, the third section discusses the Sufi influences of other American Transcendentalists, who were also inspired by earlier figures like Emerson.

The first essay, Leonard Lewisohn's "English Romantic and Persian Sufi Poets: The Wellspring of Inspiration for American Transcendentalists," does not concern the Transcendentalists directly, but provides an invaluable introduction to the root themes and images that underlie all poetry written by poets with Neoplatonic influences, including Sufis, Romantics, and Transcendentalists. Like the Romantic poets, the Sufi masters with whom they were acquainted worked with a common set of symbols that Lewisohn describes as "publicly hermetic, so that all writers and readers of Sufi poetry quickly understood its celebrated set of 'esoteric signs.'" Part of the aim of these symbols was to introduce the language of human love and physical experience as a counterpoint to the discursive and abstract language upon which mystical poetry relied to describe otherwise indescribable experiences. Well-suited to Romantic temperaments, Hafiz in particular was unmatched in the Sufi literature for his lyrics on love and wine. Hafiz was particularly revered in India, where Sir William Jones drew most of the material that introduced the West to Eastern culture and literature. Lewisohn traces examples of this and similar themes, including those of mystical death and *carpe diem*, between the works of British Romantic poets Percy

Bysshe Shelley and William Blake, and Sufi poets Rumi and Hafiz, providing insight into the little-explored relationship between Sufism and the Romantic poets as well as establishing the artistic and thematic framework occupied by the Transcendentalists later on in America.

In the first section, Ralph Waldo Emerson is given the title of "Master" for the seriousness of his commitment to Sufi doctrine, and his pervasive influence on so many other writers. These essays illustrate Emerson's conflicted relationship with exoteric Islam, his serious interest in Persian Sufi masters, and his use of the "Orient" as a framework and vocabulary to align himself with the kind of spiritual universe he yearned for all his life. They also emphasize the crucial role he played in publicizing and popularizing Sufi poetry. Emerson did not publish his first volume of verse until he was 43, but between the ages of 40 and 55 he read and was constantly inspired by the work of Sa'di in particular. He even translated over 700 lines of Persian verses, often from the German, in the free versification tradition of the eighteenth century, often adding rhyme and regularizing rhythm in order to achieve a deliberate poetic sensibility. Silently, he sometimes combined fragments of different *ghazals* in passages intended for publication, or his own translations with those of von Hammer-Purgstall.

Mansur Ekhtiyar considers these and other aspects of Emerson's background in his essay "Chronological Development of Emerson's Interest in Persian Mysticism," in which he traces the gradual development of Emerson's interest in Eastern thought in general, and in Islamic and Persian mysticism specifically. Beginning with Emerson's college years, Ekhtiyar unravels how Emerson became interested in Hindu and Zoroastrian thought first, and then, through English and German translations of such Persian Sufi poets as Hafiz and Sa'di, came to develop an intense interest in Islamic mysticism. In his *Works*, the *Essays*, and the *Journals*, Emerson's enthusiasm for the Eastern use of imagery and symbolism is evident, although he consistently struggles with the Islamic sense of fatalism he found in Sufism. Still, the struggle did not prevent him from expounding upon Hafiz's use of "wine" or playing with the notions of solitude and exile.

In the next chapter, Marwan M. Obeidat takes a more analytical approach to the eminent Transcendentalist. Marking Emerson's interest in Oriental thought "as the beginning of interest in comparative religion in America," the author offers an insightful analysis of Emerson's uneasy and conflicted relationship with Islamic mysticism. While Emerson remained intensely interested in Oriental thought to the end, Obeidat shows how the poet's Western mindset still considered the Occidental identity superior; as Emerson himself asserted, "Orientalism is Fatalism, resignation: Occidentalism is Freedom and will." This chapter also suggests that Platonism and Neoplatonism provided a common language with which the American Romantics understood and related to Islamic mysticism.

The following essay, Parvin Loloi's "Emerson and Aspects of Sa'di's Reception in America," primarily concerns the means by which Emerson became acquainted with Sufism and Persian mystical literature, and the poems of Sa'di in particular. Emerson became aware of Sufism when he was only eleven years old, but it was not until he became acquainted with German and French translations that his interest grew and matured into scholarly thought. His preoccupation with these translations both influenced his own transcendentalist sentiments and gave him a preexisting yet flexible linguistic framework to express them. As demonstrated in the autobiographical poem "Saadi" (1842), which Loloi quotes in full, Emerson came to identify Sa'di as the ideal poet, as well as an aspect of himself. In analyzing the poem, Loloi also traces its Romantic elements, including an emphasis on nature and its relation to "divine essence." Loloi affirms the role that Plantonism and Neoplatonism played in interesting the Romantics in Oriental literature. Neoplatonism in particular made it possible for a common discourse and metaphysical language to emerge, as the author explores in the latter part of her essay.

The influence of Hafiz on Emerson is the subject of the next chapter. Farhang Jahanpour's essay, "Emerson on Hafiz and Sa'di: The Narrative of Love and Wine," is divided into four sections. In the first section, Jahanpour traces Emerson's interest in Persian poetry from his exposure as a teenager to the poetry of Sa'di, Hafiz, and Jami, to his more mature encounters with Firdawsi and Sa'di's *Gulistan*. The second section discusses the German translations that served as guides to Hafiz's difficult esoteric language, and quotes passages from Emerson's *Journals* in which he expresses sincere appreciation of Hafiz's poetry. The third section focuses on Emerson's own translations; of the approximately 700 lines of Persian poetry he translated into English, about half of them are from the work of Hafiz. Although Emerson's dedication to the translations is unquestioned, his faithfulness to the originals varies; often, he attempted a literal translation, while other times he mixed poems together or elaborated upon them himself. The article ends with a section that traces the echoes of Hafiz's poems in Emerson's writings, both Oriental and involving other subject matter. This section features some of Emerson's own renditions of Hafiz's poems in English and compares them to the original Persian.

Whitman existed in the same cultural milieu that saw Ralph Waldo Emerson embrace Sufi poetry to justify his own belief in self-reliance by reinterpreting Sa'di's didacticism and libertarian sentiments into a doctrine of democracy and self-equality in Nature. Whitman saw evidence of divinity in the most commonplace people and objects, and celebrated the material world as part of the divine Logos and as proof of the underlying humanity in a nation that was increasingly divided by sectional differences. Like Hafiz, Whitman also accepted the ineffability topos that implicitly accompanied all Sufi mystical poetry. The interpretation of Walt Whitman as a mystical poet gained popularity among scholars in the 1960s. "He is the one mystical writer of any consequence America has produced," Karl Shapiro wrote, "the poet of the greatest achievement."[1]

Eastern mysticism in particular seemed to resonate with Whitman, as V. K. Chari and T. R. Rajasekharaiah have examined at length using Hindu and Buddhist texts. Based on comparisons between poems and the contents of Whitman's unpublished journals and notes, Rajasekharaiah concludes persuasively that the poet was in fact well-read on the subject of Vedantic philosophy by the end of his life, though his understanding of Eastern mysticism was likely more intuitive than academic when the first edition of *Leaves of Grass* was published in 1855.

The next series of essays, grouped under the title "The Disciple: Walt Whitman," is meant to acknowledge the idea that the same connection between poet and philosophy holds true of Whitman and Sufism as well. The traditional starting point from which to test this connection is Ralph Waldo Emerson, the main conduit of Sufi poetry into the Transcendentalist literary community. Whitman was an avid reader of Emerson, and would in all likelihood have read the poem "Saadi" when it was published in 1842. Additionally, the influence of Hafiz is quite clear in Emerson's 1848 poem *Bacchus*, though it is not a direct translation of a Hafiz sonnet. Whitman may also have read the series of "Ethical Scriptures" from the sacred books of the Orient that Emerson and Thoreau published in *The Dial* in 1842 and 1843, or the translations of several fragments of mystical poetry that Emerson provided *The Atlantic Monthly* and *The Liberty Bell* in 1851. Like Emerson, Whitman found his path to Sufism through German translations of Persian poetry, and various Sufi doctrines, such as the annihilation of the Self in God (*fana' fi'llah*), had a deep effect on his life and work. In the first essay of this section, Mahnaz Ahmad, in "Whitman and Hafiz: Expressions of Universal Love and Tolerance," presents a biographical and analytical study and also illustrates Whitman's own concept of love, as depicted in the character of the "graybeard Sufi" in his poem "A Persian Lesson," alongside Ahmad's own exquisite translations of Hafiz's difficult *ghazals*.

Massud Farzan continues the study of Whitman in the essay "Whitman and Sufism: Towards 'A Persian Lesson.'" Farzan compares the mystical experiences Whitman evokes in writings such as "Song of Myself," and "A Persian Lesson" to the Sufi concept of ecstasy, especially as explored in some of Rumi's poetry. Whether it is in Sa'di's *Gulistan* or Rumi's *Mathnavi*, "argument, abstraction, and getting stuck in logistics are anathema to Whitman and Persian poet-mystics alike," Farzan states. The chapter continues with a discussion of Whitman and Sufi concepts of the self, wherein the selfish "I" is juxtaposed with the divine "thou," and concludes with the idea of the mystical death of the self and unity with God.

In the next essay, Arthur Versluis discusses other authors in his "'Islamic' Magic and Mysticism of Thomas Lake Harris, Lawrence Oliphant, and Paschal Beverly." He uses a biographical approach to highlight the similarities between three notable figures involved in both the American Transcendentalist and indigenous esoteric traditions of other religions. Thomas Lake Harris' work reflects aspects of Sufism, even though his direct familiarity with the "Sufi tradition" was nebulous at best. The case of Laurence Oliphant is different, for his travel to the Middle East and Palestine in particular may well have put him in contact with an array of Sufi groups. Oliphant specifically references Druze, whom he calls the "Druse," a splinter Shi'ite group with a strong esoteric orientation. Finally, Versluis compares the experiences of Paschal Beverly Randolph, who also traveled to the Middle East and claimed contact with some of the more esoteric and mystical orders. Versluis questions the legitimacy of some of their teachings, but notes that whether it came in the form of intimate knowledge of esoteric traditions or simply a projection of what they imagined such traditions to entail, the influence of Sufism and its themes on these three figures was considerable.

The next essay, by John D. Yohannan, focuses on a number of specific figures who were primarily disciples of Emerson: Thoreau, Whitman, Longfellow, Lowell, Melville, and Lafcadio Hearn. Each of these figures made a serious literary investment in studying Oriental mysticism, although for some the allure was stronger than for others. Thoreau, for instance, echoed Emerson's identification with Sa'di: "I know, for instance, that Saadi entertained once identically the same thought that I do, and thereafter I can find no essential difference between Saadi and myself. He is not Persian, he is not ancient, he is not strange to me."[2] This more exaggerated assessment stems from Thoreau's limited understanding of Persian poetry. Less well-read than Emerson, he cared about the ideas themselves, not their sources, and it mattered little to him whether the poetry that expressed Sufi wisdom was well-translated or entirely fraudulent. Nor was he above deliberately misinterpreting Sa'di's aphorisms to suit his own philosophical agenda. Yet, however far from traditional Sufi doctrine, the expansive, subjective philosophy of Sufism allowed for such interpretations on his part, as well as on the parts of other Transcendentalists. Yohannon also examines authors of less renown, including Amos Bronson Alcott, whose interest in Eastern wisdom led him to Sa'di and Firdawsi, and William Rounesville Alger, whose anthology *The Poetry of the Orient* (1856) served as an invaluable source of information for Walt Whitman, and which indicates the extent of his fascination with Sa'di, Hafiz, and other Persian Sufi masters. Yohannan also mentions Moncure Daniel Conway, a second-generation Transcendentalist who helped establish a link between the American and English devotees of Persian Literature and was instrumental in drawing attention to Omar Khayyam. The rest of the essay is devoted to Longfellow, Lowell, Melville, and Lafcadio Hearn, and shows their indebtedness to Emerson while quoting specific Sufi texts that helped shape their mystical orientation.

The next essay, Philip N. Edmondson's "The Persians of Concord," examines how the city of Concord became the locus of Transcendentalist writers, attracting literary minds such as Margaret Fuller, Nathaniel Hawthorne, Henry David Thoreau, George William Curtis, and Ralph Waldo Emerson. Edmondson also elaborates on how transcendentalism utilized a similar ideology and set of themes similar to that of Romanticism as a preestablished linguistic framework to communicate Muslim mystical concepts.

In the final essay, Mehdi Aminrazavi traces the impact of Omar Khayyam's *Ruba'iyyat* upon an American audience. Khayyam was a polarizing poet: he was elevated to the level of prophet by some and demoted to that of demon by others. He gained immense popularity among the New England literary circles shortly after the 1859 publication of FitzGerald's exquisite rendition of the *Ruba'iyyat*. The Omar Khayyam Club of America was formed in 1900 as an opportunity for literary figures to celebrate the great Persian sage, and produced a small school of Omarian poets. Even though Omar Khayyam was not a Sufi in the strictest sense of the word, his *Ruba'iyyat* were understood to espouse the same esoteric Eastern wisdom that American audiences perceived in the Sufi mystical poets. Aminrazavi shows the extent of his influence, both among less famous literary figures and more notable authors like Mark Twain, T. S. Eliot, and Ezra Pound.

Mark Twain refers to the "wise old Omar Khayyam" for the first time in 1876, yet his life-long interest in the author of the *Ruba'iyyat* is well-known. Alan Gribben, in his essay "Bond Slave to FitzGerald's Omar: Mark Twain and the Ruba'iyyat," brings to light this little-known influence of Twain's and provides helpful context for understanding the place the *Ruba'iyyat* occupied in Twain's personal and poetic life. The sense of rebellion against the cruelty of life in the *Ruba'iyyat* resonated with Twain in the face of his own hardships. Gribben ends with a selected number of Twain's more burlesque *Ruba'iyyat*, while the complete version of the poems follows in the next chapter.

The original idea for this volume arose from a discussion with colleagues on the lack of a single volume highlighting the reception of Islamic mysticism by the academy, and the difficulty of accounting for increasing interest in Sufism after the turn of the nineteenth century. While there are many books dealing with the current interest in Sufi literature, particularly in the context of such popular authors as Rumi and Hafiz, there is no notable work on the historical background of Sufism's enthusiastic reception by eminent masters of classical American literature. It is hoped that including a variety of essays that bring together figures of the nineteenth- and early twentieth-century American literary scene in a single volume will make this an important contribution to the understanding of the complex web of ideological similarities that existed between Islamic mysticism and American Transcendentalism. Even without Emerson's background in the terminology and available translations of Persian poetry, the often-contradictory themes of mystical ecstasy, Oriental serenity, the divinely intoxicated intellect, and love for the emancipation of Soul—just to name a few of Emerson's favorites—would have appealed to poetic imaginations such as those of Whitman and Thoreau. The use of the language of human love as a cipher for mystical knowledge of the Divine, the revelation of a new moral code as evidence of otherwise ineffable experiences, and the importance of embracing and transcending the physical world all find eloquent expression in the poetry of Emerson, Whitman, and a multitude of other writers, but they attain even greater clarity when compared to similar philosophical concepts illustrated by the Sufi masters.

Today, their interest lives on in the form of continued interest in Sufi poetry and prose, and it is thanks to the works of early masters of American literature that translations of Rumi have remained among the best-selling works of poetry in the last decade in America.

It should be noted that for historical reasons, I have left the transliterations of names and phrases in Persian and Arabic by the nineteenth-century American authors, as they have used them, which are often transliterated incorrectly. I have provided the correct transliterations in the glossary at the end of the volume.

Finally, I would like to express my debt of gratitude to a number of people who assisted me in preparing this volume. I am grateful to Dr. Leonard Lewisohn for his invaluable suggestions regarding the choice of articles and contributors. I would particularly like to thank my research assistant, Annie Kinniburgh, for her thorough reading of this manuscript and extensive editorial suggestions. Her recently completed thesis listed in the Bibliography provided me with new information which I found to be very helpful in recasting of the introduction.

I am grateful to Dr. Robert H. Hirst and the Mark Twain Project at the Bancroft Library of the University of California in Berkeley for granting me the permission to print all of the *Ruba'iyyat* of Mark Twain.

Mehdi Aminrazavi
April 2014

Notes

1. J. E. Miller, K. Shapiro, and B. Slote, *Start With the Sun: Studies in Cosmic Poetry* (Lincoln: University of Nebraska Press, 1960), 58.

2. Henry David Thoreau, *Journal of Henry D. Thoreau*, ed. Bradford Torrey and Francis H. Allen (Boston: Houghton Mifflin, 1949), vol. IV, 48.

The English Romantic Background

English Romantics and Persian Sufi Poets

A Wellspring of Inspiration for American Transcendentalists[1]

Leonard Lewisohn

Platonism in Romantic and Sufi Poetry

Cross-cultural studies focusing on comparative mysticism between Muslim Sufi and Western poets have been seldom made; when made, have seldom been successful.[2] Despite this, homologies both of content and intent in the verse of the classical Persian Sufi poets and the English Metaphysical and later Romantic poets are clearly present insofar as a huge common intellectual ground between both poetic traditions exists. The closest corresponding school of English poetry to Persian Sufi poetic imagery, aside from the Romantics, is that of the Metaphysical—Neoplatonic and Meditative—poets of the seventeenth century such as Donne, Marvell, Herbert, Crashaw, Traherne, and Vaughn.[3] The fraternity of Poetic Genius between the Sufis and Romantics is not only animated by the metaphysics of the Imagination, as Henry Corbin's researches have shown,[4] but grounded in the mutually shared Platonism and Neoplatonism nurturing both poetic traditions, not to mention many similar metaphysical worldviews, cosmogonies, theoerotic, and ethical doctrines which Christianity and Islam hold in common and which transcend their exoteric theological divergences (such as Islam's rejection of the Christian dogmas of the Incarnation, Trinity, and Crucifixion).

Regarding Platonism and Neoplatonism in particular, before attempting any comparison it should be underlined that there is far less known about the literary history of the Platonic tradition in mediæval Islam than there is about it in Christianity. For instance, not one single Persian Sufi poet has ever directly quoted a Platonic dialogue to my knowledge.[5] "It remains difficult to say just how much of Plato, whether in integral translation or in epitomes," F. E. Peters underlines, "the medieval Muslim actually possessed. No Arabic version of a Platonic dialogue has been preserved."[6] This stands in direct contrast to the situation found among the late eighteenth- and early nineteenth-century English Romantics, nearly all of whom were immersed in the actual study of Plato's dialogues and studied him in the original Greek. Almost all of the main English Romantic poets were steeped in Plato, which they read in Greek, and Neoplatonic commentaries on Plato written in Latin.

Percy Bysshe Shelley (1792–1822), for instance, whose rendition of Plato's *Symposium* from Greek to English is a superb work of prose translation,[7] was one of the most erudite scholars of Greek history, literature, and poetry of his day. When translating the *Symposium,* Shelley kept Marsilio Ficino's commentary in Latin on it—probably the most influential work of the Renaissance on romantic and divine love—constantly at his side.[8] For years, Shelley had immersed himself in Thomas Taylor's translations of Plato.[9] As James Notopoulos has exhaustively demonstrated in his monumental work on *The Platonism of Shelley,*[10] Shelley was a *poeta doctus* who knew in depth and detail the precise metaphysical references of his romantic imagery. In addition to his Platonic studies, Shelley was also well versed in Indian, Kabbalistic, and Hermetic works of metaphysical gnosis. More importantly for this essay, he also influenced by Persian Sufi poetry, having composed imitations of some of the *ghazals* of Hafiz.[11] It is thus entirely in order to compare his type of Platonic hermeticism with traditions of Islamic gnosis found in poets of the Persian Sufi tradition.

The same pattern emerges with all the other English Romantic poets. Coleridge as a schoolboy had read the Neoplatonists in the writings of Thomas Taylor the Platonist, the first translator of Plato into the English language during the last two decades of the eighteenth century. In his own writings he frequently cites Plato and Neoplatonic texts in the original Greek.[12] Keats likewise was steeped in Thomas Taylor's translations. William Blake was a personal friend of Thomas Taylor; in fact, he was so intimate with Taylor's translations of Plato that some of the speeches made by the gods in his Prophetic Books paraphrase Taylor's commentary on Plato's dialogues, myths, and symbols exactly.[13] Blake was especially attentive to Taylor's translations of Plotinus's Tractates, which he illustrated in his paintings and verse. The American Transcendentalists, who were largely inspired by Romantic philosophy,[14] were all well-versed in Plato's writings: Thoreau, Emerson, and Whitman knew their *Phaedo, Phaedrus, Republic* and *Symposium,* not to mention Pythagoras, Iamblichus, and Plotinus, quite well.[15]

Of course, it would be a gross simplification of the cultural complexity of the Romantic sensibility to say that the religious and philosophical influences on the Romantics were limited to, or even largely defined by Platonism or Neoplatonism, since the terrain for Romantic poetics was based on a number of other pietistic and theosophical undercurrents of the Enlightenment.[16] Yet the fact remains that, despite the difference in the reception-history of Plato in the Christian West and Muslim Persia (which no one should overlook when attempting a comparative understanding of these civilizations), *Plato's thought and Neoplatonism are the most important part of the mutual philosophical heritage shared by these Christian Romantic and Muslim Persian Sufi poets and mystics.*

Given the temporal span of five centuries separating the classical Persian Sufi poets from the Romantics, the geographical distance that separates Persia from Europe and North America, the varieties and differences in the reception history of Platonism in Islam and Christianity, not to mention theological divergences between the eminent *poeta theologi* in both traditions, it might appear that the pursuit of parallels and convergences between Sufis and Romantics is a kind of quest for the horn of a unicorn. However, this is not the case and there today exists a small but important coterie of authors, such as Luce Lopez-Baralt, Maria Rosa Menocal, Parvin Loloi, and Massud Farzan,[17] who have already charted some of the correspondences that do exist with much success. In their writings the presence of such correspondences, heretofore largely intuitively appreciated, have received solid scholarly substantiation.

Comparative Persian–English Poetics: Archetypal and Anagogic Criticism

Northrop Frye provides us with two important theoretical approaches to comparative literature that offer useful tools to explore and expose the common ground between the two schools of poets separated by so much time and space. He delineates these approaches as comprising, respectively, "archetypal" and "anagogic criticism." "Archetypal criticism" is described as tracing the associative clusters of symbols within a body of literature, in which the critic is essentially concerned with a poem's "relationship to the rest of literature."[18] This type of criticism explores poetry's communicable symbols and conventions in order "to fit poems into the body of poetry as a whole."[19] Archetypal criticism, which involves the "study of literary symbols as parts of a whole,"[20] applied to the study of Persian Sufi poetry, is concerned with, for instance, the elaboration and expression of the technical terms (*istilahat*) of Sufi symbolism in poetry.[21] The Sufi symbolic lexicon was publicly hermetic, so that all writers and readers of Sufi poetry quickly understood its celebrated set of "esoteric signs"—images, metaphors—used by poets, spelled out in detail, for example, in the classical commentaries on Shabistari's *Garden of Mystery* (*Gulshan-i raz*)[22] or in traditional mystical exegeses on the *Divan* of Hafiz.[23] From the standpoint of comparative literature, at this level of criticism it is difficult to make any valid comparisons between Western Romantics and the Sufis since often their respective uses of poetic symbols and signs are quite different. The *topoi* of the cypress and the narcissus, for instance, have entirely opposite symbolic meanings in Persian Sufi and in English Classical and Romantic poetry. However, even on this level one can still find certain archetypal themes that pervade both traditions.

One of the most obvious of these is *carpe diem*. From the perspective of archetypal criticism, *carpe diem* is a common, universal, grand theme that pervades classical English literature as well as ancient Egyptian, Greek (e.g., Aeschylus), Latin (e.g., Horace, Catullus), Renaissance Italian (e.g., Lorenzo de Medici), Sanskrit, and Persian poetry.[24] Indeed, virtually all of the world's literatures contain similar expressions of this timeless idea. Consider, for instance, the sentiment expressed by this quatrain by 'Umar Khayyam (d. c. 1132), quoted here from Fitzgerald's translation—which for once follows the Persian original[25] closely enough to make the comparison valid:

> Ah! Fill the cup: what boots it to repeat
> How time is slipping underneath our feet:
> Unborn Tomorrow, and dead yesterday,
> Why fret about them if today be sweet![26]

Between this quatrain and the following poem attributed to Henry David Thoreau, itself entitled *Carpe Diem,* an exact homology exists:

> Build not on tomorrow
> But seize on today
> From no future borrow
> The present to pay
> The task of the present
> Be sure to fulfil
> If sad or if pleasant
> Be true to it still
> God sendeth us sorrow
> And cloudeth our day
> His sun on it morrow
> Shines bright on our way.[27]

Both Khayyam and Thoreau encourage their readers to cloud not their delight in the present moment with melancholic reveries about the brevity of life. At the same time both poets express in nearly identical terms the same archetypal theme of the perception of the eternal within the transitory.

Another common archetypal theme that the Sufi poets shared with Romantic poets is the ethical teaching that salvation lies in overlooking the faults in one's neighbours and in "seeing no evil," which appears to be held in common both as a tenet of moral philosophy and an insight based on poetic intuition. Blake's view that abstaining from censure of one's neighbours leads to salvation in this verse:

> Mutual forgiveness of each vice
> Such are the Gates of Paradise.[28]

is identical in spirit and substance to Hafiz's doctrine that salvation lies in finding no fault and seeing no evil expressed in his famous verse:

> I said to the master of the tavern: "Which road is
> The road of salvation?" He called for wine and said,
> "Not revealing the faults of other people."[29]

Above and beyond the comparison of such grand archetypal themes, there is another literary approach that Frye calls "anagogic criticism." Viewed from the anagogic perspective, almost all such comparisons now make much better sense because this approach allows us to transcend all civilization-specific and ethnocentric interpretations of literature and discern the "universal symbols" underlying the exoteric literary archetypes. Frye thus explains that "in the anagogic phase, literature imitates the total dream of man, and so imitates the thought of a human mind which is at the circumference and not at the center of its reality. . . . When we pass into anagogy, nature becomes, not the container, but the thing contained, and the archetypal universal symbols, the city, the garden, the quest, the marriage, are no longer the desirable forms that man constructs inside nature, but are themselves the forms of nature."[30] 'Attar understood this well when he sang:

> Both earth and heaven must fit within your own soul
> If on love's path you'd be distinguished and unique.
> 'Attar, could you but free yourself *in toto* from your 'self,'
> All ninefold cobalt vaults of heaven will find place within your soul![31]

Andrew Marvell referred to the same phenomenon when he spoke of

> . . . The mind, that Ocean where each kind
> Does straight its own resemblance find;
> Yet it creates, transcending these,
> Far other worlds, and other seas. . . .

At the anagogic level, the writer becomes a seer who is "caught up into the life of the Universe," as Emerson well understood in his essay on "The

Poet"—"his speech is thunder, his thought is law, and his words are universally intelligible as the plants and animals." Such a poet "has yielded us a new thought ... unlocks our chains, and admits us to a new scene. This emancipation is dear to all men, and the power to impart it, as it must come from greater depth and scope of thought, is a measure of intellect. Therefore all books of imagination endure, all which ascend to that truth, that the writer sees nature beneath him, and uses it as his exponent. ... All the religions of the world are the ejaculations of a few imaginative men."[32] The universe of the anagoge, Frye continues, is not to be "contained within any actual civilization or set of moral values, for the same reason that no structure of imagery can be restricted to one allegorical interpretation. ... The *ethos* of art is no longer a group of characters within a natural setting, but a universal man who is also a divine being, or a divine being conceived in anthropomorphic terms. The form of literature most deeply influenced by the anagogic phase is the scripture or apocalyptic revelation."[33] A good example of the unity of the microcosm and macrocosm within that "universal man," as Frye calls it here, appears in Blake's *Four Zoas*:

... Man looks out in tree & herb & fish & bird & beast
Collecting up the scatter'd portions of his immortal body
Into the Elemental forms of everything that grows.
... In pain he sighs, in pain he labours in his universe
Screaming in birds over the deep, & howling in the wolf
Over the slain, & moaning in the cattle & in the winds ...
And in the cries of birth & in the groans of death his voice
Is heard throughout the Universe: wherever a grass grows
Or a leaf buds, The Eternal Man is seen, is heard, is felt
And all his sorrows, till he resumes his ancient bliss.[34]

Frye's use of word "anagoge" here was derived from the medieval Biblical Christian hermeneutics, according to which there existed a fourfold meaning to Scripture: literal, allegorical, moral, and anagogical.[35] In Islam, a very similar theory, propounding that four levels of meaning existed within the Qur'ān,[36] was advanced; thus Prophet said that "The Koran has an outer sense (*zahiri*), an inner sense (*batini*), a tropological sense (*haddi*), and an anagogic sense (*matla'i*) which itself further extends unto seven, nine and seventy inner senses."[37] Both in medieval Christian poetics,[38] and in classical Sufi poetics, therefore, not only God's word in the revelation of divine scripture, but inspired poetry could be thus read as polysemous works hiding higher parabolic senses.[39] M. D. Chenu, in his *Nature, Man, and Society in the 12th Century*, in describing "The Symbolist Mentality" of Christian Neoplatonism, reveals that: "this upwards reference of things—this *anagoge*—was constituted precisely by their natural dynamism as symbols. The image of the transcendent was not some pleasant addition to their natures; rather, rooted in the 'dissimilar similitudes' of the hierarchical ladder, it was their very reality and reason for being."[40] He notes that the anagogic approach to symbols was "essentially a method of approach to intelligible reality, not an explanation of the world of sense by means of that reality. [It was] an ascent that began from the lowest material level, on which the mind of man found its connatural objects—objects whose value for knowledge, for sacred knowledge, lay not in their coarse material natures but in their symbolic capacity, their 'anagogy.'"[41] Thus Coleridge believed that without "symbolical" perception, one merely lives a world of shadows:

> For all that meets the bodily sense I deem
> Symbolical, one mighty alphabet
> For infant minds; and we in this low world
> Place with our backs to bright Reality
> That we may learn with young unwounded ken
> The substance from the shadow.[42]

This is of course the same thing that Mircea Eliade meant when he noted that for *homo religiosus* all of nature is a cosmic hierophany.[43] Persian Sufi poetics understood the anagogic references of images and metaphors to be of quintessential importance. Interpreting "The Philosophy of Persian Art," Ananda Coomaraswamy reveals how "anagogic values can be read" in all Persian works of art, for "the divine Artist is thought of now as an architect, now as a painter, or potter, or embroiderer; and just as none of His works is meaningless or useless, so no one makes pictures . . . without an intention."[44] This is what Sa'di meant, for example, in the following verse from his *Bustan*:

> That student of weaving spoke well as he wove
> The shapes of the elephant, phoenix, giraffe . . .
> "My own hand it's not that configures these forms,
> Except if the Maker above for me weave them first."[45]

Sa'di here versifies Plato's doctrine enunciated in the *Symposium* and *Phaedrus* that the arts are but phantom reflections and shadows of the Forms of Ideal Beauty and the progeny of Heavenly Love.[46] In his essay, "The Poet," Emerson thus quotes Spenser's famous stanza in *The Faerie Queen* which teaches that the soul makes the body:

> So every spirit, as it is most pure,
> And hath in it the more of heavenly light,

> So it the fairer body doth procure
> To habit in, and it more fairly dight,
> With cheerful grace and amiable sight.
> For, of the soul, and body form doth take,
> For soul is form, and doth the body make.[47]

In *Prometheus Unbound* Shelley too had set this same doctrine to verse:

> And lovely apparitions,—dim at first,
> Then radiant, as the mind arising bright
> From the embrace of beauty (whence the forms
> Of which these are phantoms) casts on them
> The gathered rays which are reality—
> Shall visit us, the progeny immortal
> Of Painting, Sculpture, and rapt Poesy,
> And arts, though unimagined, yet to be . . .[48]

Therefore, on the anagogic level the theological, religious and cultural distinctions that otherwise separate the Persian Sufi from the English Romantic poets evaporate and leave not a rack behind, insofar as literature at this level, to quote Frye again, is viewed as "existing in its own universe, no longer a commentary on life or reality, but containing life and reality in a system of verbal relationships."[49] That is because at this phase, as Frye says, for the poet, "only religion or something as infinite in its range as religion, can possibly form an external goal."[50]

Anagogic Correspondences Between Sufi and Romantic Poetry

At this juncture it will be asked: how exactly "anagogic criticism" may enable us to better grasp the correspondences between Sufi and Romantic poetry? Below, six anagogic themes found in both Sufi and Romantic poetry will be examined—*Carpe diem, Nunc aeternum, Mundus imaginalis,* Annihilation and Mystical Death (*fana'*), the Earthly Mirror of Divine Beauty in the Eternal Feminine, and the Unity of Religions—and an attempt to disclose some of the allusive anagogic correspondences between the two poetic traditions will be made.

Carpe Diem

If from the anagogic perspective we approach now the same theme of *carpe diem* discussed above, we find correspondences that are entirely different from what archetypal criticism had yielded us. Here, the theme of *carpe diem* becomes an expression of the poet's realization of the *nunc aeternum,* which in Sufism is termed "metaphysical time" (*waqt*[51]): the Eternal Now transcending dull, horizontal, serial temporality, beyond our personal obsession with events future or past, living within the presence of "Eternity's sunrise" which sustains "the moment as it flies" as Blake understood. Instead of considering *carpe diem* merely as a universal literary theme, we now contemplate it as expressing an *anagogic truth* about the higher vertical *reality* of the interface of Time with Eternity. Remarkably, we also discover that the Persian Sufi poets' anagogic conception of *carpe diem* is expressed in almost precisely the same way it is by the English Romantics Blake and Shelley, or for that matter, in exactly the same way that Ralph Waldo Emerson's approached the songs of Hafiz which he translated (from the German albeit) in a manner that has been accurately described by one commentator as a "spiritual *carpe diem*."[52] However, it will be impossible to clarify the anagogic sense of *carpe diem* without examining the anagogic reality of the concept itself and entering into the realm of the Eternal Now.

Nunc Aeternum

Several quite clear expressions of the transcendence of serial time in the eternal moment in Persian Sufi poetry can be found in the poetry of Shabistari (d. after 1340) and Hafiz's (d. 1389) *Divan*. In the introduction to his *Garden of Mystery*, Shabistari describes his experience of the "metaphysical moment of time" (*waqt*) as being transported outside of serial time, during which he was able to compose his whole poem in an hour or so:

> So after all their earnest pleas
> that I compose a reply in verse
> I started out with this response.
> With words exact I knit quite terse,
> concise a text. I wrote
> these words in just a moment's space
> among a throng of men all free of ties,
> —I took no pause to think, without
> reflection or any repetition, it all flowed out. . . .[53]

In another of his poems, he clarified the mystical doctrine underlying the moment of poetic inspirations as follows:

> What spiritual vision *(nazar)* senses
> in a breath of mystic consciousness
> no pen can write in the space of fifty years.
> Nor in a moment's span can anyone write
> What treading the way takes years to teach.[54]

In his poem "Milton," William Blake describes in similar terms exactly the same phenomenon of trans-temporal poetic inspiration, where the poet realizes the "eternal now" of "metaphysical time"—

> Every Time less than a pulsation of the artery
> Is equal in its period & value to Six Thousand Years
> For in this Period the Poet's Work is done, and all the Great
> Events of Time start forth & are conceiv'd in such a Period,
> Within a Moment, a Pulsation of the Artery.[55]

Blake penned numerous descriptions of metaphysical time, which he called the moment of inspiration, asserting, for instance, later on in the same poem, that:

> There is a Moment in each Day that Satan cannot find,
> Nor can his Watch Fiend find it; but the Industrious find
> This Moment & it multiply, & when it once is found,
> It renovates every Moment of the Day if rightly placed.[56]

In his poem on erotic mystical love, *Epipsychidion*, which, as Notopoulos states, best manifests "the complex nature of Shelley's Platonism,"[57] the poet recounts how the metaphysical moment, rightly opened and amplified, can fill each day with fresh inspiration:

> Mind from its object differs most in this:
> Evil from good, misery from happiness;
> The baser from the nobler; the impure
> And frail, from what is clear and must endure.
> If you divide suffering and dross, you may
> Diminish till it is consumed away;
> If you divide pleasure and love and thought,
> Each part exceeds the whole; and we know not
> How much, while any yet remains unshared,
> Of pleasure may be gained, of sorrow spared.
> This truth is that deep well, whence sages draw
> The unevied light of hope; the eternal law
> By which those live, to whom this world of life
> Is as a garden ravaged, and whose strife
> Tills for the promise of a later birth
> The wilderness of this Elysian earth.[58]

In these verses the poet had based himself on Proclus's *Elements of Theology*, propositions 26–27 which taught that "in giving rise to the effect the cause remains undiminished and unaltered,"[59] and Diotima's doctrine of love, according to which, as Socrates in the *Symposium* narrates, the vision of supreme intellectual beauty is "eternal, unproduced and indestructible; neither subject to increase nor decay . . . All other things are beautiful through participation of it, with these conditions, that although they are subject to production and decay, it never becomes more or less, or endures any change."[60]

But Shelley's verses also speak of the spiritual elongation of moments of "pleasure and love and thought" by which the quality of the transient and temporal is itself deepened by the "light of hope." Similarly, the Sufis celebrate that spiritual *carpe diem*, which is the knowledge or gnosis of time, called *waqt-shinasi*, as Hafiz expounds in this verse:

> Rise and come! Those cognizant of time, earth and heaven sell
>   freely
> For an idol's company and a cup of drossless wine.[61]

Elsewhere, in his dramatic poem *Hellas,* Shelley gives the following description of the *nunc aeternum,* the Eternal Now which encompasses the past, present and future, as narrated by Ahasuerus, the Wandering Jew (who corresponds to Khiḍr in the Sufi tradition[62]):

> All is contained in each.
> Dodona's forest to an acorn's cup
> Is that which has been or will be, to that
> Which is—the absent to the present, Thought
> Alone, and its quick elements, Will, Passion,
> Reason, Imagination, cannot die;
> They are what that which they regard appears,
> The stuff whence mutability can weave
> All that it has dominion o'er—worlds, worms,
> Empires, and superstitions. What has thought
> To do with time, or place or circumstance?
> Wouldst thou behold the future?—ask and have!
> Knock and it shall be opened—look and lo!
> The coming age is shadowed on the past
> As on a glass.[63]

Shelley's mention of the immortal powers of Imagination leads us directly into the third anagogic theme that the Romantics share alike with the Sufi poets:

Mundus Imaginalis

When Shelley states here that "Will, Passion, Reason, Imagination, cannot die," he refers here to the latent power of these internal faculties and senses to open up, in Blake's words, "the immortal Eyes of Man into the Worlds of Thought, into Eternity Ever Expanding in the Bosom of God, the Human Imagination."[64] This expansion of consciousness occurs because, as Coleridge later explained, Imagination is, in its primary power, "the reflection in the finite mind of the eternal act of creation of the infinite I AM."[65] Sufis refer to this phenomenon of "reflection" of "the finite mind . . . in the infinite" as *tafakkur*: contemplative meditation or visionary reflection.[66] In a verse which sums up Coleridge's sentence in a single epigram, Shabistari thus says,

> Reflection is passing from the false to the Truth
> To behold the Infinite Whole within the finite part.[67]

Imagination is the key word here. "The notion of imagination, magical intermediary between thought and being, incarnation of thought in image and presence of the image in being, is a conception of the utmost importance, which plays a leading role in the philosophy of the Renaissance and which we meet again in the philosophy of Romanticism."[68] As Henry Corbin points out, both in Sufism and in Christian esoteric thought of the Renaissance and the later Romantic period,

> We encounter the idea that the Godhead possesses the power of Imagination, and that by imagining the universe God created it; that he drew the universe from within Himself, from the external virtualities and potencies of His own being; that there exists between the world of pure spirit and the sensible world an intermediate world which is the idea of "Idea Images," as the Sufis put it, the world of "supersensory sensibility," of the subtle magical body, "the world in which spirits are materialized and bodies spiritualized"; that this is the world over which Imagination holds sway; that in it the Imagination produces effects so real that they can "mold" the imagining subject, and that the Imagination "casts" man in the form (the mental body) that he imagined.[69]

For the Sufis[70] as for the Romantics as Rene Wellek pointed out, Imagination was "not merely the power of visualization, somewhere in between sense and reason, as it had been for Aristotle . . . but a creative power by which the mind 'gains insight into reality,' reads nature as a symbol of something behind or within nature."[71] More than this though, "Imagination was the fundamental ground of human knowledge"[72] for all the Romantic poets. For Coleridge and for Shelley in the above-cited verses, as well as for Blake[73]—who spoke of God as being the Poetic Genius,[74] and the "Imagination or the Divine Body in Every

Man"[75]—Imagination is fundamentally identical with the Platonic *nous*[76] and is, as Emerson put it, the "cardinal human power."[77]

Furthermore, according to Blake, Shelley, Coleridge . . . *and* the Sufis, the powers of passion, feeling, reason, and imagination themselves *comprise the quintessence of Being itself,* because *existence itself is thought*. Blake thus proclaimed that "Mental Things are alone Real; what is called Corporeal, Nobody knows of its Dwelling Place, it is a Fallacy, and its Existence an Imposture . . . Vision or Imagination is a representation of what Eternally exists." In other words, everything non-mental is immaterial, a truth which Shelley later has Ahasuerus proclaim in *Hellas:*

> The future and the past are idle shadows
> Of thought's eternal flight—they have no being;
> Nought is but that which feels itself to be.[78]

Blake was a Berkeleyan immaterialist who shared with Shelley and Coleridge the Platonic notion that thought alone has created—and continues to create—the world. "The Universe is the externalisation of the soul," said Emerson. "The earth, and the heavenly bodies, physics, and chemistry, we sensually treat, as if they were self-existent; but these are the retinue of that Being we have."[79] The same idea we encounter in the Persian Sufi tradition. The world is but a single thought generated by the Universal Mind,[80] as Rumi affirms. It is utter ignorance to consider the world to be "real" and our thoughts "unreal," since any grandeur the former may possess ultimately derives from the wonder of the latter.

> If just a single thought comes in your consciousness
> A thousand different worlds fall head over heels.
> The Sultan's bodily form is one in its outer show,
> And yet behind it squadrons and battalions go.
> Yet still that good king's form is but a silhouette
> Which follows the decree of thought unmanifest.
> From just one single thought, a crowd has filled the plain
> Like sluices opened when the floodgates are let drain.
> That thought, the mass of men thinks insignificant,
> But puny thought gushed through the world and ate it.
> And so you see from just one thought, all trades and crafts
> Throughout the world subsist: all residences
> And villages, all manor houses and palaces,
> All hills and peaks and parks and fields, brooks and streams,
> The sun above, this firmament and earth and sea
> Like fish within the sea, by thought all live and breathe.[81]

To sum up, both the Sufi and Romantic poets apprehend and affirm the creative power of Imagination to animate, and Thought to generate, the cosmos. Both have similar anagogic approaches to the metaphysical moment of poetic inspiration. Such ideas are not merely *topoi* and literary themes according to Sufi and Romantic belief but rather a shared symbolic discourse based on an anagogic perspective of the role of the Imagination in human creativity and consciousness that sets into vibration planes of reality and awareness other than that of the sensible world.

Annihilation, Mystical Death, *Fana'*

Mystical death and dissolution of the self is another theme that English Metaphysical and Romantic and Persian Sufi poets share in common. Since this theme is so profoundly native to classical Christian mysticism,[82] it will be helpful to see how it was expressed by more explicitly pietistic poets of seventeenth century before exploring its appearance among the Romantics in the nineteenth century.

The sentiments of the English Metaphysical poets are more often than not completely Sufiesque in their metaphors and imagery. Consider Richard Crashaw's stanza in his poem "The Flaming Heart upon the Book and Picture of the Seraphical Saint Teresa":

> By all of Him we have in Thee
> Leave nothing of my SELF in me.
> Let me so read thy life, that I
> Unto all life of mine may dy.

Likewise, the tone of John Donne's address to God in his Holy Sonnet XIV can be seen as identical to the spiritualized eroticism of the Persian Sufi poets:

> Take mee to you, imprison mee, for I
> Except you'enthrall mee, never shall be free,
> Nor ever chast, except you ravish mee.

Both verses elaborate the idea of self-annihilation in God couched in an erotic imagery wherein God figures as the lover and man the ravished beloved. Both the doctrine and imagery of such verses are startlingly close to the classical Sufi concept of *fana'* as the "annihilation of particular, self-consciousness in the divine, universal consciousness," a doctrine which was elaborated in Islamic lands as an essential element of the mystic experience from the early ninth century onward.[83] Some three hundred years after the death of the Prophet Muhammad, a Persian Sufi by the name of Abu'l-Qasim al-Junayd (d. circa 908), known by the epithet, the "Leader of the Sufis" for his sober intellectual expression of the most subtle of the Sufis' ecstatic experiences, elaborated the various stages of *fana'*, the last of which he described as being "that you cease to be conscious of your ecstatic experience [of God], as a result of an overwhelming vision of God's witness (*shahid*) to you. At this stage you die as well as live, and you live in reality, for you die to yourself and live by God. Your personal characteristics (*rasm*) survive, but your independent identity (*ism*) vanishes."[84]

While in their specifically Christian context such verses function as a kind of poetic commentary on the famous words of the Gospel: "Anyone who wants to be a follower of mine must renounce self; day after day he must take up his cross, and follow me. Whoever wants to save his life will lose it, but whoever loses his life for my sake will save it." (Luke 9:23–4; Matthew 16:24–6), their resonances in Sufi doctrine and poetry are so obvious as to be virtually identical to that of the English poets. Consider the parallels in theme and imagery to the verses from Donne's Sonnet IV cited above in the following two verses from a Sufi poem by Muhammad Shirin Maghribi (d. 808/1410):

> Enravish me, usurp me from me, oh beloved
> in your rapture
> Seize me, seize me, in spirit-filled attraction
> But me, me! there is no other veil like me
> Before me—!
>
> How, how, tell me how
> I can get just one step outside my self
>   and go beyond everything that is 'me' and 'I'
> If and since my very *being* stands in the way
>   roadblocking me.[85]

A similar idea of annihilation and dissolution of the Selfhood appears in all the Romantics. It is probably most clearly expressed in Blake's poem *Milton*, which inculcates the teaching that ego-centrism is itself Death. Annihilation, or as the Sufis call it, *fana'*, on the other hand, is in fact not annihilation at all, but a liberation from the constrictions of the selfhood, expressed as follows in Shabistari's *Garden of Mystery*:

> Go! Take this 'self' which bars the path;
> Each moment engage yourself in Faith anew.
> Inside us all the lower soul's an infidel:
> Rest not content with this Islam of outer form.[86]

And that is also why Blake's Milton, a symbol for the inspired man of Poetic Genius, clearly announces his pursuit of annihilation:

> I will go down to self annihilation and eternal death,
> Lest the Last Judgment come & find me unannihilate
> And I be seiz'd & giv'n into the hands of my own Selfhood.[87]

Through annihilation of self, one attains to what is known as "subsistence-in-God" (*baqa'*) in the lexicon of Persian Sufism,[88] an idea that Blake also enunciates perfectly later on in his poem where he attacks Satan, his symbol for the Infidel Selfhood (in the Sufi lexicon termed *nafs-i kafar*), and has Milton exclaim:

> I come to Self Annihilation.
> Such are the Laws of Eternity, that each shall mutually
> Annihilate himself for others' good, as I for thee.
> Thy purpose & the purpose of thy Priests & of thy Churches
> Is to impress on men the fear of death, to teach'
> Trembling & fear, terror, constriction, abject selfishness.
> Mine is to teach Men to despise death & to go on
> In fearless majesty annihilating Self, laughing to scorn
> Thy Laws & terrors, shaking down thy Synagogues as webs.
> I come to discover before Heav'n & Hell the Self righteousness
> In all its hypocritic turpitude ... to put off
> In Self annihilation all that is not of God alone,
> To put off Self & all I have, ever & ever. Amen.[89]

Similarly, Rumi maintains that the best sort of existence is found only when a man annihilates his "self." Although vis-à-vis the divine Attributes, he writes in the *Mathnawi*, the mystic may seem to be "annihilated," his "annihilation" (*fana'*) is in fact a higher form of 'being-in-God (*baqa'*).[90] "Since by way of Annihilation you have discovered how to survive in life (*in baqaha az fanaha yafti*)," Rumi reproaches the reader, "how is it you turn your back on Annihilation? ... Since the latter is superior to the former—pursue Annihilation, and adore the One-who-changes."[91] Elsewhere, he counsels: "Die, if you would see Him who brings forth Eternal Life bring forth a living person from this mortified person. Become Winter as you would see how Spring is manifest. Be Night if you would behold the advent of Day."[92]

We may compare this advice with the counsel given by Shelley in his ode to his friend Keats, *Adonais*:

> Die!
> If thou wouldst be with that which thou dost seek!
> Follow where all is fled!—Rome's azure sky,
> Flowers, ruins, statues, music, words, are weak
> The glory they transfuse with fitting truth to speak.

> ... 'Tis Adonais calls! Oh, hasten thither,
> No more let Life divide what Death can join together.[93]

Eternal Feminine: Earthly Mirror of Divine Beauty

> O wrangling schooles, that search what fire
>   Shall burn this world, had none the wit
> Unto this knowledge to aspire
>   That this her feaver might be it?
>
>   John Donne (1572–1631)

As Jill Line has demonstrated in her insightful book on Shakespeare, the philosophical doctrine sustaining these verses by John Donne can be traced back to the Neoplatonic erotic theory in Marsilio Ficino's commentary on the *Symposium* of Plato,[94] and in particular to the idea that by medium of earthly forms and terrestrial beauty the soul engages in loving contemplation of the divine beauty of God.[95] This fundamental mystical idea appears in Petrarch's sonnets celebrating Laura, in Dante's *La vita nuova* honoring his love of Beatrice, and again in all the great artists and poets of the Renaissance. Donne's contemporary, Spenser in *The Fairie Queen* (1596) paraphrased this Platonic doctrine of the Beautiful reflected in the fair things of the earth as follows:

> That wondrous pattern, whosoe'er it be
>   Whether in earth laid up in secret store,
> Or else in heaven, that no man may it see
>   With sinful eyes, for fear it to deflower,
>   Is perfect Beauty, which all men adore.
>   Whose face and feature doth so much excel
>   All mortal sense, that none the same may tell.
>
> Thereof as every earthly thing partakes,
>   Or more or less by influence divine
> So it more fair accordingly it makes,
>   And the gross matter of this earthly mine
>   Which encloseth it, thereafter doth refine,
>   Doing away the dross which dims the light
>   Of that fair beam, which therein is empight.[96]

Several decades later, Shakespeare (d. 1616) likewise referred to that same divine Beauty, the heavenly prototype of all earthly beauty,[97] as being an unmoving, unchanging, immutable "substance," expressing exactly the same Platonic doctrine in his Sonnet 53:

> What is the substance, whereof are you made
> That millions of strange shadows on you tend?
> Since everyone hath, every one, one shade,
> And you, but one, can every shadow lend.
> Describe Adonis and the counterfeit
> Is poorly imitated after you;
> On Helen's cheek all art of beauty set,
> And you in Grecian tires are painted new.
> Speak of the spring and foison of the year,
> The one does shadow of your beauty show,
> The other as your bounty doth appear;
> And you in every blessed shape we know.
>   In all external grace you have some part,
>   But you like none, none you, for constant heart.

The same Platonic teaching concerning the reflection of divine beauty in the mirror of the Eternal Feminine found in Donne, Spenser, and Shakespeare also reappears in the nineteenth-century English Romantics and the American Transcendentalists. One of the most beautiful poems ever composed in any language on the manifestation of Divine Beauty in earthly forms—and in this case, the Eternal Feminine—is Shelley's *Epipsychidion*,[98] where the supreme expression of this Platonic doctrine among the English Romantics appears. In the following verses the poet celebrates his ethereal beloved and praises the deathless reflection of the perfect forms of heavenly beauty upon earth in her:

> See where she stands! a mortal shape indued
> With love and life and light and deity,
> And motion that may change but cannot die;
> An image of some bright Eternity;
> A shadow of some golden dream; a Splendour
> Leaving the third sphere pilotless; a tender
> Reflection of the eternal Moon of Love
> Under whose motions life's dull billows move.[99]

Later on in the same poem, delighting in the poetic hyperbole which insists on beholding the divine original perpetually reviving the mortal exemplar, penetrating "into the height of Love's rare universe," he actually refers to the same heavenly "substance," which was the divine source of his longing:

> Our breath shall intermix, our bosoms bound,
> And our veins beat together; and our lips

> With other eloquence than words, eclipse
> The soul that burns between them, and the wells
> Which boil under our being's inmost cells,
> The fountains of our deepest life, shall be
> Confused in Passion's golden purity . . .
> In one another's substance finding food,
> Like flames too pure and light and unimbued
> To nourish their bright lives with baser prey,
> Which point to Heaven and cannot pass away. . . .[100]

Shelley's doctrine here, as Richard White pointed out, is a poetic paraphrase of the speech on love made by the comic poet Aristophanes in Plato's *Symposium*, who speculated to the gathering that the lover might regain his lost original wholeness through merging into the beloved.[101]

The Neoplatonic doctrine that the soul is an emanation of the One[102] expressed in these verses was also enunciated in similar terms in Rumi's *Mathnawi*,[103] in the *Fusus al-hikam* by Ibn 'Arabi,[104] as well as in other works on romantic and divine love by Ibn 'Arabi's later poet-disciples in the Persian Sufi tradition—specifically the *Divine Flashes (Lama'at)* of Fakhr al-Din 'Iraqi and the *Divine Scintillations (Lawayih)* of Jami. Although space does not here permit elaboration in any detail of the intricacies of the Sufi metaphysics of love[105] or the Akbarian doctrines of theophany (*tajalli*) and theomonism (*wahdat al-wujud*) which animate the Sufi poetry of these two great poets, suffice it to say that the Platonic theory underlying Shelley's above verses is quite close to the doctrine in chapter XXIV of the *Divine Flashes* of 'Iraqi. All the lover's attributes in truth belong to the Beloved, 'Iraqi asserts, for the lover "cannot be called a partner, for partnership in attributes would demand two separate essences. But in the lover's contemplative eye there exists in all reality but one single existent Essence."

> A hundred things
> a million or more
> are one.

"Thus all attributes pertain to the Beloved alone, leaving no ontological attribute to the lover."[106]

This is exactly Shelley's doctrine of love as well, where he says in *Epipsychidion*, vv. 573–4:

We shall become the same, we shall be one
Spirit within two frames, oh wherefore two?[107]

After the fashion of some classical Persian Sufi poet, Shelley describes in his poem *Adonais* his vision of the One beyond the temporal realm of generation and decay, seeming to inculcate a kind of Platonic Sufi *tawhid* (the notion of divine unity which is the basis of Islamic faith) in verses which approach the Sufi vision of Unity within multiplicity:

> The One remains, the many change and pass;
> Heaven's light forever shines, Earth's shadows fly;
> Life, like a dome of many-coloured glass,
> Stains the white radiance of Eternity
> Till Death tramples it to fragments.[108]

Exactly the same metaphor of the shadow of earthly beauties acting as prisms mirroring and relaying the reflection of the One's heavenly radiance to the soul appears in Rumi's *Mathnawi*. "That which made you wonder and marvel at the faces of the Fair is the light of the Sun reflected through a glass prism. It is that many-coloured glass which makes that one Light appear as so many hues like this to you. So make yourself fit to gaze on that Light without a glass, lest when the glass is broke, you be left blind."[109] Here, we see the same archetypal poetic topos and anagogic insight shared by the Romantic and Sufi poet alike. Shelley's metaphor of the dome of many-colored light refracting the Light of Eternity had first been coined in these verses by the Sage of Konya it appears. Had Byron perhaps on their sailing trips recited these verses from the Rumi's *Mathnawi* to Shelley? This same kind of anagogic mirror metaphor was utilized by a number of other Persian Sufi poets,[110] and was mentioned repeatedly by 'Iraqi in his *Divine Flashes*. The following passage is typical:

> In each mirror, each moment the Beloved shows a different face, a different shape. Each instant reflections change to suit the mirror, image follows image in harmony with the situation.
>
> > In each mirror, each moment
> >   a new face reveals His beauty
> > Now he is Adam, and now
> >   He appears in the robes of Eve.
>
> Thus, He never twice shows the same face; never in two mirrors does one form appear. Abu Talib al-Makki says, "He never shines through one shape twice nor manifests as one form in two places."
>
> > His loveliness owns
> >   a hundred thousand faces;

> gaze upon a different fair one
>   in every atom;
> for He needs must show
>   to every separate mote
> a different aspect
>   of His Beauty.
> "One" is the fountainhead
>   of all numbers:
> each split second wells up
>   a new perplexity.

Thus it is that every lover gives a different sign of the Beloved and every gnostic a different explanation; every realized one seems to point to something different, yet each of them declares:

> Expressions are many
>   but Thy loveliness is one
> Each of us refers
>   To that single Beauty. (al-Nuri)[111]

And in Jami's mystical epic Joseph and Zulayka (*Yusuf va Zulaykha*), this doctrine is carefully enunciated as well.[112] A few stanzas later on in *Adonais*, Shelley celebrates the divine light and love that fill the universe and is woven through the wool of life, diffusing a fiery glow that illuminates each person according to his or her capacity to receive its light:

> . . . That Light whose smile kindles the Universe,
> That Beauty in which all things work and move,
> That Benediction which the eclipsing Curse
> Of birth can quench not, that sustaining Love
> Which through the web of being blindly wove
> By man and beast and earth and air and sea,
> Burns bright or dim, as each are mirrors of
> The fire for which all thirst.[113]

Shelley's verses here (penned to celebrate his beloved "Emilia as a Platonic theophany on earth . . . the earthly vision of Platonic Beauty, Love, and Immortality"[114]) have many close correspondences in the Persian Sufi poets' erotic theology, where we are told that the divine Beloved created the world like a mirror wherein God's Beauty and Grandeur are reflected and adored.[115] This Sufi view of the cosmic hierophany is based on the common metaphysical symbolism shared by medieval Islamic and Christian thinkers alike, according to which "all things are like so many mirrors," as the late Roman author Macrobius said, "which reflect in their beauty the unique visage of God."[116] In the Persian Sufi tradition, one of most famous verses which describes the reflection of divine beauty in Eternity *a parte ante* (*azal*) which causes "love" (*'ishq*) to appear and "set ablaze" the entire world was composed by Hafiz:

> One day in pre-Eternity a ray of your beauty
> Flashed forth in a blaze of theophany.
> Then Love revealed itself and cast down
> Its fire that razed the earth from toe to crown.[117]

Hafiz speaks here of the "Pre-eternal" role of Beauty which permeates and infiltrates the creation and Love which ultimately consumes it. Inspired by Ibn 'Arabi's theory of divine self-manifestation or theophany (*tajalli*: the same Arabic term used by the poet here), Hafiz describes how God's beauty 'showed itself forth' (that is: theo-phany = *tajalli*) in two distinct manners. Firstly, His Beauty appeared through an essential theophany (*tajalli-yi dhati*) which corresponds to the level of 'the most holy emanation' (*al-fayd al-aqdas*). Secondly, His Love appeared through the "theophany of the divine Attributes" (*tajalli-yi sifati*), which is the level of "the holy emanation" (*al-fayd al-muqaddas*).

All creation thus serves as a mirror reflecting God's Beauty and Love according to Hafiz's metaphysic, appearing through two basic types of "self-manifestation" or theophany (*tajalli*) of the Absolute. During the second theophany, Love emerges from its invisible, purely intelligible condition, appearing in external phenomena, permeating every aspect of existence. Both through the love of human beings for one another (which the Sufis call figurative love: *'ishq-i majazi*), and through that love which human beings have for God (which Sufis call divine love: *'ishq-i haqiqi*), the fire of Love sets everything in the world ablaze.[118] Shakespeare, referring to the "right Promethean fire" of the Eternal Feminine's apparition, espouses this same "doctrine" as follows:—

> From women's eyes this doctrine I derive:
> They sparkle still the right Promethean fire;
> They are the books, the arts, the academes,
> That show, contain, and nourish all the world.[119]

Now, the metaphysical topos of Love's fiery apparition through Beauty in the mirror of the world has a completely Christian (and Islamic) Platonic pedigree. It is clearly enunciated in *The Divine Names* of Pseudo-Dionysius,[120] "a work which describes the universe as an inexhaustible irradiation of beauty, a grandiose expression of the ubiquity of the First Beauty, a dazzling cascade of splendours."[121]

Centuries later it appears in Ficino's commentary on Plato's *Symposium* (which inspired Shakespeare's verse cited above[122]), where we read how "the single face of God shines successively in three mirrors." These "mirrors" are the Angel, the Soul, and the Body of the World. The Angel here corresponds to what Muslim philosophers and Sufis call the First Intellect; the Soul corresponds exactly to the *Anima Mundi* or Universal Soul (*nafs-i kulli*) of Peripatetic thinkers such as Avicenna, a doctrine endorsed by all Sufis and the Illuminationist philosophers (*Ishraqi*) of Islam. The Body of the World is of course the *materia* of the world. "The Angelic Mind," Ficino continues, "sees that face of God imprinted in its own breast. It immediately admires what it has seen. It cleaves passionately to it forever. The grace of that divine face we call beauty. The Angel's passion, clinging inwardly to the face of God, we call Love."

Precisely the same doctrine is also taught by Hafiz here who envisions in his verse the pre-Eternal ray of divine Beauty setting the world ablaze with love. So identical are the Neoplatonic theoerotic doctrines of the Sufis to Renaissance Christian-Platonism that glossing Hafiz's verse by Ficino's exegesis of the *Symposium* works perfectly in this case. Ficino explains that "beauty is a certain lively and spiritual grace infused by the shining ray of God, first in the Angel, and thence in the souls of men, the shapes of bodies, and sounds; a grace which through reason, sight, and hearing moves and delights our souls; in delighting, carries them away, and in carrying them away, inflames them with burning love."[123] This apparition of beauty—first to the Angel and then to men, detailed in depth by Ficino here—is in fact precisely recorded by Hafiz in the next verse in his poem:

Your Face revealed itself. It saw the Angels had
No Love; so then it turned like fire consumed
With jealous rage, and struck the soul of man.

If we now review Shelley's stanza cited above ("That Light . . ."), we see that the light imagery of Shelley and Hafiz both anagogically descry the same reality. That "Light whose smile kindles the Universe," which fills Shelley with such enthusiasm and that generates that "sustaining Love" reflected in the mirrors of "man and beast and earth and air and sea" throughout all levels of the Body of the World, is essentially identical to the pre-Eternal epiphany of beauty envisioned by the Persian Shirazi poet. Furthermore, this is exactly the same metaphysical doctrine that had been taught by Spenser who described how "every earthly thing partakes" of the "influence divine," and so refines the dross of that "gross matter" which had dimmed "the light of that fair beam."

To conclude this study of the anagogic correspondences between Persian Sufi and English Romantic poetry it is fitting that we consider how both Platonic traditions are united by their shared ecumenical approach to religious diversity. Their intellectual fraternity is best reflected in the similarity of their understanding of the topos of the unity of religions.

The Unity of Religions

Arthur McCalla informs us that "Romanticism holds that the essential content of myths and religions is the same everywhere and at all times (that is, the unfolding of Spirit), [so] it follows that differences among them are only superficial and that there is no absolute distinction between Christianity and other religions. . . . Romanticism practices an analogical hermeneutics of myth and religion that discovers an inner unity beneath the surface differences that seem so striking."[124] This ecumenical outlook on the higher unity of religious diversity on the part of Romanticism bears comparison with the traditional Sufi standpoint of the transcendental Unity of Religions (*wahdat al-madhahib*).[125] Consider, for instance, these verses by Shaykh Baha'i (d. 1030/1631), a leading Persian Sufi poet of seventeenth-century Persia and one of the greatest Shi'ite divines and scientists of the entire Safavid epoch:

> I visited the hermitage of pietists and priests;
> I witnessed they all knelt in awe and reverence
> Before her visage there. Since in the winecell of the monk
> And in the chapel of the pietist I was
> At home, it's there I dwell. At times I make my residence
> The mosque, at times the cell: which is to say, it's you
> I seek in every place, both in the tavern and the church.
>
> Whatever door I knock upon, the Lord within
> The house is always you, and every place I go
> The light that shines therein is always you.
> The One beloved in bodega and convent you:
> From Ka'ba or pagoda all my quest and aim
> Again, is you. You, *you*, are what I seek therein:
> The rest—pagoda or the Ka'ba—all is but a ruse.[126]

In these verses Shaykh Baha'i follows a Sufi tradition that can be traced back at least to the thirteenth century, if not earlier, in Persian poetry, which espoused the ecumenical idea that, as one modern commentator on Hafiz's verse has put it: "the relish for the spiritual quest exists in everyone, and all the various religions have the same basic spiritual aim. Moreover, divine Love is not restricted to Sufi mystics alone, for both the mosque and the temple are places of love."[127] The commentator on Hafiz was referring to two different verses where the poet tells us that all the various faiths and sects of mankind comprise multiple expressions of a single Truth:

> Let's forgive the seventy-two sects for their ridiculous
> Wars and misbehaviors.[128] Because they couldn't take in
> The path of truth, they took the road of moonshine.[129]

> Whether we are drunk or sober, each of us is making
> For the street of the Friend. The temple, the synagogue,
> The church and the mosque are all houses of love.[130]

Many of the Romantic poets held similar if not nearly identical views to those of Hafiz. Tennyson, for instance, writing in his poem "Akbar's Dream" (composed not incidentally after reading and translating Hafiz from the original Persian—a passion that he shared with his friend Edward FitzGerald), espoused exactly the same open-minded pluralistic attitude towards religious diversity:

> the never-changing One
> And ever-changing Many, in praise of whom
> The Christian bell, the cry from off the mosque,
> And vaguer voices of Polytheism
> Make but one music, harmonising "Pray."[131]

Aside from being touched by the "Tongue of the Invisible" (Hafiz), Tennyson's views here had also been inspired by the Indian Sufi poets who wrote in Persian at the court of Akbar the Great (ruler of Mughal India, reg. 1542–1605) in praise of religious syncretism. Poets such as 'Urfi, Faydi and Raha'i had all penned verse in praise of a transcendental religious unity, aiming to assimilate, accept and absorb the differing views of Hindus, Muslims, and Zoroastrians. 'Urfi's famous verse sums up the spirit of their ecumenical endeavor:

> The lover's drunk and senseless; he
> Knows neither Islam or infidelity.
> He's like a moth empassioned over fire
> So one appears to him the burning pyre
> Outside the Hindu's pagoda
> Or candle burning in the Ka'ba.[132]

Tennyson's attitude toward religious diversity, obviously influenced by his reading of Persian and Mughal Sufi poetry, are echoed in Byron's comment (jotted down in a footnote to his poem *The Giaour* [l. 734] written in 1813) that "On a still evening, when the Muezzin has a fine voice ... the effect is solemn and beautiful beyond all the bells in Christendom."[133] Byron, like Tennyson, knew Persian poetry quite well.[134] He had read Hafiz and Saʻdi,[135] and was himself adept in the doctrines (and quite probably an initiate of) the Bektashi Order of Sufis in Ottoman Turkey.[136] Blake, it also should be recalled, in 1788, had etched a short tract entitled "All Religions are One," where he preaches that "The Religions of all Nations are derived from each Nation's reception of the Poetic Genius, which is every where call'd the Spirit of Prophecy."[137] This ecumenical outlook on religious diversity amongst the Romantics is ultimately traceable back to the seventeenth-century Cambridge Platonists such as Henry More (1614–80), whose doctrine on this matter was quite close to the seventeenth-century Persian Platonists of the School of Isfahan,[138] as Marshall Hodgson and Corbin have pointed out.[139]

Conclusion: Platonic Poetics and the Science of Anagogic Criticism

From the foregoing, it can be seen the epistemological key to understanding the Platonic poetics of both Persian Sufi and English Romantic poetry is to be found in the science of anagogic criticism. As demonstrated above, if we approach both the English Romantic and the Persian Sufi poetic traditions *anagogically*, contemplating their *topoi,* myths, and symbols as fundamental *expressions of universal symbols,* there appear to be far more parallelisms than divergences of perspectives between poets in both mystical traditions. This is particularly the case if we study the *spiritual* sentiments of Sufis and Romantics. Anagogically speaking, as shown above, they point to essentially the same metaphysical truth and reality, which are expressed poetically in a lexicon which is predominantly Platonic/ Neoplatonic, whatever their exoteric religious persuasions—Christian (Romantic) or Muslim (Sufi)—may be.

To demonstrate this, it may be *helpful,* but not always *necessary* to know how much Persian, for instance, Tennyson knew, or whether Byron and Shelley had actually read Saʻdi and Hafiz. But even without knowing these helpful bio-bibliographical details, I think it may be demonstrated that *anagogically* they were expressing fundamentally similar spiritual visions. Geographically, of course, because "the favourite location of English poetry" that was composed by Romantics such as Shelley, Byron, and Robert Southey, "in the second decade of the nineteenth century becomes the Eastern Mediterranean and the Middle East,"[140] there was a tendency on the part of almost all the Romantics to favour the Muslim Orient and sometimes even to celebrate Islam.[141] Likewise, in terms of literary influence, one also notices that at the end of the eighteenth and beginning of the nineteenth centuries "there came into existence a small but significant body of work translated from Persian,"[142] works which clearly did have an effect on the English and American Romantic movements. Yet even without these literary influences and tendencies, which are significant, it should be reiterated that the anagogic perspective partook of the shared Islamic–Christian Platonic heritage that was quintessentially *both* Romantic *and* Sufi.

Apart from the Platonic and Neo-Platonic heritage, M. H. Abrams has shown in his monumental study of romanticism *Natural Supernaturalism*[143] how deeply the Romantic poets were steeped in Hermetic and esoteric currents of thought. Just as the Romantics shared a fascination with Platonic philosophy and Neoplatonic esoteric doctrines, so the Persian poets were steeped in Sufi mystical doctrine and symbolism; for this reason any comparative study of Romantic and Sufi poetry must take such forms of esoteric speculation seriously, not dismissing it to the realm of the fanciful and fantastic. Unfortunately, the common ground of the esoteric has been all but eradicated from the study of literature by what can only be described as the secular mind's inherent distaste for metaphysical speculation. This is the product of a "subtle, unacknowledged form of agnosticism" that, as Henry Corbin puts it, "consists in raising a frontier between what is commonly known as philosophy and what is known as theology." Although the origins of this frontier are situated remote in time, "it has particularly made itself felt in the countries of so-called Latin civilization . . . where philosophy as such has lost contact with 'the phenomenon of the Holy Book' which, if it makes its presence known, there are philosophers to claim that it is no longer philosophy." But it is only by grace of the *esoteric dimension* that philosophy and theology may operate as a unity. For this reason, as Corbin reminds us,

> There is no such thing as Christian philosophy, or Judaic philosophy or Islamic philosophy. If we trace carefully the origins of this declaration, we collide with the frontier erected between philosophy and theology, and there it can be seen to be a consequence of the refusal of the esoteric, which is nevertheless common to the 'religions of the Book.' It is that esoteric which traditional philosophy and sciences postulate, and which has isolated them from official philosophy and theology to the extent which, in the West, these refuse what remains the axis of oriental thought.[144]

For the purposes of this essay, the most relevant aspect of this secular "refusal of the esoteric" is our dismissal of the role that anagogic criticism must play in comparative literature. The Poetic Genius and Imagination, as understood by both the Romantics and Sufis, has access to an anagogic, parabolic Reality.[145] Once this is admitted, and once the esoteric symbolism and doctrines sustaining that Reality are appreciated and understood, then, whether the poetic expression of that vision be phrased in Latin or Greek, Turkish or Hindi, Arabic or English, Persian or Japanese, becomes almost a secondary consideration. As the Sufi poet Sana'i teaches us:

> When the song you sing is for the sake of Faith,
> Who cares if it is in Syriac or in Hebrew sung?
> When the place you seek is for the sake of Truth,
> What matter if your abode is Jabalqa or Jabalsa?[146]

Notes

1. The article included here was originally entitled "Correspondences between English Romantic and Persian Sufi Poets: an Essay in Anagogic Criticism" and published by the author in *Temenos Academy Review* (12:2009), pp. 189–226.

2. The reason for this is primarily scholars' poor grasp of the nuances of Sufi mysticism and doctrine. For instance, the Syrian-Lebanese poet Adonis attempted to read Rimbaud as "an oriental-Sufi poet" in his *Sufism and Surrealism* (London: Saqi 2005) (p. 194), but because of his unwillingness to seriously engage with the mystical doctrines which the French *voyant* shared with the Sufi visionaries, his comparisons remain provocative at best and unconvincing at worst. His work stands in contrast to Azize Özgüven's "Two Mystic Poets: Yunus Emre and William Blake," in A. Turgut Kut and Günay Kut, *In Memoriam Abdülbaki Gölpinarli*, in *Journal of Turkish Studies*, 20 (1996), pp. 234–47, who provides not only some interesting parallels in their thought, but several deep insights.

3. Cf. Eric Schroeder's remarks in his "Verse Translation and Hafiz," *Journal of Near Eastern Studies*, VII/4 (1948), p. 216 on the similarity of Hafiz and Donne, and the interesting observations between correspondences between European and Persian poets made by Robert Rehder, "Persian Poets and Modern Critics," *Edebiyat*, II/1 (1977), pp. 98–99. However, I do not wish to exaggerate these similarities, but merely to observe there is more room for making comparisons—in respect to rhetorical and poetic devices, poetic forms (e.g., between sonnet and *ghazal*) symbolism, metaphysical and cosmological theory, erotic theology, etc.—between these schools of poetry than there is reason to accentuate their differences.

4. Cf. *Creative Imagination in the Sufism of Ibn 'Arabi* (Princeton, NJ: Princeton University Press 1969), pp. 179ff. and parts 2–3 below.

5. While it is true that "the Arabs observed the passage of philosophy from Hellas to Islam," as F. E. Peters tells us (Peters, "The Origins of Islamic Platonism: the School Tradition," in Parviz Morewedge, ed., *Islamic Philosophical Theology*, [Albany, NY: SUNY 1979]), p. 14), "and carefully recorded its progress," the transmission of the thought of Aristotle in the Islamic world is far more easy to trace than that of Plato. As a consequence, we do not know as much about the transmission of Platonism in Islam as we do about Platonism's transmission in Christianity. There were also many varieties of Platonism and Neoplatonism in Islam—from that of the free-thinker Muhammad ibn Zakariyya al-Razi (d. 925), to the intellectual mysticism of the Isma'ilis, to the ecstatic meditations of the

Sufis, to the Pythagoreanizing Neoplatonism of the Ishraqi thinkers—all of whom in diverse manners, drew on Plato's thought for inspiration, as Peters (ibid.) observes. The contributions to Parviz Morewedge, ed., *Neoplatonism and Islamic Thought* (Albany NY: SUNY 1992) illustrate this diversity of the heritage of Plato in Islam. As Richard Walzer points out, Platonism was nearly always conflated with Neoplatonism in Islam, for "the Plato to whom al-Farabi (with the exception of his theory of the ideal state), Ibn Sina, Ibn Badjdja and Ibn Rushd refer is, whether explicitly or implicitly, always the Plato of Plotinus and his followers." Richard Walzer, "Aflatun," *Encyclopædia of Islam*, 2nd edition, I, p. 234. Having said this, after nearly 200 years of scholarship on Islamic mysticism, there is not even one good study—nay, hardly even one mediocre essay—comparing Sufi theosophy to Platonic/Neoplatonic thought. A good place to begin reading, however, is John Walbridge's *The Wisdom of the Mystic East: Suhrawardi and Platonic Orientalism* (Albany, NY: SUNY 2001).

6. Peters, "The Origins of Islamic Platonism," p. 15.

7. In Richard Holmes, ed., *Shelley on Love: Selected Writings* (London: Flamingo 1996), pp. 97–156,

8. As Richard Holmes in his biographical study of *Shelley: the Pursuit* (London: Flamingo 1995), p. 431, observes. Shelley also translated Plato's *Phaedo, Ion* and several other dialogues.

9. See J. A. Notopoulos, "Shelley and Thomas Taylor," *PMLA*, LI (1936), pp. 502–17.

10. *The Platonism of Shelley: A Study of Platonism and the Poetic Mind* (Durham, NC: Duke University Press 1949). While it is surprising to find Shelley's spiritual teachings based on Plato's writings are still misunderstood by scholars, it is utterly astounding that a learned poet and critic such as T. S. Eliot could accuse him of not having any "metaphysical or philosophical mind," and imagine that his verse was the effusions of a "confused . . . [and] a cloudy Platonist." In his "Keats and Shelley," in *The Use of Poetry and the Use of Criticism* (Cambridge: Harvard University Press 1933, rprt. 1996, 6th printing), p. 81.

11. See F. Jahanpour, "Western Encounters with Persian Sufi Literature," in L. Lewisohn and D. Morgan (eds.) *The Heritage of Sufism: Late Classical Persianate Sufism: the Safavid and Mughal Period* (Oxford: Oneworld 1999), pp. 50–51.

12. Kathleen Raine, "Traditional Symbolism in 'Kubla Khan,'" in idem., *Defending Ancient Springs* (Suffolk: Golgonooza Press 1985), pp. 88–104.

13. Kathleen Raine has shown this in so many of her erudite studies. In particular see her monumental two-volume study of the Platonic sources of Blake's symbolism and terminology: *Blake and Tradition* (Bollingen Series XXXV/11; Princeton: Princeton University Press 1968).

14. American Transcendentalism has been described as an offshoot of Romanticism's basic ideas, comprising "an agreeable summary of the less difficult phases of romantic thought—contempt for the rationalist side of the eighteenth century . . . exaltation of intuition, spirit, sensibility, imagination, faith, the unmeasurable, the wordless." Crane Brinton, "Romanticism," in Donald Borchert (ed.), *Encyclopedia of Philosophy*, 2nd edition (Farmington, MI: Thomson/Gale 2006), VIII, p. 488. Martin Halliwell thus describes transcendentalism as "closely associated with the flowering of American Romanticism in New England in the 1830s and 1840s." "Transcendentalism," in Christopher Murray

(ed.), *Encyclopedia of the Romantic Era, 1760–1850* (New York: Fitzroy Dearborn 2004), II, p. 1149. Ian D. Copestake ("Emerson, Ralph Waldo," Ibid., I, p. 318) described Emerson as "the embodiment of American Romanticism."

15. See Jay Bergman, "Neoplatonism and American Aesthetics," in Aphrodite Alexandrakis and Nicholas Moutakfakis (eds.), *Neoplatonism and Western Aesthetics* (Albany, NY: SUNY 2002), pp. 177–92, who details the influences of, for example, Pythagorus on Thoreau (p. 186) and Thomas Taylor on Emerson (p. 178).

16. Kurt Weinberg, "Romanticism," in Alex Preminger (ed.), *The Princeton Encyclopedia of Poetry and Poetics* (London: Macmillan 1986), p. 720.

17. Luce Lopez-Baralt has mainly concentrated on the influence of Sufism on medieval Spanish Catholic poets such as San Juan de la Cruz, as in her remarkable *San Juan de la Cruz y el Islam* (Mexico City/San Juan: Colegio de México/University of Puerto Rico Press 1985), but has also touched on the influence of Sufism on contemporary Spanish prose literature in her *Islam in Spanish Literature: from the Middle Ages to the Present*, tr. Andrew Hurley (Leiden: Brill 1992). Menocal's *Shards of Love: Exile and the Origins of the Lyric* (Durham, NC: Duke University Press 1994) explores (among other things) the influence of medieval Islamic literature on modern poets such as Ezra Pound and rock musicians such as Eric Clapton. Part 1 of Parvin Loloi's *Hafiz, Master of Persian Poetry: A Critical Bibliography, English Translations Since the Eighteenth Century* (London: I. B. Tauris 2004) provides a good account of the influence of Hafiz on the English Romantics. M. Farzan's many studies of this subject include, among others, his "Whitman and Sufism: Towards 'A Persian Lesson,'" in *American Literature*, 41/1 (1976), pp. 572–82, which is reprinted in the present volume.

18. *Anatomy of Criticism: Four Essays* (Princeton: Princeton University Press 1957), p. 100.

19. *Anatomy of Criticism*, p. 99.

20. *Anatomy of Criticism*, p. 118.

21. The ground-breaking work in this field is Javad Nurbakhsh, *Sufi Symbolism: The Nurbakhsh Encyclopedia of Sufi Terminology*, translated by various authors (London and New York: KNP 1984–2004), 16 vols.

22. See my *Beyond Faith and Infidelity: the Sufi Poetry and Teachings of Mahmud Shabistari* (London: Curzon Press 1995), chap. 6.

23. The vast literature in Persian on this is covered in Leonard Lewisohn (ed.), *Hafiz and the Religion of Love in Classical Persian Poetry* (London: I. B. Tauris 2010).

24. Roger Hornsby, "Carpe Diem," in Alex Preminger (ed.), *The Princeton Handbook of Poetic Terms* (Princeton, NJ: Princeton University Press 1986), p. 28.

25. *Az day kah gudhasht hich az u yad makun. Farda kah nayamada-ast, faryad makun. Bar namada u gudhashta bunyad makun: hali khwush bash u 'umr bar bad makun.*

26. In Edward Fitzgerald (trans.), *Rubáiyát of Omar Khayyám*, edited with an introduction and notes by R. A. Nicholson (London: Adam and Charles Black 1909, reprinted Tehran: British Council 2003, with facing Persian text; introduction in Persian by Husayn Ilahi-Qumsha'i), Quatrain XXXVII.

27. Cited in Husayn Ilahi-Qumsha'i, *Dar qalamru-yi zarrin: 365 ruz-i ba adabiyat-i Inglisi* (Tehran: Sukhan 1386/2007), pp. 163–64.

28. *Blake: Complete Writings,* ed. G. Keynes (London: OUP 1972), p. 761 ("For the Sexes: the Gates of Paradise").

29. *Divan*, ed. Khanlari, ghazal 385: 4. In Robert Bly and Leonard Lewisohn (trans.) *The Angels Knocking on the Tavern Door (Thirty Poems of Hafez)* (New York: Harper Collins 2008). Although Khanlari's *lectio* is *raz* (secret), three of his MSS. read: *'ayb* (fault), which is the reading we follow here (this is also Qazwīnī & Ghanī's *lectio*). As will be seen from the following story, a homily on the evils of fault-finding is the most likely soteriological message the poet meant to convey here. Commenting on this verse, a seventeenth-century commentator on Hafiz relates an interesting tale from a certain "Treatise on the Benefits of Belief" (*Risala-yi fawa'id al-'aqa'id*) about the ascension of the Prophet. "Having returned from the divine Presence, the Prophet found himself standing in the midst of Paradise. He was given a robe of honour to put on. He thought to himself 'How nice it would be if the members of my community might also receive some benefit from this robe as well.' Gabriel at that moment appeared and said, 'Indeed, the members of your community will benefit from this robe of honour but on one condition.' Upon return to his terrestrial abode, the Prophet summoned his elect Companions and related other particulars of his spiritual journey, before concluding with the above account. He commented, 'Now, I wonder if there is any among you who can fulfil that condition so I may give him this robe?' 'Umar, Uthman and Abu Bakr each rose and offered their own views about the meaning of Gabriel's binding condition, yet one by one the Prophet bade them be seated. Finally when it came the turn of 'Ali, the Prophet asked, 'So 'Ali, to fulfill this condition, what would you do?' 'Ali replied, 'I would reveal the upright virtues (*rast*) of God's devotees and conceal their faults.' 'That, indeed, is the condition!' the Prophet said, bestowing upon 'Ali that robe of honour (*khirqah*), which has been passed ever since down to the Sufi masters of the present day. Indeed, being a dervish totally consists in concealing the faults of people." Abu'l-Hasan 'Abd al-Rahman Khatmi Lahuri, *Sharh-i 'irfani-yi ghazalhā-yi-i Hafiz*, edited by Baha' al-Din Khurramshahi, Kurush Mansuri, and Husayn Muti'i-Amin (Tehran: Nashr-i Qatrah 1374 A.Hsh./1995), vol. IV, p. 2563.

30. *Anatomy of Criticism*, p. 119.

31. *Divan-i 'Attar*, ed. T. Tafadduli, 3rd ed. (Tehran: Markaz-i Intisharat-i 'Ilmi va Farhangi 1362 A.Hsh./ 1983), *ghazal* 776, vv. 8, 10. All translations from the Persian are my own below, unless otherwise indicated.

32. *Ralph Waldo Emerson: Essays and Lectures*, ed. Joel Porte (New York: Library of America 1983), p. 463.

33. *Anatomy of Criticism*, p. 120.

34. *Blake: Complete Writings*, ed. G. Keynes, p. 355. Cited by Kathleen Raine, "The Human Face of God," in James Lawrence (ed.), *Testimony to the Invisible: Essays on Swedenborg* (West Chester, PA: Chrysalis Books 1995), p. 72.

35. "The medieval world of allegory was confined to the affairs of the Hebrews. The events recounted in the Bible were ordered as a vast message, expressed through its literal sense but pointing towards a spiritual meaning. The spiritual had various aspects. It was *allegorical* whenever the persons and events of the Old Law prefigured those of the New Law; it was *moral* whenever the actions of Christ indicated how we should live; and it was *anagogical* when it referred to the things of heaven." Umberto Eco, tr. H. Bredin, *The Aesthetics of Thomas Aquinas* (Cambridge, MA: Harvard University Press 1988), p. 151.

36. For an overview of which, see Annebel Keeler, *Sufi Hermeneutics: The Qur'an Commentary of Rashid al-Din Maybudi* (Oxford: OUP 2006), pp. 69–73.

37. John Wansbrough, *Qoranic Studies* (Oxford: OUP 1977), p. 242–3, compares these four hermeneutic degrees in Koran exegesis to the hermeneutics of the Biblical lexicon, drawing equivalences as follows: *zahir* = *historia; batin* = *allegoria; had* = *tropologia; matla'* = *anagoge.*

38. Cf. Eco, *The Aesthetics of Thomas Aquinas,* pp. 160ff.

39. Cf. Bürgel, *The Feather of Simurgh: the "Licit" Magic of the Arts in Medieval Islam* (New York: NYU Press 1988), pp. 59–60; Lewisohn, *Beyond Faith and Infidelity,* chap. 6.

40. *Nature, Man, and Society in the 12th Century,* translated from French by J. Taylor and L. K. Little (University of Chicago Press, 1968), p. 123.

41. *Nature, Man, and Society in the 12th Century,* p. 82. Thus, Emerson states that the inspired poet who understands the "universality of the symbolic language" becomes "apprised of the divineness of this superior use of things, whereby the world is a temple, whose walls are covered with emblems, pictures and commandments of the Deity, in this, that there is no fact in nature which does not carry the whole sense of nature; and the distinctions we make in events, and in affairs, of high and low, honest and base, disappear when nature is used as a symbol." (*Essay and Lectures,* p. 454).

42. From *The Destiny of Nations,* in Ted Hughes, *A Choice of Coleridge's Verse* (London: Faber & Faber 1996), p. 217. For further discussion of this idea, see Elémire Zolla, "The Uses of the Imagination and the Decline of the West," *Sophia Perennis,* I/1 (1975), pp. 33–59.

43. M. Eliade, *The Sacred and the Profane* (New York: Harcourt Brace 1959), p. 12.

44. "Notes on the Philosophy of Persian Art," in Roger Lipsey (ed.), *Coomaraswamy: Selected Papers, Traditional Art and Symbolism* (Princeton, NJ: Princeton University Press 1977), vol. I, pp. 261–62.

45. *Kulliyat-i Sa'di,* ed. Muhammad 'Ali Furughi (Tehran: Amir Kabir 1363 A.Hsh./1984), *Bustan,* ch. V: story 7, pp. 327–28. Cited by Coomaraswamy, ibid., but my own translation.

46. Edith Hamilton & Huntington Cairns (eds.), *Plato: The Collected Dialogues* (Princeton: Princeton University Press 1961), *Symposium,* 209–212 and *Phaedrus,* 250c., pp. 497, 560–63.

47. *Emerson: Essays and Lectures,* pp. 482–83.

48. *Prometheus Unbound,* III.iii, 49–56, in Shelley, *Complete Poems,* p. 192. For an analysis of Neoplatonic philosophy in these verses, see Notopoulos, *The Platonism of Shelley's Poetry,* p. 254–55.

49. *Anatomy of Criticism,* p. 122.

50. *Anatomy of Criticism,* p. 125.

51. On the meaning of this technical term in Sufism see Dr. Javad Nurbakhsh, *Spiritual Poverty in Sufism,* trans. Leonard Lewisohn (London: KNP 1984), ch. 6: "Metaphysical Time," pp. 134–39.

52. George Williamson, "Emerson the Oriental," *University of California Chronicle,* vol. XXX (1928), p. 281; cited by John Yohannan, *The Persian Poet Hafiz in England and America,* MA Thesis, Columbia University (1939), p. 139.

53. *Gulshan-i raz,* in *Majmu'a-yi athar-i Shaykh Mahmud Shabistari,* edited by Samad Muwahhid (Tehran: Kitabkhana-i Tahuri 1986), p. 69, vv. 45–47

54. Ibid., *Sa'adat-namah,* p. 169: vv. 352–53.

55. *Blake: Complete Writings,* ed. G. Keynes, "Milton," 28: 62; 29: 1–3, p. 516. I have previously compared these two passages in my *Beyond Faith and Infidelity*, pp. 22–23.

56. *Blake: Complete Writings*, p. 526; "Milton," 35: 42–45.

57. Notopoulos, *The Platonism of Shelley*, p. 275.

58. Shelley, *Complete Poems*, p. 301.

59. See E. R. Dodds, *Proclus: The Elements of Theology* (Oxford: Clarendon Press 2000, rprt.), p. 214. Cited by Notopoulos, *The Platonism of Shelley*, p. 285.

60. From Shelley's translation of the Symposium (211b), see Holmes, *Shelley on Love*, p. 142; Notopoulos, *The Platonism of Shelley*, p. 285.

61. *Divan*, ed. Khanlari, no. 465: 6.

62. For a deeper comparison between Shelley's Ahasuerus and the Muslim Khidr, see my "From the 'Moses of Reason' to the 'Khidr of the Resurrection': the Oxymoronic Transcendent in Shahrastani's *Majlis-i Maktub . . . dar Khwarazm,*" *Fortresses of the Intellect: Ismaili and other Islamic Studies in Honour of Farhad Daftary,* ed. Omar Ali-de-Unzaga (London: I. B. Tauris and the Institute of Ismaili Studies 2011), Shelley, pp. 407–33.

63. Shelley, *Complete Poems*, Hellas, II: 792–806, p. 334.

64. These are the opening lines of his poem "Jerusalem," in *Blake: Complete Writings,* ed. G. Keynes, p. 623.

65. Coleridge, *Biographia Literaria: or Biographical Sketches of My Literary Life and Opinions,* ed. George Watson (London: Everyman 1975), ch. XIII, p. 167. On this oft-quoted passage, see Anca Vlasopolos, *The Symbolic Method of Coleridge, Baudelaire and Yeats* (Detroit: Wayne State University Press 1983), pp. 37–40. J. Robert Barth in his "Theological Implications of Coleridge's Theory of Imagination," in Christine Gallant (ed.), *Coleridge's Theory of Imagination Today* (New York: AMS Press 1989), p. 5, comments—I believe correctly—that the passage implies that "the imagination is in fact a faculty of the transcendent, capable of perceiving and in some degree articulating transcendent reality—the reality of higher realms of being, including the divine."

66. For a long treatment of *tafakkur* in the Sufi tradition, see my *Beyond Faith*, ch. 7: "The Thought of the Heart."

67. *Beyond Faith*, p. 217.

68. Alexandre Koyré, *Mystiques, Spirituels, Alchimistes due XVIème siècle allemand* (Paris 1955) p. 60, n. 2; cited by Henry Corbin, *Creative Imagination in the Sufism of Ibn 'Arabi*, p. 179.

69. Corbin, *Creative Imagination in the Sufism of Ibn 'Arabi*, p. 182.

70. See W. C. Chittick, "The World of Imagination and Poetic Imagery according to Ibn 'Arabi," *Temenos*, X (1989), pp. 98–119. For a survey of how Corbin's concept of *mundus imaginalis* has been related to Renaissance Romantic poetics, see Marieke J. E. Van den Doel, Wouter J. Hanegraff, "Imagination," in *Dictionary of Gnosis and Western Esotericism*, II, pp. 606–17; and also Tom Cheetham, *The World Turned Inside Out: Henry Corbin and Islamic Mysticism* (Woodstock, CT: Spring Journal Books 2003), ch. 4.

71. René Wellek, "The Concept of 'Romanticism' in Literary History," *Comparative Literature,* I/1 (1949), pp. 1–23, 147–72. Cited by Wouter J. Hanegraaf, "Romanticism and the Esoteric Connection," in Roelof van den Broek and Wouter J. Hanegraaf (eds.), *Gnosis and Hermeticism from Antiquity to Modern Times* (Albany, NY: SUNY 1998), p. 243.

72. Kathleen Raine, *W. B. Yeats and the Learning of Imagination* (Ipswich: Golgonooza Press 1999), p. 23.

73. See Kathleen Raine, *The Human Face of God: William Blake and the Book of Job* (London: Thames and Hudson 21982), p. 14.

74. See Blake's *Marriage of Heaven and Hell*, in *Blake: Complete Writings*, ed. G. Keynes, p. 153.

75. From Blake's Annotations to Berkeley's *Siris*, in *Blake: Complete Writings*, ed. G. Keynes, p. 773.

76. Raine, *The Human Face of God*, p. 14,

77. *The Complete Works of Ralph Waldo Emerson*, ed. E. W. Emerson (Boston: Houghton Mifflin & Co. 1903–12), X, p. 243; cited by Thomas McFarland, "Imagination and Its Cognates: Supplementary Considerations," in Gallant (ed.), *Coleridge's Theory of Imagination Today*, p. 23.

78. Shelley, *Complete Poems*, p. 334 (Hellas, II: 782–84).

79. "The Poet," in *Ralph Waldo Emerson: Essays and Lectures*, p. 453.

80. *The Mathnawí of Jalálu'ddín Rúmí*, translated and edited by R. A. Nicholson (London: E. J. W. Gibb Memorial Trust 1924–40; 2 rprt. Gibb Memorial Series N.S. 1971), II, v. 978.

81. *Mathnawi*, ed. Nicholson, II, vv. 1029–35.

82. E. Underhill's classic study of *Mysticism* analysed this notion in much detail. The Sufi notion of *fana'* seems present in San Juan de la Cruz's exposition of mystical death: see George Tavard, *Poetry and Contemplation in St. John of the Cross* (Athens: Ohio University Press 1988), pp. 203–07.

83. Cf. Qamar-ul Huda, "Reflections on Muslim Ascetics and Mystics: Sufi Theories of Annihilation and Subsistence," in *JUSUR: The UCLA Journal of Middle Eastern Studies*, 12 (1996), pp. 17–35.

84. A. H. Abdel Kader, *The Life, Personality and Writings of al-Junayd* (London 1962), 55. Cited by M. A. H. Ansari, "The Doctrine of One Actor: Junayd's View of *Tawhid*," in *The Muslim World* (1983), p. 45.

85. *A Critical Edition of the Divan of Muhammad Shirin Maghribi*, edited in the original Persian by Leonard Lewisohn with notes and an introduction by Annemarie Schimmel (Tehran: Tehran University Press; London: SOAS Publications 1993), Ghazal CXV. Translation mine.

86. *Gulshan-i raz*, for an analysis of these verses and the doctrine of the infidel selfhood in Sufism, see my *Beyond Faith*, pp. 295–98.

87. *Milton*, I.14: 22–24, in *Blake: Complete Writings*, p. 495. Citing these same verses by Blake in his article on "Intellectual Fraternity," which compared Shakespeare with Indian philosophies, Ananda Coomaraswamy comments that "it is significant that one could not find in Asiatic scripture a more typically Asiatic purpose than is revealed in his [Blake's] passionate will to be delivered from the bondage of division." *The Dance of Shiva* (New York: Sunwise Turn, Inc. 1924), p. 113.

88. For an overview of the concept of *fana'* in Sufism, see Leonard Lewisohn, "In Quest of Annihilation: Imaginalization and Mystical Death in the *Tamhidat* of 'Ayn al-Qudat Hamadani," in L. Lewisohn (ed.) *The Heritage of Sufism*, vol. I: *Classical Persian Sufism from its Origins to Rumi (700–1300)* (Oxford: Oneworld 1999), pp. 284–336. See also G. Böwering, "*Baqa' wa Fana'*," in *Encyclopedia Iranica*, III, pp. 722–24.

89. *Milton*, II.38: 35–42, 48–49, in *Blake: Complete Writings*, p. 530.
90. *Mathnawi*, IV: 398–99.
91. *Mathnawi*, V: 796, 798.
92. *Mathnawi*, V: 551–52.

93. *Adonais*, LII–LIII, in Shelley, *Complete Poems*, p. 316. Tracing the doctrine of this poem back to Plato, Notopoulos paraphrases these lines as follows: "Mortality is simply an illusion like all the phenomena of nature; it is only in death that we really live and the soul finds its true home in the Platonic reality above and beyond the physical world" (*The Platonism of Shelley*, p. 291). He also points out (ibid., p. 301) that these verses are modelled on this passage (68b) in Plato's *Phaedo*: "Surely, there are many who have chosen of their own free will to follow dead lovers and wives and sons to the next world, in the hope of seeing them and meeting there the persons whom they loved. If this is so, will a true lover of wisdom who has firmly grasped this same conviction—that he will never attain to wisdom worthy of the name elsewhere than in the next world—will he be grieved at dying? Will he not be glad to make that journey? We must suppose so, dear boy, that is, if he is a real philosopher, because he will be of firm belief that he will never find wisdom in all its purity in any other place" (trans. from *Plato: The Collected Dialogues*, p. 50).

94. Marsilio Ficino, *Commentary on Plato's* Symposium *on Love*, tr. Sears Jayne (Woodstock, Conn.: Spring Publications 1985), VI.10, pp. 125ff.

95. Jill Line, *Shakespeare and the Fire of Love* (London: Shepheard-Walwyn 2004), pp. 70–71.

96. Cited by Kathleen Raine, *Defending Ancient Springs* (Suffolk: Golgonooza Press 1985), p. 173.

97. This Platonic doctrine in this sonnet is commented on by both Raine and Line (cited in the previous two notes), and also underlined by most scholars of the sonnets: see, e.g., Helen Vendler, *The Art of Shakespeare's Sonnets* (Cambridge: Harvard University Press 1997), p. 258, and Stephen Booth, *Shakespeare's Sonnets: Edited with an Analytic Commentary* (New Haven: Yale University Press 2000), p. 224.

98. In a letter to a friend, Shelley explained the mystical nature of the poem's inspiration as follows: "The *Epipsychidion* is a mystery; as to real flesh and blood, you might as well go to a gin-shop for a leg of mutton, as to expect anything human or earthly from me." Percy Bysshe Shelley, *Complete Poems* (London: Softback Preview 1993), p. 298.

99. In Holmes, ed., *Shelley on Love*, p. 197.

100. In Holmes, ed., *Shelley on Love*, p. 209.

101. Richard White, *Love's Philosophy* (New York: Rowman & Littlefield 2001), p. 56. See also Notopoulos, *The Platonism of Shelley*, p. 288 on these lines.

102. See ibid.

103. *Mathnawi*, V: 372–74.

104. See R. J. W. Austin, "The Sophianic Feminine in the Work of Ibn 'Arabi and Rumi," in L. Lewisohn, ed. *The Heritage of Sufism*, vol. 2: *The Legacy of Mediæval Persian Sufism* (Oxford: Oneworld 1999), pp. 233–45.

105. For an overview of such doctrines of love, see my "Romantic Love in Islam," in *Encyclopædia of Love in World Religions*, ed. Yudit Greenberg (New York: Macmillan Reference & Thomson Gale 2007), vol. II, pp. 513–15.

106. Fakhruddin 'Iraqi, *Divine Flashes*, tr. William Chittick and Peter Wilson (London: SPCK 1982), pp. 118–19.

107. *Epipsychidion*, vv. 573–4.

108. Shelley, *Adonais*, LII, in *Complete Poems*, p. 316; see Notopoulos, *The Platonism of Shelley*, pp. 297–301 for a good study of the Platonic doctrines in these famous lines.

109. *Mathnawi-yi ma'nawi*, V: 988–91.

110. See Akhtar Qamber, "The Mirror Symbol in the Teachings and Writings of Some Sufi Masters," *Temenos*, XI (1990), pp. 163–79; Jacquelyn Bralove, "The Mirror in Sufi Poetry, *Sufi*, 20 (1993), pp. 29–32.

111. 'Iraqi, *Divine Flashes*, trans. Chittick/Wilson, Flash V, pp. 81–82.

112. *Yusuf va Zulaykha*, in Jami, *Mathnawi-yi haft awrang*, ed. A'la khan Afdahrad and Husayn A. Tarbiyat (Tehran: Nashr-i Mirath-i Maktub 1378 A.Hsh./1999), vol. 2, pp. 34–36, particularly vv. 324–337, where he speaks of the pre-Eternal Beauty's reflection in the mirrors of created beings, "for it is Her Beauty that everywhere appears / She's the One behind the veil of everyone beloved" (v. 334).

113. "Adonais," LII, LIV, in Shelley, *Complete Poems*, p. 316.

114. Notopoulos, *The Platonism of Shelley*, p. 281.

115. See A. Schimmel, *A Two-Coloured Brocade: the Imagery of Persian Poetry* (Chapel Hill: University of North Carolina Press 1992), p. 102.

116. *In Somnium Scipionis*, I, 14. Cited by Eco, *The Aesthetics of Thomas Aquinas*, p. 139. On various aspects of the mirror motif in Islamic thought, see J. C. Bürgel, *Feather of Simurgh*, pp. 138–58.

117. *Diwan-i Khwajah Shams al-Din Muhammad Hafiz*, ed. Parviz Natil Khanlari (Tehran: Intisharat-i Khawarazmī 1359 A.Hsh./1980), ghazal 148: 1.

118. My interpretation of Hafiz's verse is based on Baha' al-Din Khurramshahi's commentary on this poem. See his *Hafiz-namah: sharh-i alfaz, i'lam, mafahim-i kilidi va abyat-i dushvar-i Hafiz* (Tehran: Intisharat-i Surush 1372 A.Hsh./1993), I, p. 600.

119. *Love's Labour Lost*, IV.3, 346–49.

120. *Pseudo-Dionysius: the Complete Works*, trans. by Colm Luibheid and Paul Rorem (New York: Paulist Press 1987), 701D–704A, pp. 76–77.

121. Umberto Eco, tr. Hugh Bredin, *Art and Beauty in the Middle Ages* (New Haven: Yale University Press 1986), p. 18.

122. On the Platonic doctrine derived from Ficino in these verses, see Line, op. cit., pp. 1–12.

123. Ficino, *Commentary on Plato's* Symposium *on Love*, V: 6, p. 95.

124. "Romanticism," in Wouter J. Hanegraaff (ed.), *Dictionary of Gnosis and Western Esotericism* (Leiden: Brill 2005), II, pp. 1003–04.

125. Traditionalist approaches to this concept appear in the classic work by F. Schuon, *The Transcendental Unity of Religions* (London: Theosophical Publishing House 1984) and S. H. Nasr, "Principial Knowledge and the Multiplicity of Sacred Forms," in idem., *Knowledge and the Sacred* (Albany, NY: SUNY 1989), pp. 280–308. On the theory of the transcendental unity of religions in Sufism, see my "The Transcendental Unity of Polytheism and Monotheism in the Sufism of Shabistari," in L. Lewisohn (ed.), *The Heritage of Sufism*, II, pp. 379–406.

126. From Baha' al-Din Muhammad al-'Amili, *Kulliyat-i ash'ar va athar-i farsi Shaykh Baha'i*, ed. 'Ali Katibi (Tehran: Nashr-i Chakāma, n.d.), p. 348. Translation mine.

127. Husayn 'Ali Haravi, *Sharh-i ghazalha-yi Hafiz* (Tehran: Nashr-i Naw 1367 A.Hsh./1988), I, p. 365.

128. An allusion to a famous *hadith* of the Prophet: "Verily, after me my community will be subdivided into seventy-three different sects, out of which one will be saved, and the seventy-two others will be in hell."

129. *Diwan-i . . . Hafiz*, ed. Khanlari, *ghazal* 179.

130. *Diwan-i . . . Hafiz*, ed. Khanlari, ghazal 78: 3. Tr. Robert Bly and Leonard Lewisohn.

131. *The Poems of Tennyson*, ed. Christopher Ricks (London: Longmans 1969), pp. 139–43; cited by Parvin Loloi, "Tennyson, Fitzgerald, and Cowell: A Private Relationship with Public Consequences," in Sabine Coelsch-Foisner, Holger Klein (eds.), *Private and Public Voices in Victorian Poetry* (Tübingen: Stauffenburg Verlag 2000), pp. 15–16.

132. Cited by Khaliq Ahmad Nizami, *Akbar and Religion* (Dehli: Idarah-i Adabi-yat-i-Dehli 1989), p. 210. Translation mine. For the original see *Kulliyat-i 'Urfi Shirazi*, ed. Muhammad Vali al-Haqq Ansari (Tehran: Tehran University Press 1378 A.Hsh./1999), vol. 1, p. 116.

133. *Byron's Letters and Journals*, ed. Leslie Marchand (London: John Murray 1973–82), vol. III, p. 199; cited by Mohammed Sharafuddin, *Islam and Romantic Orientalism* (London: I. B. Tauris 1994), p. 237.

134. See Bernard Blackstone, "Byron and Islam: the triple Eros," *Journal of European Studies*, IV (1970), pp. 325–63.

135. H. Javadi, "Persian Literary Influence on English Literature," *Indo-Iranica*, XXVI/1 (1973), p. 22.

136. Blackstone, "Byron and Islam: the triple Eros," p. 350.

137. *Blake: Complete Writings*, p. 98.

138. See L. Lewisohn, "Sufism and the School of Isfahan: *Tasawwuf* and *'Irfan* in Late Safavid Iran ('Abd al-Razzaq Lahiji and Fayd-i Kashani on the Relation of *Tasawwuf, Hikmat* and *'Irfan*,')" in L. Lewisohn and D. Morgan (eds.), *The Heritage of Sufism*, vol. III: *Late Classical Persianate Sufism: the Safavid and Mughal Period* (Oxford: Oneworld 1999), pp. 63–134. Cf. More's defence of "Liberty of Conscience," in David Mullan, ed., *Religious Pluralism in the West* (Oxford: Blackwell 1998), pp. 159–65. The doctrine of the Cambridge Platonists on the subject was latter versified by Alexander Pope (d. 1744) in his *Essay on Man* (IV, 307–09):

> For Modes of Faith, let graceless zealots fight;
> His can't be wrong whose life is in the right:
> In Faith and Hope the world will disagree
> But all Mankind's concern is Charity:
> All must be false that thwart that One great End
> And all of God, that bless Mankind and mend.

139. Hodgson, *The Venture of Islam* (Chicago: University of Chicago Press 1974), III, p. 52.

140. Mariyn Butler, "Romanticism in England," in Roy Porter, Mikulás (eds.), *Romanticism in National Context* (Cambridge: Cambridge University Press 1988), p. 59.

141. See Sharafuddin, *Islam and Romantic Orientalism*, introduction.

142. M.J. Ahmad, *Persian Poetry and the English Reader from the Eighteenth to the Twentieth Century* (M.Litt diss., University of Newcastle 1971), p. 41.

143. *Natural Supernaturalism: Tradition and Revolution in Romantic Literature* (New York: Norton & Co. 1971).

144. H. Corbin, "Traditional Knowledge and Spiritual Renaissance," trans. Kathleen Raine, *Temenos Academy Review*, I (1998), pp. 37–38.

145. An interesting essay which applies Corbin's notion of the Islamic *mundus imaginalis* to English and American literature of the Romantic period is David Mitchell, "Nature as Theophany," *Temenos: A Journal Devoted to the Arts of the Imagination*, VII (1986), pp. 95–114.

146. *Divan-i Hakim Abu'l-Majdud ibn Adam Sana'i Ghaznavi*, ed. Mudarris Radavi (Tehran: Intisharat-i Kitabkhana-i Sana'i 1362 A.Hsh./1983), p. 52. Jabalqa and Jabarsa are cities of the subtle world of the Imagination. Jabalqa is the *mundus archetypus* located to the East, an interworld between the visible and supersensory worlds, containing all the archetypes of the universe. Jabarsa is located in the West, and is the world of Image-exemplars: the interworld in which Spirits dwell after they have left the terrestrial realm. See Henry Corbin (trans. N. Pearson), *Spiritual Body and Celestial Earth: from Mazdean Iran to Shi'ite Iran* (London: I. B. Tauris 1990; reprint of the Princeton University 1976 ed.), pp. 160–61. (Jabalqa corresponds roughly to Blake's Beulah and Jabarsa to his Golgonooza).

The Master:
Emerson and Sufism

2

The Chronological Development of Emerson's Interest in Persian Mysticism[1]

Mansur Ekhtiyar

When Emerson recognized the beauty of Oriental thought, his interest in Persian poetry and Persian mysticism began to develop. For the sake of clarity, the process and the growth of his contact with the Orient in general, and with Persians in particular, are shown chronologically.

In 1820, at the age of seventeen when he was in college, he pointed out, "All tends to the mysterious East . . . from the time of the first dispersion of the human family to the Grecian rise."[2] In the year 1820, however, there seems hardly any influence of the East traceable in his writing, even though there are hints of its mysteriousness, the unknown Oriental thought, in the *Journals* and in the *Letters*.

When Emerson was in college from 1817 to 1821, he expressed an ambition to compose a long masterly poem entitled "Asia"; but he never brought his wish to fulfillment.[3] He always defined Asia as a land of "unity" and Europe as the world of "variety."[4] He even grew to love the Orient so ideally that later he called his wife, Lidian Emerson, "Mine Asia."

Before 1820 only a few general allusions to the East are found in the *Journals*. His first contact with Persian thought was with the *Zend Avesta* in which he retained his interest throughout his life. He consulted different versions of this Zoroastrian Bible in German, French, and English. Perhaps he was anxious to compare some of the *Avesta* scriptures with the original versions in Pahlavi or Avestai, for on two or three occasions he checked out books in ancient Persian from the Boston Athenaeum[5] and studied them for several months.

In October 1820, he recorded in the *Journals*, "I begin to believe in the Indian doctrine of eye fascination."[6] On July 6, 1822, he wrote a soliloquy on God, and at the end of it he quoted Sir William Jones's translation of *Narayena*.[7] From 1822 onward Emerson maintained an interest in this English translator and eminent statesman. He was impressed by Joseph Dennie's assertion in the *Gazette of the United States* (1800), in which he mentioned Sir William Jones, along with Swift, as an Englishman whose literary achievements American scholars would do well to imitate.

In 1823, after reading *Arabian Nights,* Emerson wrote to his Aunt Mary, who shared his interest in the Orient, and referred to Indian thought. A few days earlier he had received a warm letter from her concerning a visit from an Oriental gentleman, who showed her a fine representation of the incarnation of Vishnu, and in a later letter, Mary sent him a few lines of poetry from Sir William Jones's "Hymn to Narayena."[8]

Early in 1823, when he was in his twenties, he addressed a significant letter to his Aunt Mary containing a question which had in it the germ of the Orientalism manifest in all of his most mature thought.[9]

Robert Southey's "The Curse of Kehama" (1810) had an important influence on Emerson during his Harvard years, not so much for the poem itself as for the rich background notes and quotations which Southey placed at the end of the work. It is not surprising that such a harvest of Oriental lore continued to interest Emerson even after his college days. Evidence of this interest may be found in a short story which Emerson composed for his pupils in 1823, based upon extracts from Mark Wilk's *Historical Sketches of the South of India*. Emerson's adaptation, intended for young women, romanticized the original, removed sexual implications, and purged certain details. He clearly read the *Sketches* with care; they should certainly be considered a part of his accumulated knowledge of the Orient. Southey's bibliography, as reconstructed by Kenneth W. Cameron, is beneficial for the traces of Emerson's experience of the East.[10] Arthur Christy reaffirms that the sacred books of the Orient, including those of the Persians, were sources of influence that shaped Emerson's understanding of the East.[11]

Late in 1823, Emerson contrasted Sir Isaac Newton, as representative of the Occident, and Juggernaut, as symbolic of the East, in favor of the former, stating that the admiration of a few observers to the intellectual supremacy of one page will hardly be counted, in the eye of the philanthropists, as an atonement for the squalid and desperate ignorance of untold millions who breathe the breath of misery in Asia, in Africa, and all over the globe. Emerson, in fact, did not study much about the Orient in 1823, but he resumed his investigation in the following year.

Early in 1824, he pointed out that he was eager not to live in isolation, or to be "contemptible in a corner."[12] In this light he composed his "Asia," in which he expressed the view that "Asia is not dead, but sleepeth."

Asia

Sleep on, ye drowsy tribes whose old repose
The roaring oceans of the East enclose;

Old Asia, nurse of man, and bower of gods,
The dragon Tyranny with crown and ball
Chants to thy dreams his ancient lullaby.[13]

At the same time Emerson speaks of the contrast of the modern noisy world with Asia's peaceful solitude. He addresses Americans, saying that Europe is their father and "they should bear him on their Atlantean shoulders, but Asia is thy grand desire and should give him his freedom."[14]

In 1829, he read Marie Josef de Gernado's *Histoire Comparée des systèmes de philosophie*, and he acquired a taste for the *Bhagavat* from Victor Cousin's *Cours de philosophie*. Emerson read these books because he was interested in having a clear idea concerning the Oriental approach to the "Over-Soul," "Fate," and the concept of "Free-will."

Late in 1830 he read Gernado's publication again; it was there that he had been introduced to the philosophy of the various schools of thought in India and ancient Persia. Through these works Gernado compiled, Emerson entered the path that led him to the springs of the religion and philosophy in the Orient.[15] From the four volumes of Gernado, he extracted enough material to fill fifteen pages of the *Journals*.[16]

In 1831, he was impressed with the philosophy of Plotinus and by its effects on Oriental thought. While Plotinus's work is covered in his reading list for that year, he probably read some of Plotinus's ideas in Gernado. Emerson's interest in Plotinus arose when he discovered the close kinship between Neoplatonism and Oriental thought. 1831 was, in fact, the year in which he seriously began the study of Neoplatonic philosophy, and his interest in Zoroastrianism, which had already started during his college days, developed in a parallel manner. On April 17, 1832 Emerson wrote about "Persian Scriptures." He asserts that "a strong poem is Zoroastrianism."[17]

The parallelism of Emerson's study and his interest in Neoplatonism and Orientalism are significant and quite easily traceable. Late in 1832, Emerson asserted that Plato's forms or ideas seem almost tantamount to the "Fravashi" of Zoroaster, which are the symbols of good action, good thought, and good words. Then he added that of all the "Ferours" of beings that should exist in the world, the most precious in the eyes of Ormuzd (Ahura Mazda), were that of Law, that of Iran, and that of Zoroaster. In the journal entry for July (1832), he quoted a passage from *Academie des Inscriptions*:[18]

> "Fire," the sun of Ormuzd, was also created. He represented, though imperfectly, the original "fire" which animates all beings, forms the relations which exist between them and which in the beginning was a principle of union between Ormuzd and time.

In 1832 Emerson composed a scholarly article concerning the character of Zartosht, or Zoroaster, whom he praised highly in his *Journals* on various occasions when he happened to mention Oriental men of character.

In 1834, he listed the Chinese *Sheking* in his reading list and he spoke of the *Vedas* in his *Journals*. Late in 1836, he studied *The Code of Manu*[19] and an account of the extracts from Confucius. He had already read *Arabian Proverbs* late in 1834; but he studied it again in 1836.

In 1836, Emerson also studied Hindu philosophy from different sources.[20] The *Avesta* (*Zend-Avesta de Zoroaster*) was perhaps one of the earliest books of Oriental philosophy he studied; the *Manu* was the second, and it was from this text that he quoted a passage for the motto of the first edition of *Nature*.

Early in 1837, Emerson read a steadily increasing number of Oriental books: *Chalidasa*, the *Code of Manu*, Zoroaster's *Zend-Avesta*, the sayings of the Buddha, the *Vedas*, the *Koran*, and the *Vishu Sarna*.[21] Emerson read some of the Persian *Divans* (anthologies) in German and some Persian poems in English in *The Asiatic Journal*, but he did not mention them in his reading list for 1837.

From 1839 to 1840 Emerson read more Neoplatonism than Oriental thought. The idea of "transmigration of souls" so impressed him that he reflected on it in his essay *History*.[22] However, in his *Journals* he spoke of his appreciation of the Buddhists' understanding of laws of friendship. While Emerson was discussing friendship, he mentioned the laws of hospitality among Buddhists, touching on the fact that they do not believe in "flattering benefactors."[23]

Emerson's reading of Oriental material introduced him to *Akhlaq-i Jalali* (Jalalian Ethics), a mystical handbook translated into English in 1839. It is a reference which shows the way in which the philosophy of Plato and Aristotle were introduced to Persian mysticism. Emerson read the translation of *Akhlaq-i Jalali* by W. F. Thomson, published in early 1839. *Akhlaq-i Jalali* was written about 1467–1477 by Jalal al-Din Davani (1410–1488), who wrote the book for Owzan Hassan Aq-Ghoyenlu. The book contains discussions on ethics, politics, and philosophy. He also read Samuel Miller, who had written a chapter about Persian language and literature, in which he stated that the study of Persian thought was an object of considerable attention in America during the eighteenth century;[24] and it was, of course, during Emerson's time to a large degree.

On May 4, 1840, Emerson wrote to Margaret Fuller about his recent readings and the impressions that he acquired from the Zoroastrian style.[25]

In 1841, Emerson's first series of *Essays* appeared in which there were only a few vague references to the East. Later in that year his interest in Persian thought grew to such an extent that he read many verses of Persian poetry in the German translation of von Hammer-Purgstall.[26]

Beginning about 1837, he read more and more Oriental ideas until, in 1845, he became an Orientalist in earnest.

Early in 1841, in the essay *Compensation*, he furnished himself with material for the essay *Fate*. The change in title and point of view in the two essays is largely due to the progress of his Oriental reading. Emerson also showed his antagonism toward the concept of fate, which he found among Arabian poets and some Persians. He was quite aware of the fact that "fate" and "no free will" had different connotations to a Persian mystic. To a Sufi, the will of God is called "love." A lover follows the will of the Beloved, so his "will" is always the will of the Divine. Shams of Tabriz, the teacher of Rumi (d. 1273) and a Sufi of the thirteenth century, who is called Shami in the present study, asserts:

They say, "What is love?" Say "Renunciation of the will,"
Who so has not escaped from will, no will hath he.[27]

In *Spiritual Law*, Emerson suggests a view quite similar to that of Rumi's concept of "will." He says that a little consideration of what takes place around us every day would show us that a higher law than that of our will regulates events that our painful labors are unnecessary and fruitless. He adds that there is a soul at the center of nature over the will of every man, so that none of us can wrong the universe.[28]

It is necessary here to note Emerson's and the Persian mystics' distinction between "private will," which is, in reality, "willingness and self-annihilation," and the "Divine will," which is the "eternal tendency to the good of the whole," active in every atom and every moment. Late in 1841, Emerson's interest was drawn to the doctrine of "Beautiful Necessity" and to the notion of Destiny; his eagerness led him again to the concept of "variety" in Hinduism and to Oriental mysticism.

In a *Journal* entry for 1841, he records that he found an analogy to the fact of life in the Asiatic sentences and that the Oriental genius has no dramatic or epic turn,[29] but that antiethical contemplative delights in it as in Zoroastrian Oracles, in the *Vedas*, and in Manu.[30] Emerson is not quite correct in this statement, because Firdawsi, the most famous epic writer of Persia, who lived ten centuries ago and was appreciated by Emerson for his fabulous tales, is an exception to this rule. Very late in 1841, for the first time in his *Journals*, Emerson shared the appreciation of Hafiz's thought, his Divine ecstasy, his eternal pride, and his boundless joy.

In a journal entry for 1842, Emerson writes of Sa'di that he celebrates the omnipotence of a virtuous Soul. When Emerson's interest in Persian mystic thought developed in the early 1840s, he wrote his poem "Saadi" for *The Dial* (1842). It is one of his longest poems—about 176 lines—and is, at the same time, one of his finest compositions, whose truth to its subject and poetic organization are of considerable importance. In later years, Emerson appears to have been stimulated by Hafiz, whom he named "the prince of Persian poets"—even though Sa'di was his first love. Indeed, he adapted his name in its various modifications for the ideal poet, and under it described his own language and his most intimate experience. In whatever way Emerson came on Sa'di's verse, his *Letters* show that he did not know *The Gulistan* until 1848 and in that year wrote in his *Journal* that he found in Sa'di's *Gulistan* many traits which compare favorably to the portrait he drew. In the beginning of "Saadi" Emerson defines his character:

> Yet Saadi loved the race of men,—
> No churl, immured in cave or den;
> . . .
> But he has no companion;
> Come ten, or come a million,
> Good Saadi dwells alone.[31]

Early in 1843 Emerson wrote of Sa'di that, like Homer, Dante, and Chaucer, he possessed a great advantage over poets of cultivated times, as the representative of thought to his countrymen.[32] By this time Emerson was quite familiar with the mystical terminology of the Orient. He spoke of Sa'di on different occasions and introduced him as a *Sacayi* (or *saqqa*), or water-drawer in the Holy Land, until he was found worthy of an introduction to the prophet Khizr,[33] who moistened his mouth with the water of immortality (Kousar). C. F. Strauch has discovered that Emerson confused the prophet Khizr (Khezr) in the original account, with the fountain Keuser (Kousar), which is the spring of immortality.[34] In a journal entry for 1843, Emerson refers to an interesting tale of Persian literature in which Amir Khusraw-yi Dehlavi (Emerson spells his name Delhi), asked for a mouthful of this inspiring beverage, but was told that Sa'di had received the last sip.[35]

From 1842 to 1843 Emerson joined with Thoreau in publishing a series of "Ethical Scriptures" from the sacred books of the Orient in *The Dial*. The idea came to them under the influence of Neoplatonism. At this time Emerson spoke of Oriental mysticism and of Swedenborg's contact with the mystical thought of the East and of Neoplatonism. In this year his attention was especially drawn to the philosophy of Proclus. It appears that of all the Platonic philosophers, he loved Proclus next only to Plato himself. In a journal entry for 1843, he asserts:

> I take many stimulants and often make an art of my inebriation.
> I read Proclus for my opium; it excites my imagination to let sail before me the pleasing and grand figures of Gods and daemons and demonical men.[36]

In 1844 the second series of *Essays* was published, in which there were comparatively few and vague reminiscences of his Oriental views. Emerson uses the same language in speaking of Shakespeare and Hafiz and of Homer and Sa'di, joining them all together; because both Hafiz and Shakespeare expressed for him "hilarity," "divine ecstasy," "joy," and gave emancipation; and both Homer and Sa'di "lay in the sun."[37] The expression "the Poet," used often in different passages speaking of the Orient, seems to be an allusion to Hafiz, whom he equates with Shakespeare.

Late in 1844, Emerson praised the Oriental serenity and, in a journal entry for this year, said of Hafiz and Sa'di that "some men have the perception of difference predominant, and are conversant with surfaces and trifles, with coats, coaches, faces and cities; these are the men of talent . . . . And other men abide by the perception of Identity; these are the Orientals, the philosophers, the men of faith and divinity, the men of genius."[38]

The year 1845 was the time of Emerson's most enthusiastic Oriental reading. There are two passages in the *Journals* dealing with the central idea of "Brahma." He versified one passage in the *Journals* and gave its prose form in *Plato; or the Philosopher* (1845), in which he mentioned that among secular books only Plato is entitled to the fanatical compliment of Omar to the Qur'an, when Omar, the second Kaliph of Islam, said, "Burn the libraries; for their value is in *this* book."[39]

Late in 1845, Emerson translated two interesting verses from the *Vedas*, and some from the *Avesta* from German sources. He mentioned two verses of them in *Plato; or the Philosopher*. There are clear allusions to Rumi,[40] one of the eminent Persian mystics, when Emerson uses the metaphoric Sufi terms, "flute" and "river" in this essay:

> As one diffusive air, passing through the perforations of a *flute*, is distinguished as the *notes* of a *scale*, so the nature of the Great Spirit is single, though its forms be manifold, arising from the consequences of acts.[41]

Emerson's predominant tone in *Illusion* is Oriental, not a direct influence of Greek or Neoplatonic philosophy. Late in 1845, he tried to read Machiavelli's histories to apply their philosophy to further understand his [Emerson's] mystic concept of illusion and fate; but, as he has stated, he found it difficult to read and understand. In August 1845, he read it again, and studied Hindu and Zoroastrian teachings alongside it. In an entry in his *Journals* for this year, he writes, "Yes, the Zoroastrian, the Indian, the Persian scriptures are majestic, and more to our daily purpose than this year's almanac or this day's newspaper."[42] Rather late in 1845, his interest in Persian mysticism and in its origin seemed to amount to an enthusiasm, for in this year alone his *Journals* contain references to and quotations from the Orient.

In July 27, 1846, Emerson wrote to Elizabeth Hoar, mentioning that he had recently written some verses called *Mithridates*, others called *Merlin*, others called *Alphonso of Castille*, and some called *Bacchus*; they were not, however, translated from Hafiz.[43] At the same time he pointed out in the *Journals* that "Hafiz, whom I at first thought a cross of Anacreon and Horace, I find now to have the best blood of Pindar in his veins. Also of Burns."[44]

Bacchus had been written in July 1848, only a few days before he wrote to his friends about it. In his own copy of *The Poems*, he wrote a motto to *Bacchus*, which is taken from Plato: "The man who is his own master knocks in vain at the doors of poetry." The influence of Hafiz's ecstasy is quite traceable in *Bacchus*, though it is not a translation of a Hafiz sonnet.

J. I. Harrison has asserted that Hafiz used "wine" as a theme for verse, but its symbolic use in Emerson's poem is purely Platonic.[45] Bacchus, explains Proclus, is the mundane intellect from which the soul and the body of the world are suspended. But the theologians, he adds, frequently call Bacchus "wine," from the last of his gifts.[46] Wine, both to Emerson and to Hafiz, is a symbol of the spiritual ecstasy in which Hafiz's sonnets were written. Emerson is quite aware that Hafiz's use of wine, roses, maidens, birds, rivers, flutes, *tubas*, *mushk* (the perfume of the Beloved), *moles* (attraction of the Divinity), taverns or *meikhane* (the place of emanation), and the veil (a hindrance which falls between the Man and the Over-Soul) are symbolic and that Hafiz praises them to give vent to his immense response to joy and beauty. In 1845, Emerson expressed the same idea in *Experience* and defined wine as a vehicle to elevate Man from one level to another.[47] When Emerson speaks about a movement toward a higher spiritual level in *Bacchus,* he, in fact, considers wine to be a wine of reminiscence. Late in 1846, he spoke of poetry as "God's wine" and then he added in *Poetry and Imagination*:

> O celestial Bacchus! drive them mad. . . . every man may be, and at the same time a man is, lifted to a platform whence he looks beyond sense to moral and spiritual truth, and in that mood deals sovereignly with matter, and strings worlds like beads upon his thought.[48]

There are numerous allusions to wine in the *Works*, the *Essays*, and the *Journals,* which all suggest the concept of divine ecstasy. In *Persian Poetry*, he quotes this line from Hafiz:

> I will be drunk and down with wine;
> Treasure we find in a ruined house.[49]

Emerson reminds us that love, or the wine of Hafiz, is not to be confused with a vulgar debauch. It is the spirit in which the song is written with full joy. While Edward Browne of Cambridge interprets "Hafiz's wine" to be a physical wine, the allusion to wine is merely divine wine and purely a symbolic wine of emancipation; especially owing to the metaphorical use of "loosen the knots:"

> O will it be that they will reopen the doors of the taverns,
> And will loosen the knots from tangled affairs?
> Cut the tresses of the harp [in mourning] for the death of pure wine,
> So that all the sons of Magians may loosen their curled locks![50]

We may conclude that the wine for which Hafiz and Emerson pray becomes the divinely intoxicated intellect, which is to float through all being; this intoxication is only the inspiration that the true poet should have. Charles Molly appreciates the concept of symbolic wine and calls *Bacchus* the best poem written by Emerson. He believes *Bacchus* is one of the world's greatest poems, the one in which the highest degree of emancipation is penetrated.[51] The tone of the freedom and of exaltation in *Bacchus* is similar to that of Hafiz's sonnets. As Carpenter says, three lines of the poem are perhaps as fine as any Emerson over wrote:

> Wine that is shed
> Like the torrents of the Sun
> Up the horizon walls.[52]

There is, in fact, a considerable influence of the Persian style of versification in *Bacchus* that is apparent in every line. Joel Benton suggests that Emerson blends some of his principles with the joy, ecstasy, and exaltation of Hafiz. The thought of *Bacchus* is Emersonian; he holds, but it appears that the spirit and the mystical terms are Oriental, therefore, *Bacchus*, Benton says, is the result of these combinations. In *Emerson in Concord* Edward Emerson wrote:

> Another influence now came in on the side of grace and finish, the Oriental poetry, in which he [Ralph Waldo Emerson] took very great interest, especially the poems of Hafiz, many of which he rendered into English from the German or French translation in which he found them.[53]

Several critics have made attempts to find out the sonnet of Hafiz from which *Bacchus* originated. There are many conjectures, most of them bearing some pertinence and marked by a great deal of similarity. W. R. Alger's discovery is interesting. He suggests that while Emerson was composing *Bacchus*, he was inspired by a *ghazal* of Hafiz entitled *Bring Me Wine*.[54] To a certain extent, one finds justification for Alger's view; nevertheless, it appears that Emerson was most influenced by the long poem of Hafiz, entitled *Wine* or *The Saqi[55] Song*, which is too long to be called a sonnet or a *ghazal*.[56] There are other indications to back up this hypothesis. J. D. Yohannan, in his article, *The Influence of Persian Poetry on Emerson's Work in American Literature*,[57] has also supported this view. In 1842 Emerson was fascinated by the Persian mystic term *Saki* or *Saqi*, while he was versifying his poem "Saadi."[58] Besides, there are similar mystic metaphors, comparable verse structure, and repetition of words in *Bacchus* similar to those in *The Saki Song*, such as "wine," "saqi," "pour," and "intoxication." Therefore, one may conclude that while Emerson was composing *Bacchus* he was influenced by *The Saki Song (Saqi Namah)*.[59] Late in 1847 he wrote to Edward Bangs:

> For you must allow me an affectionate expression—me so far off and you so young,—I take the first moment that really serves me to recite the title of the book I neglected to send you before leaving home—and which is, as follows: Der Dievan von Mohammed Schemseddin Hafiz.[60]

Again in 1847 he mentioned in his *Journals* that he had translated about twenty lines of Hafiz, which are from one of the finest Hafiz poems. It appears that on the eve of Emerson's forty-fourth birthday he recited a few lines of his translation and later, on May 15, 1847, spoke of Hafiz and tried to symbolize him as the right example of "freedom expresser." Emerson declares, "The proudest speech that free will ever made is in Hafiz'[s] Divan:"

> It stands written on the Gate of Heaven
> Woe to him who suffers himself to be betrayed by the Fate.[61]

Rather late in 1847, Emerson read Firdawsi's *Shah Namah* (The Book of Kings); he checked out two versions of this book from two libraries within four months. He was interested, perhaps, in comparing two or three translations, in verifying the fabulous tales in this heroic book. Late in this year he read more of Hafiz and consulted the *Divans* of Sa'di, and Farid al-Din Attar in Chadzko's translation of *Specimens of Ancient Persian Poetry*. In September, in the *Journals*, he discussed the concept of transition and its nature. Here he points out that Hafiz is characterized by a perfect intellectual emancipation, which he also provokes in the reader. Further on, he notes that nothing stops Hafiz, that he makes the "dare-God," and "dare-Devil" experiment. Emerson adds that Hafiz is not to be scared by a name or a religion; he fears nothing.[62]

Late in this year the rough drafts of *Song of Nature* and *Days* appeared, (they were published in 1852) in which one finds several allusions to Oriental mysticism like "mirror images." It is, therefore, worthwhile to stress the influence of Persian material and its mystical entities on Emerson's thought; especially because shortly after his entry on "the beauty in the mythology of Arabia," he was fascinated by the legendary epic tales of Firdawsi. Late that year Emerson extracted Sufi terms from Persian poems translated into German and used them in his writings. Persian mystic terms like "the Tuba" or "der Lieblingsbaum des Paradieses," and the fountain Keuser (as I have noted before, Emerson confused the name of the prophet Khizr with this holy fountain) appeared in his writings. Emerson refers also to the Seal of Solomon, the magic ring that symbolizes lordship over human beings, animals, and demons. The *Anka* (Anqa or Simorgh is roughly equivalent to Griffin or Phoenix), the fabulous bird of wisdom, mentioned by Firdawsi in the *Shah Namah*, represented the kingdom of the birds at the court of Solomon, but *Anqa* was eventually withdrawn and banished to the mythical mountain of *Kof* (Qaf). These fabulous mystical tales engaged Emerson's mind during the whole period from 1847 to late 1850.[63] Very late in 1847, Emerson spoke of an Oriental tale to suggest the idea for *Oriental Superlative* in which he spoke of the story of Khoja Yakul, who brought to Kurraglu the miniature of the handsome Aynas. Incidentally, the dialogue between Kurraglu and a shepherd, who came into the picture of the story afterward, so attracted Emerson that he quoted more than two pages of their conversation in the *Journals*.[64] In *The Transcendentalists and Minerva*, Kenneth W. Cameron refers to this fabulous story, and notes that the book is written by Abdulkurreem (Abdu'l Karim), and is called *The Memoirs of Khojeh Abdulkureem*, which was translated into English by Francis Gladwin in 1788.

From 1849 through 1850 Emerson read some of the interesting Persian poems more fully in the German anthology of von Hammer-Purgstall, and to a certain extent in Chadzko's *Specimens of Ancient Persian Poetry*. Emerson had previously been in contact with these two anthologies early in the 1840s. In early 1850 he began to keep a separate journal entitled *The Orientalist*. In this journal he brought together the philosophy of the Hindus, Oriental thought, Persian poetry, and the wisdom of the Oriental lands. In this year he studied the *Account of the Writings of Hinds*, Firdawsi's the *Shah Namah*, and several *Divans* (anthologies) of Persian poets, most of which were checked out from the Boston Athanaeum Library during the period of 1849 and early 1850.

In 1851, he concentrated on Persian mystic poets and translated several fragments from them for *The Atlantic Monthly* and for *The Liberty Bell*. Among the verses in his second volume of poetry, which was entitled *May Day and Other Poems* (1867), he placed two translations from Hafiz (these poems were omitted from the *Selected Poems* and neglected by J. F. Cabot in his *Revised*

Edition). Joel Benton, who has compared some quatrains of Hafiz[65] with what Emerson translated, has asserted that the translation of Hafiz's pieces, reflected in the *Poems* of the Centenary Edition (1918), seemed to him a little more like Emerson than Hafiz. In *Emerson as a Poet,* Cabot contends,

> The balance is more than preserved by his steeping his own original quatrain in a little tincture of the wine and spirit of Oriental thought.[66]

In *Fragments* found in *Poems* of the Centenary Edition, he translated four lines of a Hafiz sonnet entitled *Friendship* and tried to imitate or keep the Persian style in its translation.[67] Late in 1849, while he was discussing the concept of intellect, he declared:

> What is the effect of thought? Hafiz very properly inquires,—
> Why changes not the inner mind
> Violet earth into musk?

After this discussion, Emerson concludes that the reason for the aversion from metaphysics is the voice of Nature.[68]

Early in 1850 the concept of solitude and the idea of serenity in Khawjah Kermani's poems, a contemporary of Hafiz so impressed Emerson that he composed a fine poem entitled *From the Persian Kermani,* or *The Exile.* Perhaps the poem had been written before the one which was called *From Hafiz* and it carries the same idea. In October 1850, in *Superlative,* Emerson stated that the reader of Hafiz would infer that all food is either candy or wormwood.[69]

In 1851, Emerson's interest in Persian poetry grew so much that he became quite familiar not only with the thought of the prominent Persian mystic poets, but also with the views of those who were not considered first-class in this school of thought. He translated only two quatrains from Omar Khayyam entitled, *From Omar Khayyam*; one quatrain appeared in his essay *Persian Poetry*[70] and the other in *Translation.*[71] Emerson, like most Orientalists, was somewhat fascinated with Khayyam's philosophy. In fact he anticipated that he would have an appeal to the public but, at the same time, he was critically attracted to Khayyam's fatalistic view and his idea of ignoring the function and the spirit of hope and perspectivity. Khayyam declares his retrospective view in his *Ruba'iyyat* (*Robaiyat-quatrains*) thus,

> Ah, my Beloved, fill the Cup that clears
> Today of past Regret and Future Fears
> Tomorrow—why, tomorrow I may be
> Myself with yesterday's sev'n thousand years.[72]

The following quatrain of Khayyam will delineate his fatalistic concept which is quite contradictory to his view of hope, eternity, emancipation, and ecstasy:

> Ah, make the most of what we yet may spend,
> Before we to the *dust* descend;
> *Dust* into *dust*, and under *dust* to lie
> Sans Wine, sans Song, sans Singer, and—sans End![73]

Late in 1851, he translated two lines from Ali Ben Abu Taleb ('Ali Ibn Abu Talib),[74] the fourth Caliph of Islam, concerning friendship; four lines from Ibn Yamin, a well-known Arabian mystic poet; a quatrain from Hilali, which he entitled *The Flute*; two lines from Enweri, (Anvari) the famous Persian lyric writer, which he titled *To Shah Anvari*; Ilqo, laureate of the Saljuq emperor Sanjar, reckoned among the greatest composers of odes; about twenty lines from Kermani, entitled *The Exile*; twenty lines from Hafiz termed *From Hafiz*; and, lastly, about thirty-four lines from Seyd, which he called *Song of Seyd Nimetollah of Kuhistan*, whose proper name is Seyyd Ni'matullah Vali and his pseudonym, Vali, meaning the Master. The mystics sing his poems while they perform their astronomical dances, during which they repeat their Master's recital and, at the same time, imitate the movements of the heavenly bodies. This last poem was authentically translated by Emerson and first appeared in *The Liberty Bell* in 1851,[75] wherein he explained the process of this astronomical mystic dance in the introduction.[76]

From 1852 to 1858, he read more of Sa'di's *Gulistan* and appreciated his extreme tendency toward freedom, his love for the emancipation of Soul, his eternal joy, and his Divine ecstasy.

In March of 1852, he showed a great deal of interest in Eastern philosophy. He composed *Days* and wrote in the *Journals* that he did not remember the composition or the correction of *Days*.[77] Furthermore, he confessed that he would not be able to write such a work again. *Days* becomes a kind of poetic parable of the tragic mortality of man and it appeals particularly to those who see life in terms of human tragedy rather than of divine comedy.[78] Strauch, speaking to Carpenter's question of the source of the fifth line of *Days*, "To each they offer gifts after his will," proposes the following lines of Hafiz:

> Surely I have no treasure,
> Yet am I richly satisfied;
> God has given that to the Shah
> And this to the beggar.[79]

There is undoubtedly a flavor of Persian mystical thought in *Days*. It is perhaps the result of his close contact with the concept of fate and faith in Oriental mysticism that drew his attention to this idea.

Before he wrote *Persian Poetry* (1858), he had translated several stanzas from Hafiz and entered many quotations in his *Letters* and in the *Journals*. In an entry in the *Journal* for 1855, he stated that the chief fact in the history of the world is the penury with which the stream of thought runs. Then he reproduced this concept from Hafiz in the following lines:

> O follow, O see the sonnet's flight!
> Thou seest a fleet career,
> O child, begot in a night,
> That travels a thousand year.[80]

During the period of the 1850s his interest in Persian poetry grew considerably. On September 26, 1855, he wrote to James Eliot Cabot: "The Eastern poetry I looked through, but find the Persian still the best by far, and shall stay by Von Hammer with all the more content."[81] Later on, in his letter to Cabot and to William Emerson, he made similar statements and, furthermore, added that he took a great interest in the *Gulistan* of Sa'di in which he found a high degree of exaltation.[82]

In 1858 he wrote his essay *Persian Poetry*, which first appeared in the *Atlantic Monthly* for January, 1859. For many years he had been interested in finding a solution to the problem of evil, a quest that led him eventually to search for its solution in the Oriental concept of unity, which is above all the dualism of good and evil. *Persian Poetry* is, to a certain extent, an answer to his problem. It is, in fact, a scholarly combination of his ideas about Hafiz, Sa'di, Firdawsi, Nizami, and Farid al-Din Attar.

In his lecture *The Fugitive Slave Law*, he referred to Sa'di's affectionate feeling for mankind. He paraphrased two verses of Sa'di into one sentence thus: "Beware of hurting the orphan; when the orphan sets a-crying, the throne of the Almighty is rocked from side to side."[83]

For a long time he had considered collecting his notes and publishing a book—a first book in his life—on *Persian Poetry*, but he was unable to bring his desire to fulfillment. Late in his life, this idea so developed that in April, 1874, he wrote to Octavius Brook Frothingham thus, "One of the papers I have thought of putting into the new book is *Persian Poetry*, printed in the Old 'Atlantic' and the very design will show you how niggardly the Muse is."[84] In April 1858, in a letter to Edwin Percy Whipple, he mentioned his interest in *Persian Poetry* and how his essay on this theme was proceeding.[85]

In an entry in the *Journal* for 1858, making a distinction between Eastern and Western poets, Emerson declares that the finest genius in England or France would feel the absurdity of making fables for his queen or emperor about their saddles, though Hafiz and Enweri (Anvari) did not.[86] He was actually impressed by the fact that Hafiz, Rumi, and Shams considered a simple Sufi intoxicated by the Divine Wine to be closer to the Eternal than an emperor who is bound to his arrogance and is absorbed in his earthly wishes.

During the period of 1858 to 1864 he studied mysticism of the East. He checked out several editions of the *Gulistan* from the Boston Athenaeum Library[87] and asked other libraries to secure them for his use. Late in 1863 he consulted Malcolm's *History of Persians*, volumes I and II, as well as the different translations of the *Gulistan*; he referred to a few of them in his entries in the *Journals* and in the *Letters*.

In October 1863, he made reference to Sa'di's idea of joy and friendship. He paraphrased the following passage from the Hammer-Purgstall translation of Sa'di's *Gulistan*:

No Soul has he who no friend has;
Little joy has he who no garden has.
Who with a moon-face can refresh his heart
Enjoys a luck which has no bounds.
A dungeon is that house which solitude fills,
If they have not, like Saadi, a rose bed.[88]

He defines the genius of Sa'di and points out that the human race is interested in Sa'di, whilst the cynical tone of Byron, which helps nobody, owes its lingering longevity only to his genuine talent for melodious expression. Then he concludes: "Saadi is the poet of friendship, serenity, and of the divine Providence."[89]

In February 1864, he reflected his extensive studies of Sa'di's thought in a preface which he wrote for the first edition of the *Gulistan*, translated from the original by Francis Gladwin in 1865. He recorded that Sa'di, though he has not the lyric flights of Hafiz, has wit, practical sense, and just moral sentiment. He has, like Franklin, the instinct to teach. He is the poet of friendship, love, self-devotion, and serenity. Sa'di, Emerson adds, has been by turns a student, a water-carrier (*saqqa*), a traveler, a soldier, a prisoner employed to dig trenches before Tripoli, and lastly, an honored poet. Through his experiences and his Persian tongue, he speaks to all nations, and like Homer, Shakespeare, and Montaigne is perpetually modern. Emerson appreciates the sense of joy in Persian poetry but criticizes any kinds of fatalism. From such attitudes Hafiz perfectly freed himself, though Sa'di is slightly subject. Khayyam, however, is considerably tainted by fate, and a few Persian poets are still imprisoned in his limitations.

From 1864 to the last day of his life, he had a close contact with the Hindu philosophy, Neoplatonism, Oriental mysticism, and Persian poetry. Particularly late in Emerson's life, Hafiz remained, in his opinion, the favorite poet of Persia; he praises his "Cheerfulness" again in the last entries in the *Journals*, in his last letters, and in his essays published after 1870, such as *Society and Solitude*, *Letters and Social Aims*, and *Lectures and Biographical Sketches*.

In the last *Journals* he represents Hafiz's hypothesis for liberty and the emancipation of the soul from its earthly limitation while discussing Hegel's definition of liberty. Hafiz plays with magnitudes, but without ulterior aim; he fears nothing, he sees far and he sees throughout. There are several references to Persian thought in the last *Journals* (1875), in which Hafiz's view about fate seems to him most logical and most fascinating. In the last pages of the *Journals* and *Letters* Emerson noted Hafiz's theory of fate thus:

It stands written on the Gate of Heaven
Woe to him who suffers himself to be betrayed by Fate.[90]

Further on, Emerson affixes a like note to this idea of Hafiz, saying, "For he who loves is not betrayed, but makes an ass of Fate."[91]

Since in the last six years of his life he did not add entries to the *Journals* and wrote nothing (for he could hardly answer a letter), the above cited statements from Hafiz's *Divan* (an entry in the *Journals* for 1873) may be considered as his last item of contemplation. Very late in his life, perhaps in his last letter, on one or two occasions, he referred to the Persians and their talents in mystical thought.

Notes

1. This section has been adapted from *The Chronological Development of Emerson's Interest in Persian Mysticism*, by Mansur Ekhtiyar (Tehran: Tehran UP, 1976).
2. Ralph Waldo Emerson, *Journals, 1820–1876*. (1820), 21–22.
3. Ibid., 69.
4. Ralph Waldo Emerson, *Works*, IV, 52–53.
5. Kenneth W. Cameron, *Ralph Waldo Emerson's Reading* (New York: Haskell House, 1941), 22–23.
6. Emerson, *Journals*, I (1820), 69.
7. Ibid., 157.
8. Emerson, *Letters*, I (1822), 114.
9. Ibid., 114–115.
10. Kenneth W. Cameron, *The Transcendentalists and Minerva* (Hartford, CT: Transcendental Books, 1958), II, 435–437.
11. Arthur Christy, *The Orient in American Transcendentalism* (New York: Columbia University Press, 1932), 63.
12. Emerson, *Journals*, I (1824), 380.
13. Emerson, *Journals*, I (1824), 380.
14. Emerson, Joel Porte (*Emerson in his Journals*. Harvard University Press, 1982), 41.
15. Ibid., II (1830), 329.
16. Ibid., 329–344.
17. Ibid., 473.
18. *Academie des Inscriptions*, Vol. 37, 23.

19. *Menu* (or Manu), *Institute of Hindu Law; or the Ordinance of Menu according to the Glossary of Culluca*, translated from Sanskrit with the preface by Sir William Jones (Calcutta, 1796).

20. In "Nature" (1836), Emerson mentions Vayasa incorrectly as a philosopher.

21. Frederic Ives Carpenter, *Emerson and Asia* (Cambridge: Harvard University Press, 1930), 12.

22. Ibid., 105.

23. "Do not flatter your benefactors. The bread that you give me is not thine to give, but mine when the great order of nature has seated me today at your table. Do not let me deceive you by thanks with the notion that you are aught but the moderator of the comparing for the hour, though you call yourself rich man and great benefactor, perhaps." Emerson, *Journals*, V, 408.

24. Samuel Miller. *The Brief Retrospect of Eighteenth Century* (New York: T and J Swords, 1803), I, 72.

25. Emerson, *Letters*, II (1840), 294.

26. Joseph von Hammer-Purgstall, *Mohammed Schemsed-din Hafis. Der Diwan*, 2 vols. (Stuttgart and Tübingen, 1812–13).

27. Shams of Tabriz, *guyand ishq chist bagu tarka ikhtiyar. har ko ze ikhtiyar narast ikhtiyar nist.*, trans. Reynold A. Nicholson in *Divan-i Shams-i Tabrizi* (Cambridge: Routledge, 1952), 50–51.

28. Emerson, *Works*, II, 137–139.

29. Carpenter, *Emerson and Asia*, 162.

30. Emerson, *Journals*, V (1840), 570.

31. Emerson, *Works*, IX, 130.

32. Emerson, *Journals*, VI (1843), 463.

33. Khizr is often identified with *Enoch* in Islamic mystical literature.

34. C. F. Strauch, "Emerson's Sacred Science," *PMLA* 73 (June 1958), 242.

35. Emerson, *Journals*, VI (1843), 463.

36. Ibid., 375.

37. Carpenter, *Emerson and Asia*, 170.

38. Emerson, *Journals*, VI (1844), 493–494.

39. Emerson, *Works*, IV, 39.

40. Arthur J. Arberry, *Persian Poems* (London: Everyman's Library, 1954), 127.

41. Emerson, *Works*, IV, 50.

42. Emerson adds the rest of his statement in "Society and Solitude," *Works*, VII, 219, 22; See *Journals*, VII (1845), 241–242.

43. Emerson, *Letters*, III (1846), 341.

44. Emerson, *Journals*, VII (1846), 170.

45. J. I. Harrison, *The Teachers of Emerson* (New York: Sturgis & Walton Co., 1910), 275.

46. Proclus, *On the Theology of Plato* (London: Law, 1816), I, 216.

47. Emerson, *Works*, III, 44.

48. Ibid., VIII, 70.

49. Ibid., 246.

50. Edward G. Browne, *A Literary History of Persia* (Cambridge, UK: Routledge, 1928), III, 278.

51. "The Poems of Emerson," *The Coming Age*, XXNII (1940), 504.

52. Emerson, *Works*, IX, 126. See, also, Carpenter, *Emerson and Asia*, 189.

53. Edward Waldo Emerson, *Emerson in Concord* (Cambridge, MA: The Riverside Press, 1889), 231.

54. W. R. Alger, *The Poetry of the East* (Boston: Kissinger Publishing, 1856), 166.

55. One who serves wine.

56. J. D. Yohannan, "The Influence of Persian Poetry upon Emerson's Work," *American Literature*, 20. (March 1943), 260.

57. *American Literature*, XV (March 1943), 26–41.

58. Emerson, *Journals*, IV, 465.

59. Literally translated as "A Treatise by Saqi."

60. Ibid., 529. A copy of it is still in Emerson's Library at the Antiquarian House.

61. Emerson, *Journals*, VII (1847), 269.

62. Ibid., 328.

63. Emerson, *Works*, VIII, 263.

64. Emerson, *Journals*, VII (1847), 281.

65. Emerson, *Works*, IX, 299–300, 303.

66. Joel Benton. *Emerson as a Poet* (New York: M. F. Mansfield & A. Wessels, 1833), 29.

67. Emerson, *Works*, IX, 363.

68. *Journals* (1849), VIII, 19.

69. Ibid., 129–130.

70. Emerson, *Works*, VIII, 244.

71. Emerson, *Works*, IX, 301.

72. Edward Fitzgerald, *Rubaiyat of Omar Khayyam and the Soloman and Absal of Jami* (London, n.d.), 73.

73. Ibid., 74.

74. Emerson, *Works*, IX, 302.

75. *The Liberty Bell* (Boston, 1851), 78–81.

76. Emerson, *Works*, IX, 304.

77. Emerson, *Journals*, VIII (1852), 421.

78. E. S. Oliver, "Emerson's 'Days,'" *New England Quarterly* 19 (December 1946): 520. See, also, Carpenter, *Emerson Handbook* (New York: Hendricks House, 1953), 188–189.

79. Carl F. Strauch, "Mss. Relationship of Emerson's 'Days,'" *Philological Quarterly* NXVIII (April, 1950): 199. See, also, Carpenter, *Emerson and Asia*, 186–188. He asserts that the following statement in the *Journals* for May 24, 1847 has a clear allusion to the lines cited from Hafiz: "The days come and go . . . but they say nothing, and if we do not use the gifts they bring, they carry them as silently away." On the eve of his forty-fourth birthday, Emerson wrote this sentence later embodied in his poem "Days." See *Journals*, VII, 277.

80. Perhaps a better and more accurate translation of the last two lines would be: "A child that is one night old takes a trip a hundred years long." See *Journals*, VIII (1858), 542.

81. Emerson, *Letters*, IV (1855), 530–531.

82. Emerson, *Letters*, V (1857), 92.

83. Emerson, *Works*, XI, 238.

84. Emerson, *Letters*, VI (1874), 260.
85. Ibid., V (1858), 104.
86. Emerson, *Journals*, IX (1858), 145–46.
87. Cameron, *Ralph Waldo Emerson's Reading*, 33, 34.
88. Emerson, *Journals*, IX (1863), 545.
89. Ibid., 562.
90. Emerson, *Journals*, X (1873), 473.
91. Emerson, *Journals*, X, 55.

3

Ralph Waldo Emerson and the Muslim Orient

Marwan M. Obeidat[1]

> Life in the East is fierce, short, hazardous, and in extremes. Its elements are few and simple, not exhibiting the long range and undulation of European existence, but rapidly reaching the best and the worst.
>
> —Emerson, *Persian Poetry*

The involvement of Emerson, Thoreau, and Alcott in Oriental thought is essentially part of the beginnings of comparative religion as a field for further study, but it goes beyond that. In Emerson's case it influences his writing—particularly his interest in and admiration for the Sufi poets, and especially Hafiz and Sa'di. In 1822, a year after his graduation from college, writing to his mentor and favorite aunt, Mary Moody Emerson, who informed him of Oriental books she had recently come upon, Emerson remarks:

> I am curious to read your Hindu mythologies. One is apt to lament over indolence and ignorance, when he reads some of those sanguine students of the Eastern antiquities, who seem to think that all the books of knowledge, and all the wisdom of Europe twice-told, lie hid in the treasures of the Bramins and the volumes of Zoroaster. When I lie dreaming on the possible contents of pages, as dark to me as the characters on the Seal of Solomon, I console myself with calling it learning's El Dorado. Every man has a fairy land just beyond the compass of his horizon . . . and it is very natural that literature at large should look for some fanciful stores of mind which surpassed example and possibility.[2]

It seems probable that Emerson had already known something of the Orientals before he wrote this letter to his aunt, as Frederic I. Carpenter suggests,[3] but as yet he is not fully aware of them. The course of correspondence between Mary Moody Emerson and her nephew marked not only the presence of the Orient at the dawning of Emerson's intellectual development, but also his admiration for it. In turn, Aunt Mary's enthusiasm led to and encouraged the youth's life-long habit of speaking of the Orient. A few months earlier Emerson had written:

> I was the pampered child of the East. I was born where the soft western gale breathed upon me fragrance of cinnamon groves and through the seventy windows of my hall the eye fell on the Arabian harvest. A hundred elephants, appareled in cloth of gold, carried my train to war, and the smile of the Great King beamed upon Omar. But now—the broad Indian moon looks through the broken arches of my tower, and the wind of desolation fans me with poisonous airs; the spider's threads are in the tapestry which adorns my walls and the rain of night is heard in my halls for the music of the daughters of Cashmere.[4]

At this stage Emerson's Orientalism, Arthur Christy suggests, was not yet "disciplined by many books."[5] Though undisciplined it may be, the early phase of Emerson's Orientalism shows an awareness of the outlandish and the inaccessible—the other half of the world—an awareness of its attractiveness, romance, poetry, and religion. Such an awareness of the Orient constitutes only fragments of fantasy that reflect Emerson's preoccupation with exoticism. "The Arabian harvest" is at variance with Indian Cashmere, and is of course a different taste; and Omar, whether the second Muslim Caliph or not, is difficult to associate with the beams of the Indian moon. But Emerson did not linger much on these matters. What concerned him is the romantic suggestiveness of the "cinnamon groves," "the broken arches," "the cloth of gold," and "the broad Indian moon" as a source of literary enchantment with the Orient. These early quotations show little knowledge on Emerson's part of Oriental literatures and religions. As Frederic Carpenter perceptively suggests, Emerson's immature interest in the Orient varied between "fascination and aversion."[6] However, the feeling of aversion predominated in his early writing. For thirteen years, from the age of twenty-one to thirty-four (the period from 1824 to 1837), Emerson did not record any significant ideas or concern with the Orient, either Islamic or non-Islamic. Perhaps this lack of interest was due to the difficulty in obtaining sufficient information. Later in his career Emerson exploited the attractive mystery of the Orient and appropriated much of its culture to his own uses. But he was not an Orientalist himself, though he gradually began to rediscover Oriental material and to read all the Islamic books he came upon.[7]

There is no certain proof, observes Arthur Christy, as to when Emerson practically came under the influence of Oriental thought.[8] But it is evident that Greek Platonism was the chief element in formulating his Orientalism, which was a relatively late development in his career. "The kernel of Emerson's Orientalism,"[9] to use Carpenter's words, lies in his series of Occidental biographical lectures, *Representative Men* (1850). Though it did not offer much space for specific Islamic material, the book contained references to it, especially in the essay *Plato*. The first sentence in the essay reads: "Among secular books, Plato only is entitled to Omar's fanatical compliment to the Koran, when he said, 'Burn the libraries; for their value is in this book.'"[10] The application of Omar's statement to the Qur'an (alleged to be said at the conquest of Alexandria) to Plato's work brings East to West whereby certain boundaries and categories are set up, associations and distinctions made. The Orient is given a space where it stands vis-à-vis the Occident. While in Egypt, "Plato . . . imbibed the idea of one Deity," writes Emerson, "in which all things are absorbed," and thus,

> The unity of Asia, and the detail of Europe; the infinitude of the Asiatic soul and the defining, result-loving, machine-making, surface-seeking, opera-going Europe,—Plato came to join, and, by contact, to enhance the energy of each. The excellence of Europe and Asia are in his brain. Metaphysics and natural philosophy expressed the genius of Europe; he substructs the religion of Asia, as the base.[11]

While Asia is associated with the soul and "religion," Europe is associated with the mind and "metaphysics and natural philosophy." This distinction suppresses Asiatic religions to a substructural level. But their presence as "the base" of European culture is, though reductionist, of significance. Plato's arrival in ancient Egypt is an arrival of defining, and "[t]his defining is philosophy."[12] "At last, comes Plato," writes Emerson, "the distributor who needs no barbaric paint, or tattoo, or whooping; for he can define. He leaves with Asia the vast and superlative; he is the arrival of accuracy and intelligence."[13] From the very outset Emerson initiates his analysis by what he considers as "the one, and the two," or Unity and Variety.[14] The split had appeared and reappeared in many forms: as the one and the many, being versus intellect, rest versus motion, and finally East versus West. The key passage follows: "The country of unity, of immovable institutions . . . of men faithful in doctrine and in practice to the idea of a deaf, unimplorable, immense fate, is Asia. . . . On the other side, the genius of Europe is active and creative." East and West are intellectually defined here. The difference between them is neither geographical, nor racial. It is a difference in the cultures that distinguishes the two worlds. In any case, Emerson's pro-Western stance is too evident to be missed: he speaks of "immovable institutions" and of a "deaf, unimplorable fate" in characterizing the Orient, but emphasizes the "active" and "creative" in characterizing the Western mind, which clearly stands higher. And finally Europe is "a land of arts, inventions, trade, freedom. If the East loved infinity, the West delighted in boundaries."[15] Certainly it is not out of dislike that Emerson subordinates the Orient to the Occident; but it is specifically out of his belief in a consequential movement of history, a movement which would establish the Occident as superior and the Orient as inferior. In the "Divinity School Address" Emerson writes,

> I look for the hour when that supreme Beauty which ravished the souls of those Eastern men, and chiefly of those Hebrews, and through their lips spoke oracles to all time, shall speak in the West also. The Hebrew and Greek Scriptures contain immortal sentences, that have been bread of life to millions. But they have no epical integrity; are fragmentary; are not shown in their order to the intellect. I look for the new Teacher that shall follow so far those shining laws that he shall see them come full circle.[16]

In Plato Emerson saw a "new Teacher," a teacher who prefigures America's "strong man" who, in turn, "has entered the race."[17] Thus, Emerson attempts to identify himself with Plato, and his identification with the Greek philosopher implicates him in the westward movement of civilization; it suggests America's preeminence in world history, a preeminence which is part of a sequential movement that involves a transition from the Oriental to the Occidental and from Europe to America.

Emerson's assessment of world civilization is not motivated by any kind of bias against the Orient. On the contrary, there is strong evidence to believe that he has a unique admiration for it. The essay *Persian Poetry*, for instance, his fascination with the Sufi poets, his imitation of Hafiz and Sa'di, his numerous quotations from the Qur'an and other Islamic literature, his efforts to appropriate Indian and Brahmin mythology, all suggest a uniquely sympathetic attitude.[18] In the essay *Plato* Emerson points out that the Orient had something the Greek "Teacher" could not possess, something that kept him from influencing the multitude: "It is almost the sole deduction from the merit of Plato, that his writings have not,—what is no doubt incident to this regnancy of intellect in his work,—the vital authority which the screams of prophets and the sermons of unlettered Arabs and Jews possess."[19] Emerson was deeply attracted to the Oriental mind, to its "vital authority," unity, spirituality, and mysticism. All were among the several things that drew him toward the Orient—not as a place, but certainly as a cultural idea. But Emerson's Western preference is more overt, though he grants the Orientals (Arabs, Persians, Indians) a fair position on the scale of civilization: "If it comes back to the question of final superiority," Emerson writes, "it is too plain that there is no question that the star of empire rolls West."[20] Emerson's concern here is with the superiority of an Occidental West as opposed to the inferiority of an Oriental East. Being Occidental is being better: "Orientalism is Fatalism, resignation: Occidentalism is Freedom and Will. We Occidentals are educated to wish to be first."[21] Suffice it to say that Emerson read and admired the Orientals without abandoning an awareness of his ascendancy and superiority. His final verdict is "we read the Orientals, but remain Occidental."[22]

In the lecture *Natural Religion*, which he read to a group of religious liberals known as "Radicals" at their meeting held in Boston in 1869, Emerson, while discussing the doctrines of the existence of Christ, is reported in the newspapers as having said that

> We measure all religions by their civilizing power. We account Mohammedanism, Mormonism, Thugism, Agapism, and other sects, old or new, which gratify the passions, as mischievous and therefore false. Christianity, on the other hand, throve against the physical interests and passions of men, and needs no other stamp of truth.[23]

That the Muslim Orient is characterized by a religion which gratifies "the physical interests and passions of men" Emerson accepts, at this point, by ignoring the spiritual foundation of the religion, but in the same lecture he points out, somewhat apologetically, that although the "character of Mohammed is, on the page of history, very bad," there is "a certain spiritual elevation in [the Prophet's character], which appeared in his followers. And certainly in the Koran, whether they have borrowed the Christian Scriptures or not, there is abundance of noble sentences."[24] Even with this assumption of borrowing from the Christian scriptures, Emerson recognized in the Qur'an an "abundance of noble sentences" which certainly struck his mind to the furthest extremes. Emerson's interest in the Muslim Orient, however, reveals that he was more prepared to be involved in certain manifestations of the outer form of the religion—as is indicated in specific sayings and utterances—than in its philosophical, theoretical dogmas. Thus Emerson imbued his writing with Islamic quotations, or brief, incidentally confused, references to Islamic metaphysics and made these subservient to his views.

In the essay *Fate*, which appeared in *The Conduct of Life* (1860), Emerson displays his understanding of the concept at hand.

> Great men, great nations, have not been boasters and buffoons, but perceivers of the terror of life, and have manned themselves to face it. The Spartan, embodying his religion in his country, dies before its majesty without a question. The Turk, who believes his doom is written on the iron lead in the moment when he entered the world,

rushes on the enemy's saber with undivided will. The Turk, the Arab, the Persian, accepts the foreordained fate:—

"On two days, it steads not to run from they grave,
   The appointed, and unappointed day;
On the first, neither balm nor physician can save,
   Nor thee, on the second, the Universe slay."[25]

Emerson comes to the conclusion that the doctrine of fatalism may be turned to a beneficent force, if it is properly understood. But is can also be a social evil if accepted passively or resignedly. Emerson's understanding of the concept is enhanced by the succeeding essay, *Power*. The essay develops the idea of freedom over against surrender to fate, which, to Emerson, is a characteristic of Islamic Orientalism: "Orientalism is Fatalism, resignation." A complete resignation to fate Emerson dismisses as distasteful. In the preface that Emerson wrote for Sa'di's *Gulistan*, in 1865, he describes the Persian poets as fatalists: "In common with his countrymen, Saadi gives prominence to fatalism, a doctrine which, in Persia, in Arabia, and in India, has had in all ages a dreadful charm. 'To all men,' says the Koran, 'is their day of death appointed, and they cannot postpone or advance it one hour.'"[26] Emerson illustrates his point with a quotation from the Qur'an which in turn expresses its own fatalist nature. Emerson's argument here constitutes his own understanding of an Oriental system of determinism, a determinism which distinguishes two predestinate points in every man's life: the day of his birth and that of his death. In the essay *Persian Poetry*, Emerson characterizes the Persians, stressing their fatalism: "Religion and poetry are all their civilization. The religion teaches an inexorable destiny. It distinguishes only two days in each man's history,—his birthday, called *the Day of the Lot*, and the Day of Judgment. Courage and absolute submission to what is appointed for him are his virtues."[27]

But Emerson found much more in the Persian poets than fatalism. The Sufi poets influenced Emerson more profoundly than any other group of Oriental writers. The affinity between Emerson's thought and the Persian poets is tangible. But his remarks on them and their poetry remain rather general. Even though he developed an ideal concept of Hafiz and Sa'di, Emerson did not seem to have attempted to characterize them as poets, to see in what way, or ways, they were similar, and how they differed. Yet he admired their poetry and accepted it as ideal, and he viewed them as poets of intellectual liberty. While they believed in a designated fate, the Persian poets enjoyed an "intellectual freedom" that was part of a joyful attitude toward life.[28] In *Fate*, Emerson admires the "sallies of freedom," "One example of which is the verse of the Persian Hafiz, 'Tis written on the gate of Heaven, 'Woe to him who suffers himself to be betrayed by Fate!'"[29] And again:

We learn that the soul of Fate is the soul of us, as Hafiz sings,
"Alas! till now I had not known,
My guide and fortune's guide are one."[30]

In the essay *Persian Poetry*, in reference to Hafiz's "heroic sentiment and contempt for the world," Emerson writes:

And sometimes his . . . world [is] only one pebble more in the eternal vortex and revolution of Fate:—
"I am what I am
My dust will be again."[31]

In the essay Power, while he discusses the forms of power and the ideas of freedom, Emerson speaks of "this affirmative force . . . 'On the neck of the young man,' said Hafiz, 'sparkles no gem so gracious as enterprise.'"[32] And at the end of The Conduct of Life, in the essay Illusions, Emerson writes, pointing out the charm of illusions and the necessity of recognizing them,

It would be hard to put more mental and moral philosophy than the Persians have thrown into a sentence,
"Fooled thou must be, thou wisest of the wise:
Then be the fool of virtue, not of vice."[33]

Undoubtedly Emerson liked this quality of freedom and mental force which the Persian poets had. Speaking of the relative recklessness toward life which they expressed in their poetry, Emerson quotes Hafiz:

I batter the wheel of heaven
   When it rolls not rightly by
I am not one of the snivelers
   Who fall thereon and die.[34]

Again:

Loose the knots of the heart; never think on thy fate:
No Euclid has yet disentangled that snarl.[35]

It is this bold but joyful attitude toward life that Emerson admires most; for, like Hafiz, he believed that the force of men's thoughts lies in the way of uttering them. "Loose the knots of the heart" is in effect a statement that shows the willingness to die when the appointed time comes.

This quality of recklessness is also a quality of rejoicing and intellectual vastness. As Emerson tells us, "Hafiz praises wine, maidens, boys, birds, mornings, and music, to give vent to his immense hilarity and sympathy with every form of beauty and joy. . . . Those are the natural topics and language of his wit and perception. But it is the play of the wit and joy of song that he loves."[36] Emerson goes on to say, comparing Hafiz and Shakespeare, "A saint might lend an ear to the riotous fun of Falstaff; for it is not created to excite the animal appetites, but to vent the joy of the supernal intelligence."[37] So, in the overall analysis, the merit of expressing "the joy of supernal intelligence" becomes a "certificate of profound thought" and "intellectual liberty."[38] If Hafiz vented supreme joy, Sa'di was "the joy-giver and the enjoyer."[39] In the essay on *Shakespeare; or the Poet*, Emerson remarks:

> One more royal trait properly belongs to the poet. I mean his cheerfulness, without which no man can be a poet,—for beauty is his aim . . . Beauty, the spirit of joy and hilarity, he sheds over the universe. . . . Homer lies in the sun-shine; Chaucer is glad and erect, and Saadi says, "It was rumored abroad that I was penitent, but what have I to do with repentance?"[40]

While he refers to Shakespeare, Homer, Dante, and Chaucer, Emerson simultaneously mentions Sa'di and brings them all together. If Hafiz and Shakespeare are poets of "joy" and "emancipation," Sa'di was the poet of "cheerful temper," a poet in whose poetry "suns rise and set."[41] In the poem "Saadi," Sa'di emerges as "The cheerer of men's hearts."[42] The "wisdom of God is he."[43] And in the Preface to *Gulistan* Emerson writes:

> [Sa'di] exhibits perpetual variety of situation and incident, and an equal depth of experience with Cardinal de Retz in Paris, or Doctor Johnson in London. He finds room on his narrow canvas for the extremes of the lot, the play of motives, the rule of destiny, the lessons of morals, and the portraits of great men.

Emerson adds, "though he has not the lyric flights of Hafiz, [Sa'di] has wit, practical sense, and just moral sentiments. He has the instinct to teach, and from every occurrence must draw the moral. . . . He is the poet of friendship, love, self-devotion, and serenity."[44] In other words, to Emerson, Sa'di is a man of real genius, or morality, of "practical sense," and "just moral sentiments." He is both a teacher and a poet, an enjoyer and a joy-giver. In brief, Sa'di is not only a poet of "friendship" and "self-devotion," but he is also a teacher of "the lessons of morals," an example of "great men."

Emerson saw yet another feature in the Persian Sa'di: self-reliance. Near the opening of the poem "Saadi," Emerson suggests that Sa'di had such a quality.

> Yet Saadi loved the race of men,—
> No churl, immured in cave or den;
> . . . .
> But he has no companion;
> Come ten, or come a million,
> Good Saadi dwells alone.[45]

This virtue takes on other forms in Sa'di's writing as well as in that of Hafiz. It becomes an expression of self-assurance, independence, and authority. In the like manner Emerson writes of Hafiz:

> That hardihood and self-equality of every sound nature, which result from the feeling that the spirit in him is entire and as good as the world, which entitle the poet to speak with authority, and make him an object of interest . . . are in Hafiz, and abundantly fortify and ennoble his tone.[46]

This feeling of self-assurance helped the Persian poets accomplish self-reliance and justify it to the common man by means of self-expression. Since, in a Sufi sense, the whole nature evidences divinity, absolute beauty is reflected in all natural objects and thus in every self-reliant man who could use nature as his language. Emerson wrote of Sa'di: "He has also that splendor of expression which alone, without wealth of thought, sometimes constitutes a poet, and forces us to ponder the problem of style."[47] In an entry in the *Journals* this quality of self-expression is more clear. "Expression," writes Emerson, influenced by the reading of Hafiz,

> is all we want: not knowledge, but vent: we know enough; but have not leaves and lungs enough for a healthy perspiration and growth. Hafiz has: Hafiz's good things, like those of all good poets, are the cheap blessings of water, air, and fire [the elements of Nature] . . . "Keep the body open," is the hygeian precept . . . Large utterance![48]

Emerson believed that for the ideal poet (Sufi poets were generally ideal to Emerson) the splendid expression is Nature. And Nature is language, a language that the good poets alone can make and communicate to their fellow men.

To use Frederic I. Carpenter's judicious judgment, "to Hafiz and Saadi as ideal poets Emerson ascribed freedom of thought and freedom of spirit, which resulted in their feeling of absolute joy in the world; how they showed him a sincerity and self-reliance, which assured them of the basic value of life; and finally how they possessed for him a perception of beauty in Nature and in Man, which inspired their poetic expression."[49] Obviously Emerson admired and spoke highly of both Hafiz and Sa'di not because they had "partially freed themselves from Mohammedanism," as Carpenter explains,[50] but because they were poets of intellectual liberty, of "hilarity," of "serenity," in their own Sufi way. Although he still identified them as fatalists, Emerson, I believe, admired the Persian poets because of the quality of mental vastness they enjoyed; the variety of subjects they treated, and, more specifically, because they had a "perception of beauty in nature and in Man." They praised "wine [wine in a Sufi sense is a symbol of intoxication with Divinity], maidens, boys, mornings, and music"[51] in expressing their love of beauty. It is the use of wit and the expression of Beauty that gave Sa'di and Hafiz the assurance of pleasing the Almighty with their poetry. "Like Homer and Dante and Chaucer, Saadi [and Hafiz]," asserts Emerson,

> possessed a great advantage over the poets of cultivated times in being the representatives of learning and thought to [their] countrymen. Those old poets felt that all wit was their wit, they used their memory as readily as their invention, and were are once the librarian as well as the poet, historiographer as well as the priest of the Muses.[52]

The Sufi poets were the inspired men of their people. And they used their cultivated thought and memory and wit to demonstrate their admiration for the beautiful and, more importantly, for the divine. In *Eloquence* Emerson writes:

> The Persian poet Saadi tells us that a person with a disagreeable voice was reading the Koran aloud, when a holy man, passing by, asked what was his monthly stipend. He answered, "Nothing at all." "But why then do you take so much trouble?" He replied, "I read for the sake of God." The other rejoined, "for God's sake, do not read; for if you read the Koran in this manner you will destroy the splendor of Islamism."[53]

The fact that Sa'di himself wrote poetry for the sake of God is revealed when Emerson writes of the "angels descending with salvers of glory in their hands. On asking one of them for whom those were intended, he answered, 'For Shaikh Saadi of Shiraz who has written a stanza of poetry that has met with the approbation of God Almighty.'"[54] Though fabulous, such a note shows Emerson's appreciation of the quality of eloquence which Sa'di held. In much the same manner, Hafiz replied to the pilgrim returning from Mecca: "Boast not rashly, prince of the pilgrims, of thy fortune. Thou hast indeed seen the temple; but I, the Lord of the temple. Nor has any man inhaled from the musk-bladder of the merchant or from the musky morning wind that sweet air which I am permitted to breathe every hour of the day."[55] Indeed in seeing and simultaneously expressing Beauty, Hafiz appears to have seen the Lord; and likewise Sa'di has written a stanza of verse so eloquent that it has pleased God the Almighty.

Suffice it to say that Emerson's interest in and admiration for the Sufi poets is so evident that they can hardly go unnoticed. Though as flattering and sympathetic as Emerson's stance toward the Islamic Orient is, it is yet imbued with certain simplifications of Islam and the Prophet. However, these are only scattered, sometimes confused, remarks. As early as 1841, in an entry in the journals, arguing to the conclusion that worship of saints and worship in general are diversions "from the insight of the soul," Emerson observes:

> The various matters which men magnify, as trade, law, creeds, sciences, paintings, coins, manuscripts, histories, poems, are all pieces of *virtue* which serve well enough to unfold the talents of the man, but are all diversions form the insight of the soul. Saints' worship is one of these,—the worship of Mahomet or Jesus,—like all the rest, a fine field of ingenuity wherein construct theories.[56]

The quoted passage does not accurately highlight the spirit of Islam. Muhammad, like all the Muslims, worshipped and believed in Allah, and Emerson's comparison between the worship of Jesus in Christianity and the worship of Muhammad in Islam is untenable since it disregards the fact that the Prophet is not God and should not be worshipped. In the essay *Social Aims*, while he discusses the bases of civil society that include social and individual manners, labor, public action, conversation, and education, Emerson points out:

> True wit never made us laugh. Mahomet seems to have borrowed by anticipation of several centuries a leaf from the mind of Swedenborg, when he wrote in the Koran:—"On the day of resurrection those who have indulged in ridicule will be called to the door of Paradise, and have it shut in their faces when they reach it. Again, on their turning back, they will be called to another door, and again, on reaching it, will see it closed against them; and so on *ad infinitum*, without end."[57]

While Emerson errs if he means literally that Muhammad wrote the Qur'an, he correctly perceives that the Prophet encouraged and urged the Muslims to have a sound sense of seriousness in many of his utterances and occasional remarks. The Qur'an, of course, is God's words that the Prophet, by God's decree, was to deliver to the Muslims and non-Muslims alike. In any case, Emerson found the Prophet's words congenial. He uses them to illustrate his point that an excess of humor is incompatible with sincerity and seriousness. Again, while he attributes seriousness to the Prophet, Emerson suggests that "Mahomet seems to have borrowed by anticipation of several centuries a lead to the mind of Swedenborg." Such a remark, though it may not be taken literally, seems to imply that the Occident too had its own moral, religious strictness which Muhammad had anticipated. At any rate, Emerson's tendency to take the liberty of incorporating Islamic quotations and ideas into his own thought shows an interest in their inspirational and cultural value.

Discussing social laws that include labor, trade, property, and faith, in a lecture on *Man the Reformer*, Emerson points out that the spread of Islam occurred because of the impelling power of its beliefs and its fanatical enthusiasm.

> Every great and commanding moment in the annals of the world is the triumph of some enthusiasm. The victories of the Arabs after Mahomet, who, in a few years, from a small and mean beginning, established a larger empire than that of Rome, is an example. They did they knew not what. The naked Derar, horsed on an idea, was found an overmatch for a troop of Roman cavalry. The women fought like men, and conquered the Roman men. They were miserably equipped, miserably fed. They were temperance troops. There was neither brandy nor flesh needed to feed them. They conquered Asia, and Africa, and Spain, on barley.[58]

Indeed Islam spread in a relatively short period of time, and the Muslims conquered Asia, Africa, and Spain. However, the religion had a power of faith, too, which is what Emerson means by enthusiasm, and once in the battlefield, the Muslims, though "miserably fed" and "miserably equipped," believed that the cause of God—or, as the Qur'an puts it, the *sabil Allah*[59]—was well worth the struggle. To Emerson, Christendom, unlike Islam, had a less fanatic but more gracious faith, though this he criticizes as dead, moribund except in name. In the same lecture Emerson says:

> But there will dawn ere long on our politics, on our modes of living, a nobler morning than that Arabian faith, in the sentiment of love. This is one remedy for all ills, the panacea of nature. . . . This great, overgrown, dead Christendom of ours still keeps alive at least the name of a lover of mankind.[60]

The implicit contrast between his idea of a new faith, based on a sentiment of love, and Oriental Islam as well as dead Christianity, reveals Emerson's distrust of the civilizing power of Islam or any other formal religion. For in the early inspiration of Christianity (now formalized and dead) he sees a "nobler morning than that Arabian faith." So if Islam suggested to Emerson an impelling enthusiasm and religious heroism, Christendom brought to mind "the name of a lover of mankind."

In an entry in his journals, which he entitles *Mahomet and Woman*, Emerson brings in ideas about the transformation of Islam as a religion into practical, enthusiastic power, and he associates these ideas with a certain Mr. Vethake of New York.

> Mr. V[ethake]'s opinion was that Mahomet had tried power, and Jesus, or, I think, John, persuasion; that Mahomet has felt that persuasion, this John-persuasion had miserably failed . . . and he said, I will try this Oriental weapon, the sword, which never, never will go West; and he said to Ayesha, "I have found out how to work it. This woman element will not bear the sword; well, I will dispose of woman: She may exist; but henceforward I will veil it" so he veiled Woman. Then the sword could work and eat . . . I smelt fagots . . . Fagots![61]

Muhammad used the sword in much the same way as he used persuasion. But Emerson's acquaintance, Vethake, perhaps reiterating the centuries-old tradition of equating Islam with religious tyranny, views Muhammad as a Prophet who transformed religion into an impelling power by granting full license to the sword and by suppressing women—the most civilizing element in society. In the passage, however, we are told that "This woman element [could] not bear the sword . . . So he [Muhammad] veiled it." Even though this "veiled" element of society was neither disposed of, nor dismissed as incapable of "sufficient moral or intellectual force,"[62] it is suggested here that such an element could be suppressed. On the contrary, in the passage just quoted from *Man the Reformer*, Emerson tells us: "The [Muslim] women fought like men, and conquered Roman men." The view which Emerson held there is obviously at variance with Vethake's in that it shows more admiration than distrust for this sense of enthusiasm he found in Islam.

By and large, however, Emerson found the Muslim East congenial. His fascination for as well as criticism of the Muslim Orient may perhaps be explained as stemming from a mixture of condescension and admiration. Emerson read the Orientals, and used all his reading in his writings, but he still identified his thought closely with the Western World. He read them in order to get vocabulary for his ideas (he did not want to get the Oriental ideas for their own sake).[63] In other words, Emerson preferred to remain Occidental. And his interest in Oriental philosophy and religions remains a manifestation of a lightly prejudice-colored but preeminently sympathetic attitude, a demonstration of the Western preeminence in world history. What Emerson wanted to do was to transform the Orient into a framework, or rather a vocabulary, of his own. Admittedly he was successful in incorporating the Oriental material as an exotic element, and, on occasion, as in the case of the Sufi poets, he showed a profound interest in and fascination for the Sufi ideals for their own sake.

Notes

1. This article was first published in *The Muslim World*, vol. 78, no. 2 (1988), 132–145.
2. Ralph L. Rusk, ed., *The Letters of Ralph Waldo Emerson*, 6 vols. (New York: Columbia University Press, 1939), I, 116–17.
3. Frederic I. Carpenter, *Emerson and Asia* (Cambridge: Harvard University Press, 1930), 3–4.
4. William H. Gilman, et al., eds., *The Journals and Miscellaneous Notebooks of Ralph Waldo Emerson*, 16 vols. (Cambridge: Harvard University Press, 1930), 3–4. Subsequent references refer to this edition; henceforth cited as *JMN*.
5. Arthur Christy, *The Orient in American Transcendentalism: A Study of Emerson, Thoreau, and Alcott* (New York: Columbia University Press, 1932), 68.
6. Carpenter, *Emerson and Asia*, 9.
7. In 1837 Emerson lists the *Historia Muslemica* of Abulfeda, and, in 1840, Simon Ockley's *History of the Saracens*. In 1841 he read Thomas Carlyle's book *On Heroes and Hero Worship* (which included a lecture on the Prophet). And in 1845 he read *Akhlaq-i Jalali*, an interesting book which shows how Greek philosophy was introduced into Islamic mysticism. And as early as 1822 Emerson read the *Arabian Nights*, and at the same time he was reading Gibbon's *Decline and Fall of the Roman Empire*, chapters 50 to 52 of which describe the rise and fall of the Muslim Caliphate.
8. Arthur Christy, "Emerson's Debt to the Orient," *The Monist*, 38 (Jan. 1928), 44.
9. Carpenter, *Emerson and Asia*, 14.
10. Edward W. Emerson, ed., *The Complete Works of Ralph Waldo Emerson*, 12 vols. (Boston: Houghton Mifflin, 1903–1904), IV, 39. Unless otherwise indicated, subsequent references are to this edition; hereafter cited as *Works*.
11. Emerson, *Works*, IV, 53–54.
12. Ibid., 47.
13. Ibid.
14. Ibid.
15. Ibid., 52.
16. Robert E. Spiller, et al., eds., *The Collected Works of Ralph Waldo Emerson* (Cambridge: Harvard University Press, 1971), I, 92–93.
17. *JMN*, II, 218.
18. In 1850 Emerson began to keep a separate journal entitled "The Orientalist" where he entered, observes Carpenter, "the philosophy of India, the poetry of Persia and Arabia, and the wisdom of all the Oriental countries at once. And from this source he drew much of the richness which he was to put into his later essays." Carpenter, *Emerson and Asia*, 22.
19. Emerson, *Works*, IV, 76.

20. Emerson, *Works*, X, 179.
21. *JMN*, X, 90. In another entry in the journals Emerson writes: "With our Saxon education and habit of thought we all require to be first. Each man must somehow think himself the first in his own career," *JMN*, IX, 218–19.
22. *JMN*, XIV, 166.
23. Clarence Gohdes, ed., *Uncollected Lectures by Ralph Waldo Emerson* (New York: William E. Rudge, 1932), 54.
24. Ibid. 60.
25. Emerson, *Works*, VI, 5.
26. Sa'di, *The Gulistan: Rose Garden of Saadi*, trans. Francis Gladwin (Boston: Ticknor and Fields, 1865), ix.
27. Emerson, *Works*, VIII, 238–239.
28. Ibid., 418.
29. Emerson, *Works*, VI, 29.
30. Ibid., 40.
31. Emerson, *Works*, VIII, 250.
32. Emerson, *Works*, VI, 57.
33. Ibid., 325.
34. Emerson, *Works*, VIII, 244–245.
35. Ibid., 246.
36. Ibid., 249–250.
37. Ibid., 250.
38. Ibid.
39. Emerson, *Works*, IX, 13.
40. Emerson, *Works*, IV, 205–206.
41. Emerson, *Works*, IX, 134.
42. Ibid., 132.
43. Ibid., 130.
44. Gladwin, *Gulistan*, v–vii.
45. Emerson, *Works*, IX, 130.
46. Emerson, *Works*, VIII, 247.
47. Ibid., ix.
48. *JMN*, IX, 68–70.
49. Carpenter, *Emerson and Asia*, 179.
50. Ibid., 171.
51. Emerson, *Works*, VIII, 249–50.
52. *JMN*, IX, 38.
53. Emerson, *Works*, VIII, 121.
54. *JMN*, IX, 39.
55. Emerson, *Works*, VIII, 254.
56. *JMN*, VII, 452.
57. Emerson, *Works*, VIII, 98.
58. Spiller, *The Collected Works*, I, 157.
59. Literally meaning "by way of God," is an expression meaning "doing something for God."
60. Spiller, *The Collected Works*, I, 158–59.

61. *JMN*, VIII, 342.

62. In the essay on "Woman," read before the Woman's Rights Convention, held in Boston in 1855, Emerson criticizes "Mahomet's opinion that women have not a sufficient moral or intellectual force to control the perturbations of their physical structure." *Works*, XI, 417.

63. *JMN*, V, 343.

4

Emerson and Aspects of Saʿdi's Reception in Nineteenth-Century America

Parvin Loloi

Saʿdi has been known in the West since 1634 when André du Ryer produced French selections of the *Gulistan* entitled *L'Empire des Roses*. In his introduction he called Saʿdi the "prince des Poétes Turcs et Persans." He emphasized the need to translate and study those authors who were most valued in the East. This sentiment was to be echoed very forcefully a century and a half later by Sir William Jones. In 1651 the Dutch Orientalist, George Gentius (Gentz), published an edition of the *Gulistan* with a complete translation into Latin as *Rosarium*. The first full (though free) German translation of the *Gulistan* was published in 1654 by Adam Olearius (Ölschlager) under the title of *Der Persianischer Rosenthal*. This was quickly translated into Dutch by J.V. Duisberg, and the German version itself was reissued three times before the end of the century. In a later edition, Olearius appended a translation of the *Bustan* (as *Der Baumgarten*) which he had made from a Dutch version. These translations, and the various further adaptations made from them, were very influential in the next century in Europe. In France, Voltaire presented his *Zadig* as a translation from Saʿdi; Johann Herder in Germany, and Joseph Addison in England, both adapted fables from the *Bustan* and the *Gulistan*. Herder's *Blumen aus Morgenländischen Dichtern Gesammelt* was made up mainly of quotations from the *Gulistan*.[1] The European image of Persian literature during the seventeenth and eighteenth centuries can be understood from Herder's admiring words; it was highly appreciated by intellectuals:

> Saʿdi, "the pleasant teacher of morals," as he says, "seems to have plucked the flower of moralizing poetry in his language . . . as his poetry was and still is regarded as a rose of the Persian tongue." His simple but elegant style, his practical wisdom, his charming anecdotes

made him a poet who appealed greatly to the Europeans, especially during the Age of Reason, and he has rightly been considered the Persian poet whose work is easiest for Westerners to understand. "His genius is less alien to the West than that of others, his imagination less overbearing," as Joseph von Hammer-Purgstall wrote in 1818, and this indefatigable Austrian orientalist chose two of Sa'di's verses to be engraved on his tombstone.[2]

Toward the end of the eighteenth century, particularly with the publication of Sir William Jones's voluminous works and translations from Eastern languages into English, French, and Latin, the center of Oriental studies shifted, and now flourished in Britain. Jones, in his *Persian Grammar*, recommends to the student of Persian that the first book that he should read ought to be "the *Gulistan* or *Bed of Roses*, a work which is highly esteemed in the East," and in his *History of the Persian Language* Jones writes that "SADI, a native of this city [Shiraz], flourished in the thirteenth century, . . . his life was almost wholly spent in travel; but no man who enjoyed the greatest leisure, ever left behind him more valuable fruits of his genius and industry."[3] Jones, despite his fondness for Hafiz, translated several passages from Sa'di including the fables of *The Scented Mud* (*Gel-i Khushbu*), the *Rain Drop*, and a passage which shows Sa'di's use of Arabic and Persian.[4] The first full English version of the *Gulistan*, by Francis Gladwin, did not, however, appear until 1822; it was followed by James Ross's translation in 1823.[5]

In America, as in Europe, Sa'di's fables were known from the early seventeenth century onward, even if the anonymous form in which they were usually known made plagiarism easy.[6] The flourishing of Oriental studies in Europe meant that American periodicals such as *The Literary Magazine* and *American Register*, *The American Quarterly Review*, *Portfolio*, and others[7] reviewed German, French, and English translations from Persian, as well as reprinting some of the English translations and articles on Persian poetry. There were also frequent translations from German and French into American English. A variety of published studies and translations also found their way across the Atlantic soon after publication. These proved fertile ground for the Oriental interests of the Transcendentalists of New England, particularly those based in Concord and headed by Ralph Waldo Emerson. As early as 1814, Emerson was reading Jones and his six-volume folio edition of Sir William Jones's *Works*, with all its many translations from Arabic, Hindi, and Persian, as well as Jones's various scholarly essays on a range of Oriental subjects. As in Britain, Jones's Works were "among the most influential Oriental books read in Concord."[8] For the most part Sa'di and other Persian poets were thought of as insignificant—as one reviewer of the French *Gulistan* wrote in *The American Quarterly Review*, in 1830; he

fervently expressed the hope that there would not be in America such vogue of Persian Poetry as there had been in Europe. He considered as doggerel those would be translations which sought to merit that name by the mere "infusion of such words as gul, bubul, harem, peri." He regarded much of Persian poetry as puerile . . . [and] proceeded to attack not only the popularizers of Persian Poetry but also the father of English Orientalism, Jones himself, whom he compared unfavourably with the French Orientalist d'Herbelot.[9]

Despite such opinions, Sa'di and Hafiz became the most widely read Persian poets in nineteenth-century America, in part because of the governing spirit of the age. As Arthur Christy so aptly writes:

> To understand the "orientalism" of the nineteenth century we must comprehend the Romantic temper, which included more than mere poetic interest in something "far away and long ago." It was the expression of a state of mind rather than a literary movement.[10]

It was precisely this state of mind which created the Romantic Movement both in Europe and in America. The beginning of the nineteenth century saw the emergence of Romanticism in America, which reached its peak by the middle of the century. This, in the words of Luther S. Mansfield,

> suggests a unity or basic similarity among at least the major writers of that period which is not superficially apparent. Clearly many distinctive features of European Romanticism were echoed in American writing. In contrast to the neo-classicism of the eighteenth century with emphasis on the norm, the timeless, the standards and conventions of the group, Romanticism, here as elsewhere, stressed the bizarre, the unique, the individual.[11]

Mansfield points out that

> [t]his peak period of American literary Romanticism has been called "the golden day" by Lewis Mumford, and "the American Renaissance" by F. O. Mathiessen . . . and by Van Wyck Brooks under headings of "the flowering of New England" and "the age of Melville and Whitman." Just as properly and perhaps more descriptively, it may be labelled the age of Emerson or somewhat explicitly, the age of the Emersonian idiom. *Nature*, *Self-Reliance*, *The Poet*, *Experience* and *Fate* are essential essays for defining this idiom. Any attempt to deal

> with the authors of the period . . . should begin with at least this much of the Emerson canon.[12]

Here we need to concern ourselves with two of these essays: "The Poet," and "Nature."

In his essay, "Books," Emerson writes that the religious books of each nation are the best. They are, according to his idiom, "sacred." There is also another group of books which

> have acquired a semi-canonical authority in the world, as expressing the highest sentiment and hope of nations. Such are "Hermes Trismegistus," pretending to be Egyptian remains; the "Sentences" of Epictetus; of Marcus Antoninus; the "Vishnu Sarma" of Hindoos; the "Gulistan" of Saadi; the "Imitation of Christ," of Thomas a Kempis; and the "Thoughts" of Pascal.
>
> All these books are the majestic expressions of the universal conscience, and are more to our daily purpose than this year's almanac or this day's newspaper. But they are for the closet, and to be read on bended knees. Their communications are not to be given or taken with the lips and the end of tongue, but out of the glow of the cheek, and with throbbing heart. . . . They are not to be held by letters printed on a page, but are living characters translatable into every tongue and form of life. I read them on lichens and barks; I watch them on waves on the beach; they fly in birds, they creep in worms; I detect them in laughter and blushes and eye-sparkles of men and women. These are Scriptures which the missionary might well carry over prairie, desert, and ocean, to Siberia, Japan, Timbactoo. Yet he will find that the spirit which is in them journeys faster than he, and greets him on his arrival,—was there long before him.[13]

If Emerson thought of the *Gulistan* as a "sacred" book with universal spirit, then it is reasonable to suggest that Sa'di himself—along with some other writers of Europe and the East—was one of his ideal poets.

Emerson's interest in Sa'di began when he was only eleven years of age. In his early *Journal* of November 1814 he writes about originality, declaring that "so there are fountains all around Milton or Saadi or Menu from which they drew."[14] Elsewhere he juxtaposes two names: "Chaucer Saadi."[15] "By October 1843 he had 'had the Gulistan of Saadi,' on whom he had earlier written verses in *The Dial*."[16] However, Emerson bypasses Sa'di in his essay *Persian Poetry*, published in 1858, except for the mention of his name in the first paragraph.[17] It seems evident from Emerson's *Journals* that he had read little of Sa'di at this date—or perhaps he was saving his thoughts for later. He had known at least the names of many Persian poets since his student days at Harvard and read some of their works in Jones but did not study their work systematically. In January of 1861 he had started reading and translating from the *Bustan*. His sources were the German translations by K. F Graf, *Moslichedden Sadi's Lustgarten (Bustan)*, and *Moslichedin Sadi's Rosengarten, (Gulistan)*, as well as Joseph von Hammer-Purgstall's *Geschichte der schonen Redekunste Persiens mit einer Bluethenlese aus zweyhundert persischen Dichtern*. By 1863 Emerson was fully immersed in the study of Sa'di, as his *Journal* of this year amply illustrates. His notes and translations from Sa'di during this period found their way into his introduction to the first American reprint of the *Gulistan* by Francis Gladwin, published in Boston in 1865, and into his poem *Saadi*.[18] Some of the translations he read were also influential in other areas of his own poetry, as noted by Yohannan.[19] Yohannan has also identified the various German sources that Emerson used for his English versions.[20]

One English editor of Emerson's prose works describes him as "a moral and intellectual preacher for a free platform. His soul, imbibing the lessons of all ages, in communion with the springs of Nature, fervently sympathising with aspirations of his fellow men. . . ."[21] It is, then, hardly surprising that Emerson should have been attracted to the most explicit moralist amongst the poets of Persian literature. These two poets, Emerson and Sa'di, have more in common than first meets the eye. Both poets seem to have launched themselves on journeys of discovery round about their thirtieth years of age—Sa'di's travels occupying about thirty years—but both poets owe many of their creative insights to their roamings. Sa'di wrote his *Bustan* and *Gulistan* soon after his return to his birthplace of Shiraz around 1256, and Emerson's first essay, "Nature," was published in 1836, two years after his first trip to Europe. Therefore, for Emerson, Sa'di was a kindred soul whose

> varied and severe experience took away all provincial tone, and gave him a facility of speaking to all conditions. But the commanding reason of his treatment, expands the local forms and tints to a cosmopolitan breath. Through his Persian dialect he speaks to all nations, and like Homer, Shakespeare, Cervantes, and Montaigne, is perpetually modern.[22]

At the beginning of his *Preface* Emerson betrays some of the common assumptions underlying Western views of Oriental literature in this period:

> At first sight, the Oriental rhetoric does not please our Western taste. Life in the East wants the complexity of European and American existence; and in their writing a certain monotony betrays the poverty of the landscape, and of social conditions. We fancy we are soon familiar with all their images. Medschun [Majnun] and Leila, rose

and nightingale, parrots and tulips, mosques and dervishes . . . insane compliments to the Sultan, borrowed from the language of prayer; Hebrew and Gueber [Zoroastrian] legends molten into Arabesque;— 'tis a short inventory of topics and tropes, which incessantly return in Persian poetry. I do not know but, at first encounter, many readers take also an impression of tawdry rhetoric, an exaggeration, and a taste for scarlet, running to borders of negrofine.[23]

A few lines later he not only refutes this line of thought but blames it on a lack of understanding on the part of European and American readers of Persian poetry. He goes on to say that

[t]hese blemishes disappear or diminish on better acquaintance. Where there is real merit, we are soon reconciled to differences of taste. The charge of monotony lies more against the numerous Western imitations than against the Persians themselves, and though the torrid, like the arctic zone, puts some limit to variety, it is least felt in the masters. It is the privilege of genius to play its game indifferently with few as with many pieces, as Nature draws all her opulence out of a few elements.[24]

In his *Journal* of 1847 Emerson expounds his thoughts on dictionaries and autobiography and writes that:

An autobiography should be a book of answers from one individual to the main questions of the time. Shall he be a scholar? . . . Shall he seek to be rich? Shall he go for the ascetic or the [popular] conventional life? He being aware of the double consciousness.—Shall he value mathematics? Read Dante? Or not? Aristophanes? Plato? Cosmogonies, & scholar's courage. What shall he say of Poetry? What of Astronomy? What of Religion?

Then let us hear his conclusions respecting government & politics. Does he pay taxes and record his deeds? . . . does Goethe's Authobiography answer these questions? So of love, of marriage, so of playing providence. It should be a true Conversation's Lexicon for earnest men. Saadi's Gulistan is not far from this. It should confirm the reader in his best sentiment. It should go for imagination & taste. It should aspire & worship.[25]

Here, "Conversation's Lexicon" refers to F. A. Brockhaus's German *Konversations-Lexikon*—a monumental encyclopaedia, which later became known simply as Brockhaus and is still used today. It is interesting to note that as early as 1847

Emerson had Sa'di's *Gulistan* in his mind as an encyclopaedic work which ranked among some of the major European works of this nature. These thoughts were reflected in his *Preface* to the *Gulistan*. Eighteen years later Sa'di is compared to two of the most renowned lexicographers of France and Britain.

> Saadi exhibits perpetual variety of situation and incident, and an equal depth of experience with Cardinal de Rez in Paris, or Doctor Johnson in London. He finds room on his narrow canvas for the extremes of lot, the play of motives, the rule of destiny, the lessons of morals, and the portraits of great men. He has furnished the originals of a multitude of tales and proverbs which are current in our mouths, and attributed by us to recent writers; as, for example, the story of "Abraham and the Fire-worshipper," once claimed for Doctor Franklin, and afterwards traced to Jeremy Taylor, who probably found it in Olearius.[26]

Comparing Hafiz and Sa'di, Emerson asserts that

> Saadi, though he has not the lyric flights of Hafiz, has wit, practical sense, and just moral sentiments. He has the instinct to teach, and from every occurrence must draw the moral, like Franklin. He is the poet of friendship, love, self-devotion, and serenity. There is a uniform force in his page, and conspicuously, a tone of cheerfulness, which has almost made his name a synonym for this grace. The word "Saadi" means "fortunate." In him the trait is no result of levity, much less of convivial habit, but first of a happy nature, to which victory is habitual, easily shedding mishaps, with sensibility to pleasure, and with resources against pain. But it also results from habitual perception of the beneficent laws that control the world. He inspires in the reader a good hope. What a contrast between the cynical tone of Byron and the benevolent wisdom of Saadi![27]

After vilifying one the most famous of the English Romantic poets, Emerson goes on to discuss the style of Persian poetry in general and of Sa'di in particular:

> To the sprightly and indolent Persians, conversation is a game of skill. They wish to measure wit with you, and expect an adroit, a brilliant, or a profound answer. Many narratives, doubtless, have suffered in the translation, since a promising anecdote sometimes heralds a flat speech. But Saadi's replies are seldom vulgar. His wit answers to the heart of the question, often quite over the scope of the inquirer. He has also that splendor of expression which alone,

without wealth of thought, sometimes constitutes a poet, and forces us to ponder the problem of style. In his poem on old age, he says: "Saadi's whole power lies in his sweet words: let this gift remain to me, I care not what is taken."[28]

A couple of pages later, Emerson speaks again of the discontinuity of themes in Persian Poetry, especially those written in the form of the *ghazal* and the *qasidah*—a failure to understand the thematic unity of Persian poetry which was common among both translators and scholars of Persian poetry from the late eighteenth to the mid twentieth century in both Europe and America.[29] Emerson continues:

> In a country where there are no libraries and no printing, people must carry wisdom in sentences. Wonderful is the inconsecutiveness of the Persian Poets. European criticism finds that the unity of a beautiful whole is everywhere wanting. Not only the story is short, but no two sentences are joined. In looking through Von Hammer's anthology, culled from a paradise of poets, the reader feels this painful discontinuity. 'Tis sand without lime,—as if the neighboring desert had *saharized* the mind. It was said of Thomson's Seasons, that the page would read as well by omitting every alternate line. But the style of Thomson is glue and bitumen to the loose and irrecoverable ramble of Oriental bards. No topic is too remote for their rapid suggestion. The Ghaselle or Kassida is a chapter of proverbs, or proverbs unchaptered, unthreaded beads of all colors, sizes, and values. Yet two topics are sure to return in any and every proximity, the mistress and the name of the poet. Out of every ambush these leap on the unwary reader. Saadi, in the Gulistan, by the necessity of the narrative, corrects this arid looseness, which appears, however, in his odes and elegies, as in Hafiz and Dschami [Jami]. As for the incessant return of the poet's name,—which appears to be a registry of copyrights,—the Persians often relieve this heavy custom by wit and audacious sallies.[30]

Emerson could not have consciously contrived a more graphic picture of his total failure to comprehend characteristic Persian poetical forms. He has here reproduced once more exactly the charges which have repeatedly been laid against Hafiz. As regards the philosophy of Sa'di, however, he redeems himself by writing that the

> Sheik's (Sheikh's) mantle sits loosely on Saadi's shoulders, and I find in him a pure theism. He asserts the universality of moral laws, and the perpetual retributions. He celebrates the omnipotence of a virtu-

ous soul. A certain intimate and avowed piety, obviously in sympathy with the feeling of his nation, is habitual to him. All the forms of courtesy and of business in daily life take a religious tinge, as did those of Europe in the Middle Ages.

With the exception of a few passages, of which we need not stop to give account, the morality of the Gulistan and Bostan is pure, and so little clogged with the superstition of the country, that this does not interfere with the pleasure of the modern reader: he can easily translate their ethics into his own. Saadi praises alms, hospitality, justice, courage, bounty, and humility. . . .[31]

Finally Emerson concludes his introduction by going a long way toward negating his earlier statements when he referred to the Persians as "indolent." He writes,

> The Persians have been called "the French of Asia;" and their superior intelligence, their esteem for men of learning; their welcome to Western travellers, and their tolerance of Christian sects in their territory, . . . would seem to derive from the rich culture of this great choir of poets, perpetually reinforced through five hundred years, which again and again has enabled the Persians to refine and civilize their conquerors, and to preserve a national identity. To the expansion of this influence there is no limit; and we wish that the present republication may add to the genius of Saadi a new audience in America.[32]

Emerson's poem *Saadi* was first published in *The Dial* in 1842. As we have seen, he had not yet studied Sa'di thoroughly at this date, but Sa'di had nevertheless become one of his ideal poets. Some years later, after writing his introduction to the *Gulistan*, he is thought to have gone back to the poem to make sure that he had understood and written about Sa'di correctly in those early years.[33] His poem *Saadi* has hitherto received very little critical study,[34] so it is apt to attempt a more detailed account here. The poem, despite its length, deserves quotation in full:

Saadi

Trees in groves,
Kine in droves,
In ocean sport the scaly herds,
Wedge-like cleave the air the birds,
To northern lakes fly wind-borne ducks,
Browse the mountain sheep in flocks,

Men consort in camp and town,
But the poet dwells alone.

God, who gave to him the lyre,
Of all mortals the desire,
For all breathing men's behoof,
Straitly charged him, 'Sit aloof;'
Annexed a warning, poets say,
To the bright premium,—
Ever, when twain together play,
Shall the harp be dumb.

Many may come,
But one shall sing;
Two touch the string,
The harp is dumb,
Though there come a million,
Wise Saadi dwells alone.

Yet Saadi loved the race of men,—
No churl, immured in cave or den;
In bower and hall
He wants them all,
Nor can dispense
With Persia for his audience;
They must give ear,
Grow red with joy and white with fear;
But he has no companion;
Come Ten, or come a million,
Good Saadi dwells alone.

Be thou ware where Saadi dwells;
Wisdom of the gods is he,—
Entertain it reverently.
Gladly round that golden lamp
Sylvan deities encamp,
And simple maids and noble youth
Are welcome to the man of truth.
Most welcome they who need him most,
They feed the spring which they exhaust;
For greater need

Draws better deed:
But, critic, spare thy vanity,
Nor show thy pompous parts,
To vex with odious subtlety
The cheerer of men's hearts.

Sad-eyed Fakirs swiftly say
Endless dirges to decay,
Never in the blaze of light
Lose the shudder of midnight;
Pale at overflowing noon
Hear wolves barking at the moon;
In the bower of dalliance sweet
Hear the far Avenger's feet:
And shake before those awful Powers,
Who in their pride forgive not ours.
Thus the sad-eyed Fakirs preach:
'Bard, when thee would Allah teach,
And lift thee to his holy mount,
He sends thee from his bitter fount
Wormhood,—saying, "Go thy ways,
Drink not the Malaga of praise,
But do the deed thy fellows hate,
And compromise thy peaceful state,
Smite the white breads which thee fed,
Stuff sharp thorns beneath the head
Of them thou shouldst have comforted;
For out of woe and out of crime
Draws the heart a lore sublime."'
And yet it seemeth not to me
That the high gods love tragedy;
For Saadi sat in the sun,
And thanks was his contrition;
For haircloth and for bloody whips,
Had active hands and smiling lips;
And yet his runes he rightly read,
And to his folk his message sped.
Sunshine in his heart transferred
Lighted each transparent word,
And well could honouring Persia learn
What Saadi wished to say;

For Saadi's nightly stars did burn
Brighter than Dshami's day.

Whispered the Muse in Saadi's cot.
'O gentle Saadi, listen not,
Tempest by thy praise of wit,
Or by thirst and appetite
For the talents not thine own,
To sons of contradiction.
Never, son of eastern morning.
Follow falsehood, follow scorning
Denounce who will, who will deny
And pile the hills to scale the sky;
Let theist, atheist, pantheist,
Define and wrangle how they list,
Fierce conserver, fierce destroyer,—
But thou, joy-giver and enjoyer,
Unknowing war, unknowing crime,
Gentle Saadi, mind thy rhyme;
Heed not what the brawlers say,
Head thou only Saadi's lay.

'Let the great world bustle on
With war and trade, with camp and town:
A thousand men shall dig and eat;
At forge and furnace thousand sweat;
And thousand sail the purple sea,
And give or take the stroke of war,
Or crowd the market and bazzar;
Oft shall war end, and peace return,
And cities rise where cities burn,
Ere one man my hill shall climb,
Who can turn the golden rhyme.
Let them manage how they may,
Heed thou only Saadi's lay.
Seek the living among the dead,—
Man in man is imprisoned;
Barefooted Dervish is not poor,
If fate unlock his bosom's door,
So that what his eye has seen
His tongue can paint as bright, as keen;
And what his tender heart hath felt

With equal fire thy heart shalt melt.
For, whom the Muses smile upon,
And touch with soft persuasion,
His words like a storm-wind can bring
Terror and beauty on their wing;
In his every syllable
Lurketh nature veritable;
And thou he speaks in midnight dark,—
In heaven no star, on earth no spark,—
Yet before the listener's eye
Swims the world in ecstasy,
The forest waves, the morning breaks,
The pastures sleep, ripple the lakes,
Leaves twinkle, flowers like persons be,
And life pulsates in rock or tree.
Saadi, so far thy words shall reach:
Suns rise and we set in Saadi's speech!'

And thus to Saadi said the Muse:
'Eat thou the bread which men refuse:
Flee from the goods which from thee flee;
Seek nothing,—Fortune seeketh thee.
Not mount, nor dive; all good things keep
The midway of eternal deep.
Wish not to fill the isles with eyes
To fetch thee birds of paradise:
On thine orchard's edge belong
All the brags of plume and song;
Wise Ali's sunbright sayings pass
For proverbs in the market-place:
Through mountains bored by regal art,
Toil whistles as he drives his cart.
Nor scour the seas, nor sift mankind,
A poet or a friend to find:
Behold, he watches at the door!
Behold his shadow on the floor!
Open innumerable doors
The heaven where unveiled Allah pours
The flood of truth, the flood of good,
The Seraph's and the Cherub's food.
Those doors are men: the Pariah hind
Admits thee to perfect Mind.

> Seek not beyond thy cottage wall
> Redeemers that can yield thee all:
> While thou sittest at thy door
> On the desert's yellow floor,
> Listening to the gray-haired crones,
> Foolish gossips, ancient drones,
> Saadi, see! They rise in stature
> To the height of mighty Nature,
> And the secret stands revealed
> Fraudulent Time in vain concealed,—
> That blessed gods in servile masks
> Plied for thee thy household tasks.'[35]

Emerson's poem is essentially an exercise in Romanticism. The first stanza creates the image of the poet as solitary. It is not that he is anti-social, but rather that the activity of poetic creativity is by its very nature solitary, and thus "the poet dwells alone." In the second stanza we are told that the poet's gift as a musician of words is God-given, and for this reason, too, he "sits aloof," separate from others; even were another poet to join him the two would not be able to strike a harmonious chord together, since each must, of necessity, create in solitude; thus Sa'di, who is wise, "dwells alone." This solitude on the part of the poet does not grow from contempt for common humanity—"Saadi loved the race of men." Indeed the poet needs the whole of "Persia for his audience" who "must give ear" to his poetry; and yet, paradoxically, even if Sa'di finds a million for his audience, he is still alone. The refrain in the third stanza refers to Sa'di as "Good," so our Persian is not only wise, but he is also an emblem of moral goodness in his solitude. In the first three stanzas the use of the refrain intensifies the notion of the poet's loneliness—an ideal of Western Romantic thought.

The fourth stanza reflects on the kind of dwelling place that Sa'di occupies. Emerson warns the reader "Be thou ware where Saadi dwells." This kind of caution is again a Romantic notion, when it comes to attitudes towards the poet. Emerson might have had Samuel Taylor Coleridge's *Kubla Khan* in mind, where Coleridge writes:

> I would build that dome in air,
> That sunny dome! Those caves of ice!
> And all who heard should see them there,
> And all should cry, Beware! Beware![36]

Sa'di, the man of "truth," dwells in a place of light where woodland nymphs, "Sylvan deities," also inhabit and where the simple and the innocent are welcome. "They feed the spring which they exhaust." "Spring" as the source of pure water, in both the Western poetical tradition and in Persian Sufi poetry, is a symbol of poetic inspiration, so here while the youth and the innocent play their part in inspiring the poet they also exhaust the spring's sources for their own needs. In Sa'di's garden of light, the critics "who show [their] pompous parts, / To vex with odious subtlety / The cheerer of men's hearts" are not welcome. The next stanza illustrates the preaching of the puritanical moralists the—"Sad-eyed Fakirs"—who do not sit in the "light," but rather in darkness and who, even in the height of the day with its bright sun, bark like wolves; like an "avenger" in the sweet smelling garden they admonish the poet, saying that he should use his God-given power to offer teachings from the "bitter fount" of life and its misery, that he should not be drinking the wine—the "Malaga"—"of praise." He should make his audience suffer, "For out of woe and out of crime / Draws the heart a lore sublime." Emerson then offers the suggestion that the gods do not love tragedy, because "Saadi sat in the sun" and, despite his suffering, he had "smiling lips" and read the "runes" (mysteries) correctly and thus "Sunshine in his heart transferred / Lighted each transparent word." The images used here of righteous Fakirs and "critics" may have come from Emerson's reading of Hafiz, as Yohannan has pointed out.[37] If, further, we compare these lines to a passage from the *Bustan*, it becomes evident that Emerson's idea of a poet of light is actually Sa'di's own description of himself:

> All the lines of these books are veiled,
> Which will fall down for a heart-ravishing face.
>
> There are hidden meanings in every black letter,
> Like a veiled beloved and a moon under the clouds.
>
> In Sa'di's heart there is no room for sadness,
> Since he has many beautiful faces behind the veil.
>
> My words light up an assembly,
> They, like fire, exude light and warmth.[38]

This seventh stanza of Emerson's poem concludes by comparing Sa'di with Jami,[39] whose days lack the brightness of Sa'di's nights.

In the eighth stanza of the poem, Sa'di is described as "gentle," a poet whose muse whispers in his ears while still a babe in his cot and advises him not to listen to the warring creeds, whether "theist, atheist, pantheist," because they are "Fierce Conserver[s], fierce destroyer[s]," whereas Sa'di is a "joy-giver and enjoyer," who does not know any war or crime (this is obviously Emerson's early idealistic notion which is corrected in the Preface, p. viii). The poem finishes with the advice "Heed thou only Saadi's lay" which is repeated half way down the next stanza, after continuing the same theme but with more vivid images of a war, not clearly either Western or Eastern. Through the chaos and destruction only "one man my hill shall climb, / Who can turn the golden rhyme." The imagery of the warring nations conjures up a famous line of Hafiz:

> Excuse all the wars of the seventy two nations,
> Since they did not see the way of truth, they chose the way of fable.[40]

The second half of the ninth stanza could be interpreted as, in essence, a statement of a key Sufi doctrine. "Man in Man is imprisoned," suggests that the soul is imprisoned in the cage of the body and that the "barefooted dervish," presumably Sa'di, is not poor, in truth. He has seen what no ordinary man has, and therefore "his tender heart hath felt, / With equal fire thy heart shall melt." The muses shine on every word of Sa'di, whose "words like a storm-wind can bring / Terror and beauty on their wing; / In his every syllable / Lurketh nature veritable." Nature is an important aspect of almost all mystical philosophies, as will be discussed later. This stanza finishes with more images of light and faraway lands where Emerson hopes that Sa'di's "words shall reach" because the light of the day belongs to him.

The last stanza continues with the muse's advice to Sa'di—that he should be moderate because "all good things keep / the midway of eternal deep." He should not seek the "birds of paradise," since the boundaries of his humble "orchard wall" hold all that he needs—and more—because just as words and sayings of the prophet's cousin and son-in-law, Ali, have become common knowledge and found their way to every "market-place," so too will Sa'di's. Sa'di is advised that whatever is valuable is already near him. He only has to look and see with his mind's eye, and then he can open "innumerable doors." "Those doors are men"—even the social outcast amongst men, any "pariah," can open the door to the sanctuary of the "unveiled Allah," where he will be flooded with "truth" and "good," where angels will give him heavenly food and he can be admitted to the presence of the "perfect Mind," the Supreme Intelligence or God. The poem concludes with a quintessentially Emersonian concept of Man and Nature. The speaker, who is still the "muse," tells Sa'di "not to look beyond thy cottage wall," because the redeemer is within him. When he sits on his doorstep and watches the old, the decrepit, and the ugly gossip foolishly in their monotonous tones, he should recognise that even they can reveal the true and lofty nature of man, and thus reveal the secret which even "Time," has failed to steal. If Sa'di looks closely and understands, he will recognize that even his household servants are "gods" in disguise. They, too, can also reveal the essence of nature and thus of God.

Emerson's philosophical view of Nature, and of Man as its supreme being, is closely related to the ideas of Neoplatonism—but there are also many common doctrines shared between Sufism and Neoplatonism. Without space or time to attempt any full account of the complex metaphysical theories of the Persian philosophers and mystics, a mere couple of examples will have to suffice here. In a note to Affifi's[41] Commentaries on the most famous of the Western Muslim Sufis, Ibn 'Arabi, Henry Corbin writes:

> [t]here is the metaphysical theory that Man (mankind) is the most perfect revelation of all the Divine Attributes, and there is the mystical theory that certain men, partaking of the category of the Perfect Man, attain to a level of consciousness in which they experience the significance of their unity with the divine reality. On this realization depends the truth of perfect man as a microcosm *in actu*. . . . But this microcosmic truth . . . must in turn, when one speaks of the Perfect Man as a cosmic principle, lead us not to confuse the *Haqiqat al-Haqa'iq* (Muhamadic essence, *Nous*, Holy Spirit) and its concrete manifestations, namely the class of men (prophets and saints) entering into this category of Perfect Man.[42]

A second example can be taken from Hermeticism. Avicenna, the most famous of those Persian philosophers thought to have been influenced by Greek philosophy, especially that of Aristotle, and whose philosophy has in turn been influential in the west, notably on Dante,[43] holds similar notions of the "Perfect Man." Henry Corbin, in comparing *The Recital of Hayy ibn yaqzan* by Avicenna and Suhrawardi's *The Recital of the Occidental Exile (al-Ghurbat al-gharbiyyah)* with the Hermetic vision of Poimandres writes:

> Just as, in Avicenna and Suhrawardi, the "reciter" receives his vision either in sleep or in a state between waking and sleep, so the *Nous* (*'aql, khrad*) appears to Hermes while "his bodily senses were under restraint" during a deep sleep. It seems to him that a being of vast magnitude appears before him, calls him by name, and asks: "'What do you wish to hear and see, to learn and come to know by thought?' 'Who are you?' I said. 'I,' said he, 'am Poimandres, the Mind [*Nous*] of Sovereignty. . . . I know what you wish, for indeed I am with you everywhere' . . . Forthwith all things changed in aspect before me, and were opened out in a moment. And I beheld a boundless view; all was changed into light, a mild and joyous light; and I marvelled when I saw it." Later in the course of the vision: "He gazed long upon me, eye to eye, so that I trembled at his aspect. And when I raised my head, again, I saw in my mind [*Nous*] that

> the light consisted of innumerable Powers, and come to be . . . a world without bounds . . . And when I was amazed, he spoke again, and said to me, 'You have seen in your mind [*Nous*] the archetypal form, which is prior to the beginning of things, and is limitless.' Thus spoke Poimandres to me." It is of this ecstasy of Hermes that there is a trace in Suhrawardi, when the Form of Light replies to Hermes: "I am thy Perfect Nature."[44]

While it cannot be demonstrated that Emerson was directly influenced in any way by Persian poets and philosophers like Avicenna or Suhrawardi, he certainly knew Hermes Trismegistus and his work when he wrote "Saadi." Between 1841 and 1843, Emerson

> came most fully under the influence of Neoplatonism, while at the same time he was enlarging his knowledge of the Orient. In 1841 he was reading Proclus, Porphyry, Iamblichus, Hermes Trismegistus, Synesius, and others . . . and was confiding to his *Journals* his most enthusiastic praise of the 'Trismegisti' or 'Platonists.'[45]

Emerson's study of Platonism, Neoplatonism and Orientalism were concurrent. In 1845 he published a volume entitled Representative Men, made up those of the Occident, with no room for the direct reflection of his Oriental reading; yet in the process of writing his first essay, on Plato, he manages to convert "the Greek philosopher into half an Orientalist, devoting a large part of the essay to Oriental aspects of his thought."[46] Therefore "[h]is essay on Plato is the locus classicus for the expression of Orientalism in Emerson's writings."[47] Carpenter argues that "Emerson's curious concept of Platonism" can be explained by the history of his reading. He identified Plato with Platonism, declaring in his essay "it is fair to credit the broadest generalizer with all particulars deducible from his thesis." Further, he identified Platonism with Neoplatonism. He credited Plato with the doctrines that the Neoplatonists of Alexandria had deduced from his philosophy, and these doctrines bore a strongly Oriental tinge. They represent, historically, the fusion of Greek Platonism with a mysticism brought from the Orient by way of Alexandria.[48] Emerson's statement, as described by Carpenter, is rather flawed. Alexandria was, of course, the center of education and as the ancient texts were translated into both Arabic and Latin, but the exchange was a two way discourse, thus the Greek philosophy made its mark on Muslim philosophers as well. To clarify Emerson's viewpoint, a couple of passages from Plato will have to suffice. Talking about Indian philosophy, Emerson also clearly sets out his own ideas:

> The same, the same: friend and foe are of one stuff; the ploughman the plough and the farrow are of one stuff; and the stuff is such and so much that variations of form are unimportant . . . It is soul,—one in all bodies, pervading, uniform, perfect, pre-eminent over nature, exempt birth, growth and decay, omnipresent, made up of true knowledge, independent, unconnected with unrealities, with name, species, and the rest, in time past, present and to come. The knowledge that this spirit, which is essentially one, is in one's own and in all other bodies, is the wisdom of one who knows the unity of things. As one diffusive air, passing through the perforations of a flute, is distinguished as the notes of a scale, so the nature of the Great Spirit is single, though its forms be manifold. . . .[49]

Earlier in the same passage Emerson writes, that

> [i]n all nations there are minds which incline to dwell in the conception of fundamental Unity. The raptures of prayer and ecstasy of devotion lose all being in one Being. This tendency finds its highest expression in the religious writings of the East. . . .[50]

Thus we can safely assume that the above passage could also easily be applied to Sufi doctrines, as well as to Neoplatonic philosophy. Indeed at one point in *Plato*, Emerson compares a passage from the Qur'an with Plato:

> The East is explicit on this point of caste. "Men have their metal, as of gold and silver. Those of you who were the worthy ones in the state of ignorance, will be the worthy ones in the state of faith, as soon as you embrace it." Plato was no less firm. "Of the five orders of things, only four can be thought to generality of men." In the Republic he insists on the temperaments of the youth, as first of the first.[51]

Elsewhere he emphasizes that "the notion of virtue is not to be arrived at except through contemplation of the divine essence."[52]

"Divine essence" is the key to the study of Nature, as was seen by the Romantics in Europe and America. It is also a major doctrine of the Sufi philosophers. The study of Nature was, therefore, an important preoccupation of the Concordian friends, Amos Bronson Alcott (1799–1888) and Henry David Thoreau (1817–1862), headed by Emerson. The three friends shared all the books they read. Emerson was a founding member of *The Dial* in 1840, and the first volume of the magazine contains an article entitled The Divine Presence in Nature and in Soul. The author is identified by the letter "P." The article sets out the basic principles of Nature as an emanation of God—a philosophical doctrine which is shared in almost all religions. The Omnipresence of God is described thus:

> He [God] fills the world of outward nature with his presence. The fullness of divine energy flows inexhaustibly into the crystal of the rock, the juices of the plant, the splendor of the stars, the life of the bee and Behemoth. . . . Hence Nature ever grows, and changes, and becomes something new, as God's all pervading energy flows into it without ceasing.

The author goes on to say that "[i]t is an important fact that all parts of nature are in perfect harmony with God's will, and therefore reveal all of God that can be made manifest to the eye, the ear, and other senses of man." As regards the manifestation of God in Man, "P" writes "But yet God is present in man as well as out of him. The divine energy and substance possess the human soul, no less than they constitute the law and life of outward nature." "P" further writes that "His presence revealed in all that is magnificently great, or elegantly little, renders the world of nature solemn and beautiful."[53] It is then hardly surprising that Sa'di, who proudly but succinctly proclaims,

> In the eye of the wise, each leaf of the green trees,
> is manifestation of the mysteries of God[54]

should be one of the favorite men of this group of American thinkers, a "Perfect Man" in terms of both the Sufi and Neoplatonic doctrines. Sa'di's lines, naturally, could have been influenced by either Islamic thought or by the Neoplatonists. In Islamic philosophy,

> man seeks to transcend nature and nature herself can be an aid in this process provided man can learn to contemplate it, not as an independent domain of reality but as a mirror reflecting a higher reality, a vast panorama of symbols which speak to man and have meaning for him.[55]

Thus,

> a Plotinus, an Avicenna, or a St. Albert the Great would . . . [say] that in nature there is nothing more evident than the essences of things, since these manifest themselves in the 'forms' themselves. Only, they cannot be discovered by 'laborious work of investigation' nor measured quantitatively; in fact the intuition that grasps them relies directly on sensory perception and imagination, inasmuch as the latter synthesizes the impression received from outside.[56]

Dante expresses a similar notion in the *Divine Comedy*:

> ... Le cose tutte quante
> Hann' ordine tra loro: e questo è forma
> Che l'universo a Dio fa simigliante.
>
> ... *All things whatsoever*
> *observe a mutual order; and this is the form*
> *that maketh the universe like unto God.*[57]

It is not, therefore, surprising that Sa'di should have become one of the most revered of poets for the Transcendentalists of New England. Emerson, influenced by his readings of the Western and Eastern philosophers, developed a complex doctrine of "Nature," discussion of which is beyond the scope of this article, but the essence of his thoughts can be summed up in the poem he attached to his essay on "Nature."

Nature

> The rounded world is fair to see,
> Nine times folded in mystery:
> Though baffled seers cannot impart
> The secret of its labouring heart,
> Throb thine with Nature's throbbing breast,
> And all is clear from east to west.
> Spirit that lurks each form within
> Beckons to spirit of its kin;
> Self-kindled every atom glows,
> And hints the future which it owes.[58]

For Emerson, Sa'di was, above all, a poet of Nature; this is clear from his poem *Saadi* and from a *Fragment on the Poet* where he writes;

> Those idle catches told the laws
> Holding Nature to her cause.
> ...
> God only knew how Saadi dined;
> Roses he ate, and drank the wind.
> ...
> He felt the flame, the fanning wings,
> Nor offered words till they were things.
> ...
> Sun and moon fall amain
> Like sower's seeds into his brain,
> There quickened to be born again.[59]

Emerson believed that an ideal poet should speak through the symbolic language of Nature and its many splendid images. In his essay "The Poet," Emerson writes that "nature has a higher end, in the production of new individuals, . . . namely *ascension*, or the passage of the soul into higher forms,"[60] which is a similar notion to that of Ibn 'Arabi as quoted above. The poet thus has access to a "better perception" through which

> he stands one step nearer to things, and sees the flowing or metamorphosis; perceives that thought is multiform: that within the form of every creature is a force impelling it to ascend into a higher form; and following with his eyes the life, uses the forms which express that life, and so his speech flows with the flowing of nature.[61]

Poets are thus liberating gods.[62]

For the Romantics withdrawal into nature was a way towards understanding the complexities of nature. For such reasons, these three friends in Concord regularly went to the wildernesses of New England, Thoreau more fully than the others. Emerson wrote "We nestle in nature, and draw our living as parasites from her roots and grains, and we receive glances from the heavenly bodies, which call us to solitude and foretell the remotest future."[63] It was the related affinity which these friends felt towards Sa'di which made Thoreau write in his *Journal* of 8 Aug. 1852, that

> . . . entertaining a single thought of a certain elevation makes all men of one religion . . . I know, for instance, that Sadi entertained once identically the same thought that I do, and there after I can find no essential difference between Sadi and myself. He is not Persian, he is not ancient, he is not strange to me. By the identity of his thoughts with mine he still survives. It makes no odds what atoms serve us. Sadi possessed no greater privacy or individuality that is thrown open to me . . . Truth and a true man is something essentially public, not private. If Sadi were to come back to claim a *personal* identity with the historical Sadi, he would find there were too many of us; . . . By sympathy with Sadi I have embowelled him. In his thought I have a sample of *him*, a slice from his core.[64]

Important Persian poets, as well as other Oriental writers, were, as we have seen, the objects of serious study by the Romantics of New England. Sa'di and Hafiz were the only two Persian poets, taking their place amongst other Oriental religious texts and writers, for whom Emerson in particular showed long lasting interest. Sa'di fascinated him more than Hafiz and this was also the case with his Transcendentalist friends. Sa'di lived long and travelled for many years and wrote most of his work in the later part of his life; his work, perhaps in consequence, has a kind of astute wisdom and moral judgment which appealed to Emerson and his friends. Moreover, Sa'di was a "joy-giver" and "enjoyer" of Nature—very attractive qualities; therefore Sa'di

> appears much oftener as an ideal poet in Emerson's writings than Hafiz. Probably a reason for this is that Emerson felt himself much more nearly akin to him. Most of the qualities which he ascribes to the Persian might be used to describe Emerson's own writing.[65]

The American Transcendentalists were very much influenced by Kantian and other German philosophical ideas; but they were also Romantics in the broader European sense, and like many of their European predecessors they were fundamentally Neoplatonists. Their interest in Oriental Scriptures, as they called anything with religious and mystical qualities, was part of a desire for Universal Knowledge. Emerson in particular employed Sa'di, like other Oriental writers, to give illustrative substance to his own thoughts and ideas. He was fascinated by Goethe and Swedenborg; the first was greatly influenced by Persian poetry and the second heavily influenced by esoteric Islam. Emerson chose them both amongst his Representative Men. He is thought to have tinkered with the idea of including Sa'di as well, but eventually decided against doing so. Whatever reasons there might have been behind this change of heart, the fact remains that Sa'di remained among the authors whom Emerson held in his mind until late in his life. His *Journal* of 1872 mentions the Persian poet by name. A lot more might be written on Sa'di and his influence on American writers, especially if a philosophical comparison were undertaken between Sa'di's views of humanity and man's place in Nature and those of the American authors. Unfortunately, the confines of this essay have made it impossible to offer more than a cursory look at Thoreau, Emerson's disciple and friend, as well as forcing me to overlook writers such as Alcott, Alger, Taylor, and others. Still, it was Emerson who was centrally responsible for the popularity in America of Sa'di, supreme humanist and moralist of the Persian poets.

Notes

1. For this initial information I am indebted to John D. Yohannan's works on Sa'di, which include "The Poet Sa'di: A Persian Humanist," *Persian Studies Series*, no. 11 (New York, 1987); "Persian Literature in Translation," *Persian Literature*, ed. Ehsan Yarshater, (New York: Bibliotheca Persica, 1988); "Persian Poetry in England and America: A Two Hundred Year History," *Persian Studies Series* no. 4 (New York: Delmar, 1977).

2. Annemarie Schimmel, "The Genius of Shiraz: Sa'di and Hafiz," *Persian Literature* (1988): 214–25. The quotation occurs on 214–15.

3. Lord Teignmouth, ed., *The Works of Sir William Jones*, 6 vols. (London, 1799), V, 178, 433.

4. These can be found consecutively in Ibid., vol. V, p. 309, 434–6. The fable of the "Rain drop" is translated into Latin in vol. VI, pp. 273–4.

5. A full list of these early translations of Sa'di into English is provided by Yohannan, *Persian Poetry*, 315–16.

6. Yohannan in his volume *The Poet Sa'di* points out some of the uses made of Sa'di's fables in the West, 3–4.

7. A complete list of periodicals of the time can be found in Yohannan, *Persian Poetry*, 107–14.

8. Arthur Christy, *The Orient in American Transcendentalism* (New York: Columbia University Press, 1972), 285.

9. Yohannan, *Persian Poetry*, 110.

10. Arthur Christy, *The Asian Legacy and American Life* (New York: The John Day Co., 1945), 37.

11. Luther S. Mansfield. "The Emersonian Idiom and The Romantic Period in American Literature," *Romanticism and the American Renaissance*, ed. Kenneth Walter Cameron (Hartford, 1977), 23–28. The quotation is taken from 23.

12. Ibid., 23–4.

13. Ralph Waldo Emerson, "Books," *Society and Solitude*, from *Emerson's Complete Works*, 12 vols. (London: Riverside Edition, 1883–94), vol. VII, 208–9 (henceforth, *Works*).

14. *The Journals and Miscellaneous Notebooks of Ralph Waldo Emerson*, various editors, 16 vols. (Cambridge, MA, 1976), vol. VIII, 67. (henceforth, *J&N*)

15. Ibid., XII, 362.

16. Ralph L. Rusk, *The Life of Ralph Waldo Emerson*, (New York: Charles Scribner's Sons, 1949), 310.

17. Ralph Waldo Emerson, "Persian Poetry," *The Atlantic Monthly*, vol. 1 (April 1858), 724–34.

18. *J&N.*, XV, 89, 354–78, 382–386, 396, 399–400. The editors have identified the passages which were later incorporated into his introduction to the *Gulistan*.

19. J. D. Yohannan, "The Influence of Persian Poetry Upon Emerson's Work," *American Literature*, vol. 15, no. 1, (1944), 25–41, and his *Persian Poetry*, 127–32.

20. J. D. Yohannan, "Emerson's Translations of Persian Poetry from German Sources," *American Literature*, vol. 14, no. 4, (Jan. 1943), 407–420.

21. Ralph Waldo Emerson, *The Complete Prose Works of Ralph Waldo Emerson, With a Critical Introduction* (London: Ward, Lock, and Bowden, 1889), v.

22. Ralph Waldo Emerson, "Preface" to *The Gulistan, Or Rose Garden by Musle-Huddeen Saadi of Shiraz*, trans. Francis Gladwin (Boston: Ticknor and Fields, 1865), viii.

23. Ibid., iv–v.

24. Ibid., v.

25. *J&N*, X, 48.

26. Emerson, "Preface" to *Gulistan*, v.

27. Ibid., vii–viii.

28. Ibid., viii–ix

29. For a comprehensive discussion of the various theories about unity in the *ghazals* of Hafiz see Parvin Loloi, *Hafiz, Master of Persian Poetry: A Critical Bibliography; English Translations since the Eighteenth Century* (London: I. B. Tauris, 2004), 13–45.

30. Emerson, "Preface" to *The Gulistan*, xi–xii.

31. Ibid., x.

32. Ibid., xv.

33. Yohannan, *Persian Poetry*, 116, 280, note 329.

34. Though the brief discussion in Lawrence Buell's *Emerson* (Cambridge: Harvard University Press, 2003) is of interest, not least for his observation that Emerson "imagines [Sa'di] as a kind of cheerful hippie, content to live in squalor and take what inspiration brings" (141).

35. Emerson, *Works*, IX, 114–19. Emerson's poem has been translated into Persian by Farhang Jahanpour in "Sa'di va Emerson," *Iran Nameh*, vol. 3, no. 4, 1985, pp. 690–704.

36. Samuel Taylor Coleridge, *The Poetical Works of Samuel Taylor Coleridge*, ed. Ernest Hartley Coleridge (Oxford: Oxford University Press, 1912), 298.

37. John Yohannan, "The Influence of Persian Poetry upon Emerson," 31.

38. Sa'di, *Bustan*, ed. Gholam-Hossein Yusofi (Tehran, 1369/1990 (first published 1359/1980)), 167, ls. 3228–31. (The translations are by myself unless otherwise stated.)

39. Emerson employs German spellings for the names of Persian poets, derived from his reading of German translations.

40. Hafiz, *Divan*, ed. Parviz Natel-Khanlari, (Tehran, 1362/1983), 374, l., 4.

41. Ibn Arabi, *Fusus al-hikam*, Abu'l 'Ala 'Affifi, ed., (Cairo, 1365/946). 2 vols.: first volume contains the text and the second is the commentary. He also published *The Mystical Philosophy of Muhyid-Din Ibn al-'Arabi*, (Cambridge, 1939).

42. Henry Corbin, *Creative Imagination in the Sufism of Ibn 'Arabi*, trans. from French by Ralph Manheim, Bollingen Series XCI (Princeton, NJ: Princeton University Press, 1969), 319, no. 79.

43. For further information on Avicenna's influence on Dante see Étienne Gilson, *Dante and Philosophy* (New York: Harper and Row, 1963) and Bruno Nardi, *Dante e la Cultura Medievale* (Bari: Laterza, 1985).

44. Henry Corbin, *Avicenna and the Visionary Recital*, trans. from French by Willard R. Trask (Dallas: University of Dallas, 1980), 22.

45. Frederic Ives Carpenter, *Emerson and Asia* (New York: Haskell House, 1968), 46.

46. Ibid., 14.

47. Ibid., 43.

48. Ibid., 15.

49. Emerson, "Plato," in *The Representative Men*, *Works*, IV, 50–51.

50. Ibid., 50.

51. Ibid., 65–6.

52. Ibid., 63–4.

53. P., "The Divine Presence in Nature and in the Soul," *The Dial; A Magazine for Literature, Philosophy, and Religion*, vol. I (1841), 58–70. The quotations are taken consecutively from 59, 61–62, 66.

54. Sa'di, *Kuliyat*, ed. Mazahir Musaffa (Tehran, 1340/1961), 472, line 11.

55. Seyyed Hossein Nasr, *The Encounter of Man and Nature; The Spiritual Crisis of Modern Man* (London: George Allen and Unwin, 1968), 95.

56. Titus Burckhardt, *Mirror of the Intellect*, trans. William Stoddart, (Albany, NY: SUNY Press, 1987), 24.
57. *Paradiso*, I, 103 in Burkhardt, *Mirror*, 86.
58. Emerson, "Nature," *Works*, III, 161.
59. Carpenter, *Emerson and Asia*, 176.
60. Emerson, "Poet," *Essays, Second Series, Works*, III, 28
61. Ibid., 25.
62. Ibid., 33.
63. Ibid., 165.
64. Henry David Thoreau, *The Journals of Henry D. Thoreau*, ed. Bradford Torrey and Francis H. Allen, 14 vols. bound in two, Dover, (1855–61) (New York: Dover Publications, 1962). The quotation is taken from IV, 290.
65. Carpenter, *Emerson and Asia*, 193.

5

Emerson on Hafiz and Sa'di

The Narrative of Love and Wine

Farhang Jahanpour

Although Emerson's philosophical and religious ideas were mainly influenced by Hindu sources, the greatest literary influence from the East was that of Persia, in particular Hafiz and Sa'di who occupied a special place among Persian poets who influenced Emerson. It may not be extravagant to claim that, with the exception of English literature, Persian literature constituted the most important literary influence on Emerson's work.[1]

Emerson's biographers and critics recognized early on that there was a connection between his literary and mystical works and Persian literature. Emerson's son, describing the sources of influence on his father's writings, wrote: "Another influence now came in on the side of grace and finish, the Oriental poetry, in which he took very great interest, especially the poems of Hafiz."[2] An early critic of Emerson, Joel Benton, discovered the similarity of style in the poems of Emerson and Persian poets, especially translations of the works of Hafiz. He concluded that if the translations seem "a little more like Emerson than it does like Hafiz, the balance is more than preserved by his steeping his own original quatrain in a little tincture of the wine and spirit of Oriental thought. When he translated Hafiz, he was probably thinking of his own workmanship; when he described him, he was simply absorbed in the poet."[3]

Emerson's Encounter with Persian Literature

Many scholars writing on Emerson's familiarity with Persian literature, however, have wrongly assumed that his first contact with Persian literature started in 1841 when he read Joseph von Hammer-Purgstall's translations from Persian poetry.[4] However, before immersing himself in von Hammer's translations, Emerson had already come across many other translations from Persian poetry and references to Persian poets. A study of Emerson's *Journals*, and especially an examination of the often neglected literary journals that he borrowed from various Boston and Harvard libraries, shows that Emerson's familiarity with Persian poetry goes back to his youth.[5]

Emerson's acquaintance with Persian poetry started in his teen years; when he read *The Asiatick Miscellany*, which contained a number of translations from the poems of Sa'di, Hafiz, and Jami.[6] Later on, through the works of Sir William Jones that he read in 1821 and subsequently, he gained more knowledge of Persian poetry.[7] Emerson's *Journals* from 1822 also refer to *The Thousand and One Nights: Or the Arabian Nights Entertainments*,[8] which provided him with a treasure-trove of Persian and Arabic tales. In 1836, Emerson read Anquetil Duperron's *Zendavesta, Ouvrage de Zorostre*,[9] which was the complete translation of the Zoroastrian scripture *Zend-Avesta*, excerpts of which Emerson had already read in 1832. Emerson was clearly interested in Iran's ancient religion, because a year later he read *The Phoenix: A Collection of Old and Rare Fragments*.[10] The second section of this book contained *The Oracles of Zoroaster, the Founder of the Persian Magi*. This was prefaced with *An Abstract of the Persian Theology of Zoroaster*. This section seems to have particularly interested Emerson, from which he quoted a few passages in his *Journals*.[11]

In 1840 Emerson borrowed all the six volumes of Sir William Jones's *Works*,[12] which contained a great deal of information about Oriental literature, including translations from Hafiz.[13] Jones's *Works* seem to have further stimulated Emerson's interest in Persian poetry because, in the following year, he read Joseph von Hammer-Purgstall's voluminous anthology of Persian poetry and his translation of the *Divan* of Hafiz into German.[14] These works marked a watershed in Emerson's interest in Persian literature and especially in the *Divan* of Hafiz which, as we shall see later, lasted to the end of his life. He also read Aleksander Chodzko's *Specimen of the Popular Poetry of Persia*,[15] which is recorded in his *Journals* in 1846, and from which he made several quotations.[16] In the same year, he read James Atkinson's translation of the *Shah Nameh* (The Book of Kings) of Firdawsi[17] and James Ross's translation of the *Gulistan* of Sa'di.[18]

Emerson's reading lists in later years are full of references to Persian poets, and his Eastern studies between 1845 and 1855 were mainly dominated by Persian literature. Among the most important books on Persian literature that Emerson read during these years were: W. R. Alger's *The Poetry of the East*;[19] James Atkinson's translation of *The Shah-Nameh*;[20] James Ross's translation of Sa'di's *Gulistan* (The Flower Garden);[21] the German translation of the *Divan* of the celebrated Persian mystic Jalal al-Din Rumi;[22] David Shea and Anthony

Troyer's translations of *The Dabistan, or School of Manners*;[23] and numerous other English and German translations of the works of Hafiz and Sa'di.

Emerson's Writings on Persian Mystical Literature

Apart from numerous references to different Persian poets, Emerson wrote two long essays and two poems dealing with Persian poetry, and he translated as many as seven hundred lines of Persian poetry mainly from German sources, more than half of them from the work of Hafiz. One of his essays is *Persian Poetry*, in which he spoke mainly about Hafiz and briefly referred to some other Persian poets.[24] The other is the preface that he supplied to the first American edition of Sa'di's *Gulistan* translated by Francis Gladwin was published in 1865 by Ticknor and Fields.[25] The two poems dealing specifically with Persian poetry consisted of a long poem under the title of *Saadi*,[26] and *Fragments on the Poet and the Poetic Gift*.[27]

In his essay on "Persian Poetry," Emerson commences with a general comment on the work of von Hammer-Purgstall as a translator. Of the specimen of two hundred Persian poets that this German translator had given to the Western world, Emerson writes:

> That for which mainly books exist is communicated in these rich extracts . . . There are many virtues in books, but the essential value is the adding of knowledge to our stock by the record of new facts, and, better by the record of institutions which distribute facts, and are the formulas which supersede all histories.[28]

But soon after a general account of Persian poetry, Emerson writes about Hafiz and shows his appreciation of this great Persian poet. He writes:

> Hafiz is the prince of Persian poets, and in his extraordinary gift adds to some of the attributes of Pindar, Anacreon, Horace, and Burns the insight of a mystic, that sometimes affords a deeper glance at Nature than belongs to either of these bards. He accounts all topics with an easy audacity.[29]

Then Emerson approvingly translates a few lines from Hafiz that show his self-reliance, a quality that greatly appealed to Emerson:

> I batter the wheel of heaven
> When it rolls not rightly by

> I am not one of the snivellers
> Who fall thereon and die.[30]

and:

> Alas! Till now I had not known
> My guide and Fortune's guide are one.[31]

and:

> 'Tis writ on Paradise's gate,
> "Woe to the dupe that yields to Fate!"[32]

The other quality that Emerson praises in Hafiz is his frankness and dislike of hypocrisy. Emerson writes:

> Hypocrisy is the perpetual butt of his arrows:
> Let us draw the cowl through the brook of wine![33]
> I will be drunk and down with wine,
> Treasure we find in a ruined house![34]

In Hafiz, Emerson finds the qualities that are the surest signs of greatness to him. He says:

> That hardihood and self-equality of every sound nature, which result from the feeling that the spirit in him is entire and as good as the world, which entitled the poet to speak with authority, and makes him an object of interest, and his very phrase and syllable significant, are in Hafiz, and abundantly fortify and ennoble his tone. His was the fluent mind in which every thought and feeling came readily to the lips. "Loose the knots of the heart" he says.[35]

Another admirable quality that Emerson finds in Hafiz is his spiritual independence and the power of overcoming his surroundings. He writes:

> The other merit of Hafiz is his intellectual liberty, which is a certificate of profound thought . . . Wrong shall not be wrong to Hafiz, for the name's sake. A law or statute is to him what a fence is to a nimble schoolboy,—a temptation to jump.
> "We would do nothing but good, else would shame come to us on the day when the soul must hie hence; and should they

then deny us Paradise, the Houris themselves would forsake that, and come out to us!"

His complete intellectual emancipation he communicates to the reader. There is no example of such facility of allusion, such use of all materials. Nothing is too high, nothing too low, for his occasion. He fears nothing, he stops for nothing. Love is a leveller, and Allah becomes a groom, and heaven a closet, in his daring hymns to his mistress or his cupbearer. This boundless character is the right of genius.[36]

Hafiz's poetry mirrors forth his mind: the same confusion of high and low, the clarity of flight and allusion which our colder muses forbid, is habitual to him. From the plain text:

> The Chemist of love
> Will this perishing mould,
> Were it made out of mire,
> Transmute into gold,[37]

He proceeds to the celebration of his passion; nothing in his religious or his scientific traditions is too sacred or too remote to afford a token of his mistress. The moon though she knew his own orbit well enough, but when she saw the curve on Zuleika's cheek, she was at a loss:

> And since round lines are drawn
> My darling's lips about,
> The very moon looks puzzled on,
> And hesitates in doubt
> If the sweet curve that rounds thy mouth
> Be not her true way to the South[38]

In one of his *Journals* entries, Emerson used similar words to praise Hafiz. He wrote:

> He is not scared by a name or a religion. He fears nothing. He sees too far, he sees throughout; such is the only man I wish to see and to be. The scholar's courage is as distinct as the soldier's or statesman's and the man who has it not cannot write for me.[39]

One of the main merits of Persian poets, especially Hafiz, which Emerson admires in them is their love of beauty and their joy in life. Hafiz was living at one of the darkest periods of Iranian history, when his homeland was attacked by the ferocious and fanatical armies of Tamerlane (Timur Lang) and his descendants, and his native town of Shiraz witnessed the slaughter of thousands of its inhabitants and at least five of its short-lived rulers. But, in spite of the darkness that surrounded him, Hafiz remained calm and serene in the depth of his soul and occupied himself with praising the beauty of nature. Hafiz's serenity of heart and his boundless search for beauty fascinated Emerson:

> Hafiz praises wine, roses, maidens, boys, birds, morning and music, to give vent to his immense hilarity and sympathy with every form of beauty and joy; and lays the emphasis on these to make his scorn of sanctimony and base prudence . . . Sometimes it is a glance from the height of thought, as thus:—
> "Bring wine: for in the audience-hall of the soul's independence, what is sentinel or Sultan? What is the wise man or the intoxicated?"
> And sometimes his feast, feasters and world are only one pebble more in the external vortex and revolution of Fate:—
> "I am: what I am
> My dust will be again."[40]

Finally, one more device of Hafiz which pleased Emerson, was his skill in mentioning his name in his poems. Emerson describes that "The law of the ghaselle [*ghazal*], or shorter ode, requires that the poet inserts his name in the last stanza. It is itself a test of skill, as this self-naming is not quite easy . . . But it is easy to Hafiz . . . He tells us 'The angels in Heaven were lately learning his last pieces.' He says, 'The fishes shed their pearls out of desire and longing as soon as the ship of Hafiz swims the deep.'"[41]

> Out of the East and out of the West, no man understands me;
> O, the happier I, who confide to none but the wind!
> This morning heard I how the lyre of stars resounded,
> Sweeter tones have we heard from Hafiz.
> . . .
> 'When Hafiz sings, the angels hearken, and Anaitis, the leader of the starry host, calls even the Messiah in heaven out to the dance.'[42]

Again:

> 'O Hafiz, speak not of thy need;
> Are not those verses thine?

> Then all the poets are agreed,
> No man can less repine.'[43]

He asserts his dignity as bard and inspired man of his people. To the vizier returning from Mecca he says:—"Boast not rashly, prince of pilgrims, of thy fortune. Thou has indeed seen the temple; but I, the Lord of the Temple. Nor has any man inhaled from the musk-bladder of the merchant, or from the musky morning wind, that sweet air which I am permitted to breathe every hour of the day."[44]

In his essay on *Persian Poetry*, Emerson concentrated his attention on Hafiz, but in the *Preface to Gulistan* he dwelt mainly on Sa'di, although he still made frequent references to Hafiz. As its title denotes, Emerson's poem on *Saadi*, first published in *The Dial* in 1842, also mainly dealt with Sa'di, whom he chose as an example of a representative poet. Contrary to the assertion of some critics that the poem *Saadi* was merely a device for writing about poets as a whole, there is plenty of evidence to show that he had the Persian poet in mind when writing that poem. Not only do many references to "Saadi" correspond with what he had written about Sa'di in his *Journals*,[45] he clearly states that it was a portrait of the Persian poet. Emerson wrote that poem after reading many translations of the works of Sa'di. A year after writing it, he read the full text of the *Gulistan*, and in a telling passage in the *Journals* he declared: "In Saadi's Gulistan I find many traits which comport with the portrait I drew [in the poem Sa'di]."[46]

In *Fragments on the Poet and the Poetic Gift*, Emerson again concentrated on Sa'di (here referred to as Said) and on Hafiz. Both of them were hungry for truth and beauty and went everywhere searching for it:

> There are beggars in Iran and Araby,
> Said was hungrier than all;
> Hafiz said he was a fly
> That came to every festival.[47]

In this poem Emerson mixes the praise of the two poets together and sometimes what he says of one is more true of the other. At the beginning of the poem there are some lines about Hafiz, which definitely apply more to Sa'di:

> He came a pilgrim to the Mosque
> On trail of camel and caravan,
> Knew every temple and kiosk
> Out from Mecca to Isphahan . . .

These lines are hardly true of Hafiz who never visited Mecca and seldom left his beloved Shiraz, but they can refer to Sa'di who travelled widely and made eight pilgrimages to Mecca.

On the other hand, the following lines attributed to Sa'di are truer of Hafiz:

Said Saadi, 'When I stood before
Hassan the camel-driver's door
I scorned the fame of Timour brave'
Timour, to Hassan, was a slave . . .

When Sa'di was living, Tamerlane was not even born, but Hafiz's alleged encounter with the Tartar ruler is famous. Emerson himself in his essay on *Persian Poetry* relates that story:

It is told of Hafiz that, when he had written a compliment to a handsome youth,—

Take my heart in thy hand, O beautiful boy of Shiraz!
I would give for the mole on thy cheek Samarcand and Buchara!

The verses came to the ears of Timour in his palace. Timour taxed Hafiz with treating disrespectfully his two cities, to raise and adorn which he had conquered nations. Hafiz replies, 'Alas, my lord, if I had not been so prodigal, I had not been so poor!'"[48]

It is evident that in the poem *Fragments on the Poet and the Poetic Gift*, Emerson refers freely to these two poets and his descriptions could be true of either of them. He writes about Sa'di:

The Dervish whined to Said,
"Thou didst not tarry while I prayed."
But Saadi answered,
"Once with manlike love and fear
I gave thee for an hour my ear,
I kept the sun and stars at bay,
And love, for words thy tongue could say.
I cannot sell my heaven again
For all that rattles in thy brain."

Yet in his *Journals,* Emerson had praised Hafiz in the same tone: "He is not scared by a name or a religion. He fears nothing. He sees too far, he sees throughout; such is the only man I wish to see and to be. The scholar's courage is as distinct as the soldier's or statesman's and the man who has it not cannot write for me."[49]

Or, again in this poem, Emerson praises Hafiz in similar terms that he had used to praise Sa'di in the poem bearing his name as its title:

His music was the south-wind's sigh,
His lamp, the maiden's downcast eye,
And ever the spell of beauty came
And turned the drowsy world to flame.
By lake and stream and gleaming hall
And modest copse and the forest hall,
Where'er he went, the magic guide
Kept its place by the poet's side

Referring to Sa'di, Emerson wrote in verse what he had written about him in prose in his *Journals*. He had noted Sa'di's interest in high and low and, as a result, all people's interest in him. He wrote: "The human race is interested in Saadi . . . Saadi is the poet of friendship, of love, of heroism, of self-devotion, beauty, serenity, and the divine Providence."[50]

Apart from the above sources wherein Emerson speaks in detail about Persian poets there are many other references to them scattered in his *Works* and *Journals*. Emerson often put Hafiz and Shakespeare in the same category. In one of his poems he wrote of the two poets as teachers who taught and inspired without preaching:

"A new commandment," said the smiling Muse,
"I give my darling son, Thou shalt not preach;—"
Luther, Fox, Bohmen, Swedenborg grew pale,
And, in the instant, rosier clouds upbore
Hafiz and Shakespeare with their shining choirs.[51]

In his poem on *The Poet*, Emerson speaks about poets in general and does not specify any by name. But there are certain passages in that poem that in the light of what he had written elsewhere of Hafiz can be easily distinguished as referring to him. For example, he writes:

He sowed the sun and moon for seeds . . .
But oh, to see his solar eyes
Like meteors which chose their way
And rived the dark like a new day!
No lazy grazing on all they saw
Each chimney-pot and village picket fence,
But, feeding on magnificence,
They bounded to the horizon's edge
And searched with the sun's privilege.[52]

These lines recall what he had written of Hafiz in his *Journals*: "Hafiz's poetry is marked by nothing more than his habit of playing with all magnitudes, mocking at them. What is the moon, or the sun's course or heaven, and the angels to his darling's mole or eyebrow?"[53] Again, he had written about the same poet: "He is restless, inquisitive, thousand-eyed, insatiable, and as like a nightingale intoxicated with his own music; never was the privilege of poetry more haughtily used."[54]

There is another passage in *The Poet*, which may refer to Hafiz:

He whom God has thus preferred,—
To whom sweet angels ministered,
Saluted him each morn as brother,
And bragged his virtues to each other . . .[55]

With these lines are to be compared the following prose translations from Hafiz made by Emerson for the essay on *Persian Poetry*: "When Hafiz sings, the angels hearken, and Anaitis, the leader of the starry host, calls even the Messiah in heaven out to the dance." And, "I heard the harp of the planet Venus, and it said in the early morning, I am the disciple of the sweet-voiced Hafiz."[56]

There is an entry in the *Journals* that was written shortly after Emerson read Hafiz: "Expression is what we want: not knowledge, but vent: we know enough; but have not leaves and lungs enough for a healthy perspiration and growth. Hafiz has! . . . 'Keep the body open,' is the hygiene precept . . . Large utterance!"[57]

Emerson was attracted to Hafiz as soon as he came to know him. The very first entry about Hafiz is as follows:

Hafiz defies you to show him or put him in a condition inappropriate or ignoble. Take all you will, and leave him but a corner of Nature, a lane, a den, a cowshed . . . he promises to win to that scorned spot the light of the moon and stars, the love of men, the smile of beauty, and the homage of art.[58]

There are further references in the *Journals* that show other qualities that Emerson liked in Persian poets, especially Hafiz. One was the inspirational quality of women. In his second series of *Essays* there is a striking passage asking:

Was it Hafiz or Firdawsi that said of his Persian Lilla, She was an elemental force, and astonished me by her amount of life, when I saw her day after day radiating, every instant, redundant joy and grace on all around her. She was a solvent powerful to reconcile all heterogeneous persons into one society: like air or water, an element of such a great range of affinities, that it combines readily with a thousand substances. Where she is present, all others will be more than they are wont. She was a unit and whole, so that whatsoever she did, became her. She had too much sympathy and desire to please, than that you could say, her manners were marked with dignity, yet no princess could surpass her clear and erect demeanour on each occasion. She did not study the Persian grammar, nor the books of the seven poets, but all the poems of the seven seemed to be written upon her. For, though the bias of her nature was not to thought, but to sympathy, yet was she so perfect in her own nature, as to meet intellectual persons by the fullness of her heart, warming them by her sentiments; believing, as she did, that by dealing nobly with all, all would show themselves noble.[59]

Another quality that Emerson admired about Hafiz was his disregard of the material world. He quoted a poem from Hafiz where he says: "Our father Adam sold Paradise for two kernels of wheat; then blame me not if I hold it dear at one grapestone."[60] Yet another trait of the Persian poet that Emerson admired was his love of beauty and his dislike of religious formalism. He quotes Hafiz approvingly when he addresses the leader of the pilgrims to Mecca that he only sees the surface and the building while Hafiz sees the Lord of the building: "To the vizier returning from Mecca he says:—Boast not rashly, prince of pilgrims, of thy fortune. Thou has indeed seen the temple; but I, the Lord of the Temple."[61] Again, in his *Journals*, Emerson praised Hafiz's disdain of literal religion in these words: "He is not scared by a name or a religion. He fears nothing. He sees too far, he sees throughout; such is the only man I wish to see and to be. The scholar's courage is as distinct as the soldier's or statesman's and the man who has it not cannot write for me."[62]

In the notebook called *Orientalist* are the following passages, mostly transcribed from the *Journals* during his forties when Emerson became familiar with German translations of Hafiz:

> Hafiz has only just arrived as a competitor to our occidental lyricists, as the Pasha of Egypt challenged so lately the English men of the turf, and our theologians left out till now the Bhagavat Geeta [*Bhagavad Gita*]. Nothing stops him; he makes the dare-God and dare-devil experiment; he is not to be scared by a name, or a religion; he fears nothing, he sees too far, and sees throughout.
>
> Hafiz's scepticism is only that of a deep intellect: he pays homage to virtue. Wine stands poetically for all that symbolizes, and not as in Moore's verse for Best Port. He who sees the horizon may securely say what he pleases of any tree of twig between him and it. He takes his life in his hand, and is ready for a new world . . . 'Talk not to me of mosques or of dervishes, God is my witness, I am where he

dwells.' Hafiz does not write of wine and love in any mystical sense, further than that he uses wine as the symbol of intellectual freedom.

In this passage, Emerson makes a very important statement about Hafiz's symbolism. Contrary to many who see his use of wine either as a sign of debauchery or see it purely as a symbol for mystical intoxication, Emerson points out that above all it is a symbol of "intellectual freedom." At a time of religious fanaticism and bigotry when drinking wine could result in harsh penalties, Hafiz uses wine as a way of transcending religious strictures and expressing his disgust of hypocrisy and sanctimonious religiosity.

In his *Journals* for 1846, Emerson wrote: "Hafiz, whom I at first thought of a cross of Anacreon and Horace, I find now to have the best blood of Pindar also in his verses." [63]

Emerson's Translations from Hafiz

Emerson translated about 700 lines of Persian poetry, about half are translations from the poems of Hafiz. Apart from Hafiz who has the lion's share of Emerson's translations, the following poets furnished the sources of Emerson's other translations: Fereideddin [Farid al-Din] Attar (54 lines), Sa'di (34 lines), Nimatollah [Ni'matullah] of Kuhestan (34 lines), Ibn Jamin [Ibn Yamin] (22 lines), Nizami (21 lines), Enweri [Anvari] (20 lines), Kermani (20 lines), Omar Chiam [Khayyam] (12 lines); and Adschedi [Asjudi], Feizi, Dschami [Jami] and Dscheladdin [Jalaluddin] Rumi (4 lines each).[64] As von Hammer-Purgstall's German translations of Persian poetry provided the origins for most of Emerson's translations he adopts the German spelling of Persian names. For example, he writes Medschnun for Majnun, Dscheladdin for Jalaluddin and Dschami for Jami.

To Emerson should, doubtless, go the credit for being one of the first translators of some quatrains from the *Ruba'iyyat* of Omar Khayyam in the United States, and also for introducing the Persian Ruba'i (quatrain) into English. His translations of the *Ruba'iyyat* preceded those of Fitzgerald by many years. To him also goes the distinction of prophesying that Omar Khayyam deserved and would become better known by Western readers. Writing in the Atlantic Monthly for April 1858, Emerson pointed out: "The seven masters of Persian Parnassus, Firdousi, Enweri, Nisami, Dschelaleddin, Saadi, Hafiz and Dschami, have ceased to be empty names; and others, like Fereideddin Attar, and Omar Chiam, promise to rise in Western estimation."[65]

The first category of his translations consists of attempts to render a literal translation of the original. In his translations of Hafiz, Emerson sometimes produced the verbal translation and later on improved upon his original rendition. One example is the translation of a few lines of the following *ghazal*:

> See, the chemist of love
> Will the dust of the body
> Convert into gold
> Were it never so leaden.
> O Hafiz, do churls Know the worth of great pearls?
> Give the high-prized stone
> Only to sacred friends alone.

When he came to quote this poem in his essay on *Persian Poetry*, this is how he rendered it:

> The chemist of love
>   Will this perishing mould
> Were it made out of mire,
>   Transmute into gold.
> Thou foolish Hafiz! Say, do churls
>   Know the worth of Oman's pearls?
> Give the gem which dims the moon
>   To the noblest or to none.[66]

Sometimes Emerson tried to produce exact translations of the original poems, but misunderstood the meaning of the German translations, and as a result changed the meaning of ideas expressed in the original poems. For example, it is a familiar sentiment in the poems of both Hafiz and Omar Khayyam that one should treasure the moment, as when one leaves this world one will not come back. Emerson, translating a line expressing this idea, wrote: "When thou goest, come not back," which has a completely different meaning.

The second category of translations includes selections from different poems, mixed together to form a single poem. An example of this category is a poem which Emerson called *Of Passionate Abandonment*, and which is formed out of two odes of Hafiz:

> I know this perilous love-lane
>   And whither the traveller leads,
> Yet my fancy the sweet scent of
>   Thy tangled tresses feeds.
> In the midnight of thy locks,
>   I renounce the day;

> In the ring of thy rose-lips
> My heart forgets to pray.[67]

Sometimes, we come across some translations that have more than the German text for a source. It is evident that Emerson has made use of the notes of von Hammer's translations or has been acquainted with some English versions of those poems. For example, in the following translation, *From Hafiz*, Emerson has exactly rendered the Persian original that had been distorted in the German text:

> I said to heaven that glowed above,
> O hide yon sun-filled zone,
> Hide all the start you boast;
> For in the world of love
> And estimation true,
> The heaped-up harvest of the moon
> Is worth one barley-corn at most,
> The Pleiads's sheaf but two.

In fact, E. B. Cowell had already translated that particular ghazal of Hafiz and Emerson might have read it.[68]

The third category of selections includes poems that can hardly be called translations. In this group belong poems that have some Persian source, but Emerson has elaborated on the translation and many lines have been added to the original. In this category may be included the poems that Emerson wrote about Hafiz, but which were inspired by some of the poems by Hafiz. The similarity is so striking that it is difficult to decide whether to classify them as translations or imitations. For instance, among the quatrains we come across a poem entitled Hafiz:

> Her passions the shy violet
> From Hafiz never hides;
> Love longings of the raptured bird
> The bird to him confides

There is a poem by Hafiz translated by Emerson, which probably suggests the above lines:

> By breath of beds of roses drawn,
> I found the grove in the morning pure,
> In the concert of the nightingale
> My drunken brain to cure.

With unrelated glance
    I looked the rose in the eye;
The rose in the hour of gleaming
    Flamed like a lamp hard-by.

She was of her beauty proud,
    And prouder of her youth,
The while unto her flaming heart
    The bulbul gave his truth.

The sweet narcissus closed
    Its eye, with passion pressed,
The tulips out of envy burned
    Moles in their scarlet breast.

The lilies white prolonged
    Their sworded tongue to the smell;
The clustering anemones
    Their pretty secrets tell.[69]

Echoes of Hafiz's Poems in Emerson's Verse

Through the frequent reading of the poems of Hafiz and other Persian poets, Emerson's poems were influenced by them, and in some of his most famous poems the influence is too clear to be missed. The influence is manifest in several ways: in the similarity of style and the use of imagery, the correspondence of thoughts and feelings, and the use of the same material. Emerson's style has been described as being original among the Western writers. His familiarity with and imitation of Persian poetry might provide some of the answers for the unique qualities of Emerson's verse. Persian poetry served to enrich the stone of his imagery and to introduce many new forms of expression to him, but it is not only in Emerson's use of imagery and language that one can discover the influence of Persian poetry. Many of his ideas were also borrowed from the same source.

One of the poems that was inspired, in part at least, from his reading of Persian poetry is the poem *Days*. This poem is short and may be quoted entirely:

Daughter of Time, the hypocritic Days,
Muffled and dumb like barefoot dervishes,
And marching single in an endless file,

Bring diadems and fagots in their hands.
To each they offer gifts after his will,
Bread, kingdoms, stars, and sky that holds them all.
I, in my pleachèd garden, watched the pomp,
Forgot my morning wishes, hastily
Took a few herbs and apples, and the Day
Turned and departed silent. I, too late,
Under her solemn fillet saw the scorn.

There is an entry in the *Journals* for May 24, 1847, as follows: "The days come and go like muffled and veiled figures sent from a distant friendly party, but they say nothing, and if we do not see the gifts they bring they carry them as silently away."[70] In a note, Edward Emerson has observed that this sentence was later embodied in the poem *Days*.[71] At the time of expressing these sentiments, Emerson was reading Persian poetry and this sentiment is expressed often in the poems of Hafiz and Omar Khayyam. The interesting point is that the second entry in *Journals* for May 24, 1847, is a translation of a *ghazal* by Hafiz, in which occur the following lines:

Surely I have no treasure,
Yet am I richly satisfied;
God has given that to the Shah,
And this to the beggar.

Apart from expressing a similar idea to that of *Days*, these lines clearly suggest the line "To each they offer gifts after his will." In the next line of the poem *Days*, Emerson makes use of a trick of Hafiz, which he had remarked upon in his essay on *Persian Poetry*, namely Hafiz's habit of "playing with magnitudes:" "Bread, kingdoms, stars and sky that holds them all."

The term "barefoot dervishes" clearly echoes the use of the term in some Persian poems, which also appear in many of Emerson's translations of them. But, most important of all, the moral and general idea of the poem is basically Oriental and several poems of Hafiz contain the same thought.

Another poem of Emerson that has a parallel in his translations of Persian poetry is the poem entitled "To J. W." This poem bears a striking resemblance to a *ghazal* of Hafiz that Emerson translated in 1847. In order to see the similarity between the two poems, I quote both poems below:

Set not thy foot on graves;
Hear what wine and roses say;
The mountain chase, the summer waves,
The crowded town, thy feet may well delay.

Set not thy foot on graves;
Nor seek to unwind the shroud
Which charitable time
And nature have allowed
To wrap the errors of a sage sublime.

Set not thy foot on graves;
Care not to strip the dead
Of his sad ornament;
His myrrh, and wine, and rings,
His sheet of lead,
And trophies buried;
Go get them where he earned them when alive,
As resolutely dig or dive.

Life is too short to waste
The critic bite or cynic bark,
Quarrel, or reprimand;
'Twill soon be dark;
Up! mind thine own aim, and
God speed the mark.

The translation of the poem by Hafiz that Emerson entitled *Ghaselle: From the Persian of Hafiz II* is as follows:

Of Paradise, O hermit wise,
Let us renounce the thought.
Of old therein our names of sin
Allah recorded not.

Who dear to God on earthly sod
No corn-grain plants,
The same is glad that life is had,
Though corn he wants.

Thy mind the mosque and cool kiosk,
Spare fast, and orisons;
Mine me allows the drink-house,
And sweet chase of the nuns.

O just fakeer, with brow austere,
Forbid me not the vine;

On the first day, poor Hafiz clay
Was kneaded up with wine.

He is no dervise, Heaven slights his service,
Who shall refuse
There in the banquet, to pawn his blanket
For Schiraz's juice.

Who his friend's shirt, or hem of his shirt,
Shall spare to pledge,
To him Eden's bliss and Angel's kiss
Shall want their edge.

Up, Hafiz; grace from high God's face
Beams on thee pure;
Shy then not hell, and trust thou well,

Heaven is secure.

These two poems have many points in common. Both of them forbid the reader to put his mind on the next life, and teach him to enjoy God's bounties in the here-and-now rather than in the hereafter. Both offer wine and roses as sources of pleasure in life, and both end on the optimistic note that a gracious God will overlook the faults of men and will bestow salvation. Apart from similarities in contents, there are some similarities in expression as well. "Sage sublime" in the one, and "hermit wise" in the other; in both of them the closing apostrophe begins with the word 'Up.'

The third stanza of *Ghaselle*, with its reference to a frequent claim of Hafiz that he had been predestined towards wine from birth may also have provided the inspiration for the following lines from *May-Day*:

Poets praise that hidden wine
Hid in milk we drew
At the barrier of Time,
When our life was new.
We had eaten fairy fruit,
We were quick from head to foot,
All the forms we looked on shone
As with diamond dews thereon.

Another poem by Emerson, which even more clearly reflects Emerson's debt to Hafiz, is the famous poem called *Bacchus*. Most commentators have readily admitted that this poem was inspired by Persian sources. Emerson himself was aware of the fact and thought *Bacchus* might be taken as a translation of a poem by Hafiz. In July 1846, in a letter to Elizabeth Hoar he wrote that he had been working on some poems that he felt impatient to show her, "especially some verses called Bacchus . . . not, however, translated from Hafiz." But although he rightly points out that the poem is not a direct translation of Hafiz, it shows great resemblance to another translation that he made of a famous poem of Hafiz, called "*Saqi-Namah*." Let us first quote Emerson's poem:

> Bring me wine, but wine which never grew
> In the belly of the grape,
> Or grew on vine whose tap-roots, reaching through
> Under the Andes to the Cape,
> Suffer'd no savour of the earth to 'scape.
>
> Let its grapes the morn salute
> From a nocturnal root,
> Which feels the acrid juice
> Of Styx and Erebus;
> And turns the woe of Night,
> By its own craft, to a more rich delight.
>
> We buy ashes for bread;
> We buy diluted wine;
> Give me of the true,
> Whose ample leaves and tendrils curl'd
> Among the silver hills of heaven
> Draw everlasting dew;
> Wine of wine,
> Blood of the world,
> Form of forms, and mould of statures,
> That I intoxicated,
> And by the draught assimilated,
> May float at pleasure through all natures;
> The bird-language rightly spell,
> And that which roses say so well:
>
> Wine that is shed
> Like the torrents of the sun
> Up the horizon walls,
> Or like the Atlantic streams, which run
> When the South Sea calls.

Water and bread,
Food which needs no transmuting,
Rainbow-flowering, wisdom-fruiting,
Wine which is already man,
Food which teach and reason can.

Wine which Music is,—
Music and wine are one,—
That I, drinking this,
Shall hear far Chaos talk with me;
Kings unborn shall walk with me;
And the poor grass shall plot and plan
What it will do when it is man.
Quicken'd so, will I unlock
Every crypt of every rock.
I thank the joyful juice
For all I know;
Winds of remembering
Of the ancient being blow,
And seeming-solid walls of use
Open and flow.

Pour, Bacchus! the remembering wine;
Retrieve the loss of me and mine!
Vine for vine be antidote,
And the grape requite the lote!
Haste to cure the old despair;
Reason in Nature's lotus drench'd—
The memory of ages quench'd—
Give them again to shine;
Let wine repair what this undid;
And where the infection slid,
A dazzling memory revive;
Refresh the faded tints,
Recut the agèd prints,
And write my old adventures with the pen
Which on the first day drew,
Upon the tablets blue,
The dancing Pleiads and eternal men.

If one compares the above poem with Emerson's translation of *Saqi-Nameh* by Hafiz one will see many common features between the two:

Butler, fetch the ruby wine,
Which with sudden greatness fills us;
Pour for me who in my spirit
Fail in courage and performance;
Bring the philosophic stone,
Karun's treasure, Noah's life;
Haste, that by thy means I open
All the doors of luck and life.
Bring me, boy, the fire-water
Zoroaster sought in dust.
To Hafiz revelling 'tis allowed
To pray to Matter and to Fire.
Bring the wine of Jamschid's glass
That shone, ere time was, in the Néant.

Give it me, that through its virtue
I, as Jamschid, see through worlds.
Wisely said the Kaiser Jamschid,
This world's not worth a barleycorn.
Bring me, boy, the nectar cup,
Since it leads to Paradise.
Flute and lyre lordly speak,
Lees of wine outvalue crowns.
Hither bring the veiled beauty
Who in ill-famed houses sits:
Lead her forth: my honest name
Freely barter I for wine.
Bring me, boy, the fire-water,
Drinks the lion—the woods burn.
Give it me, that I storm heaven,
Tear the net from the arch-wolf.
Wine, wherewith the Houris teach
Angels the ways of Paradise.
On the glowing coals I'll set it,
And therewith my brain perfume.
Bring me wine, through whose effulgence
Jam and Chosroes yielded light:
Wine, that to the flute I sing
Where is Jam, and where is Kauss.

Bring the blessing of old times;
Bless the old departed Shahs;

Bring it me, the Shah of hearts.
Bring me wine to wash me clean,
Of the weather-stains of care,
See the countenance of luck.
While I dwell in spirit-gardens,
Wherefore sit I shackled here?
Lo, this mirror shows me all.
Drunk, I speak of purity,
Beggar, I of lordship speak.
When Hafiz in his revel sings,
Shouteth Sohra in her sphere.

Fear the changes of a day:
Bring wine which increases life,
Since the world is all untrue,
Let the trumpets thee remind
How the crown of Kobad vanished.
Be not certain of the world;
'Twill not spare to shed thy blood.
Desperate of the world's affair,
Came I running to the wine-house.
Give me wine which maketh glad,
That I may my steed bestride,
Through the course career with Rustem,
Gallop to my heart's content.
Give me, boy, the ruby cup
Which unlocks the heart with wine,
That I reason quite renounce,
And plant banners on the worlds.
Let us make our glasses kiss,
Let us quench the sorrow-cinders:
To-day let us drink together.
Whoso has a banquet dressed,
Is with glad mind satisfied,
'Scaping from the snares of Dews.

Alas for youth! 'tis gone in wind,—
Happy he who spent it well.
Give me wine, that I o'erleap
Both worlds at a single spring,
Stole at dawn from glowing spheres
Call of Houris to mine ear;

"O happy bird! delicious soul!
Spread thy pinion, break the cage;
Sit on the roof of the seven domes,
Where the spirit takes repose."
In the time of Bisurdschimihr,
Menutscheher's beauty shined,
On the beaker of Nushirvan,
Wrote they once in eider times,
"Hear the Counsel, learn from us
Sample of the course of things;
Earth, it is a place of sorrow,
Scanty joys are here below,
Who has nothing, has no sorrow."

Where is Jam, and where his cup?
Solomon, and his mirror where?
Which of the wise masters knows
What time Kauss and Jam existed?
When those heroes left this world,
Left they nothing but their names.
Bind thy heart not to the earth,
When thou goest, come not back.
Fools squander on the world their hearts.
League with it, is feud with heaven;
Never gives it what thou wishest.

A cup of wine imparts the sight
Of the five heaven-domes with nine steps:
Whoso can himself renounce,
Without support shall walk thereon.
Who discreet is, is not wise.
Give me, boy, the Kaiser cup,
Which rejoices heart and soul;
Under type of wine and cup
Signify we purest love.
Youth like lightning disappears,
Life goes by us as the wind:
Leave the dwelling with six doors,
And the serpent with nine heads;
Life and silver spend thou freely,
If thou honorest the soul.
Haste into the other life;

All is nought save God alone.
Give me, boy, this toy of dæmons.
When the cup of Jam was lost,
Him availed the world no more.
Fetch the wine-glass made of ice,
Wake the 'torpid heart with wine.
Every clod of loam below us
Is a skull of Alexander;
Oceans are the blood of princes;
Desert sands the dust of beauties.
More than one Darius was there
Who the whole world overcame;
But since these gave up the ghost,
Thinkest thou they never were?
Boy, go from me to the Shah,
Say to him: Shah crowned as Jam,
Win thou first the poor man's heart,
Then the glass; so know the world.
Empty sorrows from the earth
Canst thou drive away with wine.
Now in thy throne's recent beauty,
In the flowing tide of power,
Moon of fortune, mighty king,
Whose tiara sheddeth lustre,
Peace secure to fish and fowl,
Heart and eye-sparkle to saints;
Shoreless is the sea of praise,—
I content me with a prayer.
From Nisami's poet-works,
Highest ornament of speech,
Here a verse will I recite,
Verse as beautiful as pearls.
"More kingdoms wait thy diadem,
Than are known to thee by name;
May the sovran destiny
Grant a victory every morn!"[72]

Apart from the general tone of the two poems, which is very similar, both of them celebrate wine and both of them refer to it as something different from the "juice of the grape." Contrary to the normal tradition of Bacchanalian poems, which celebrate the physical pleasures derived from drinking and getting drunk, both Hafiz and Emerson refer to wine as a metaphor for spiritual and metaphysical intoxication that takes man to levels beyond mere rationality. It is a juice, which in Hafiz's words with "sudden greatness fills us," or "Bring me, boy, the nectar cup, Since it leads to Paradise;" and in Emerson's words "May float at pleasure through all natures; The bird-language rightly spell, And that which roses say so well." To Hafiz, wine produces a state "That shone, ere time was, in the Néant," or "Bring the blessing of old times, Bless the old departed Shahs;" while Emerson "Shall hear far Chaos talk with me, Kings unborn shall walk with me, And the poor grass shall plot and plan, What it will do when it is man."

In the vocabulary of the Sufis, butler, wine, cup-bearer, and drunk have symbolic meanings. For instance, cup-bearer is regarded as the spiritual guide that reveals spiritual secrets. Similarly, by wine is meant the fire of the love of God, which produces intellectual liberation and spiritual ecstasy.[73] Tavern is a retreat where one communicates with the Beloved, and a drunkard is one who has gone beyond the realm of reason and has been initiated into divine mysteries. In *Bacchus*, Emerson imitates Hafiz, and speaks of wine as something which takes him out of himself and beyond time and space: "Pour, Bacchus! the remembering wine; Retrieve the loss of me and mine!" With the help of wine he wishes to unlock "every crypt of every rock." There are also many similarities of diction in the two poems, and words like heaven, world, unlock, quench, etc., are used in both of them.

After *Bacchus*, Emerson wrote another poem called *Fragmentary Bachhus*, which again reflects the influence of Hafiz. The *Fragmentary Bachhus*, as appeared in the centenary edition, is as follows:

> Pour the wine, pour the wine . . .
> It can cancel bulk and time;
> Crowds and condenses
> Into a drop a tun . . .
> On a brown grapestone
> The wheels of nature turn;
> Out of it the fury comes
> Wherewith the spondyls burn.
> And because a drop of the Vine
> Is creation's heart
> Wash with wine those eyes of thine;
> Nothing is hid, nor whole nor part.
> Wine is translated wit,
> Wine is the day of day
> Wine from the veiled secret
> Tear the veil away.

This poem should be compared with some lines from a poem by Hafiz that Emerson translated in his essay on *Persian Poetry*:

> The Builder of heaven
> Hath sundered the earth,
> So that no footway
> Leads out of it forth.
>
> On turnpikes of wonder
> wine leads the mind forth,
> Straight, sidewise, and upward,
> West, southward, and north.
>
> Stands the vault adamantine
> Until the Doomsday;
> The wine-cup shall ferry
> Thee o'er it away.

The likeness of imagery between "the wheels of nature" and the "turnpikes of wonder" is too clear to miss. To Emerson, "Wine from the veiled secret, Tear the veil away," and to Hafiz "wine leads the mind forth, Straight, sidewise, and upward, West, southward, and north." Also one might add to the above source the following from the essay on *Persian Poetry*, where Emerson contends that Hafiz thinks that wine

> "can snatch from the deeply hidden lot the veil that covers it.
> To be wiser the dull brain earnestly throbs
> Bring bands of wine for the stupid head."[74]

There is another poem of Hafiz translated by Emerson, which has influenced two of his own poems. The lines from Hafiz are as follows:

> If my darling should depart,
> And search the skies for prouder friends,
> God forbid my angry heart
> In other love should seek amends.
>
> When the blue horizon's hoop
> Me a little pinches here,
> Instant to my grave I stoop,
> And go find thee in the sphere.

The poems of Emerson, which show some resemblance to the above lines are as follows:

Hermione

(The love-sick Arab is advised by the elements . . .)
Courage! we are thine allies,
And with this hint be wise,—
The chains of kind
The distant bind;
Deed thou doest she must do,
Above her will, be true;
And, in her strict resort
To winds and waterfalls
And autumn's sunlit festivals,
To music, and to music's thought,
Inextricably bound,
She shall find thee, and be found.
Follow not her flying feet;
Come to us herself to meet.

The other poem is

Give All to Love:

(The lover is urged to be . . .)
Free as an Arab
Of thy beloved.
Cling with life to the maid;
But when the surprise,
Vague shadow of surmise,
Flits across her bosom young
Of a joy apart from thee,
Free be she, fancy-free,
Do not thou detain a hem,
Nor the palest rose she flung
From her summer diadem.

Though thou loved her as thyself,
As a self of purer clay,
Tho' her parting dims the day,
Stealing grace from all alive,

Heartily know,
When half-gods go,
The gods arrive.

"Blue horizon's hoop" used in the poem of Hafiz was a phrase that Emerson liked and used it on several occasions. In *Monadnoc* he writes:

Seen happy from afar,
Above the horizon's hoop.

In his essay on *Intellect*, Emerson wrote: "I am caught up by a strong wind and so far in one direction that I am out of the hoop of your horizon."

There is yet another translation from Hafiz that seems to have inspired one of Emerson's poems.

From Hafiz:

Oft have I said, do not stray from myself.
I am a kind of parrot; the mirror is holden to me;
What the eternal says, I stammering say again.
Give me what you will; I eat thistles as roses,
And according to my food I grow and give.
Scorn me not, but know I have the pearl
And am only seeking one to receive it.

The above poem should be compared with *Mithradates* by Emerson:

. . .
Give me agates for my meat;
Give me cantharides to eat;
From air and ocean bring me foods,
From all zones and altitudes;—
. . .
Too long shut in strait and few,
Thinly dieted on dew,
I will use the world, and sift it,
To a thousand humors shift it,
As you spin a cherry.
. . .
Hither! take me, use me, fill me,
Vein and artery, though ye kill me!
God I will not be an owl,
But sun me in the Capitol.

One can find many other examples of similarities between the poems of Hafiz and Emerson, but the above examples are sufficient to show the degree of Emerson's attachment to Hafiz's poetry. His most active period of writing poetry coincided with the period that he was studying Persian poets. His use of the images that he found in the poems of Hafiz, his deliberate imitation of Persian models, and the use of the same material are so intricately bound with his own poems that the influence is to be felt rather than proved. He was very fond of short sentences—lustres he called them—which he found in the poems of Hafiz, and he used them in a modified form in his own poems.

Joel Benton, one of the first scholars to make an intense study of Emerson's poetry, saw the relationship between Emerson's poems and those of Persian poets, especially Hafiz. He remarked:

> The kinship of the mintage is, in some aspects, curious. Shall we say on account of this homogeneity that the Oriental is but another Yankee? Or is it that the Yankee is merely the Oriental moved further West? At any rate, what Hafiz address to himself, and what Emerson says of him are wondrously alike in mode, texture and tune.[75]

But there is no more eloquent testimony to Emerson's interest in Persian poetry than his own words in the Journals, where he declared:

> I suppose every one has favorite topics, which make a sort of museum or privileged closet of whimsies in his mind, and which he thinks is a kind of aristocracy to know about. Thus, I like to know about lions, diamonds, wine, beauty and Martial and Hafiz.[76]

Notes

1. For a fuller study of the influence of Hafiz on Emerson's work, see Farhang Jahanpour's MA thesis *Oriental Influences on the Work of Ralph Waldo Emerson* (University of Hull, June 1965). Also see: John Yohannan, *The Persian Poet Hafiz in England and America* (MA thesis, Columbia University, 1939). For detailed studies of Eastern influences on Emerson see: F. I. Carpenter, *Emerson and Asia* (Cambridge: Harvard University Press, 1930); Arthur Christy, *The Orient in American Transcendentalism* (New York: Octagon Books, 1963); John D. Yohannan, *Persian Poetry in England and America: A Two Hundred Year History* (New York: Caravan Books, 1977).

2. Edward Waldo Emerson, *Emerson in Concord* (Boston: Houghton Mifflin, 1889), 31.

3. Joel E. Benton, *Emerson as a Poet* (New York: M. L. Holbrook, 1883), 29.

4. Joseph von Hammer-Purgstall, *Der Divan von Mohammed Schemseddin Hafis* (Stuttgart and Tubingen, 1812), 2 vols. Also *Geschichte der Schonen Redekunste Persien, mit einer Blutenlese aus Zweihundert Persischen Dichtern* (Wien, 1818).

5. In order to compile a full list of the books and articles that Emerson read from his youth onwards, his *Works, Letters*, and particularly *Journals* that occasionally made reference to the books that he was reading at the time are most helpful. There have been various attempts to provide a complete list of Emerson's readings. These include: Kenneth Walter Cameron, *Emerson's Early Reading List (1819–1824)* (New York: New York Public Library, 1951) reprinted in *Emerson Society Quarterly*, no. 28 (1962); *Indian Superstition, edited with a Dissertation on Emerson's Orientalism at Harvard* (New York: Cayuga, 1954); and *Ralph Waldo Emerson's Reading* (Hartford: Transcendental Books, 1962). Also see Jackson R. Bryer and Robert A Rees, *A Checklist of Emerson Criticism (1951–1961), with a Detailed Index. Bibliographical Supplement: Emerson. Fragment from Eight American Authors*, p. 424–28, "Emerson Society Quarterly," no. 37 (IV Quarter 1964). Misc. notes found with *A Checklist of Emerson Criticism (1951–1961)*. These works, however, do not provide a full list of all Emerson's readings. Cameron's book takes the list of Emerson's readings up to 1924, while the second and the third sources only provide a list of the books that Emerson borrowed from three libraries in Boston. There are a large number of books and articles on Oriental and Persian issues referred to in Emerson's *Journals, Works, Letters*, and *The Dial*, which have not been included in the above sources. Many of Emerson's friends, such as Amos Bronson Alcott and Henry David Thoreau, also possessed collections of Oriental books and they exchanged these books among them. Various volumes of "The Edinburgh Review" that Emerson borrowed also provided a rich source of material on oriental subjects. Indeed, a study of the volumes of "The Edinburgh Review" that Emerson borrowed leads one to assume that articles on Oriental topics seemed to have formed the main attraction to Emerson, as nearly all the editions of the *Review* that he borrowed contained some articles on Oriental subjects. A study of all these sources shows that his familiarity with Persian literature started much earlier than some scholars have assumed.

6. Francis Gladwin, ed., *The Asiatick Miscellany, containing of Original Productions, Translations, Fugitive Pieces, etc.*, 2 volumes, (Calcutta: Daniel Stuart, 1785–86). Emerson used volume one only, which contained some Indian hymns translated by Sir William Jones, notably the "Hymn to Narayena," as well as translations from the works of Sa'di, Hafiz and Jami. See Kenneth W. Cameron's *Emerson's Early Reading List 1819–1824* (New York 1951, 4 and 9). For a complete list of Emerson's Oriental readings see Farhang Jahanpour, 311–46. For a list of periodicals with articles on Eastern topics that he read, see Ibid., 347–75.

7. In 1821 Emerson read John Shore Teignmouth's *Memoirs of the Life, Writings, and Correspondence of Sir William Jones* (London: John Harchard, 1896). The book dealt with the life and works of Sir William Jones and provided samples of his translations from Oriental poetry. See Emerson, *Journals*, I, 82.

8. Emerson, *Journals*, I, 204. It is not clear which edition of *The Thousand and One Nights* he read, but it could be Edward Forester's translation (London, 1802)

9. Anquetil Duperron, *Zendavesta, Ouvrage de Zoroastre*, 3 vols. (Paris: Tilliard, 1771). Emerson borrowed two volumes from Boston Athenaeum Library. See K. W. Cameron's *Ralph Waldo Emerson's Reading* (New York, 1951), 54.

10. *The Phoenix: A Collection of Old and Rare Fragments: viz. the Morals of Confucius, the Chinese philosopher; the Oracles of Zoroaster, the founder of the religion of the Persian magi; Sanchoniathos's History of the creation; the Voyages of Hanno round the coast of Africa, five hundred years before Christ; King Hiempsals' History of the African settlements, translated from the Punic books; and the choice sayings of Publius Syrus.* (New York: W. Gowan, 1835).

11. See Emerson, *Journals*, IV, 254.

12. Sir William Jones, *Works* (London: G. G. and J. Robinson, 1799).

13. Emerson borrowed the *Works* from Boston Athenaeum Library. See K. W. Cameron's *Ralph Waldo Emerson's Reading* (New York, 1951), 42.

14. Joseph von Hammer-Purgstall, *Der Divan von Mohammed Schemseddin Hafis*, also *Geschichte der Schonen Redekunste Persien, mit einer Blutenlese aus Zweihundert Persischen Dichtern*.

15. Aleksander Chodzko, *Specimen of the Popular Poetry of Persia* (London, 1842).

16. For Emerson's quotations from this book see *The Journals of Ralph Waldo Emerson with Annotations*, ed. E. W. Emerson and W. E. Forbes, 10 vols., (Boston, 1909–1914), VII, 153, 280, 291.

17. *The Shah Nameh of the Persian Poet Firdausi*, trans. and abridged by James Atkinson (London, 1832).

18. Saʻdi, *The Gulistan or Flower Garden*, trans. James Ross from the Persian Text of Gentius, with an Essay on Sadi (London: Richardson, 1923).

19. William Rousenville Alger, *The Poetry of the East*, 2 vols. (Boston: Whittemore, Niles and Hall, 1856). In a letter to Alger on 18 October 1856, Emerson acknowledges the receipt of the book and adds that he was very pleased to read it. See Stanley T. Williams, "Unpublished Letters of Emerson," *Journal of English and Germanic Philology*, XXVI, 483–84.

20. James Atkinson's translation of *The Shah Nameh of the Persian Poet Firdausi*, trans. and abridged by James Wilkinson (London: Oriental Translation Fund, 1832). Emerson borrowed this book from Harvard College Library on September 2, 1846. See Carpenter, *Emerson and Asia*, 48 and 72. This was the best translation of the *Shah-Nameh*, from which Emerson made a number of quotations.

21. Emerson borrowed this book from Harvard College Library on 18 November 1846. See Carpenter, *Emerson and Asia*, 48 and 102.

22. Jalal-Ad-Din, *Auswahl aus den Diwanen des grossten mystischen Dichters Persiens Mewlana Dschalaleddin Rumi aus dem Persischen mit beigefugten original—texte und erlatenrn-den Armerkungen von Vicenz von Rosenweig* (Vienna, 1836). This book was borrowed by Emerson from Boston Athenaeum Library on 4 February 1861. See Carpenter, *Emerson and Asia*, 32, 82.

23. David Shea and Anthony Troyer, *The Dabistan, or School of Manners* (Paris: Oriental Translation Fund, 1843). See *Journals*, X, 305.

24. R. W. Emerson, *Complete Works*, ed. with a biographical introduction and notes by E. W. Emerson, 12 vols., (Boston: Centenary Edition, 1903–04) VIII, 236–65. All subsequent quotations from this essay are taken from this source. This essay was first published in "The Atlantic Monthly" in 1858.

25. Musle-Huddeen Sheik Saadi, *The Gulistan* or *Rose Garden*, trans. from the original by Francis Gladwin, with preface by R. W. Emerson (Boston: Ticknor and Fields, 1865).

26. *The Dial*, 1842. When quoting passages from Emerson, the spelling that he used to refer to Persian poets is retained.

27. Emerson wrote the first part of "Fragments on the Poet and the Poetic Gift" in 1845, published in *The Poems* (Boston 1847, dated 25 December 1846).

28. Emerson, *Works*, 237.

29. Ibid., 244.

30. Ibid.

31. Ibid., 245
32. Ibid.
33. Ibid., 248.
34. Ibid., 246.
35. Ibid., 247.
36. Ibid., 248–49.
37. Ibid., 259.
38. Ibid.
39. Emerson, *Journals*, 1847; quoted in *Works*, VIII, 417.
40. Emerson, *Works*, 249–50.
41. Ibid., 252.
42. Ibid.
43. Ibid., 254.
44. Ibid.
45. For a study of Emerson's views regarding Saʻdi, see F. Jahanpour, *Oriental Influences*, 180–234.
46. Emerson, *Journals*, VI, 463.
47. Emerson, *Works*, 390–310–320.
48. Emerson, *Works*, VIII, 251.
49. Emerson, *Journals*, 1847, quoted in *Works*, VIII, 417.
50. Emerson, *Journals*, 562.
51. Emerson, *Works*, IX, 297.
52. Emerson, *Works*, IX, 310.
53. Emerson, *Journals*, X, 167.
54. Emerson, *Works*, VIII, 417.
55. Ibid., IX, 316.
56. Ibid., VIII, 253.
57. Emerson, *Journals*, VII, 279.
58. Ibid., V, 562.
59. Emerson, *Essays*, Essay 16 on "Manners."
60. Emerson, *Journals*, VIII, 244.
61. See Emerson's essay on *Persian Poetry*, *Works*, VIII, 236–65.
62. Emerson, *Journals*, 1847; quoted in *Works*, VIII, 417.
63. Emerson, *Journals*, 418.
64. These translations appear in different places. Some of them were quoted in Emerson's *Works* and *Journals*. For the translations see: *Poems* (Boston, 1847), 209–18; *The Liberty Bell*, by Friends of Freedom (Boston, 1851), 78–81 and 156–57; *Works* (Essay on Worship), VI, 234; *Works* (Essay on Persian Poetry), VIII, 237–65; *Works*, IX, 298–305; and *Journals*, VII, 181; VII, 277–78; VIII, 542; IX, 75; IX, 538–39; IX, 544–45.
65. Reprinted in *Works*, VIII, 237. It is interesting to note that a few years later, two of the three poets that Edward FitzGerald chose for translation were those mentioned by Emerson. FitzGerald translated the *Rubaʻiyyat* of Omar Khayyam, the *Language of Birds* [*Mantiq al-tayr*] by Attar and *Salaman and Absal* by Jami. Even more interestingly, Fitzgerald compared Omar Khayyam with Emerson and wrote: "I wonder that Persia could have produced anything so like Emerson where Emerson is truest and greatest." Quoted in J. H. Thonet, "Etude sur Edward Fitz-gerald et la literature persone, d'apres les sources

originale" (Bibliotheque de la faculte de philosophie et letters de l'universite de Liege, H. Valliant-Carmann, Paris, Champion, 1929), 21–2.

66. Emerson, *Works*, VIII, from "Persian Poetry," 247.
67. Ibid., 261.
68. E. B. Cowell, "Hafiz, the Persian Poet," *Fraser's Magazine*, L, 288 ff (September 1854).
69. Emerson, *Works*, VIII, 257.
70. Emerson, *Journals*, VII, 277.
71. Ibid., 277.
72. Emerson, *Poems*, "From the Persian of Hafiz I."
73. In his notebook called *Orientalist*, Emerson wrote of Hafiz, "he uses wine as a symbol of intellectual freedom." In the essay on *Persian Poetry*, he further remarked: "But the love or the wine of Hafiz is not to be confounded with vulgar debauch. It is the spirit in which the song is written that imports, and not the topics."
74. Emerson, *Works*, VIII, 246.
75. Joel E. Benton, *Emerson as a Poet*, 28, 29.
76. Emerson, *Journals*, VIII, 488.

The Disciple:
Walt Whitman

6

Whitman and Hafiz

Expressions of Universal Love and Tolerance

Mahnaz Ahmad

The issue of universal love and tolerance is common to different cultural and poetic traditions. This is the common thread that unites the mystical poetry of the fourteenth-century Persian Sufi poet Hafiz, and the visionary outpourings of nineteenth-century American poet, Walt Whitman. In Hafiz and Whitman we have two poets who are keenly aware of their contexts and the world around them, but convey a deep sense of the spiritual oneness of all life. Their poetry is the expression of a humanistic vision of the world, with love being the primary driving force. In "Song of Myself," Whitman, in a moment of mystical insight, says,

> Swiftly arose and spread around me the peace and joy and
>   knowledge that pass all the art and argument of the earth;
> And I know that the hand of God is the elderhand of
>   my own,
> And I know that the spirit of God is the eldest brother of
>   my own,
> And that all the men ever born are also my brothers . . .
>   and the women my sisters and lovers,
> And that a kelson of the creation is love;[1]

And Hafiz writes,

> Within the Magian tavern
> The light of God I see;

In such a place, O wonder!
Shines out such radiancy.[2]

And again:

See God's creation mirrored in your own face
I send you an all-revealing mirror.[3]

Hafiz's belief in the interconnectedness of all creation stems from two important doctrines of Sufism. First is the doctrine of the "Transcendent Unity of Being" (*wahdat al-wujud*) and second is the doctrine of the "Universal or Perfect Man" (*al-insan al-kamil*). All things are theophanies of the Divine names and qualities and derive their existence from the One being who alone Is. Man is the only creature in this world who can reflect the Divine names and qualities in a total and conscious manner just as the mystic is the one who realizes all the possibilities of the human state—the Perfect Man. As such he is the microcosm, in whom are reflected all the perfect attributes of the macrocosm.

There are two sides to the concept of God and the universe: the first is the orthodox view, seeing God in terms of the sovereign will, as the creator of the world, the Almighty ruler; and the second is an outlook influenced by Neoplatonic philosophy. This conceives of the world as the emanation from the Deity and sees God as the hidden essence or reality of all things. While God is thus immanent in all things, he is yet the transcendent home and goal of all things. Under the influence of Neoplatonism, the principle of divine unity, which is fundamental to Islam, "God—there is no God but Him," came to mean that God is not merely the sole cause of existence but that He alone has real being. So far as anything else exists at all, it exists as a ray of His light. The world is thus the self-revelation of God and it is the aspiration of the mystic to pierce the veil of outer things to see the Truth. While God permeates the phenomena of the world, He still remains in His eternal being above and beyond the flux of nature.

In their conception of man, the Sufis adopt a dual attitude. On one hand they are aware of the sinfulness and imperfections of human nature, on the other hand they see the Divine light in the soul of man. The soul is a mirror that is soiled and covered with rust, but which may be cleansed and polished, so as to reflect the beauty of the higher world. Although man has descended into this world, he still possesses the inner sight (*sirr*) whereby he may rise into immediate contact with God. The deepest part of man's soul is divine.

In his "Song of Myself," Whitman takes us through his experience of awakening of the self to an awareness of a divine design, a plan transcending the self and all things animate and inanimate, seen and unseen. He acknowledges in Section 17: "These are the thoughts of all men in all ages and lands, they are not original to me."[4]

Sufi ideas found a way into Whitman's spiritual development under the influence of Emerson. James Russell in his work *Emerson and the Persians* points out that Emerson was inspired by the beauty of Sufi poetry and its underlying philosophy, which he knew through German translations. "It is a standard aspect of Persian Sufi poetry, from the earliest times, that the great mystical revelation is—or at least verges upon—pantheism. That is to say, the fully realized mystic discovers that what he thought to be his individual ego, his contingent being, is irrelevant or illusory, and vanishes altogether in the great experience of self-extinction, Arabic *fana' fi'llah*, in the One, in God."[5] According to Russell, it was Emerson's translation of Persian poets like Hafiz, and his ideas derived from "the visionary and philosophical traditions of the ancient world", that influenced Whitman. Whitman, like the Sufis, saw the transcendent expressed in humanity. He was aware of a cosmic presence in every man. The belief in the essential divinity of man is echoed in Whitman's poetry. In one of his poems he inquires, "Was somebody asking to see the soul? See, your own shape and countenance, persons, substances, beasts, the trees, the running rivers, the rocks and sands." He talks of man as the "microcosm of all creation's wildness, terror, beauty and power," and sees God in "the faces of men and women, and "in my own face in the glass."[6] There is in Whitman, as in Sufi poets, an intuitive awareness of self to God, to other men and women, and to nature. From such awareness comes tolerance and understanding:

> Each of us inevitable,
> Each of us limitless—each of us with his or her right upon the earth
> Each of us allow'd the eternal purports of the earth,
> Each of us here as divinely as any is here.[7]

This is Walt Whitman in his poem "Salut Au Monde" enfolding humanity in his embrace, accepting differences in creed, color, race, and social standing. He writes, "I think some divine rapport has equalized me with them."[8]

In Hafiz's poetry, tolerance is derived from his philosophy of unreason, which scorns reason as a way of knowing God, and which preaches self-abandonment to a greater Truth. An examination of Hafiz's poetry reveals that he does not write religious or divine poems as such, though a few poems deal purely with the mystical relationship between the soul and God. The striking thing about Hafiz's approach to the question of Sufism is the unconventionality of his ideas. Throughout his *Divan*, he takes care to distinguish himself from the ascetic *zahid* and the Sufi, and to project his own version of true and pure

Sufism. Tearing away the veil of hypocrisy, formalism, and asceticism from institutionalized religion, he reaches for the essence—the core of mysticism, as it were, by declaring himself a lover and a profligate: "Openly I declare, and I say it with glee / The slave of love am I, and from both worlds free."[9] Disassociating himself from the puritanical ascetic, he puts forward the theory that: "Whether drunk or sober all are seeking the Friend / The House of Love is everywhere, whether mosque or church."[10]

Hafiz will accept no boundaries or limitations. His belief in the infinite possibilities open to human beings in their search for Truth comes into direct conflict with the narrow sectarian beliefs and piety of the puritanical ascetic, who worship out of fear of punishment or desire for reward. Hafiz opposes the legalists who dominated so much of Islamic life in his time. The legalists were opposed to Sufism, because it claimed knowledge of God distinct from codified religion. For Hafiz, God is infinite, and the only love worthy of God is infinite. Hafiz sees himself as the liberated man. He is opposed to the ascetic who is a prisoner of the world because he is bound by conventions and taboos and thus constantly in fear of infamy: "Tell the sermonizer not to fault Hafiz, who's / left the cell, / Freeman's feet aren't restrained—if he's gone away / he's gone."[11] The ascetic who preaches one thing and practices another is hardly a true lover of God, for his main concern is with the image he presents to the world, whereas the true mystic transcends religious differences and sectarian prohibitions: "Don't consider ill fame if you're the follower of love's way, / Shaikh Sanaan left his mantle in pawn at the vintner's shop."[12]

Paul Smith talks of Hafiz's joyful humanity and love of nature, his freedom of thought and spirit, and the sincerity and self-reliance that attracted Emerson to Hafiz. These are precisely the qualities that permeate Whitman's poetry. Whitman was deeply influenced by Emerson. In "One Hour to Madness and Joy," Whitman's language of inebriation, of losing oneself to the infinite One, is reminiscent of Hafiz when he writes, "O to drink the mystic deliria deeper than any other man,"[13] and, "To ascend, to leap to the heaven of the love indicated to me! / To rise thither with my inebriate soul! / To be lost if it must be so!"

However, Hafiz's symbolism of wine and inebriation has to be understood in context of his brand of mysticism. In order to distinguish between the self-centered cleric and the true mystic, Hafiz resorts to his famous cluster of images centering on the wine-shop. The *rind* (vagrant) who drains the cup of wine to the dregs is the mystic, and the *kharabat* (tavern) itself stands as a concrete symbol in opposition to the mosque, church, or anything representing formal and institutional religion. The reprobate *rind,* intoxicated and disorderly, has drunk of the wine of love and he comes closer to the truth than the sanctimonious Sufi with his rosary and prayer-book. Hafiz writes, "On the day of reckoning I fear, the religious elder's lawful bread, / Cannot compete with our forbidden liquor."[14]

In trying to understand Hafiz's attitude toward mysticism, it is important not to underestimate his anti-orthodoxy. He was against asceticism practiced for its own sake and against the unaccommodating, sterile, and narrow religion of the ascetics. He saw the essence or religion as something vast and illimitable, something that went beyond the confines of the mosque, church, and monastery; something that could be acquired in the strangest of places, as "the magian's tavern."

Hafiz saw any form of monasticism as quite inimical to the true spirit of Islam, particularly to the mystical aspect. He stresses the relationship between the individual and a personal God outside the rigid codes laid down by ritualists, who have no comprehension of the truth, that which can be gained through love alone: "Hafiz, seek not the jewel of love in the monastery's confines, / Step abroad, if you have the desire to seek."[15]

Hafiz's mysticism is the mysticism of love. For him, the cloister and the penitential robes of the Sufi are as unsatisfying and hypocritical as the formal religion of the orthodox theologian and lawyer: "In the magian's world, a lover like me there is none, / The woolen *khirqah* lies pawned here, wine-cup and / Book there."[16] In his notebook, Whitman talks about the meeting ground of all religions: "[T]he clear atmosphere above them—There all meet—previous distinctions are lost—Jew meets Hindu, and Persian, Greek and Asiatic and European and American are joined—and any one religion is just as good as another." Whitman expresses dissatisfaction with codified religion, and proclaims an alternative which is more liberating and all-encompassing: "I do not despise you priests, all times, the world over, / My faith is the greatest of faiths and the least of faiths, / Enclosing worship ancient and modern and all between ancient and modern."[17] Like Hafiz, Whitman sees love as the unifying force in the universe. "The Mystic Trumpeter" announces the theme of love:

> Blow again trumpeter! And for thy theme,
> Take now the enclosing theme of all, the solvent and the setting,
> Love that is pulse of all, the sustenance and the pang,
> The heart of man and woman all for love,
> No other theme but love—knitting, enclosing, all diffusing love.[18]

In his essay, *Whitman and an All-Inclusive America*, James Russell has drawn an interesting parallel between Whitman and Hafiz. In his interpretation, the two poets share a vision of a world based on love. Hafiz wrote a famous ode that speaks of a "lost city of lovers" ruled by kindness, friendship, and equality. Whitman recreates this city of love in the vision of America that he projects in *Leaves of Grass*. For Whitman, his book, himself, and his nation were one and indivisible, as well as all encompassing, a home for wanderers and outcasts, like the "thoughtful Armenian" he mentions in his poem "Salut Au Monde!"[19]

Hafiz's "lost city" is a nostalgic longing for a time gone by, when lovers were inebriated by the wine of unreason: "Nobody has the taste for drunkenness—what happened to the wine-drinkers?"[20]

Hafiz tries to recreate in his poetry a world where roses bloom and nightingales sing and where "Love was to replace law, indeed, it was to be the only law." Despite the chaos and uncertainty in the world around him, Hafiz remains steadfast in his belief that this "old world will become youthful again." Whitman, on the other hand, sees the realization of his dream as imminent in his homeland, in the New World.

> I dream'd in a dream I saw a city invincible to the attacks
> of the whole of the rest of the earth,
> I dream'd that was the new city of Friends,
> Nothing was greater there than the quality of robust love, it led
> the rest.[21]

Love is the underpinning, or "kelson" of Whitman's "city of Friends." James Russell explains, "The kelson is a line of timber that fastens a ship's floor timbers to the keel: it holds together the top and bottom where the two sides of the craft meet, so it is the unifying factor in all directions, the center and soul of the structure, in touch with all, necessary to all. The kelson of the ship America is love."[22]

Love is central to Hafiz's worldview. This love is many-faceted. As Mahmud Human points out:[23] when Hafiz advocates the path of love, the love he talks about is a combination of sensual, intellectual (Platonic), and spiritual love. The love can be heterosexual or homosexual. Hafiz eulogizes love, love in all its aspects. He does not reject either the erotic, symbolized by the "venus-browed" and the "soft-bodied" (*zohreh jabinan wa nazok badanan*), or the spiritual, symbolized by the man of God, the "magian elder" (*pir-i moghan*). Love can be experienced and enjoyed in different ways by different people, depending on their vision and growth. Those who cannot fathom the mysteries of "higher love" would do well to seek the "bodies soft and delicate" and thus attain the spiritual through the physical. This idea is based on the mystical belief in the physical world as the world of illusions, which had its source in the Platonic and Neoplatonic idea that this world is but a reflection of the real world, archetypal world (*alam-i missal*),[24] and that physical beauty, human goodness, etc., are imperfect shadows, representations in crude matter of heavenly and immaterial forms of beauty and goodness. The mystic thus learns first to love earthly beauty, then, when he perceives that this is but the reflection of the eternal beauty, his love is set upon God. "Love, beloved and wine, these I'll never give up, / A hundred times I've repented, but never again."[25]

Asheq Sho (be a lover) is the cry echoing through Hafiz's poetry. The theme of inebriation and love are linked together in Hafiz's vision. Love and wine have a similar effect of releasing the ego from the phenomenal world; the lip of the beloved and the wine-bowl are complementary to each other; the wine is both the ruby-red wine of the grape and wine of divine love and ecstasy. The *saqi*, or cupbearer, is the earthly beloved and drinking partner, as well as the divine beloved. In his poetry, Hafiz ranges unobtrusively and naturally through the various nuances and meanings in the span of a single poem. The spiritual and the sensual are an integral part of his mature vision and exist together, enhancing one another. A subtle harmony and equilibrium is maintained between different spheres of being. He is not a pure sensualist nor is there a dichotomy between the physical and the spiritual in his vision. Like most Sufis, he sees the physical as a bridge to the spiritual. There is much to be enjoyed in the physical world and Hafiz scoffs at the *zahid,* or ascetic, who would deprive himself of happiness in this world in hope of the "pleasures of paradise." Addressing the *zahid* he says: "You've told all wine's defects, tell its virtues too: / Pandering to vulgar minds, don't flout logic."[26]

Yet at the same time, Hafiz is aware that nothing is untainted by the hue of mortality, and that pleasures are short-lived. The vicissitudes of mortal existence cannot be shut off from the mind by a total indulgence in the senses. Life for him is as it is for Percy Bysshe Shelley, a "dome of many-colored glass, that stains the white radiance of eternity."[27] Yet the beauty of this dome cannot be denied; in fact, the beauty reaffirms the perfect beauty of its maker.

Whitman, like Hafiz, is aware of the interdependence of the body and the soul, the physical and the spiritual. In "Song of Myself," he declares:

> I am the poet of the Body and I am the poet of the Soul,
> The pleasures of heaven are with me and the pains of hell are
>   with me,
> The first I graft and increase upon myself . . . the latter I translate
>   into a new tongue.[28]

Whitman accepts the body, not as something to be reviled and degraded, nor as a necessary evil that needs to be mortified, but as a stepping-stone to the spiritual. He describes the soul and body as intimate lovers: "the hugging and loving bed-fellow sleeps at my side through the night, / and withdraws at the peep of the day with stealthy tread."[29]

Whitman says:

> I believe in the flesh and the appetites,
> Seeing hearing and feeling are miracles, and each part and tag of
>   me is a miracle.

> Divine am I inside and out, and I make holy whatever I touch or
> am touched from.[30]

Whitman's concept of self includes both body and soul, and God can only be apprehended through the complete self. In "Song of Myself" he writes,

> Clear and sweet is my soul, and clear and sweet is all that is not
> my soul.
> I believe in you my soul, the other I am must not abase itself to you,
> And you must not be abased to the other.[31]

Like his "graybeard Sufi" in *A Persian Lesson*, Whitman sees the divine "immanent in every life and object." Sometimes Whitman uses the language of transcendence and sees God in "limitless space" and "limitless time," but God is also the "great Camerado." Using imagery from earthly love, Whitman refers to God as a lover who leaves messages for him, "I find letters from God dropt in the street, and everyone is sign'd by God's name." Massud Farzan points out that Whitman's experience of the divine, as described in section five of "Song of Myself," is closer to the beloved of the Sufi than the "abstract deity . . . the Brahman of the Indian sage."[32] Whitman's language has parallels with Sufi poets like Hafiz, who use sensuous, even erotic, imagery to describe the union of the soul with God. Hafiz views the relation between the creator and created as that of a lover and beloved. The dynamic force of love and longing inspired many mystic-poets who looked to the Qur'an for appropriate verses to justify their expression. For example, the famous *surah*, "We indeed created man; and we know what his soul whispers to him, and we are closer to him than the jugular vein,"[33] inspired many poets. Human love was seen as an analogue to the love of God. For the Sufi, the world of the senses has no final or intrinsic value or reality, but it is not a mere illusion from which one must step aside. It is a shadow, an image or reflection of the Truth, a gateway to the real world. For Whitman the world of the senses, "seeing, hearing, feeling are miracles." His aim is to purify and transfigure the physical through an acceptance of the physical world, by celebrating the body. It is through the transfigured senses that he arrives at mystical consciousness. "Through me forbidden voices / Voices of sexes and lusts, voices veil'd and I remove the veil, / Voices indecent by me clarified and transfigure'd."[34]

The most important lesson Whitman learned from the "graybeard Sufi" is that logic and discursive reasoning have never provided all the answers and that the solution to the baffling mystery of life lies in a mystical surrender of the limited human ego to the infinite self in an act of love. "Logic and sermons never convince," Whitman says in "Song of Myself." Nor is he satisfied by the "proofs" and "figures" presented by the "learn'd astronomer." In his acceptance of life in all its complexity, Whitman understands "the puzzle of puzzles / And that we call Being." Whitman's poetry echoes Hafiz's philosophy: "Be happy and let not your mind contend with Being and not-Being / For not Being is the end of everything that is."[35]

For Hafiz, not-Being, or *nisti*, is not death or oblivion, but rather an abandonment of self to a greater self, through love, tolerance, and acceptance of human frailty. In "Song of Myself," Whitman's mystical experience leads him to the conclusion that the key to human life is not "chaos or death—it is form, union, plan—it is eternal life—it is Happiness." He reiterates this realization in "Song of the Open Road."

> Here is the efflux of the soul,
> The efflux of the soul comes from within through embower'd
> gates, ever provoking questions.
>
> The efflux of the soul is happiness.[36]

Likewise, Hafiz believes that, "except through affliction, none arrives at happiness,"[37] and he embraces life as an inscrutable mystery which has to be endured. Whitman too embraces life with all its multiplicity and contradictions. "Do I contradict myself? / Very well then . . . I contradict myself; / I am large . . . I contain multitudes."[38]

Both Hafiz and Whitman seek out love as the great equalizer in a world that is full of imperfections. This love is the infinite love that pours out from God to humanity and informs every living thing. There is in both poets a belief in the oneness of creation and a sense of the divine presence in human life. Whitman looked to a time when there would be no need for priests and every man, through the divinity within him, would be his own priest. Like Hafiz, he believed that the object of life is to know and experience the divinity within each one of us, and this can be achieved through the transformation of the heart in love.

Notes

1. Walt Whitman, *Leaves of Grass* (New York: Modern Library, 1980).

2. Arthur J. Arberry, *Hafiz, Fifty Poems* (Cambridge: Cambridge University Press, 1970), 117.

3. Translated from Persian by author, from Muhammad Qazwini and Qasim Ghani, *Divan of Hafiz*, (Teheran, 1941), number 83. This will be referred to as QG throughout with the number indicated by #.

4. Walt Whitman, *Leaves of Grass*, Section 17.

5. James Russell, "Emerson and the Persians," Lecture Series: Near East in the Mind of America (Harvard, 2002).
6. Whitman, *Leaves of Grass*, Section 48.
7. Ibid.
8. Ibid.
9. Author's translation, QG, #317.
10. Author's translation, QG, #80.
11. Author's translation, QG, # 83.
12. Author's translation, QG, # 77.
13. Paul Smith, "Hafiz of Shiraz: Hafiz's influence on Western Poetry," <www.hafizofshiraz.com>.
14. Author's translation, QG, #11.
15. Author's translation, QG, #11.
16. Author's translation, QG, #386.
17. Whitman, *Leaves of Grass*, Section 43.
18. Ibid., 250.
19. Russell, "Emerson and the Persians."
20. Ibid.
21. Whitman, *Leaves of Grass*, 105.
22. Russell, "Emerson and the Persians."
23. Mahmud Human, *Hafiz che miguyad* (Teheran: 1938).
24. This idea is expounded in detail by Ibn Al-Arabi. See Annmarie Schimmel, *The Mystical Dimensions of Islam* (Chapel Hill: University of North Carolina Press, 1975).
25. Translated by author, QG, #343.
26. Translated by author, QG, #182.
27. Neville Rogers, ed., *Complete Poetical Works of Shelley* (Oxford: Clarendon Press, 1972).
28. Whitman, *Leaves of Grass*, Section 21.
29. Ibid., Section 3.
30. Ibid., Section 24.
31. Whitman, *Leaves of Grass*, Section 3.
32. Massud Farzan, "Whitman and Sufism: Towards *A Persian Lesson*" *American Literature* (January 1976), 572–582.
33. Qur'an 50:16.
34. Whitman, *Leaves of Grass*, Section 24.
35. Translated by Author, QG, #25.
36. Whitman, *Leaves of Grass*, Section 7.
37. Translated by Author, QG, #25
38. Whitman, *Leaves of Grass*, Section 51.

7

Walt Whitman and Sufism

Towards "A Persian Lesson"[1]

Massud Farzan

Interest in Whitman as a prophet and mystic is not new. Emerson and Thoreau—to mention only two famous nineteenth-century names—more than anything else praised his *Leaves of Grass* for the passion and profundity of its mystical visions and messages. However, during the early part of the twentieth century, particularly during the academic flowering of formalism and T. S. Eliot's literary theories, attention was focused on Whitman as a poet of compactly structured lyrics such as the "Lilacs" poem or segments contained in "Drum Taps." By contrast, the vast mystical panegyrics of, say, "Song of Myself" or "The Song of the Open Road" were underestimated, at times dismissed with such designations as "a needless pretext." The phrase is Eliot's.[2]

During the 1960s, with the publication of *Start With the Sun: Studies in Cosmic Poetry* by the poet Karl Shapiro and others, attention seems to have been once again redirected to Whitman's importance as a poet of mystic consciousness. "He is one mystical writer of any consequence America has produced," Shapiro writes, "the poet of the greatest achievement."[3] The consequence of such dramatic reevaluation of Whitman has been twofold. First, a number of academic scholars have investigated formal pattern and symbolic unity in "Song of Myself," discovering previously unrecognized structures. Second, critics have willingly studied and written on Whitman's mystical poetry *qua* mystical poetry. Of particular significance and value have been a number of comparative studies in which the influence on Whitman by other mystics and mystical works, as well as relevant parallelisms, have been investigated.[4] As such, by far the most typical studies have been related to Vedantic, Buddhist, and Hindu classics. The famous statement of Thoreau, upon meeting Walt Whitman in 1855, that *Leaves of Grass* was "wonderfully like the Orientals" is usually prefatory to these comparative studies.[5]

No similar studies have been made with regard to Whitman's indebtedness and similarity to Persian mystics and, more specifically, the Sufi-inspired poets such as Rumi, Sa'di, and Hafiz, even though as early as 1866 a noted British Orientalist, Lord Viscount Strangford, called attention to the astounding affinity of *Leaves of Grass*, in its spirit, content, and form alike, to Persian poetry.[6] While Strangford's comments were undoubtedly exaggerated, there is no reason why Whitman would not have been acquainted with the Sufi poets of Persia and highly influenced by their thought and poetry. His contemporary kindred soul, Ralph Waldo Emerson, was extremely interested in the Sufis, having read their works extensively and written about them, notably Sa'di and Hafiz. Thoreau too was fond of the Sufis and had quoted from Sa'di's *Gulistan* in *Walden*. More unequivocally, though, Whitman's own 1891 poem *A Persian Lesson*—originally called *A Sufi Lesson*[7]—is indeed a surprisingly accurate and inspired reflection of Persian Sufism.

All the same, the affinity between *Leaves of Grass* and the work of Persian Sufi-poets has been ignored or merely passed over. The claims of Lord Strangford have not been put to any serious test, nor has Whitman's *A Persian Lesson* received any worthwhile exploration. It is not my intention in this essay to corroborate Strangford's contention that Whitman "instead of wasting his gifts on *Leaves of Grass* . . . should have translated Rumi."[8] Nor do I intend to show that Whitman's mysticism was of an unquestionably Sufic variety: no genuine mystic draws distinctions between varieties of mysticism. Accordingly as a mystic, Whitman is neither more Sufic than Vedantic, more Christian than Hindu. Instead, it is my purpose to show that there are indeed striking similarities between Whitman and the Sufi poets, so much so that it is altogether conceivable that Whitman had been influenced more by Persian Sufi poetry than any other mystical works and that his unique old-age poem, *A Persian Lesson,* presents a marvelous fruition of a long acquaintance with and immersion in Sufism.

A Song of Myself

A famous fragment in the mystical poetry of *Leaves of Grass* is section five of "Song of Myself," which tells of the poet's metaphysical experience of a clear summer morning, during which "Swiftly arose and spread around me the peace and knowledge that pass all the argument of the earth." A noteworthy characteristic of this section is one of duality: "I believe in you, my soul, the other I am must not abase itself to you." What is of particular interest, however, is that the "soul"—and what the poet addresses as "you" in section five—is also the beloved of the "I." One could call that entity an ordinary human being—male or female—and the passage an ordinary love poem with touches of eroticism.

There is in fact enough in the lines of sexual imagery—supported by similar passages in later sections of *Song of Myself*—to warrant such a point of view:

> I mind once how we lay such a transparent summer morning
> How you settled your head athwart my hips and gently turn'd
>   over upon me,
> And parted the shirt from my bosom-bone . . .[9]

> On all sides prurient provokers stiffening my limbs,
> Straining the udder of my heart for its withheld drip,
> Behaving licentious toward me, taking no denial,
> Depriving me of my best for a purpose,
> Unbuttoning my clothes, holding me by the bare waist. . . .[10]

Yet in the language of carnal love, Whitman is actually representing mystical experiences. As such, it will be seen, Whitman's triumvirate of lover-soul-deity reveals an interesting similarity, not so much to the "abstract deity . . . the *Brahman*, or rather *Parabrahman*, of the Indian sage, devoid of all personal attributes,"[11] but to the Beloved of the Sufi poet. The Sufi's primary desire to bring the I-Thou relationship, the microcosm-macrocosm duality, to complete fusion and oneness, finds its most convenient and poetic expression in the love-sex relationship between two people. Here is Hafiz in one of his most famous *ghazals* from the *Divan*:

> Hair disarrayed, cheeks beflushed, holding the cup
> Bosom displayed, laughing, ghazal-chanting
>   Eyes challenging, lips whispering charms—

> So came my lover, at midnight, sat by my bedside
> Reached over and said with taunt:
> "Are you asleep my lover of old times?"

> A Sufi who is offered such a night-cap
> Would be a betrayer of love, if he didn't become a wine
>   worshipper.

> Go tell the ascetic not to flout the poor dreg-drainers
> Whatever was poured in eternity to our cups, we drank up—
> Whether from the wine-cellars of paradise or the corner pub.[12]

"My lovers suffocate me," Whitman says in a mock-plaintive tone, "coming naked to me at night."[13] And in a manner reminiscent of the recollection scene of section five, Rumi says in his celebrated *Divan-i Shams-i Tabrizi*:

Happy the moment when we were seated in the palace,
   thou and I
With two forms and with two figures but with one soul,
   thou and I
The colors of the grove and the voices of the birds will
   bestow immortality
At the time when we should come into the garden,
   thou and I.[14]

It should be noted that the introduction of the language of human love to Persian mystical poetry is the by-product of a larger scheme: to replace the discursive and abstract with the concrete and the tangible. Whitman explains the same point though in a somewhat different way: "This effusion of corporation of the soul is always under the beautiful laws of physiology—I guess the soul itself can never be anything but great and pure and immortal; but it makes itself visible only through matter—a perfect head, and bowels and bones to match is the easy gate through which it comes from its embowered garden."[15] Once the poet uses the language of ordinary heterosexual (or homosexual) love relationship to express mystic love, he goes all the way, bringing all the ramifications of the latter, such as jealousy and possessiveness, to the language of mystical love: "I think of rimes and the Beloved taunts / 'Don't think of aught but me'" (Rumi). Repeatedly the Sufi masters drive it home that the prime requisite for the Sufi path is the feeling of want, the *thirsting*, the *taste*. It would then be quite conceivable to find a book of mystical poetry in an "extraordinary collection of small imagist poems, versified short stories, realistic urban and rural genre paintings, inventories, homilies, philosophizing, farcical episodes, confessions, and lyric musings. . . ." This is Richard Chase's list[16] of what makes up "Song of Myself," but it could be an equally accurate designation of Rumi's *Mathnavi* or Sa'di's *Gulistan*. Argument, abstraction, and getting stuck in logistics are anathema to Whitman and Persian poet-mystics alike:

To elaborate is no avail, learn'd and unlearn'd
   feel that it is so[17]

I have no mockings or arguments, I witness and wait.[18]

Knowing the perfect fitness and equity of things,
   while they discuss, I am silent. . . .[19]

And more directly Rumi says:

The legs of logicians are of wood;
Wooden legs are mighty untrustworthy.

And elsewhere:

> I said to the Master, "Tell me the secret of the One and multiplicity."
> He said, "The wave, the foam, the eddy—they're aught but the sea."

Once in a while the poet of *Leaves of Grass* has barely started to expound on the unnamable when he becomes aware of his mistake:

> The press of my foot to the earth springs a hundred affections,
> They scorn the best I can do to relate them.[20]

And again, Rumi:

> Whatever I say about love, I hang my face once I am *in* love.
> Words are to elucidate, love can do without.
> The pen was racing on paper, until it came to love and cracked.
> The donkey of reason got bogged down in a mud-path.
> All that was finally written about love and loving was love itself.
> The sun rose as proof of the sun, feel it on your soul's face
> Why linger on the shadows as its sign?

One is reminded of Whitman's poem about attending an astronomy lecture, then coming out and gazing at stars. Or this, among many other similar lines, from "Song of Myself,"

> A morning-glory at my window satisfies me more than all the metaphysics of books.[21]

Parallelisms are too many to include in a brief introductory article such as this. The main objective is to show with a few isolated examples how, in manner and matter alike, Whitman reflects the Sufi-inspired poetry of classical Persian poets such as Rumi. In this light one may approach the puzzling identities (or "Whitman's images" as Leslie Fiedler put it) which the poet has dispersed throughout *Leaves of Grass*.

Whitman and Rumi

Who is Whitman's boisterous self-celebrating, self-singing "I?" Who is the modest, self-effacing, wondering "I?" Who is "my soul?" Who is "my fancy?" And how about the "I"'s unnamed interlocutors—who, for instance, is being addressed when we read: "Unscrew the locks from the doors! / Unscrew the doors themselves from their jamb!'"? Likewise, who is Hafiz's interlocutor in the *ghazal* starting with the following lines: "Come let us scatter roses! Splash wine into the goblets! / Destroy the world's roof and cast a new design!" and, "They call you from the heights of Arsh; / Your place is not this dingy, desolate corner." Or Rumi's "thou" in "Happy the moment when we are seated in the palace, thou and I?"

For Sufis the vocative "you" (or "thou") is usually an entity whom the poet loves or identifies with, and through whom he wants to annihilate the conscious or selfish "I." The "you" (which is sometimes named, such as Rumi's Shams), can be the master, an Ideal or Perfect Man, Love, God, soul, over-soul, and so on; or, it is the Unconscious, if you will, who, to the extent that the conscious "I" diminishes, becomes more and more real to the *salik* (Sufi neophyte). Thus the vacuum created by the emptying of the conscious self is gradually filled with the attributes of the Unknown.

In most of the "Song of Myself" and other early poems of *Leaves of Grass* the "I"—"undisguised and naked"—goes about, opening itself to all he sees in his "journey," absorbing, expanding—"And these tend inward to me, and I tend outward to them, / And such as it is to be of these more or less I am." He writes,

> I am a Southerner soon as a Northerner, . . .
> A Kentuckian walking the vale of the Elkhorn in my deer-skin
>   leggings, a Louisianian or Georgian, . . .
> Of every hue and caste am I, of every rank and religion.

In the same manner Rumi announces:

> Should there be any lover, O Muslims—it's me
> Should there be any believer, infidel, or Christian monk—it's me . . .
> None of the world's seventy-two sects and creeds
>   exist, I swear by God. Every creed
>   and sect there is—it's me.

At one point in "Song of Myself" Whitman sets about cataloguing what he thinks constitutes the I; then he concludes: "But they are not the Me myself;" and Rumi cries out:

> What is to be done, O Muslims? for I do not recognize myself,
> I am neither Christian nor Jew nor Gabr nor Muslim
> I am not of the east, nor of the west, nor of the land nor of the sea
> I am not of nature's mist nor of the cycling heavens.
> I am not of the earth, nor of water, nor of air, nor of fire. . . .
> I am not of India, nor of China, nor of Bulgaria, nor of Saq-sin. . . .

The paradoxes of these self-identifications are evident and can be stated and explained briefly: to the measure that the consciousness becomes emptied of its makeup (conditionings, prejudices, individual and racial memories, and the like), gradually the "I" becomes nothing and everything. Then the poet-mystic talks of himself in the humblest of terms, now in the most self-exalting language. It is this last aspect of Whitman's self-identification that has raised eyebrows or elicited derisive smiles.

> I celebrate myself . . .[22]
> I admire myself . . .[23]
> I dote on myself. . . .[24]

Yet, compared to some of the mystical utterances of the Sufis, Whitman's pronouncements are quite mild. "Glory to me! How great is my glory!" proclaimed the celebrated Persian Bayazid-i Bastami. And at a moment of ecstasy Hallaj cried out, "I am the Truth." He was accused of heresy, persecuted, and ultimately hung in gallows; but fortunately Bastami was diagnosed as insane and eventually set free.

So long as any consciousness of the "I" and "me" is left—even though the "I" may have been transformed and become "large" and "multitudinous"—there is an experiencer; there is an observer distinct from the observed. Consequently, there is space (between the observer and the observed) and time (the mechanism of thought as past, present, and future). Because the "I"-consciousness is the sum of whatever the mind gathers and accumulates, deliverance from it all via death and dying becomes a paramount mystical experience and gets emphatic poetic expression in mystic poetry. For Whitman and the Persian Sufi poets alike, death is renewal, freedom, and part of the progressive evolutionary movement in creation; hence the absurdity of fear and death and the recognition that indeed "to die is different from what anyone supposed, and luckier." In his *Mathnavi*, Rumi says:

> I died as mineral and became a plant
> I became animal once I died as plant
> I died as animal and became man
> Why should I then fear death?
> When was I less by dying?
>
> Once more shall I die as man
> To become what man's mind doesn't contain.

"All goes onward and outward, nothing collapses," Whitman says; and as if in chorus with Whitman, Rumi goes on:

> The urge of each particle toward another, the procreant merging
>   of the opposites
> Each desiring the other for its growth and motion
> The urge of creation: rolling along on the tide-waves of love.
> Otherwise the world would freeze upon itself
> Otherwise no mineral would yearn to be plant
> No animal would wish to die and become human.

With the mystical death (*fana'*) and consequent rebirth into "What man's mind doesn't contain" (*baqa'*), the Sufi not only journeys to the Immeasurable or God—that is, passes from plurality to unity—but becomes one with God. At this stage even the mystic's earlier statements such as "Divine I am inside and out" become meaningless. For there is still here the duality of inside and out, you and I, the lover and the Beloved. When the individual reaches the stage of complete absorption the duality ceases altogether, the boundaries are obliterated, inside and outside merge, and "All goes onward and outward" with grace and beauty. Then the poet can bid goodbye to his Fancy. Or Rumi can celebrate the death of the "I"; "Glory! Glory! I triumphed—no more do I / Know myself as me. I burn with love. . . . / Glory! Joy! No mortal mind can fathom me."[25]

It is then that the individual arrives at a profound stage of peace and humility, the highest form of freedom and love.

It is on this note that *A Persian Lesson*—published in 1891 as one of the poems of *Goodbye My Fancy*—starts and in which Whitman's own mystical peregrinations seem to have reached a new stage:

A Persian Lesson

> For his o'erarching and last lesson the greybeard Sufi
> In the fresh scent of the morning in the open air,
> On the slope of a teeming Persian rose-garden
> Under an ancient chestnut tree wide spreading its branches,
> Spoke to the young priests and students.
>
> "Finally my children, to envelop each word, each part of the rest,
> Allah is all, all, all—is immanent in every life and object,
> May-be at many and many-a-more removes—yet Allah, Allah,
>   Allah is there.
>
> "Has the estray wander'd far? Is the reason-why strangely hidden?
> Would you sound below the restless ocean of the entire world:
> Would you know the dissatisfaction? the urge and spur of every life;
> The something never still'd—never entirely gone? the invisible
>   need of every seed?

It is the central urge in every atom, (Often unconscious, often
   evil, downfallen)
To return to its divine source and origin, however distant,
Latent the same in subject and object, without one exception."

Here is presented a surprisingly compact poem in which is contained the essence and synthesis of his earlier poems. Moreover, the poem has a distinctly Sufi flavor—not only in the authenticity of setting, the repetition (in the manner of Sufi *zekr*[26]) of the word Allah, or such recognizably Sufi phrases as "the invisible need of every seed"—but mainly because the whole poem presents a marvelous coalescence of theme and tone.

As mentioned earlier, this poem was first published in 1891, when Whitman was seventy-one. It is interesting to note that Rumi's *Mathnavi* has for its prologue exactly the same "urge and spur of every life; / The something never stilled . . . / To return . . . ." I am referring to the celebrated *Mathnavi* poem about the cut-off reed (a leaf of grass?), singing of its longing to return to the reed-field, to its source. Whitman's *A Persian Lesson*, it may be concluded, is not an isolated case, the reflection of a brief interest in Sufism, without relevance to the rest of the poet's work. Rather it may very well be looked upon as a fitting coda for *Leaves of Grass*, not only because it presents a synthesis and recapitulation of the rest of the book, but also because of the marvelous sense of tranquility and wholeness it conveys. It is here finally that we see the serenity of a man who has said goodbye to his Fancy, and one wonders whether the "greybeard Sufi" of the first line is not the good grey poet himself.

Notes

1. This article first appeared in *American Literature,* Vol. 47, no. 4 (January 1976), 572–82. Republished by permission of the copyright holder, Duke University Press.

2. See T. S. Eliot, *After Strange Gods* (New York: Harcourt, Brace, and Co., 1934). The complete sentence is: "When Whitman speaks of the lilacs or the mockingbird, his theories and beliefs drop away like a needless pretext." In a 1955 article ("Images of Walt Whitman") Leslie A. Fiedler examines "the endless insistence in *Leaves of Grass* upon the first person, the deliberate confusion of the Mask and the self" and wonders with astonishment why Whitman became "the world's looked-for, ridiculous darling." See Milton Hindus, ed., *Leaves of Grass One Hundred Years After* (Stanford, CA: Stanford University Press, 1955), 55 and 73.

3. J. E. Miller, K. Shapiro, and B. Slote, *Start With the Sun: Studies in Cosmic Poetry* (Lincoln: University of Nebraska Press, 1960), 58.

4. For a list of such studies see Gay Wilson Allen, *A Reader's Guide to Walt Whitman* (New York: Farrar, Straus, & Giroux, 1970), 29, 224–228.

5. See, for example, V. K Chari, *Whitman in the Light of Vedantic Mysticism: an Interpretation* (Lincoln: University of Nebraska Press, 1964), vii.

6. Lord Strangford, "Walt Whitman," *The Pall Mall Gazette*, Feb. 16, 1866; quoted in G. W. Allen, *A Reader's Guide to Walt Whitman* (London: Farrar, Straus, & Giroux, 1970) 28.

7. Walt Whitman, *Leaves of Grass*, eds. H. W. Blodgett and S. Bradley (Chicago: 1946), 552.

8. Paraphrased in G. W. Allen, *Walt Whitman Handbook* (New York: New York University Press, 1962), 474.

9. Whitman, *Leaves of Grass*, "Song of Myself," Section 5.

10. Ibid., Section 28.

11. F. Attar, *The Conference of the Birds*. trans and intro. by Dick Davis and Afkham Darbandi (London: Penguin Books, 1984).

12. The translations from Persian poets are by the present author, unless otherwise indicated.

13. Whitman, *Leaves of Grass*, "Song of Myself," Section 45.

14. R. A. Nicholson, *Rumi, Poet and Mystic* (London: G. Allen and Unwin, 1950), 53.

15. Emory Holloway, ed., *Uncollected Poetry and Prose of Walt Whitman* (New York: P. Smith, 1921), 65.

16. Richard Chase, *Walt Whitman Reconsidered* (New York: William Sloane Associates, 1955), reprinted in C. Feidelson, and Paul Brodtkorb, eds., *Interpretations of American Literature* (New York: Oxford University Press, 1959), 180.

17. Whitman, *Leaves of Grass*, "Song of Myself," Section 3.

18. Ibid., Section 4.

19. Ibid., Section 3.

20. Ibid., Section 14.

21. Ibid., Section 24.

22. Ibid., Section 1.

23. Ibid., Section 3.

24. Ibid., Section 24.

25. Cf. Whitman's poem "Joy, Shipmate, Joy!"—"Joy, Shipmate, Joy! / Pleas'd to my soul at death I cry, / Our life is closed, our life begins. . . ."

26. *Zekr*, or *dhikr*, means "invocation" and refers to the Islamic devotional act of repeating the Names of God. In Sufism, this practice is part of daily sacred activity.

The Initiates:
Other American Authors

8

Literary "Masters" in the Literature of Thomas Lake Harris, Lawrence Oliphant, and Paschal Beverly Randolph

Arthur Versluis

Reference to American "literary masters" prompts one to think of well-known authors like Emerson and Melville, whose work certainly alludes to Persian Sufism and to Islam. Other articles in this collection discuss those kinds of works in some detail. But there is another way to understand this term, and that is with a different emphasis: we also can say "literary *masters*." In this case, we are looking not at great works of literature, but rather at works of literature that incorporate and seek to convey one form or another of what we might term adapted forms of Islamic esoteric religion. In effect, the authors present themselves—or characters in their thinly disguised fiction—as spiritual masters, and literature is the mode of initiatory transmission. But to what extent are these Anglo-American nineteenth-century literary "masters" influenced by Islamic esoteric religion, and to what extent are they creating new religions? As we shall see, they likely often are influenced by Islamic esoteric religion, but in effect create new religious syntheses.

There are, broadly speaking, several angles from which one can approach the question of Islamic influence in nineteenth-century England and America. One is clearly exoteric: it focuses on social, political, and literary influences of Islam. Such an approach is exemplified by Iraqi scholar Muhammed Al-Da'mi's *Arabian Mirrors and Western Soothsayers*,[1] a survey of Victorian depictions of Islamic culture and history that includes such figures as Thomas Carlyle, John Henry Cardinal Newman, and Washington Irving. Irving's approach is emblematic of such Victorian views of Arab lands: his voluminous works on the Moorish presence in Spain, like *Mahomet and His Successors*, look at Islamic Spain or at Islam from the outside, in the manner of extended travelogues with an eye to what in Islamic history might prove a model for the American republic. At the other extreme of approaches, we find a far less well-known esoteric angle, as exemplified by such figures as Thomas Lake Harris, Laurence Oliphant, and Paschal Beverly Randolph.

Muhammed Al-Da'mi does an excellent job of analyzing the Western-centered, orientalist and exoteric or externalist approach to Islam as exemplified in Carlyle, Newman, and Irving. Such an approach sees Islam mostly from the outside and Islamic history as "a vestigial remnant of a dead era," an attitude that, he continues, we see lingering into the twenty-first century in the Bush, Jr. administration's attempt to impose "democratic values" on Iraq by way of invasion and occupation. As al-Da'mi points out, "today's 'Western' vision of a 'new world order' derives from the West-centered reading of history promoted by such shapers of public opinion as Carlyle, Newman, and Irving, among others."[2] As documented by Edward Sa'id and many subsequent scholars, such an approach to Arab countries has a long history, and still shaped much of Western policies toward Islamic societies even into the late twentieth and early twenty-first centuries.

But there is another aspect of Western engagement with Islamic cultures that is much less well-studied or well-known, perhaps in part because it is much more ambiguous, one may even say, mysterious. There are numerous examples of esoteric authors whose works purport to reveal some secret teachings of remote forms of Islamic mysticism—indeed, this is almost a genre of esoteric works. One thinks of such twentieth-century authors as Gurdjieff, whose esoteric philosophy was said to have been drawn from his training in a remote Sufi brotherhood in far-away Mongolia; or of the various Western Sufi orders that sprang up during the twentieth century.[3] What are we to make of such individuals or groups? I think it is more productive to regard them as interesting and creative phenomena in their own right than to dismiss them out of hand or to denigrate them.

When we turn to more esoteric dimensions of cross-cultural communication, it becomes difficult to sort out exactly what was originally there in the Islamic tradition, and what was projected onto "mysterious Islam" by the Western esoteric author who sought to give his work an exotic "oriental" flavor. This is the kind of question we face when we turn to the esoteric religious philosophies of Thomas Lake Harris, Laurence Oliphant, and Paschal Beverly Randolph, all nineteenth-century authors whose works were published in the United States, and some of which were surprisingly influential. To what extent can we speak of the "Islamic" magic and mysticism of these authors? That is the question we will pursue here.

Thomas Lake Harris

The least explicitly influenced by Islam or by Sufism was Thomas Lake Harris, but we must outline some of his works here in order to tell the related story of his disciple, Laurence Oliphant. Harris was born in England, and immigrated to America in 1828. In 1845, he became a Universalist minister, a career which served him for less than two years, for in 1847 he joined the group of Andrew Jackson Davis. But shortly thereafter, Harris left that group as well, resigning because of Davis's endorsement of "free love," and joining the Swedenborgian "Church of the New Jerusalem." Although he lived with a group of spiritualists from 1850 to 1853, he subsequently returned to proselytizing for Swedenborgianism, and traveled to England to do so, where he announced his own esoteric millennialist group called the "Brotherhood of the New Life," intended for the "reorganization of the industrial world." Harris established his group at Brocton, Salem-on-Erie, New York, and finally in California. His Brotherhood was known for its avant-garde views on sexuality, and drew heavily in later years on the Western esoteric traditions.

It is clear that Harris's characteristic views had been worked out by this relatively early period, and that his subsequent, controversial life was an unfolding of them. At the end of his life, early in the twentieth century and nearly fifty years later, we find him:

1. Struggling against demonic influences and in visionary realms, while

2. Suffering related physical torments, and

3. Regarding himself as the "pivotal man" in the world, the single figure who incarnates the primal apocalyptic struggle between good and evil.

Already in the 1850s we find Harris writing about "internal respiration," about the existence of "fays" or faeries, and about the spiritual importance of male-female "counterparts," a theory that derived from the Swedenborgian idea of "conjugial" love.

Although he remains relatively little-known, Harris was a prolific author and also wrote and published a number of hymns and songs. In addition to *Arcana of Christianity: An Unfolding of the Celestial Sense of the Divine Word* (1858–1867), Harris published a collection of extemporaneous lectures entitled *The Millennial Age: Twelve Discourses on the Spiritual and Social Aspects of the Times* (1860), a monograph on "universal religion" entitled *The Breath of God with Man* (1867), and, in the book *The Golden Child* (1878), a daily chronicle of life in the

California community Harris founded. Harris also left a significant body of unpublished material. In essence, Harris joined together Christian millennialism with Swedenborgian thought, but also drew on a range of other esoteric traditions. Harris is a fairly important figure whose work deserves fuller study than it has yet received.

Hannah Whitall Smith, who was highly critical of him, wrote that Harris had spent several years "in the Orient, where he learnt a strange vocabulary," and attracted adherents from as far away as Japan.[4] Harris had not gone to Asia, but he did have Japanese followers.[5] Nonetheless, Harris was not influenced very much by Asian religions. "Redemption of the body," he tells his audience, "is to begin with internal respiration," and that might sound like some kind of Buddhist meditative practice.[6] However, Harris in fact refers to a particular kind of breathing that derives from Swedenborg and that is conceived as a result of divine grace. Harris's esotericism was certainly primarily European in origin, emerging out of Swedenborgianism.[7]

Harris's teachings concerning male-female "counterparts" might be slightly reminiscent of Tantrism, and might even have analogues in other forms of esoteric religion. But the theology—including a male-female divinity, a cult of the Mother, and a belief in an enduring transcendent male-female spiritual body—while it may have some tangential connection to the work of Jacob Böhme, is chiefly Harris's own.[8] The doctrine of counterparts is this: each individual, male or female, has a counterpart of the other gender. According to Harris, it is rare for both counterparts to be incarnated and married; in general, one's counterpart is a spiritual being.[9] One comes to know one's counterpart through an inner revelatory process, and contrary to the accusations laid against Harris's Fountain Grove community in particular, his was a quasi-ascetic arrangement whereby the sexes were largely separated. In the personal accounts of some members, there were sexual dimensions to the counterpart experiences, but those experiences were of union with nonphysical beings. But it is also evident that Harris's teachings included a joint male-female transformative process.[10]

What distinguishes Harris's visionary experiences is the pivotal role that he himself plays in the invisible worlds or dimensions. He was often referred to by his disciples as the "Primate," sometimes with the name "Faithful," and sometimes even as "Primate Pivotal Twain-in-One." His disciples regarded him more or less similarly to the way Sufi disciples are said to regard their *shaykh*. He consistently believed himself to intervene not only in local or regional metaphysical dimensions, but also on a national and international as well as cosmic scale. Harris saw himself as "the pivot," a term quite similar to the Sufi term *qutb*.

But if there were an Islamic influence on Harris, from whence would it have come? The answer is not from Harris having traveled in the Middle East, but rather from his remarkable disciple, Laurence Oliphant.

Laurence Oliphant

Laurence Oliphant (1829–1888) was born to Anthony and Mary Oliphant, and by the time he was ten, his father had been knighted. Sir Anthony and Lady Oliphant were members of the Calvinist Protestant Reformed Church, and the young Laurence grew up in Ceylon, where his father was Chief Justice, and in England. Even as a youth and young man, Laurence Oliphant traveled a great deal, spending much time in Europe as well as Ceylon. He had a lifelong close relationship with his mother. In his early adulthood, he traveled through India and Nepal, returned to England and passed the bar exam, traveled to Russia, observed the Crimean war firsthand, became Lord Elgin's private secretary on the mission that negotiated a primary treaty between Canada and the United States, and as Herbert Schneider put it, "embarked on one expedition after another with reckless abandon and almost incredible energy."[11] He had seen wars in numerous countries, served on diplomatic missions to China and Japan, and later became a widely known war correspondent for the *Times* of London; by 1865, he had been elected to the British Parliament.

The most controversial relationship of Oliphant's life was with Thomas Lake Harris, whom he met in England during Harris's visit there. To the astonishment and chagrin of his English peers, upon his election to Parliament, instead of attending to his position, Oliphant applied for membership in Harris's esoteric community in New York State, and he became known as the silent member of Parliament for his refusal to speak there—even though that had been a long-standing dream. Instead, he traveled to New York State about two years after his mother, Lady Oliphant, had become a member of Harris's community, called "the Use," at Amenia, New York. There, Oliphant, like his mother, subordinated himself to the charismatic Harris as his "Father," and worked as a farmhand, hoeing and doing other manual labor in the vineyards and on the farm for ten or more hours a day. Oliphant, formerly the archetypal man-about-town and man-of-the-world, lived in a cold corner of a shed in total isolation, cleaning out stables and hauling rubbish.

Oliphant and his mother spent years in the Brocton community, which grew to around one hundred members, and to significant relative wealth. That wealth came from the shared resources of members, significant among which were the Oliphants. Later, Harris and some select members of the community moved to a huge estate near Santa Rosa, California, where again they developed considerable vineyards, and built a mansion on a high hill overlooking the region. Oliphant returned to England, rejoined high society, married the striking Alice le Strange Oliphant, and returned with her to New York. She traveled to California to visit Harris there, but was not received well by Harris, who sent her away. Oliphant and his wife subsequently broke from Harris's community, saw Harris himself as having gone astray, and after regaining Oliphant's wealth through threatened legal action, made preparations to move to Palestine.

Oliphant later published two works that detailed his own esoteric teachings, which turned on the various esoteric relationships possible between men and women. These works bore the significant influence of his wife Alice, particularly the first of them, *Sympneumata; or Evolutionary Forces Now Active in Man* (1885) and *Scientific Religion; or, Higher Possibilities of Life and Practice through the Operation of Natural Forces* (1888), published in the year of Oliphant's death. In these books, we see Oliphant's esoteric sexual teachings outlined in considerable detail. He remained Christian to his deathbed, so these works are not a result of Oliphant's having entered into any esoteric Islamic or other orders; they are, rather, the summation of his syncretic esoteric teachings.

That his esoteric philosophy was syncretic is quite visible in Oliphant's two-volume novel *Masollam* (1886). This novel was written and published after Oliphant and his wife Alice had moved to Palestine to live, and after she had unexpectedly died there. Oliphant believed that he was in communication with her spirit, which was his spiritual counterpart. In *Masollam*, Harris's erstwhile disciple depicts himself as the hero with the transparently obvious name of "Santalba" (implying "holy" and "white") whereas Masollam (Harris) is depicted as originally having real spiritual experience and insights, but as having gone bad. Given Oliphant's and Harris's public and bitter parting of the ways, it is not surprising that in the novel, Santalba and Masollam also undergo a bitter split. While the novel is prolix—it could be less than half the length—it does include some very interesting indications of Harris's teachings.

Partway through the second volume, Santalba speaks to a Druse sheikh [Druze shaykh],[12] referring to a young woman named "Anima," who had been raised and trained by Masollam. Santalba tells the shaykh that

> the world's deliverance has come, and it has come in the form of a woman. It could not be delivered hitherto, because the sexes were divided; but in union is strength. It is only when the sexes are united according to the divine intention that the redemptive forces for the world's deliverance can play through them; and it is through the operation of the divine feminine that this union must be achieved. This is the interpretation of your vision of the twofold Word. Regard women, therefore—but especially the woman by your side [Anima]—in a different light from what you have hitherto done.[13]

Sheikh Mohanna then responds: "You have said that the highest form of inspiration could only descend by means of the operation of a conjunction of masculine and feminine elements; and that therefore its most fitting receptacle was an associated pair."[14]

Sheikh Mohanna then asks: But what about one whose partner has died, as Santalba's (and in real life, Oliphant's wife Alice) had? Santalba replies: "She who was my associate on earth, and who has passed into higher conditions, is not prevented thereby from co-operating with me . . . due to the fact that during our external union we had, by long and arduous effort and ordeal, arrived at a consummation, whereby an internal and imperishable tie had been created, the mystery of which I dare not enter upon now." Santalba asserts that his "consociation" with his dead wife is not mere mediumship, but "a permanent condition of free and independent mental association, with a pure intelligence of the upper region."[15] In ordinary spiritualism, "the bodily health is injured, the intellectual faculties are enfeebled . . . by the invasion of influences which torture the mind and body which they have made their abiding-place, and which cannot be ejected. It is the penalty which poor mortals pay for attempting to pry, by disorderly methods, into the secrets of nature, which they are not meant to penetrate." By contrast, this higher union results in "increased mental vigor and bodily strength, a consciousness of moral and intellectual freedom and spontaneity. The individuality, instead of being suppressed, is reinforced. With every accession of power, there flows in a rushing current of love for the human race, and a desire to serve it. There is no longing to pry into mysteries, because knowledge seems to ripen in the mind more rapidly than it can be acted on."[16]

One could object that what we see above are Oliphant's teachings, not those of Harris. But earlier in the novel, Masollam (Harris) tells the young Anima that "alone I am powerless; that it is only a woman who can feed me with the elements which are essential to the ultimation of my forces, which need this conjunction to render them operative. . . . For the rule of the man is naught without the woman."[17] What we see, in both characters (i.e., Harris and Oliphant), is that the spiritual union of man and woman is essential to their teachings—and is a direct reflection of their theology of a male-female God. The male-female nature of God is the secret discerned by Santalba's Druze chieftain friend Sheikh Mohanna, and it is central to the themes of the novel as a whole.[18] Those who go astray in the novel—notably Masollam and his wife—do so by detours away from spiritual union and divine service into passion or ambition. The novel is not flattering to Harris, but it does nonetheless reveal how Oliphant absorbed Harris's teachings on the spiritual counterparts of men and women, and then transposed those teachings into a Middle Eastern context.

In his travel memoir *The Land of Gilead* (1881), there are some quite interesting intimations that Oliphant encountered esoteric teachings among two groups in the Middle East: the Druze and the Ansariyeh, both of which, he says, belong to the Isma'ili tradition. Oliphant offers some quite interesting speculations about Druze esoteric teachings, including the possibility that the Druze have an emanationist dimension to their teachings, which bore connections to esoteric Buddhism. He argues that ancient Persia was host to Buddhists, and that there was cultural cross-pollination between Buddhism and esoteric Islam, as evidenced, among other things, by the Druze belief in reincarnation.[19] Both the Druze and the Ansariyeh, Oliphant insists, will assume whatever outward religious form is necessary for survival, but they both also continuously maintain esoteric teachings that are to be kept secret.

In a chapter about his visit to "an Ansariyeh village," Oliphant discusses in detail the origins, religious tenets and practices, and other customs of the Ansariyeh. In one passage, Oliphant alludes to sexual mysteries among the Ansariyeh, writing that although women are "never admitted to religious meetings," nonetheless there are "certain ceremonies, in which they must of necessity bear an important part." These ceremonies "are symbolical of the origins of man and the productive powers of nature, which are highly honored and considered sacred among them. In this they have much that was common to the Gnostics of the early Church." They are, Oliphant continues, "an offshoot from the Druze sect" because they follow the "teaching of Nusair."[20] On the whole, Oliphant's travel memoir of his time in the Middle East suggests that although his own esoteric sexual teachings did not have their origin in the Middle East, still he found there (and in scholarship like Sacy's), suggestions that there were such teachings to be found in some religious sects, notably the Ansariyeh. The mystery remains, and actually deepens with the introduction of our next author.

Paschal Beverly Randolph

Our third primary figure, Paschal Beverly Randolph, is every bit as fascinating (and, for that matter, as prolific a writer) as were Harris and Oliphant. Randolph was self-educated, grew up in the New York slums, and became one of the very first African-American novelists, as well as one of the most widely influential occultist authors of the nineteenth and twentieth centuries. Like Oliphant, Randolph was a world traveler, having sojourned not only in England and Europe, but also, he said, in Egypt, Turkey, and possibly elsewhere in the Middle East, having learned there magical practices and mystical teachings from obscure esoteric lineages, most notably, from the Nusa'iri order. Randolph's primary influence was to bring sexual practices and teachings explicitly into Western magical orders, and these teachings, he said, he learned during his journeys in the Middle East, among Islamic mystics and magicians, and from a Muslim "dusky maiden" who initiated him into the ways of esoteric sexuality.

Randolph's tales of Middle Eastern travels and of learning esoteric traditions there should not be dismissed out of hand. In fact, one has to wonder whether he also may have encountered some residual Sufism in the United States during his youth or young adulthood. In an exceptional work of reconstructive scholarship, *Black Crescent*, Michael Gomez documents how Sufi orders had moved into Black Africa prior to and during the period of the slave trade, and of how representatives or devotees of those orders may very well have found themselves in the United States. "Given the prominence of organized Sufism in West Africa during the period of the transatlantic trade," Gomez writes, "it is difficult to imagine that Sufis did not arrive on North American shores." Sufism then, it seems, intermingled with Freemasonry in the Black community, and along with Sufism may have come some Islamic forms of magic, including amulet making.[21] Such influences are shadowy, and tracing them is admittedly speculative, but it is at least possible that Randolph's later travels in the Middle East were inspired by contact with some African Americans familiar with Sufism or with variant forms of Islamic magical traditions.

Just as in the case of Harris and Oliphant, we have an exceptional book detailing their lives and something of their works (Herbert Schneider's *A Prophet and a Pilgrim*), so too we have a remarkable survey of Randolph's life and work by John Patrick Deveney: *Paschal Beverly Randolph: A Nineteenth-Century Black American Spiritualist, Rosicrucian, and Sex Magician* (1997). And here, although reconstructing Randolph's life and publication history requires some conjecture or educated guessing, nonetheless Deveney also offers great depth of documentation, at least in terms of Randolph's extensive publications and of many (though not all) aspects of his unusual life. Randolph published many pamphlets and books, and made numerous claims about his travels and esoteric connections, so sorting all this out is a Herculean task.

Here, I will offer an overview of Randolph's life and work, with an eye to his probable connections with the Arabic world. Randolph was born in New York City, the illegitimate son of a father who abandoned him to the streets. He grew up in the Five Points, a notorious slum full of brothels and taverns, but managed to teach himself to read and write—indeed, to develop a distinctive literary style and later to absorb some French, Arabic, and Turkish as well. Randolph acknowledged his African heritage when it was useful for him, but had no problem denying it if that was the more beneficial course. Randolph and his first wife, Mary Jane, both claimed Native American ancestry—at least when it suited them. By 1853, Randolph had given up being a barber and had put out his shingle as a "clairvoyant physician and psycho-phrenologist," while living in upstate New York. During this period, Deveney speculates, Randolph "must have met Thomas Lake Harris, another sexual mage, who broke with spiritualism when Randolph did (and for similar reasons) and whose name recurs in Randolph's works over the years."[22]

In 1855, Randolph began a series of trips across the Atlantic, during which he reportedly spent time in England, in Europe, and in the Middle East. While the exact itinerary of Randolph's travels is often unclear because of his tendency toward myth-making, it is clear that, like Harris and Oliphant, he rejected much of the contemporary "occult" scene, especially spiritualism, but also the libertinism of the "free love" movement, and that he met many of the most interesting esoteric authors of the period. Unlike Harris or Oliphant, Randolph was very much interested in animal magnetism and in magical traditions and orders, and claimed that he had moved in related circles both in England and in France. What is particularly remarkable about Randolph is that he apparently managed to travel so widely and to have moved in fairly esoteric circles, all without any of the resources available to someone like the wealthy Oliphant, even without the benefit of conventional education, and in a period when travel was by no means easy or fast.[23]

It was in 1861–1862 that Randolph is said to have traveled throughout the Middle East, and in particular in Egypt, Palestine, possibly in Lebanon, in Constantinople, and in Turkey. The true extent of his travels is impossible to verify, but it is clear that he returned with considerable knowledge of the use of hashish, and with some knowledge of Arabic magical traditions. One English author reported in 1862 that he had been "with the Dervishes, Persian Magicians, and miracle workers, whom he astonished and confounded with exhibitions of the higher sort of magic . . . and had received "a series of instructions in Arab medicine, Persian metaphysics, and Egyptian magic."[24] This description, like much concerning Randolph's travels in the Middle East, strikes one as wildly overblown, but it does show that at least one of his contemporaries apparently believed his claims. After this time, a mysterious initiatory figure named "Pul Ali Beg" appears in Randolph's writings—but we might note that an alchemical work had circulated in England under the name "Ali Puli" since the late seventeenth century.[25] Such coincidences do make one wonder to what extent Randolph's travels account for his "Oriental" sources, and to what extent he was drawing primarily on English Orientalism and "Oriental" archetypes, mingled with his own powerful imagination. He was, after all, a fairly well received novelist of the occult.[26]

Having settled in Boston after his earlier travels, Randolph was compelled to move by the great Boston fire of 1872, during which he unfortunately lost many of his baffling variety of publications, including numerous pamphlets, circular letters, and books by which he made his uncertain living. He moved eventually to Ohio, where he met an attractive young woman named Kate Corson, whom he may or may not have married, and who bore him a son, Osiris Budh. During this late period of his life, he apparently visited Europe once again, and published a variety of books including his most influential work of sexual magic, *The Ansairetic Mystery*, which revealed "the secret of the Ansaireh Priesthood of Syria," by which "men and women can call down to them celestial—almost awful—powers from the Spaces, thereby being wholly able to reach the souls of others, and hold them fast in the bonds of a love unknown as yet in this cold land of ours."[27] Passages like this lend at least some credence to the claims of some associated with the Theosophical Society, that Randolph was making available secrets of "black magic." It is apparently the case that, although H. P. Blavatsky, the charismatic founder of the Theosophical Society, did refer favorably to Randolph as a genuinely "half-initiated" Rosicrucian, she also was reportedly hostile to him during this late period of his life. On July 29, 1875, Randolph was found dead near his home of a gunshot wound to the head, evidently a suicide.

Randolph's widow continued to market his books, and even acquired an agent for them in England. Perhaps most famously, Maria Naglowska—herself a flamboyant figure in the French occult scene during the 1920s and 1930s—translated his works on sexual magic into French under the title *Magia Sexualis*.[28] From the prior and subsequent circulation of Randolph's works, his theories on sexual magic became quite influential in European and English magical circles, from there moving back again to the United States.[29] Thus we can see the complex circuits that Randolph and his work represented: from England and Europe to the Middle East, from the Middle East to Europe and England, from the United States to Europe and England and back again—the lines of circulation are complex enough to warrant diagramming, and one has to wonder if, in the end, anyone will be able to more thoroughly map this bewildering territory than Deveney already has.

Conclusions

There are larger questions to consider here, above all whether or to what extent Harris, Oliphant, and Randolph actually had contact with Druze or Sufi magicians or mystics? In Harris's case, it at first seems fairly clear that, because he did not travel in the Middle East or make claims about the Druze, Nusairi, or Sufi origins of his teachings, Harris was not much influenced by Islamic magical or mystical traditions. Yet one wonders. There are aspects of his work that do suggest Islamic resonances or parallels, if not outright origins. The organization of his community resembles the organization of a Sufi *tariqah* (spiritual) path, with himself as the *shaykh*. Furthermore, a major *shaykh* in Sufism is sometimes termed the "pivot" or *qutb*, a title that Harris asserted for himself as the "pivotal two-in-one." Sufism tends toward lay orders and a kind of lay monasticism rather similar to the organization of Harris's groups. Harris's secret teachings concerning the "fay" or fairy spirits are parallel to some Islamic traditions concerning *jinn* or *djinn*. Is it merely happenstance that Oliphant's fictionalized depiction of Harris and of Oliphant himself should have featured a Druze *Shaykh* and a Middle Eastern setting?

Could Harris have come into contact with Druze or Sufi teachings or traditions in England during his visit in 1860? Certainly it is highly unlikely that he did, and so all these elements are simply striking parallels or coincidences. After all, unlike Oliphant or Randolph, Harris left little reference to such Middle

Eastern traditions in his own voluminous writings, and furthermore, we know with certainty that much of his teaching derived from Swedenborg, from Andrew Jackson Davis, from English/Scottish traditions concerning fairies, and other fairly clearly Western or Western-esoteric sources. And yet one is left with lingering questions that offer no easy answers. Oliphant had traveled extraordinarily widely by the time he and his mother, Lady Oliphant, met Harris in England in 1860—he had been all the way to Ceylon and Nepal.

But in Oliphant's case, just as in Harris's, there is no direct evidence linking him to Druze or Sufi traditions during the formative years of his and Harris's esoteric teachings. It is true that Oliphant and his wife traveled to the Middle East and settled in Palestine after their acrimonious separation from Harris and the Brotherhood of the New Life. And it is undoubtedly also true that they had personal contact with a wide variety of Muslims during this period. But when we look more closely at Oliphant's novel *Masollam*, we see there that the esoteric teachings concerning men and women, and their spiritual union, come primarily *from* the Westerner Santalba and are spoken *to* the Druze *Shaykh*. In other words, the Middle Eastern setting serves as a kind of projection screen for Oliphant's Western esotericism, and the Druze *Shaykh* reflects it back to him, thereby "confirming" it.

This brings us to Randolph. While Randolph claimed to have traveled extensively in the Middle East, and furthermore to have received there essential magical teachings from the Nusairi order, there is some reason to doubt this. As Deveney points out, Randolph acknowledged in his book *Eulis* that he had made up his connections not only to the Rosicrucians, but also to the Nusa'iri, which he called "Ansairi." He wrote:

> Precisely so was it with things purporting to be Ansairetic. I had merely read Lydde's [sic] book, and got hold of a new name; and again mankind hurrahed for the wonderful Ansaireh, but incontinently turned up its nose at the supposed copyist. In proof of the truth of these statements ... the world is challenged to find a line of my thought in the whole 4,000 books on Rosicrucianism ... or in the Ansairetic works, English, German, Syriac, or Arabic.[30]

Is it really likely that a tourist who did not speak traditional languages, let alone dialects, in the course of a few months might have been so accepted into local society that he was forthwith initiated into the most secret (sexual?) mysteries of a heretical Sufi, Nusa'iri, or Druze order? It seems doubtful.

Let us look at some analogous cases. In the 1920s, another American sojourner, William Seabrook, traveled in the Middle East and made it his goal to meet Druze warriors and Yezidi "devil worshippers."[31] In a remarkable book, *Adventures in Arabia*, filled with photographs and drawings and striking descriptions, Seabrook tells of meeting Druze warriors and elders and of just how much he could learn of their sacred ceremonies and teachings.[32] Just as Randolph claims he had done seventy years before, and just as Oliphant did when he and his wife moved to Palestine, Seabrook was able to meet various dervishes, Druze elders, and even Yezidis. But there is a difference between meeting or even befriending members of various esoteric orders on the one hand, and actually becoming an initiate on the other. Seabrook was only able to get so far—as an adventurer, he could *meet* Druze elders or Yezidis, but as he tells us himself, he was never admitted into initiatory traditions. I strongly suspect that exactly the same is true of Oliphant, who after all remained Christian; thus by definition he could not have been an initiate into Islamic esoteric traditions and, for that matter, the same can be said of Randolph.

Randolph himself admits as much, when, in typically claiming that in his visit to the Middle East he became "chief" of the "mystic" "lofty brethren," he goes on to note how he became so, not by initiation or acceptance, but rather by "suggestion" and "clues" into "labyrinths of knowledge [they] themselves did not even suspect the existence of."[33] Deveney may be right in speculating that Randolph did have direct contact with Sufis, and in particular with Nusa'iri; but such contact is almost certainly not so much the origin of, as it was the *occasion* for, Randolph's complicated occult sexual philosophy, which ultimately is more about Randolph himself and his own ideas about esoteric dimensions of sexuality than it is about the traditions of Islam, Sufism, the Nusa'iri, or others.

And this is the larger conclusion that we inevitably come to when we look at these figures together. There is a kind of genre here, or an archetype—the Western occultist who travels to the Middle East and who finds there a venue from which he can draw some elements in order to create an exotic new esoteric synthesis. This esoteric syncretism is real—that is, there really may be some elements of Islamic, Druze, Nusa'iri or other forms of Middle Eastern esoteric traditions woven into these new syntheses that we see in the works of Oliphant, Randolph, or for that matter, of much more recent esoteric adventurers like Peter Lamborn Wilson, author of *Scandal: Essays in Islamic Heresy*, who also traveled in Islamic esoteric and even heretical circles in Iran and elsewhere in the Middle East. Each of these figures brought back the results of his travels to incorporate them into his own esoteric sexual philosophy, whether in the nineteenth or, as in Wilson's case, in the late twentieth century.[34]

But it is somewhat difficult to understand figures like these if one does not sufficiently recognize the role that syncretism plays more generally in the history of religions. It is easy to assert that figures like Oliphant or Randolph were simply "projecting" their own occultism onto Middle Eastern personae or traditions. But although in some respects it is true, that is much too simplistic a conclusion. It is too simplistic because it ignores the central role that syncretism plays not only in Western esotericism, but also in the history of religions more generally. By the time of Randolph's and Oliphant's sojourns in the Middle East, there had been considerable history of cultural cross-pollination. Numerous books and articles had been published in England on the Druze, on the Nusa'iri, on Islamic mysticism and magic, and there had been much commerce and intellectual exchange between England and the Middle East. Such intellectual cross-pollination inevitably resulted in what we might term "occult" syncretism, and that is exactly what we see in nineteenth-century works like those of Randolph and Oliphant.

Figures and authors like these two, and Harris, as well as later figures like Wilson, are fascinating not least because they are themselves marginal or liminal figures who represent not the authorities of a self-righteous orthodoxy, but rather the "heretical" experimenters who exist on the margins of Christianity and Islam alike, and who are far more likely than their orthodox counterparts to be open to cross-cultural or religious syncretism or, even more likely, syncrasis—that is, the absorption of practices from another tradition. Such figures are fascinating because of their place on the margins, and because they are by nature intrepid travelers and experimenters who are willing to cross not only physical borders, but also intellectual and religious ones. In the lives and works of figures like Oliphant and Randolph we see early forms of Islamic-Western esoteric synthesis that continue to this day in later currents like the Traditionalist schools of René Guénon and of Frithjof Schuon, as well as in works like those of Peter Lamborn Wilson.[35] Far from belonging only to their own day, nineteenth-century figures like Oliphant and Randolph represent examples of larger syncretic or syncrasic currents that clearly continue through the esoteric movements of the twentieth century, and right on into our own time. It would be a mistake to dismiss or ignore initiatory literature, for whatever we may conclude about particular examples, it is nonetheless an important and fascinating religious phenomenon.

Notes

1. Muhammed al-Da'mi and Daniel Walton, *Arabian Mirrors and Western Soothsayers* (New York: Peter Lang, 2002).

2. See Ibid., 176. Al-Da'mi was a professor at Baghdad University, prior to the U.S. invasion and occupation of Iraq in 2003, and observations like the one quoted here take on a certain poignancy in light of what subsequently was to happen. See also Edward Said, *Orientalism* (New York: Routledge, 1978), and *Covering Islam: How the Media and the Experts Determine How We See the Rest of the World* (New York: Pantheon, 1981).

3. See, for instance, Mark Sedgwick's *Against the Modern World* (Oxford: Oxford University Press, 2004), a critical and somewhat limited overview of the Traditionalist school of René Guénon and its offshoot, the school of Frithjof Schuon. Schuon presented himself, and was regarded by followers, as the *shaykh* of a Sufi *tariqah*.

4. Hannah Whitall Smith, *Religious Fanaticism: Extracts from the Papers of Hannah Whitall Smith*, ed. Ray Strachey (London: Faber, 1928), 121.

5. Herbert Wallace Schneider and George Lawton, *A Prophet and a Pilgrim* (New York: Columbia University Press, 1942) 154, 199–200.

6. Thomas Lake Harris, *The Millennial Age: Twelve Discourses on the Spiritual and Social Aspects of the Times* (New York: New Church, 1860), 142.

7. Thomas Lake Harris, *The Arcana of Christianity*, 2 vols. (New York: Brotherhood of the New Life, 1867), and Thomas Lake Harris, *The Breath of God With Man* (New York: Brotherhood, 1867).

8. Swainson emphasizes the parallels with Böhme's work, esp. 64 ff. W. P. Swainson, *Thomas Lake Harris and His Occult Teaching* (London: William Rider & Son, 1922).

9. Thomas Lake Harris, "The Children of Hymen," in *The Herald of Light: A Monthly Journal of the Lord's New Church* (New York: New Church, 1859), II.307.

10. Smith, *Religious Fanaticism*, 219–28; see also Herbert Wallace Schneider, *A Prophet and a Pilgrim* (New York, Columbia University Press, 1942), 534–60.

11. Schneider, *A Prophet and a Pilgrim*, 80.

12. By "Druze sheikh" he is referring to "Druze Shaykh." Druze are originally an esoteric sect of Shi`ites who now consider themselves to be an independent religion. A Druze Shaykh would be a spiritual master in such an order.

13. Laurence Oliphant, *Masollam: A Problem of the Period*, (Leipzig: Tauchnitz, 1886), II.123.

14. Ibid., II.128–29.

15. Ibid., II.130.

16. Ibid., II.130–31.

17. Ibid., I.253.

18. Ibid., II.111–12, where Sheikh Mohanna tells Santalba that he "now perceived, what has been hidden from the faithful till now, that the 'Eternal Word' was twofold, masculine and feminine, and the feminine principle was shown to me that I might understand this, and I was further made aware that my apprehension of this truth would constitute my deliverance." He sees a female figure in blinding light, who places a warning finger on her lips. His first experience "of intercourse with the gross and superficial beings in the unseen world" "helped me to work wonders and perform acts of healing." His "second experience" was "of those profounder and subtler intelligences of a more nether sphere, who delude men with the specious phraseology of occult science, and seek to draw them away from the practice of true religion, by the substitution for it of esoteric dogmas." Now he perceived the "difference between the true and false" but found it "impossible to describe," to be "apprehended only by experience; and . . . as my people were not yet ready to receive this truth, I must be silent in regard to it."

19. Laurence Oliphant, *The Land of Gilead* (New York: Appleton, 1881), 319.

20. Ibid., 56–57.

21. See Michael Gomez, *Black Crescent: The Experience and Legacy of African American Muslims in the Americas* (Cambridge: Cambridge University Press, 2005), 249. It is noteworthy that in the whole of Gomez's book, there is no mention made of Randolph, despite the prior publication of Deveney's extensive analysis of Randolph's work and significance. This is a surprising oversight, to be sure, and probably is because of Randolph's "unsavory" sexual occultism.

22. John Patrick Deveney, *Paschal Beverly Randolph: A Nineteenth-Century Black American Spiritualist, Rosicrucian, and Sex Magician* (Albany, NY: SUNY, 1997), 7–12, 13.

23. One of the sources Randolph would have known was Silvestre de Sacy, *Exposé de la Religion des Druzes* (Paris: L'Imprimerie Royale, 1838), II.559–86, "De la secte des Nosaïris." This may well have sparked Randolph's interest, and it may be a partial basis for his tales of the Ansairetic mysteries.

24. Deveney, *Paschal Beverly Randolph*, 146–47.

25. Ali Puli, *Centrum Naturae Concentratum*, trans. Edward Brice (London: J. Harris, 1696).

26. See Paschal Beverly Randolph, *The Wonderful Story of Ravelette* (New York: S. Tousey, 1863), which was subsequently translated and published in 1922 by none other than Gustav Meyrinck, under the title *Dhoula Bel*.

27. Paschal Beverly Randolph, *The New Mola!* (Toledo: P. Randolph, 1873), 17–18. See also Randolph, *The Ansairetic Mystery* (Toledo: Liberal Printing House, 1873), and *Eulis!* (Toledo: Randolph, 1874).

28. See Maria de Naglowska, *Magia Sexualis* (Paris: Télin, 1931). There were numerous subsequent editions of this work; it was on the shelf in Paris bookshops, readily available in the 1990s.

29. The sexually charged rituals of groups like the Ordo Templi Orientis, and the Fraternitas Saturni, certainly owe more than a little to the antecedent works of Randolph.

30. Deveney, *Paschal Beverly Randolph*, 216. Deveney is citing Paschal Beverly Randolph, *Eulis* (Toledo: Randolph Publishing, 1874), 47. "Lydde," he notes, is Rev. Samuel Lyde, author of *The Anseyreeh and Ismaeleh: A Visit to the Secret Sects of Northern Syria* (London: Hurst & Blackett, 1853) and *The Asian Mystery, Illustrated in the History, Religion, and Present State of the Ansaireeh or Nusairis of Syria* (London: Longman, Green, 1860).

31. Editor's comment: Though *Yezidi* can roughly be translated as "devil worshipers," their understanding of Iblis (Lucifer in Islam) is a gnostic concept. For them, Iblis is the symbol of an angel who was the true lover of God and therefore *did not* betray God by bowing to man. Some of the Sufi masters such as Ahmad Ghazzali have written on in praise of Iblis. See Ahmad Ghazzali, *Sawanih*, in *Majmu'a-yi athar ahmad ghazzali* (Tehran University Press, 1370), 69–98.

32. See William Seabrook, *Adventures in Arabia* (New York: D. Appleton, 1928).

33. Deveney, *Paschal Beverly Randolph*, 217.

34. See Peter Lamborn Wilson, *Scandal: Essays in Islamic Heresy* (New York: Autonomedia, 1988). Wilson writes there that "the 'facts' in this book (and some fictions too, perhaps) may prove of very little interest to students of Islam, and may in fact cause offense to many Muslims. It can fairly be said that the book is not really 'about' Islam" (31).

35. See Mark Sedgwick, *Against the Modern World: The Secret Intellectual History of the Twentieth Century* (New York: Oxford UP, 2004). As to Peter Lamborn Wilson, it is worth noting that he spent some years in Iran, working with Traditionalists there in the ambit of Seyyed Hossein Nasr, before branching out into his own line of what we may call mystical anarchism under the pen name "Hakim Bey." See, for example, his most influential book *Temporary Autonomous Zones* (New York: Autonomedia, 1998 ed.). My point here is that Traditionalism and its counterpart opposite in Wilson's/Bey's antinomianism both derive from Western-Islamic syntheses or syncrases.

9

American Transcendentalists' Interpretations of Sufism

Thoreau, Whitman, Longfellow, Lowell, Melville, and Lafcadio Hearn[1]

John D. Yohannan

Emerson found in Persian literature boldness of expression and a valid ethical stance. He was about to import this fairly exotic foreign literature to the New England scene in the mid-nineteenth century, not only because it was harmonious with the prevailing ethical culture, but also because it pointed to a transcendental realm beyond the pale negations of Unitarianism, where poetry and religion, the secular and the sacred, were blended. Saʻdi provided a new Bible for the world, and Hafiz was the Tongue of the Hidden. In this breadth of literature the prudent Yankee might have both his hard nut and his blissful orgy from one dispensation.

But Emerson's own performance in appropriating this literature for American uses had been so formidable that it fairly preempted the field from followers. Even those who were in conscious opposition to the sage's philosophy—like Longfellow, Lowell, and, in a different way, Melville—had to work in his shadow, that is, so far as Oriental literature was concerned. The present chapter has to do with Emerson's disciples, or, at any rate, those who were in basic sympathy with his Transcendentalist ideals.

Of these, Thoreau and Whitman had the largest individual endowments, and were thus able to go on to an equal—if not, indeed, greater accomplishment—in American literature. But in matters Oriental, they did not reach a step beyond the areas already mapped out by their mentor. The lesser figures, both of his own generation and that which followed, were content to restate his devotion to Persian and other literature as a body of secular scriptures. They preached mush and produced little of their own. Though some of them presumed to be scholars, they were not Oriental scholars, and their work was deficient in accuracy. They did not even bother to demark Persian literature from that larger corpus of writings that went by the vague name Oriental.

At Harvard College, Henry David Thoreau accepted the current prejudice against Oriental exaggeration; he even thought that the title of Sa'di's *Gulistan* or *Flower-Garden* was excessive. After he came to stay in Emerson's home in 1841, however, his friend's library reconciled him to Sa'di and even whetted his appetite for Confucius and the *Bhagavad Gita*. William E. Channing noted that Thoreau liked to read the Hindus and Sa'di, but that his interest was personal and superficial.[2] This is a fair judgment; the object of study for Thoreau was seldom the author of a book but usually the reader's self is discovered in a foreign work. In his *Journal* for March 23, 1842, Thoreau wrote that in Sa'di and the *Arabian Nights* and the *Fables of Pilpay* he found confirmation of his relationship to nature and such of its creatures as moles and titmice. "I have discovered more materials of Oriental history [in the New England noontide]," he added, "than the Sanskrit contains or Sir William Jones has unlocked."[3] The observations are a true measurement of his idiosyncratic approach to Persian and other Oriental literature.

There was a fair amount of Oriental exaggeration in what Thoreau later had to say about that literature. In *A Week On the Concord and Merrimac Rivers,* he finds fault with the English (and the Germans too) for not knowing enough about Persian and Indian literature although European literature grew up only after the decline of the Persian. This is clearly a counsel of perfection, for he had not read a great deal himself. To say, as he does, that "the reading which I love best is the scriptures of the several nations, though it happens that I am better acquainted with those of the Hindoos, the Chinese, and the Persians, than those of the Hebrews which I have come to last,"[4] is, on the face of it, untrue. No matter how little he loved them, he had certainly come to the Hebrew scriptures first. As for Persian scriptures, it is not clear what he was referring to, unless, like Emerson, he had in mind the *Gulistan* as a sort of lay scripture.

Among the "Ethnical Scriptures" that were published from time to time in the *Dial,* the short-lived journal of the Transcendentalists, the Confucian and the Buddhist sections were edited by Thoreau in July 1842.[5] His chief interest, however, appears to have been in the Hindu writings, particularly the *Bhagavad Gita*, and there is some justification for accepting his designation of himself as a Yogi.[6] But there is no justification whatsoever for the opinion of his early biographers that his poem *To the Maiden in the East* has a Hafizian quality.[7] The passionate Hafiz is the remotest possible influence on Thoreau, and Persian poetry in general plays a very minor part in his work.

When, in 1855, his English friend Thomas Cholmondeley sent him a collection of about forty-five volumes of *Orientalia*, he does not appear to have made much use of them. By then his interest in Oriental literature had considerably diminished. But even earlier, his characteristic attitude toward these writings—or, for that matter, any writings—was expressed in his defiant words: "I do not care the least where I get my ideas, or what suggests them."[8] Thus the fraudulent character of such books as the *Desatir* or the *Chaldean Oracles* did not interest him, so long as they had provocative things to say. This obviously assured not only that Thoreau would receive curious influences from his Persian readings, but also that his conception of the Persian poets would bear the stamp of his own prior bias. His taste was both more subjective and less catholic than Emerson's.

The transcendental *Week* cites both Hafiz and Sa'di in an inspirational vein: "Yesterday at dawn God delivered me from all worldly affliction; and amidst the gloom of night presented me with the water of immortality."[9] On Sa'di he observes: "In the Life of Sadi by Dowlat Shah occurs this sentence: 'The eagle of the immaterial soul of Sheikh Sadi shook from his plumage the dust of his body.'"[10] The more sociological *Walden* calls upon Sa'di to testify on the subject of philanthropy, one of Thoreau's imperfect sympathies. "Do not stay to be an overseer of the poor," says Thoreau in a typical anti-do-good mood, "but endeavor to become one of the worthies of the world." He then quotes Sa'di's description of the cypress tree as *azad,* or free, since it is not subject to the seasonal change of bloom and withering. It is, rather, always flourishing, like the spiritual *azads* or independents. He concludes in Sa'di's words: "If thy hand has plenty, be liberal as the date tree; but if it affords nothing to give away, be *azad.*"[11] The sentiment perfectly suited Thoreau's notions about the inefficacy of philanthropy; it is a good deal less typical of Sa'di, and quite contrary to the Islamic injunction on tithe-giving.

Thoreau's feelings about Sa'di and himself are best summed up in a *Journal* entry for August 8, 1852:

> The entertaining of a single thought of a certain elevation makes all men of one religion . . . I know, for instance, that Sadi entertained once identically the same thought that I do, and therefore I can find no essential difference between Sadi and myself. He is not Persian, he is not ancient, he is not strange to me. By the identity of his thought with mine he still survives. . . . Sadi possessed no greater privacy or individuality than is thrown open to me. . . . Truth and a true man is essentially public, not private. If Sadi were to come back to claim a *personal* identity with the historical Sadi, he would find there were too many of us; he could not get a skin that would contain us all. . . . By sympathy with Sadi I have embowelled him. In his thought I have a sample of him, a slice from his core, which makes it unimportant where certain bones which the thinker once employed may lie.[12]

In an age that was trying so hard to establish the identity of Persian literary culture, this must have sounded perverse. In our own time, when historicity is itself being questioned, it will no doubt recommend itself to many as a correct view of reality.

In the light of the above, one might wonder what Thoreau meant when he said that Walt Whitman was "wonderfully like the Orientals."[13] Or what Moncure Daniel Conway meant when he spoke of Whitman's "marvelous resemblance not only to Biblical but to ancient Persian poetry."[14] "Ancient" improperly describes the Persian literature known to the West in the nineteenth century—hardly anything produced before 1000 AD. Did Conway have in mind the erotic element common to Whitman, Hafiz, and *The Song of Songs*? Or the folk wisdom of the democratic bard matching the sententiousness of Sa'di and the book of Proverbs? Scholars have recently traced cogent analogies between Whitman and the *Bhagavad Gita* or the Vedantic philosophy, but the affinity with Persian poetry is difficult to see.

The question of whether Whitman had access to Persian poetry—even at second hand, through Emerson—is complicated by his denial at one time that he had read any, and his assertion at another time that he had.[15] In "Song of Myself" there are the usual references to various ethnic scriptures (sections 41, 43). In the later "Passage to India," these are more pronounced, and they include mention, among the epics of the world, of Firdawsi's *Shah-Namah*. In still another poem, Whitman describes the howling and the whirling dervishes that had already acquired a European notoriety, and he gives an accurate account of the more sober worship of Orthodox Muslims:

> I hear dervishes monotonously chanting, interspersed with frantic
>   shouts, as they spin around turning always to Mecca,
> I see the rapt religious dances of the Persians and the Arabs . . .
> I hear from the Mussulman mosque the muezzin calling,
> I see the worshippers within, nor form nor sermon, argument nor
>   word,
> But silent, strange, devout, raised, glowing heads, ecstatic faces.[16]

But there is nothing in all this to indicate a direct knowledge of the poetry of Persia.

One would suppose that Sufism, with its pantheistic philosophy, would have had a special attraction for Whitman. There are indeed passages in "Song of Myself" which have the Sufistic ring, but it would be just as correct to relate them to Hindu or indeed to European mysticism. A reader of Attar or Rumi would understand perfectly the observation in section 48 of that poem: "In the faces of men and women I see God, and in my own face in the glass," but there is nothing in the poem or in the poet's biography that explicitly connects this line with the Sufi poets who expressed the same sentiment.

That Whitman later acquired some familiarity with Sufism is demonstrated in a poem entitled "A Persian Lesson." It is perhaps as precise a statement of the pantheistic doctrine at the basis of Sufism as is to be found in such small compass. It is here given in full:

> For his o'erarching and last lesson, the greybeard Sufi,
> In the fresh scent of the morning in the open air,
> On the slope of a teeming Persian rose-garden,
> Under an ancient chestnut-tree wide spreading its branches,
> Spoke to the young priests and students.
>
> Finally my children, to envelop each word, each part of the rest,
> Allah is all, all, all—is immanent in every life and object,
> May-be at many-a-more removes—yet Allah, Allah, Allah is there.
>
> "Has the estray wandered far? Is the reason-why strangely hidden?
> Would you sound below the restless ocean of the entire world?
> Would you know the dissatisfaction? the urge and spur of every life;
> The something never still'd—never entirely gone? the invisible
>   need of every seed?"
>
> "It is the central urge in every atom,
> (Often unconscious, often evil, and downtrodden,)
> To return to its divine source and origin, however distant,
> Latent the same in subject and object, without one exception."[17]

Yet even here one has the feeling that the Persian lesson in Sufism has been sieved through German idealistic philosophy, whose vocabulary it uses, rather than poured straight from the tap of Islamic mysticism.

Equally disappointing is the encounter with Persian poetry of John Greenleaf Whittier (1807–1892). His tolerance for Buddhist, Zoroastrian, and Islamic writings probably derived more from his Quaker faith than from Emerson's Transcendentalism.[18] We are told that Whittier once saw an Arab reading his Qur'an and looking homesick while stationed with a circus in the town of Amesbury. When Whittier spoke to him, the Arab was happy "to find a friend who had also read his sacred book."[19] There is no doubt that the poet's affection for the rival faith was genuine, as evidenced in this sympathetic Islamic vignette in his poem "The Star of Bethlehem":

> Each Moslem tomb and cypress old
> Looked holy through the sunset air;
> And, angel-like, the muezzin told
> From tower and mosque the hour of prayer.[20]

There is no evidence, however, of a more than superficial knowledge of Islamic literature on Whittier's part. (The same poem credits one of Shiraz's two famous poets with sowing thought "in the warm soil of Persian hearts.") It is regrettable—and in a sense inexplicable—that Whittier, who had more than an average capacity for mysticism, as evidenced by his more serious interest in Hindu thought, did not respond to the challenge of Sufism. His treatment of Persian themes was basically sentimental.

We turn next to four writers of lesser stature who were committed to the Transcendentalist cultivation of Oriental literature. Two of these were contemporaries of Emerson, two his followers in the succeeding generation.

The prominence given by Arthur E. Christy to Amos Bronson Alcott (1799–1888) in *The Orient in American Transcendentalism* is probably only justified by the affectionate regard which the quixotic teacher inspired in Emerson and others who knew him. He thought of himself as a receiver of Emerson, and as a reader of the biblical literatures of the world. His connection with the present study is tangential to that abiding interest in his life.

Under the guidance of Emerson, Alcott began in 1849 to read the *Bhagavad Gita* and to draw up a sort of Mankind Library that would include all the scriptures of the world, a concept by now thoroughly laicized. Along with the Qur'an, the Vedic writings, and the Confucian classics, Alcott listed both Sa'di and Firdawsi. When he had trouble obtaining Sa'di's writings at the Athenaeum, he turned to the Harvard College Library or to the private collection of Henry W. Longfellow. His diary revealingly describes Sa'di as "a Persian Come-outer." When he had finally arranged a series of readings and discussions, the order of the poets and philosophers was as follows, with Jesus a sort of pivotal figure: Hermes Trismegistus, Zoroaster, Confucius, Sa'di, Aeschylus, Pythagoras, Socrates, Plato, Jesus, Dante, Behmen, Shakespeare, Milton, Swedenborg, and Goethe.[21] This was a veritable Great Books course with a strongly didactic accent on ethical culture. There is nothing to testify, however, that new insights were induced, or that Persian poetry received any special elucidation, from the labors of Bronson Alcott.

If Alcott's influence was felt mainly by those who came into personal contact with him, that of William Rounesville Alger (1822–1905) was chiefly communicated by his popular anthology *The Poetry of the East*, which was reissued in 1865 as *The Poetry of the Orient*. The change of title betokened a change of content in the wake of Emerson's influential essay on Persian poetry. Alger now alluded to Emerson in the lengthy *Historical Dissertation* which occupied one-third of his book. Citing the instance when Sa'di justified his idle existence as a poet by comparing himself with a sweet-smelling rose, Alger added:

> So our Concord Saadi sings, as if responding from today and America, over the ages and the sea, to the dead lyrist of Persia: Tell them, dear, if eyes were made for seeing, Beauty is its own excuse for being.[22]

So far as Persian literature was concerned, Alger ranged over pretty much the same ground as Emerson had in his essay. His sources were mainly German, and many of his selections simply translations of Tholuck, von Hammer, and others. But he was also well informed on English periodical literature on the subject—both the popular and the scholarly—and revealed a prodigious amount of reading. Like Emerson, he testified to the universality of Persian poetry; like him, too, he compared Hafiz ("the Bulbul of Shiraz") with "The Swan of Avon." With von Hammer as guide, he traversed Persian literature: its images, tropes, favorite themes, and the ideas of Sufism. Like a true Transcendentalist, he stressed the Sufi's denial of evil, his contempt for external religious forms, and the ecstasy of his expression. He remarked on the "delicacy of sense . . . elsewhere unparalleled" which is to be found in Persian poetry. His personal high regard for it was manifest in the original poems which he mixed with his translations and adaptations, in tribute to the Persian poets. For example:

Sweet Hafiz is not dead, although his body turned
To dust in Eastern Shiraz centuries ago.
He lives and strikes the lyre which in his hand then burned:
This day his thoughts through Western nations sound and glow.[23]

Had Alger commanded a better poetic talent than this doggerel, he would have been a formidable rival to Emerson in the introduction of Oriental poetry to mid-nineteenth-century American readers.

The link between the first generation of Transcendentalists and the second was supplied by Moncure Daniel Conway (1832–1907), who also linked the American with the English devotees of Persian literature in the later nineteenth century. His *Sacred Anthology (Oriental): a Book of Ethnical Scriptures,* published in the 1870s, was apparently begun in the fifties.[24] Going beyond Emerson and Alcott, he stretched the term scripture to include, among the Persian poets, not only Sa'di and Hafiz but also the newly discovered Omar Khayyam. In fact, Sa'di excepted, the largest number of Persian quotations came from Khayyam. However, although FitzGerald's first edition was listed as a source, there was not a single quatrain from this translation quoted in the book. Instead, the French versions of Nicolas (which, it will be remembered, assumed a Sufistic interpretation) were translated into rather literal English prose. This was an interesting accommodation, on Conway's part, to his mixed reading audience of ethical culturists and fin de siècle decadents.

Conway's book was marred by mistakes that were inevitable in a work of such ambitious dimensions. Quotations from Jalal al-Din Rumi were presented under three different heads: Rumi, Maulavi Rumi, and *Methnewi* (Mathnawi). Emerson's versions were regarded as translations in the same sense as those of Sir William Jones, even though twice removed from their Persian sources.

Nevertheless, the book was useful in propagating the liberal religion of Transcendentalism as it was beginning to merge back into the Unitarian Christianity from which it had originally emerged. In the next decade, Charles D. B. Mills's anthology of Oriental literature would draw on not only Emerson and the Germans but also on Conway's book.[25] By 1883, the Transcendentalist view of Persian poetry had reached the West Coast. A contributor to the *Overland Monthly* saw resemblances, he thought, between "eminently oriental" Hafiz and such genuinely American authors as Emerson and Thoreau. Transcendentalism and Persian poetry had come full circle.

A recent article, *The Orient in Post-Bellum American Thought*, calls our attention to a second generation Transcendentalist whose work on world religions showed a considerable knowledge of Persian literary culture.[26] Samuel Johnson (neither, of course, the eighteenth-century writer nor the president of Columbia University, but a left-wing Unitarian clergyman) never completed his three-volume study of *Oriental Religions and Their Relation to Universal Religion*. The first two volumes, on India and China, dealt with what Johnson called the "cerebral" and the "muscular" type of mind in religion. The third volume, on Persia, treated of the "nervous" mind, subsumed under Zoroastrianism and Islam. The section on Islam was further broken down into chapters on "Mahomet" and "The Shah-Nameh; or Book of Kings"; a third chapter was never written, and one wonders whether it might not have dealt with the religious implications of Sufism.[27]

The chapter on the *Shah-Namah* shows considerable erudition in German as well as English scholarship on the epic poem, which is brought into this book on religion because of a monotheistic stress that Johnson finds in Firdawsi. Quite apart from this purpose, however, considerable chunks of the story are provided in Johnson's own creditable English renditions of his German sources, some in linear verse, some in prose. Johnson was much more scholarly than either Alger or Conway, and it is to be regretted that he did not address himself to the whole range of Persian literature.

Longfellow, Lowell, Melville, and Lafcadio Hearn

Although Emerson's influence on the reading of Persian literature dominated the American scene in the mid-century, it soon had to share that role with the phenomenal translation, from abroad, of the *Rubʿiyyat* of Omar Khayyam. In fact, it was the Americans who truly discovered FitzGerald's poem. In the last quarter of the century, the *Rubʿiyyat* became the stronger influence, and there was soon very little difference between the American reader brought up on the Transcendentalist view of Hafiz, and the English reader who inherited the Cowell-FitzGerald bequest of Omar. Both groups were likely to have either read Emerson or heard him lecture, and both had their copies of the *Rubʿiyyat*. The Rev. Frederick R. Martin, an American Transcendentalist of the later era, might believe that there was a real difference between the two points of view. For him, Hafiz and Whitman were singers of themselves, an occupation which he regarded as fundamentally healthy; Omar, on the other hand, was a victim of *Selbst-Schmerz* or *Welt-Schmerz*, a spiritual malady to be guarded against.[28] Yet, Emerson himself, on his transatlantic voyage of 1873, read and re-read FitzGerald's *Rubʿiyyat* and, according to Charles Eliot Norton, found it "very lofty in its defiance."[29]

Henry Wadsworth Longfellow (1807–1882) was hardly a Transcendentalist, but like most of his American contemporaries, he took his first cue regarding Persian literature from Emerson. An entry in his journals for 1849 (two years after the publication of Emerson's first translations from Hafiz,) notes that he should go to the library for a book about Hafiz and also for Firdawsi's *Shah-Namah*. Two years later he confided that a friend had lent him German versions of both Hafiz and Saʿdi. His Catholic taste in European literature was soon further broadened to include the Asian. His library contained numerous books dealing with the East, among them several anthologies of Oriental and Persian poetry, an English version of the story of Leili and Majnoun, the *Gulistan* of Saʿdi, FitzGerald's *Rubʿiyyat* of course, and Chodzko's book on the folk poetry of Persia, from which both he and Emerson learned about the Persian Robin Hood, Kurroglou.[30]

Longfellow's poem "The Leap of Roushan Beg" is a good example of the basically romantic interest which he had in the Orient, and the characteristically didactic use which he made of Oriental material. Chodzko had introduced the story thus:

> The hero of the narrative of our work is Kurroglou, a Turkman Tuka, a native of Northern Khorassan, who lived in the second half of the seventeenth century. He rendered his name famous by plundering the caravans on the great commercial road from Persia to Turkey, between the cities of Khoi and Erzerum, and still more so by his poetical improvisations.

Longfellow's first stanza picks, chooses, and adds:

> In the land that lies beyond
> Erzeroum and Trebizond,
>   Garden-girt his fortress stood;
> Plundered khan, or caravan
> Journeying north from Koordistan,
> Gave him wealth and wine and food.[31]

It was no matter that the journey should have been north *to* Kurdistan, and place names were fair plunder for the poet. Although written in his seventieth year, the poem displays Longfellow's remarkable verve in narration, the story coming to an exciting climax as Kurroglou's renowned horse Kyrat leaps across a thirty-foot precipice and takes the bandit out of his pursuers' reach.

"The Spanish Jew's Tale" from *Tales of a Wayside Inn* reveals something more than a romantic interest in derring-do and exotic allusions to Ispahan and Samarkand. It tells the story of how Azrael,[32] appeared to the Rajah of Hindostan as he visited with King Solomon at the latter's great palace, how the Rajah begged Solomon to use his magical power to transport him back to Hindostan lest Azrael carry him away, and how the angel, seeing the Rajah whisked off, grimly observed:

> Thou hast done well in listening to his prayer;
> I was upon my way to seek him there.[33]

Worthy of a place in Sa'di's *Gulistan,* by which it was undoubtedly inspired, is Longfellow's own parable on the transiency of royal power, "Haroun Al Raschid":[34]

> One day Haroun Al Raschid read
> A book wherein the poet said:—
>
> "Where are the kings, and where the rest
> Of those who once the world possessed?
>
> "They're gone with all their pomp and show,
> They're gone the way that thou shalt go.
>
> "O thou who chosest for thy share
> The World, and what the world calls fair,
>
> "Take all that it can give or lend,
> But know that death is at the end."
>
> Haroun Al Raschid bowed his head:
> Tears fell upon the page he read.[35]

The poem "Keramos," a potter's song, owes its title and some of its philosophical tone to the *Kuzah-Namah* or potter's section of the *Rub'iyyat* of Omar Khayyam.[36] Since the poem was composed in 1877, it may even be presumed to participate in the debate over the *Rub'iyyat,* then already raging. To some extent,

Longfellow, like Browning in *Rabbi ben Ezra*, attempts to refute the philosophy of Omar Khayyam. Thus, one of the potter's songs says:

> Turn, turn, my wheel! This earthen jar
>   A touch can make, a touch can mar;
>   And shall it to the Potter say,
>   What makest thou? Thou hast no hand?
>   As men who think to understand
>   A world by their Creator planned,
>   Who wiser is than they.

Nevertheless, in its final refrain, there is a sort of concession to the melancholy fact of life's transience, a theme so persistent in the *Ruba'iyyat*:

> Stop, stop, my wheel! Too soon, too soon
> The noon will be the afternoon,
>   Too soon today be yesterday;
> Behind us in our path we cast
> The broken potsherds of the past,
> And all are ground to dust at last,
>   And trodden into clay![37]

James Russell Lowell (1819–1891) had both the scholar's interest in and the romantic poet's inclination to some of the themes which that literature had brought into the stream of English and American letters. His almost Byronic affinity with the East is exemplified in his remarks, after visiting Constantinople: "I like the Turks," and after visiting Spain, "I like the Spaniards . . . they are still Orientals."[38] His affection for Asian civilizations was extraordinary. He once said that, although he had read Asian literature only in European translations, he felt somehow "as if I had lived some former and forgotten life in the East."[39] He spoke praisefully of Firdawsi's *Shah-Namah* and regretted that there was no longer a large reading public interested in such works.[40] He had something of the well-read Englishman's feeling for the colonial phase of British Orientalism, yet his inability to understand Emerson's mystical poem "Brahma" indicates that there were perhaps decided limits to his sympathy with Oriental subjects.

    In his essay on the English poet Spenser, Lowell wrote that the nationality of a poet does not cut him off from the rest of the world but rather endears him to it. "I can understand the nationality of Firdawsi when, looking sadly back to the former glories of his country, he tells us that 'the nightingale still sings Old Persian.'"[41] In the essay on Chaucer, again, he places the *Shah-Namah* above most of the great romances of Europe: "In point of art they are far below . . . Firdausi, whose great poem is precisely the romantic type." Having quoted two passages from the French epic of Roland, he adds: "The episode of Sohrab and Rustum (Rustam) as much surpasses the former of the passages just alluded to in largeness and energy of treatment, in the true epical quality, as the lament of Tehmine over her son does the latter of them in refined and natural pathos."[42] It is clear from this reference that Lowell was not relying on Matthew Arnold's adaptation, which omits the mother's lament, but on James Atkinson's translation, which includes it. This was a worthy display of literary scholarship for the first president of the Modern Language Association.

Lowell wrote a number of his own poems in the Oriental manner. "Youssouf" (Yusuf) is an interesting parable with an affecting moral. It tells the story, so reminiscent of Sa'di or Rumi, of how a stranger came to Youssouf's tent and received generous hospitality only to reveal at the end that he is Ibrahim, who slew Youssouf's son. In a moving conclusion to the poem, Youssouf trebles the parting gift he has bestowed on the stranger saying that with him into the desert goes his one black thought. Then, invoking his dead son, he cries: "Thou art avenged, my first-born, sleep in peace."[43]

Rumi's notable parable about the friend who knocked on the door and was sent away (when, in answer to the question "Who is there?" he replied "It is I") found a strange adaptation in Lowell's thought. Rumi was of course demonstrating the pantheistic Sufi doctrine that subject and object, man and God, I and thou are one. Lowell cites the parable in his essay on democracy to prove the principle (as enunciated by Theodore Parker), not that I am as good as you are, but that you are as good as I am. Lowell relates the story thus:

> A beautiful and profound parable of the Persian poet Jelalledden (Jalal al-Din Rumi) tells us that "One knocked at the Beloved's door, and a voice from within asked 'Who is there?' and he answered 'It is I.' Then the voice said 'This house will not open and hold me and thee;' and the door was not opened. Then went the lover into the desert and fasted and prayed in solitude, and after a year returned and knocked again at the door; and again the voice asked 'Who is there?' and he said 'It is thyself;' and the door was opened to him."[44]

Like Longfellow, Lowell lived in to the era of the fame of the *Ruba'iyyat* of Omar Khayyam, and his critical writings make frequent allusions to that poem. In his own copy of the *Ruba'iyyat* he wrote the following verses to his wife in the measures of FitzGerald's famed translation; they offer the typical fin de siècle consolation of aesthetic satisfaction for the loss of religious faith:

> These pearls of thought in Persian gulfs were bred,
> Each softly lucent as a rounded moon;

> The diver Omar plucked them from their bed,
> FitzGerald strung them on an English thread.
>
> Fit rosary for a queen, in shape and hue,
> When contemplation tells her pensive beads
> Of mortal thought, forever old and new.
> Fit for a queen? Why, surely then for you!
>
> The moral? Where Doubt's eddies toss and twirl
> Faith's slender shallop till her footing reel,
> Plunge: if you find not peace beneath the whirl,
> Groping, you may like Omar grasp a pearl.[45]

Lowell has unfortunately lost some of the music of his model by leaving unrhymed the second rather than the third line of the stanza. But it was a tribute to the most significant new force in Persian poetry in America since the heyday of Transcendentalism.

Herman Melville (1819–1891) was both disciple to and apostate from Emerson. In part the apostasy was of course due to temperament, but in part simply to chronology: the oracles of self-reliance did not have as authentic a ring in Melville's late reading of them as they had had when Emerson first uttered them. Melville could therefore annotate Emerson's essays with both admiration and cynicism when they counseled that all was well and wisely put. The remedies of Transcendentalism were a mixed bag for the new age; they attracted and repelled. For that matter, Emerson himself had turned with a sense of relief to the sober realism of Sa'di's *Gulistan* after the Transcendentalist feast of moon and stars. For Melville too there would be a therapy in that book.

He appears to have begun with the standard images of the Persian poets—those long since established by Sir William Jones and very recently refined by Cowell and Emerson. In *Mardi*, first published in 1849, Hafiz is the Persian Anacreon, yet the reference to him is couched in language so reminiscent of Emerson that one is forced to the conclusion that Melville was recalling his predecessor's famous verses on Shakespeare and Hafiz. In the chapter "Dreams" the digression on writing style reads:

> Like a grand ground-swell, Homer's old organ rolls its vast volumes under the light frothy wave-crests of Anacreon and Hafiz; and high over my ocean, sweet Shakespeare soars, like all the larks of spring.[46]

It is notable, however, that, whereas Emerson had coupled Hafiz and Shakespeare, Melville separates them; for him, obviously, Shakespeare had already begun to have a unique significance.

In these early years of his literary career, Melville's acquaintance with Oriental literature appears to have been most superficial.[47] Whatever his knowledge of Persian poetry, in *Pierre* he reiterated the same standard notions about Hafiz that he had earlier accepted in *Mardi*. The hero, commenting on *Young America in Literature*, asks:

> What could Pierre write of his own on Love or anything else, that would surpass what divine Hafiz wrote so many long centuries ago? Was there not Anacreon too, and Catullus and Ovid—all translated and readily accessible?[48]

There is no question about the accessibility of any of the above authors to mid-century American readers. What is to question, with regard to Hafiz at any rate, is whether he had yet been presented in a way acceptable to the age. The Hafiz that Melville's *Pierre* was familiar with was a rather stereotypical one.

Melville nevertheless became seriously involved in the problem of the meaning of Hafiz's wine—as Emerson had been, reasoning circuitously that it stood for all that it symbolized. In *The Confidence Man*, Melville permits Francis Goodman to address the following panegyric on wine to Charles A. Noble, cosmopolitan:

> The lyre and the vine forever! . . . The vine, the vine! is it not the most graceful and bounteous of all growths? And by its being such, is not something meant? As I live, a vine, a Catawba vine, shall be planted on my grave.

But later, when the cosmopolitan is speaking with a mystic, the latter is permitted to have his say on the subject:

> But as for the wine, my regard for that beverage is so extreme, and I am so fearful of letting it sate me, that I keep my love for it in the lasting condition of an untried abstraction. Briefly, I quaff immense draughts of wine from the page of Hafiz but wine from a cup I seldom as much as sip.[49]

In a book that has been construed as a satirical jibe at Emerson's Transcendentalism, it would be easy to take this as a rejection of the extremely quintessential—to use a term Melville himself later employed satirically—character of Transcendentalist thought. W. R. Alger, for example, whose anthology was in Melville's library, separated the wine of Hafiz completely from the vine. Melville was to return later in life to the imagery of Persian poetry, but meanwhile he found no more could be done with a merely Anacreontic Hafiz than had already been done. Like many another poet of the mid-century, Melville was at a sort of spiritual dead end. Emerson's Hafiz was no help. Sustenance was to come, however, from two other Persian poets.

In 1868 Melville acquired Sa'di's *Gulistan* in Gladwin's translation (though not the 1865 edition, for which Emerson had written an introduction). In the next decade, he possessed three different editions of Omar Khayyam's *Ruba'iyyat*.[50] When, in the language of the English Victorians, he referred to Omar as "that sublime old infidel," and described his poem as "the irreligion of thinking men," it was apparent that his readings in Persian poetry had taken a new bent.[51]

Melville's copy of the *Gulistan* shows markings that tell us as much about the American owner as about the Persian author. Heavy underscorings and multiple marginal lines call attention not only to the well-known parables and apothegms of Sa'di, but also to less familiar ones which suited the reader's cynical mood at the time, such as:

> Tranquility of mind requires a fixed income.

or,

> In a season of scarcity and drought inquire not of a distressed Durwaish (Darwish) how he does, unless you mean to apply ointment to his wound by giving him sustenance.

or,

> And the sages have declared that falsehood mixed with good advice is preferable to truth tending to excite strife.[52]

The last of these looks interestingly forward to *Billy Budd*, into which the message of the inutility of unmixed good has been read.

It may well be, as Dorothee M. Finkelstein asserts in her book on Melville's Oriental interests, that his Eastern journey to the Holy Land was but an affirmation of his Western heritage. Nevertheless, the Eastern poets play a role in the dialectical discussions of *Clarel*. In a recitative from Part III (*Mar Sabe*), the poet Hafiz is allowed to respond to an inquiry regarding the relevancy of his wine and roses to the world as it is:

> To Hafiz in grape arbor comes
> Didymus with book he thumbs:
> My lord Hafiz, priest of bowers—
> Flowers in such a world as ours?

> Who is the god of all these flowers?—
> Signor Didymus, who knows?
> None the less, I take repose—
> Believe and worship here with wine
> In vaulted chapel of the vine
> Before the altar of the rose.[53]

The Hafizian joy is, to say the least, here on the defensive. Part IV of *Clarel* (*Bethlehem*) contains an even less blithe "Persian rhyme," composed, it is said, by "An Asian man" ("strange lore was his and Sadi's wit"). It describes the dying of the ancient Zoroastrian fires in lines worthy of the apocalyptic visions of William Butler Yeats. The poem ends:

> The rule, the Magian rule is run,
> And Mithra abdicates the sun.[54]

This sense of the running out of time and of a cycle of civilization was a strong undercurrent in the melancholy quatrains of Omar Khayyam, and it was that which recommended them so strongly to readers of the fin de siècle. Of these Melville must be counted as one. This is manifest in both the prose and the poetry which he wrote in the last decade or so of his life, much of it left behind in manuscript form.

An example is the story *Under the Rose*, which is described in an epigraph as "Being an extract from an old manuscript entitled 'Travels in Persia (Iran) by a Servant of My Lord the Ambassador.'" The epigraph is of course a spoof, for the work is Melville's own fabrication. It represents perhaps his recollection of James Morier's fiction as well as the poetry of Hafiz, Sa'di, and Omar Khayyam, with which he was by now on fairly good terms.

He had apparently been impressed by the illustrations for the *Ruba'iyyat* of Omar Khayyam made by the American artist Elihu Vedder, whose Pre-Raphaelitish manner of both literal and metaphysical interpretation had a large appeal for the late Victorians. Into his story *Under the Rose*, Melville imported a Vedder-like scene carved on an amber vase; it depicted in relief an angel with a spade (like a gardener) and another angel with a wine jar on his shoulder (like a cellarer), both walking toward a small Job-like character standing near a sepulcher. The vase and its figure had tempted the court poet (called in the Persian manner "Sugar-lips") to indite some verses which must now be translated from the Persian language by a renegade Greek. The latter demands wine before rendering his services because, as he says, "this same Sugar-lips' verses being all grapes, or veritably saturated with the ripe juice thereof, there is no properly rendering them without a cup or two of the same." After five drinks, "swaying his body like the dervishes hereabouts," he translates the verses, which have the mordant tone of Khayyam's more cynical quatrains and end on a line that alludes directly to one of Khayyam's stanzas: "And here comes the jolly angel with the jar!"[55]

Before concluding whether all this tends in Melville's *biographia literaria,* we must look at two late *Miscellaneous Poems* which Melville apparently consigned to the wasteland by his subtitle for them: "Weeds and Wildings Chiefly: with a Rose or Two." The first of these, called "The New Rosicrucians," is very much in the style of Emerson's "Ghazelle" of the 1847 volume, the second of his translations from Hafiz. It expresses a similar impatience with sanctimonious condemnation of those given to a sybaritic life:

> To us disciples of the Order
> Whose Rose-vine twines the Cross,
> Who have drained the Rose's chalice
> Never heeding gain or loss;
> For all the preacher's din
> There is no mortal sin—
> No—none to us but Malice.
>
> Exempt from that, in blest recline
> We let life's billows toss;
> If sorrow come, anew we twine
> The Rose-vine round the Cross.[56]

The substitution of rose-vine for grape-vine does not materially affect the thrust of the poem.

The second poem, entitled "The Rose Farmer," tells of a man who has come into possession of a large rose-garden but doesn't know whether he should reap a harvest of roses or distill them into a small but concentrated amount of Attar. A Persian gentleman rose-farmer advises him to prefer the roses to the perfume, at which all the roses in the garden nod their heads in glee in a manner often depicted by Hafiz and found so delightful by both Emerson and Tennyson. The poem continues:

> Discreet in second thought's immersion
> I wended from this prosperous Persian
> Who, verily, seemed in life rewarded
> For sapient prudence not amiss,
> Nor Transcendental essence hoarded
> In hope of quintessential bliss:
> No, never with painstaking throes,
> Essays to crystallize the rose.[57]

Melville's ambivalent attitude toward Emerson and the Transcendentalists is well illustrated in the above poems. He obviously could not countenance a metaphysical view of the materials of Persian poetry, whether rose-vine or grape-vine. He would not, "in hope of quintessential bliss," attempt "to crystallize the rose." He might accept help from Emerson in attacking the "unco guid," but the conversion of Persian hedonism into a "spiritual carpe diem" was another matter. In the then current tendency to polarize Persian poetry, so that Hafiz symbolized the Transcendentalist view and Omar Khayyam the view of the decadence, Melville was apparently pulled more strongly in the latter direction. In a late poem called "Hearts-of-Gold," he sought to take even Hafiz away from the Transcendentalists, although that meant, in effect, that he would have to fall back on the old Anacreontic view which regarded the wine of Hafiz as indeed *Moore's Best Port*.

'Twere pity, if true,
What the pewterer said
Hearts of gold be few.
Howbeit, when snug in my bed,
And the firelight flickers and yellows,
I dream of the hearts-of-gold sped—
The Falernian fellows—
Hafiz and Horace,
And Beranger—all
Dextrous tumblers eluding the Fall,
Fled? can be sped?
But the marigold morris
Is danced o'er their head;
And their memory mellows,
Embalmed and becharmed,
Hearts-of-gold and good fellows![58]

It is a pity that Melville did not include in this company Omar Khayyam, who had so well depicted the "marigold morris" danced over the heads of so many who had gone before.

More distinctly a writer of the late nineteenth-century European decadence was Lafcadio Hearn (1850–1904), but he was at the same time unusually responsive to the Transcendentalist interest in Oriental literature as a form of scripture. Exotic almost by birth, Hearn was the son of Irish and Greek parents; transported from Greece to Ireland, he later migrated to America, whence he went to Japan in 1890. There he married a native woman, assumed a Japanese name and Japanese citizenship, and died and was buried. But it was in America that he did the most considerable part of his writing, and it was there that he made his first contributions to the study of Asian literature.[59]

The poetry of Persia, and the lore of Islam generally, had a high place in his esteem. Although he had no knowledge of Near Eastern languages, he made excellent use of his command of French to gain access to the translations of Persian classics not yet available in English. So fascinated was he by the sound of Eastern words that he retained them in transliteration in his popular adaptations, which were often rejected by newspaper and magazine editors who saw no reading audience for such exotica.

Reading in the *Gulistan* the story of Bilal, the first muezzin (Moazzin),[60] Hearn became enamored of the muezzin's call to prayer, and sought to obtain from London the musical notations that would render its sounds. Later, he was taken up with the idea of writing about the music of the howling dervishes. Into a volume called *Stray Leaves from Strange Literatures*—which also contained Indian, Talmudic, Egyptian, and Finnish excerpts—went his versions of passages from *The Lights of Canopus* (a Persian variant of the Pilpay fables), the *Gulistan,* and the *Mantiq al-tayr* or *Bird-Parliament*.

While employed as a newspaper man by the *Times-Democrat* of New Orleans, Hearn wrote a number of unsigned articles, since collected, that show his steady interest in the literature of Asia. It was his hope that through the study of world literature people would eventually come to a "future universal religion." This concept of a syncretic world faith was probably inspired by Sir Edwin Arnold's sympathetic studies of Hinduism, Buddhism, and Islam. Always susceptible to what lay between the sentimental and the mystical, he marveled at the mastery of death implied in Rumi's bold lines:

> I am the mote in the sun-beam, and I am the burning sun;
> "Rest here," I whisper the atom; I call to the orb: "Roll on!"[61]

Hearn wondered if Occidental man would ever learn this secret.

In another article he praised the *Shah-Namah* (which he much preferred to Matthew Arnold's adaptation of a portion of it), and thought the cost of $150 for a set of Jules Mohl's French translations of the epic well worth it. This poem had proved, he said, that chivalry had existed in Persia long before it appeared in Europe. With more good will than political realism, he urged that the cultivation of this and other Oriental books would sooner bring about universal brotherhood than would commerce.

Hearn's course of lectures at the University of Tokyo in the years 1896–1902 have come down through the notes taken by interested students. One lecture was on FitzGerald's *Ruba'iyyat,* which he considered the supreme manifestation of Orientalism in English literature. For his Japanese students he underscored the similarity between Omar's ideas of the impermanency of life and Buddhist notions already familiar to them; and with perhaps no more license than many other interpreters took, he suggested that the *Ruba'iyyat* form was not unlike the Japanese *tanka* or thirty-one syllable poem.[62] In the light of his large service to the popularization of Japanese literature, his devotion to Persian poetry—however slight—deserves to be recorded.

Notes

1. This section has been adapted from John D. Yohannan, *Persian Poetry in England and America: A 200-Year History* (New York: Caravan Press, 1977), 135–284.

2. William E. Channing, *Thoreau the Poet-Naturalist* (Boston: Goodspeed, 1902), 50.

3. Henry David Thoreau, *Writings of Henry David Thoreau* ed. Bradford Torrey (Boston: Houghton Mifflin, 1906), VII, 344.

4. Ibid., I, 72, 148–49, and 415.

5. For Thoreau's contributions to the *Dial*, see Clarence Gohdes, *The Periodicals of American Transcendentalism* (Durham, NC: Duke University Press, 1931).

6. See Sreekrishna Sarma, "A Short Study of the Oriental Influences upon Henry David Thoreau with Special Reference to his *Walden*," *Jahrbuch für Amerikastudian* (Heidelberg, 1956), 76–92.

7. F. B. Sanborn, *Henry D. Thoreau* (Boston: Houghton Mifflin, 1895), 163.

8. Henry David Thoreau, *Journal*, ed. Bradford Torrey and Francis H. Allen (Boston: Houghton Mifflin, 1906), VIII, 135 (Jan. 23, 1856).

9. Poem by Hafiz.

10. Thoreau, *Writings*, I, 415. See also 70, 80 of same volume.

11. Ibid., II, 87–88.

12. Thoreau, *Journal*, IV, 290 (August 8, 1852).

13. Gay Wilson Allen, *Walt Whitman Handbook* (Chicago: Packard & Co.,1946), 457–58.

14. Moncure Daniel Conway, "Walt Whitman," *Fortnightly Review*, VI (Oct. 15, 1866), 538 ff.

15. See Allen, *Whitman Handbook*, who cites Lord Strangford's comparison of Whitman with Rumi.

16. Walt Whitman, *Leaves of Grass*, Comprehensive Reader's Edition, ed. Harold W. Blodgett and Sculley Bradley (New York: NYU Press, 1965), "Proud Music," 408.

17. Ibid., 553.

18. Arthur Christy, "Orientalism in New England: Whittier," *American Literature*, I (January 1930), 372.

19. Arthur Christy, "The Orientalism in New England: Whittier," in ibid., V (November 1933), 247.

20. John G. Whittier, *The Complete Poetical Works*, ed. Horace E. Scudder (Boston: Houghton Mifflin, 1894), 416.

21. Christy, *The Orient in American Transcendentalism*, 246.

22. William R. Alger, *Poetry of the Orient* (Boston: Roberts Brothers Press., 1865), 78.

23. Ibid., 147.

24. Moncure Daniel Conway, *Sacred Anthology (Oriental): a Book of Ethical Scripture*, 5th ed. (New York: Henry Holt, 1877), esp. "Preface," vi–vii.

25. Charles D. B. Mills, *Pebbles, Pearls and Gems of the Orient* (Boston: G. H. Ellis, 1882).

26. Carl T. Jackson, "The Orient in Post-Bellum American Thought," *American Quarterly* 22 (Spring 1970): 67–81.

27. Samuel Johnson, *Oriental Religions and Their Relations to Universal Religions* (Boston: Houghton Mifflin, 1885), vol. III, "Persia." A contemporary of Johnson's, James Freeman Clarke, used his knowledge of verses in creditable English (James Freeman Clarke and L. Clarke, *Exotics: An attempt to Domesticate Them*, [Boston: Houghton Mifflin, 1875, 1876]).

28. Frederick R. Marvin, *The Companionship of Books* (New York: Putnam's Sons, 1906). See also his *Poems and Translations* (Boston: Sherman, French & Co., 1914), passim.

29. Christy, *The Orient*, 316.

30. An account of Longfellow's Oriental library is given by Arthur Christy, *The Orient*, 321–23.

31. Henry Wadsworth Longfellow, *The Leap of Roushan Beg*, facsimile of the original manuscript, ed. Arthur Christy (New York: William Rudge,1931), 9, 35.

32. The Islamic angel of death, best known in Jalal al-Din Rumi's famous parable on the inevitability of fate.

33. Horace E. Scudder, ed., *The Complete Poetical Works of Henry Wadsworth Longfellow* (Boston: Houghton Mifflin, 1893), 264.

34. Harun al-Rashid.

35. Ibid., 339.

36. It is not clear to which section is the author referring to since there is no specific section in the *Rub'iyyat* known as *Kuzah-Namah* or potter's section. (Editor)

37. Ibid., 329–33.

38. James Russell Lowell, *Letters of James Russell Lowell*, ed. Charles E. Norton (New York: Harper, 1894), vol. II, 222.

39. Ibid., 234.

40. James Russell Lowell, "Fragments of an Unfinished Poem," *Complete Writings*, Elmwood edition. (Boston: Houghton Mifflin, 1904), XII, 123.

41. Ibid., IV, 227.

42. Ibid., II, 205.

43. Ibid., XII, 246.

44. Ibid., VII, 18.

45. Ibid., XIII, 132. Other references to the *Ruba'iyyat* are to be found in II, 320; VII, 86 and 316; and VIII, 275.

46. Herman Melville, *The Works of Herman Melville*, Standard ed. (New York: Russell and Russell, 1963), vol. IV, *Mardi*, Chap. 15, 53–54.

47. The chief treatment of Melville's Orientalism is by Dorothee M. Finkelstein, *Melville's Orienda* (New Haven: Yale University Press, 1961). Although she tends to make more of Melville's use of Persian poetry than it will stand, with her main conclusions I am in agreement. Another instance of this reading too much into Melville is Eleanor M. Tilton's interpretation of Melville's story "Rammon" in *Harvard Library Bulletin*, 13.1 (Winter 1959): 5–91.

48. Herman Melville, *The Works,* Vol. IX, *Pierre,* p. 350.
49. Herman Melville, *The Confidence Man* (New York: Grove Press, 1949), 199, 224.
50. For Melville's readings, see Merton M. Sealts, Jr., *Melville's Readings: a Check-List of Books Owned and Borrowed* (Madison: University of Wisconsin Press, 1966), esp. 60, 83, and 89.
51. Herman Melville, *The Letters of Herman Melville,* ed. Merrell R. Davis and William H. Gilman (New Haven: Yale University Press, 1960), 276, 282.
52. Musle-Huddeen Shaik Sady of Sheeraz, *The Gulistan or Rose-Garden,* trans. Frances Gladwin (London: Kingsbury, Parbury & Allen, 1822), copy in Beinecke Library, Yale University, 2, 249, 284.
53. Herman Melville, *Works,* vol. XV, *Clarel,* Sect. 13, 66.
54. Ibid., Part 4, "The Convent Roof," Sect. 16, 226–27.
55. Ibid., vol. XIII, "Under the Rose," 344. The FitzGerald quatrain alluded to is number 58 of the Fourth Edition.
56. Ibid., vol. XVI, 337.
57. Ibid., 348.
58. Ibid., 428.
59. The chief source of information about Hearn has been Elizabeth Bisland, *The Life and Letters of Lafcadio Hearn,* 2 vols. (Boston: Houghton Mifflin, 1906), esp. vol. 1.
60. A Moazzin is responsible for maintaining the prayer schedule of a mosque by both leading and reciting the call to prayer. Bilal the first, was chosen by Mohammad himself.
61. Lafcadio Hearn, *Stray Leaves from Strange Literatures* (Houghton Mifflin, Boston: 1922). The collections from the *Times-Democrat* were issued under the title *Essays in European and Oriental Literature* (New York: Dodd Mead, 1923).
62. Lafcadio Hearn, *Interpretations of Literature,* ed. John Erskine, 2 vols. (New York: Dodd Mead, 1929).

10

The Persians of Concord[1]

Phillip N. Edmondson

By the late 1840s, in the literary community of Concord, Massachusetts, fascination with sensual, spiritual, and psychological themes had converged to bring about an attraction to the Classical Persian poetry of Sa'di, Firdawsi, Hafiz, and Nazami. Celebrating the spiritual qualities and creative energy of the Persian poets and their characters, the Concord writers assumed these Eastern mystical personas entering their poetic realms or transferring them to a New England setting. Evidence of this influence can be found in the works and journals of Ralph Waldo Emerson, Margaret Fuller, Nathaniel Hawthorne, and Henry David Thoreau, as well as George William Curtis. From the Sufi poets and their characterizations, these American writers fashioned their ideal poet; furthermore, their literary inquiry into the psychology of artistic creativity equated a Persian feminine divinity with the creative force driving the poetic spirit.

For American readers, the tales of the Islamic East conjured up romantic images of an occult and exotic psychic space of vivid enchantment and hidden truths. As in Europe, the *Arabian Nights* had become popular family reading by the mid-nineteenth century. This book was so popular that from 1803 to 1833 there were thirty-three editions and reprints.[2] One major Concord writer, Nathaniel Hawthorne, in images inspired by the *Arabian Nights*, describes his search for the secrets of the unconscious. His son Julian recounts that his father told him:

> There lingers in me superstitious reverence for literature of all kinds. A bound volume has a charm to my eyes similar to what scraps of manuscripts possess for the Mussulman. Every new book or antique one may contain the Open Sesame, the spell to disclose treasures hidden in some unsuspected cave of truth.[3]

The popular culture of this period reveals the impact of the Islamic East on Concord. A retrospective of the period in the *Eclectic Magazine* aptly reported that Concord had become the "mecca" of Transcendentalism.[4] This account also characterized Margaret Fuller at Brook Farm as an Eastern-like mystic, replete with charms, a fortune-teller of faces. Descriptions of Islamic costumes, which the Brook Farm residents wore at masquerade picnics, indicate the presence of the exotic East in their imaginations.[5] Even the sponsors of this experimental community appeared at dress balls costumed as dervishes.[6] Indeed, this New England "mecca" opened its portals to the sensuality and mystery of the Islamic East to welcome liberating forms of literary self-expression.

Following the interest of the English and German artists in Oriental literature and *Naturphilosophie*, the Concordians turned to the Persian mystical poets for a rich new source of imagery and symbols to express their own literary purposes.[7] The Oriental Translation Fund, a British-sponsored Asiatic society, supplied scholarly information to American journals such as the *Knickerbocker* and the *American Monthly Magazine*. The society's most valued contributions were translations of Persian poetry. For example, Sir William Jones, an eighteenth-century Orientalist and linguist, provided Europe and America with the first reliable translations of Sufi poetry by the two great Persian mystics, Hafiz and Rumi.[8] J. A. Atkinson, Esq. and his son James translated two great epic poems, *Shah-Namah* by Firdawsi and *Laili and Majnun* by Nazami.

These publications made their way into the homes of Concord's writers. Among various English sources, Longfellow's library included Atkinson's translations of Nazami's classic, *Laili and Majnun*, significant for its characters and theme of the lover-Beloved relationship.[9] Majnun, the love-sick madman, rejects reason to wander the desert in search of his beloved Laila. The pain of separation from Laila causes Majnun to transform her into a beautiful, bewitching, feminine force that represents God. At the same time, the pain annihilates Majnun's attributes until he has abandoned himself for love. In considering the impact of Persian literature on mid-nineteenth-century American literature, this epic love story by Nazami proved to be as significant as the poetry of either Sa'di or Hafiz since the Concordian writers transformed Majnun into the questing poet and Laila into his creative force.

A second Persian poetic source in Longfellow's private collection was the first popular English anthology of Persian verse, *The Rose Garden of Persia* by Louisa S. Costello.[10] Though not published by the Oriental Fund, Costello must have drawn heavily from the research accumulated by this British Orientalist society. Her anthology, reviewed at length in the *Westminster Review*, assumes that its readership is rather well acquainted with the major Persian poets and their works.[11]

The contributions of the German Orientalists, particularly in the work of Joseph von Hammer-Purgstall, equaled if not surpassed the influence of English sources. The prominent German Orientalist sent a copy of his translations to

Emerson, who undoubtedly spirited this flurry of interest in Persian poetry among Concordians through his English translations.[12] Some 700 lines of poetry appear in Emerson's journals and works from Saʻdi, Hafiz, Nazami, and Anwari.[13] Theodore Parker, a Brook Farm teacher, listed among his collection of mystical and religious works a Persian anthology published in 1817 and von Hammer-Purgstall's translations of Hafiz and other major poets.[14]

Throughout the decade of the 1840s, journals and letters by this close community of writers and intellectuals disclose an ever-increasing attraction to Persian mystical poetry, based on the various sources which they shared. Margaret Fuller's letter on February 23, 1840 to Emerson on the *Shah-Namah* by Firdawsi marks one of the earliest exchanges. She relates this epic to Emerson in personal terms by seeing herself as a thirsty wanderer in the desert reminiscent of the Persian character Majnun in Nazami's classic. Fuller describes this wanderer as a "gentle-hearted, religious man" who prefers his quest to the comfort of the oasis.[15] Alcott mentioned in his journal entry of February 11, 1851 that the Boston Athenaeum had no information on the Persian poet Saʻdi, so he had to rely on the Harvard College Library and on Longfellow.[16] Longfellow also noted in his journal entry of August 30, 1849, that he wanted to borrow a work on Hafiz from the Harvard College Library.[17] On August 13, 1851, Longfellow wrote in his journal that George Curtis had lent him Daumer's translation of Hafiz and Graf's translation of Saʻdi's *Rose Garden*.[18]

Part of the reason for the interest of the Germans and the Concord writers in Persian literature was, undoubtedly, the fact that both groups had embraced a concept of artistic creativity prevalent in German Romanticism at the time, a concept of submission similar to the master-disciple relationship in Sufism. Hawthorne, for example, shared with his fellow writers the belief of the Germans that real artists had to submit to the divine force, as self-effaced vessels.[19] Although all human beings possess the creative spirit, its development depends on the observance of certain conditions, according to Hawthorne. First, the artist must gain the "soul's eyesight" through simple faith in Reality.[20] Creative imagination combines with this instinctive perception to bring about discernment of Reality, of which Nature is a shadow. The subordinate role of reason is to understand the heart's knowledge, which emanates from this instinctive perception.[21]

So great was this influence that Emerson based his ideal poet and muse on Persian sources. He first identified himself with one of Persia's greatest poets in his autobiographical poem entitled "Saadi," first published in the *Dial* in 1842. Saʻdi appealed to Emerson so much that numerous references to him appear in the Transcendentalist leader's poems. Later, Emerson changed the name *Saadi* to *Seyed* to identify his poet as a wandering dervish with a crystal soul in harmony with Nature.[22]

Thoreau best expressed his own identification, as well as that of the Concord community, with this poet in these terms:

I know, for instance, that Saadi entertained once identically the same thought that I do, and thereafter I can find no essential difference between Saadi and myself. He is not Persian, he is not ancient, he is not strange to me. By the identity of his thoughts with mine, he remains alive.[23]

Thoreau continues to express the Concordian identification with Sa'di:

If Saadi were to come back to claim a personal identity with the historical Saadi, he would find that there were too many of us; he could not get a skin to contain us all . . . By sympathy with Saadi I have embowelled him.[24]

Just as Emerson identified his ideal poet with Sa'di, so did he associate the Orient and Nazami's Lilla (Laila) with the feminine force:

Was it Hafiz or Firdousi that said of his Persian Lilla, She was an elemental force, and astonished me by her amount of life, when I saw her day after day radiating, every instant, redundant joy and grace on all around her? She was a solvent powerful to reconcile all heterogeneous persons into one society: Like air or water, an element of such great range of affinities that it combines readily with a thousand substances. Where she is present all others will be more than they are wont. . . . She did not study the Persian grammar, nor the books of the seven poets, but all poems of the seven seemed to be written upon her. For though the bias of her nature was not to thought, but to sympathy, yet was she so perfect in her own nature as to meet intellectual persons by the fullness of her heart, warming them by her sentiments.[25]

Feminist Margaret Fuller's autobiographical piece, entitled *Leila*, documents her identification with Nazami's characterization of the Beloved. At a time when the burgeoning spiritual cults of New England celebrated feminine prophecy and divinity as a countervailing force to male sexual antagonism, Fuller exceeds Emerson's portrayal of Laila as "joyful sympathy" to empower her instead with boundless knowledge and impelling force. Fuller's Laila overwhelms men rather than reconciles them as Emerson envisages:

Most men, as they gazed on Leila were pained; they left her at last baffled and well-nigh angry. For most men are bound in sense, time, and thought. They shrink from the overflow of the infinite; they cannot a moment abide in the coldness of abstractions; the weight of an idea is too much for their lives.[26]

While both writers acknowledge that Laila possesses the elemental powers of Nature, Fuller points out that "to the thought of the pious wild man, Leila manifests the regulatory powers of conscience and retribution."[27] Only the poet, through the release of his creativity, could escape the madness to which she could drive men. Fuller views Laila as a prophetess of "pure ministry" who holds the "secret of mental alchemy."[28] She is the "moving principle" in unity with God:[29] "She knows all, and is nothing."[30]

Of all the Concord writers, George William Curtis was the most romantic Orientalist, and the only member of his community to travel extensively in the Middle East. He even assumed the rather affected sobriquet *howadji*, a corruption of *haji*, the Arabic word for "pilgrim." During his attendance at the Brook Farm school, where he and Hawthorne became friends, Curtis referred to himself as Hafiz, one of the greatest of the Persian poets.[31] In his *Nile Notes*, Curtis equates Hafiz with the mystery and poetry of the East. Whether he was in Beirut or in Damascus, Curtis felt that he was in Shiraz, home of Hafiz. Curtis maintains this comparison in his second work, *The Howadji in Syria*, in which he states that the *Arabian Nights* and Hafiz's poetry better express the "spirit and splendor of Oriental life than all the books on Eastern travel ever written."[32]

Throughout the month of March 1851, Hawthorne read aloud nightly to his wife Sophia *The Nile Notes*, a work which enchanted them. In a letter of April 29, 1851, to Curtis, Hawthorne praised the "descriptive power" of the travelogue to transport the reader.[33] Hawthorne again commends Curtis and his travelogues in the foreword to *The Blithedale Romance*.

The following excerpt from *The Howadji in Syria*, regarding the cafes of Damascus, must have caught Hawthorne's attention because of its reference to Zenobia, a female character in *The Blithedale Romance* fashioned after the legendary Queen of Palmyra:

> Here is the golden atmosphere of romance and the natural picturesque. The cafes of Damascus are passionate poems. It is the difference between a mild-eyed milkmaid and the . . . magnificence of Zenobia. . . . The best Western suggestions of these Damascus delights are those German gardens in pleasant arbors. . . . But here again is all the difference between Albrecht Durer and Hafiz. . . . There is a marked vein of prose in everything German. The cafes of Damascus are pure poetry.[34]

Edward Sa'id has pointed out that the Orient was a place of pilgrimage for European writers throughout the nineteenth century.[35] In America, as well, the Concord literary community took this pilgrimage to the imaginary space of Sufi literature to activate their creative urge. The Persian-inspired models of the ideal poet and prophetess/creative force ruled the Transcendental Pantheon in the mid-nineteenth century. The act of identification with Persian persona—

writers and characters—transported these New England literary pilgrims to an imaginative Orient, a space in which their creative processes were ignited. That these American writers conceived of the creative process in terms of Sufi poetry signifies the impact of this mystical literature on New England writing of the mid-nineteenth century.[36]

Notes

1. This article was originally published in *Sufi: The Magazine of Khaniqah-i Ni'matullahi,* 3 (Autumn 1989), 14–18.

2. The *National Union Catalogue Pre-1956 Imprints,* 19 (Chicago: Mancell, 1969), 44–48, lists the first edition of the *Arabian Nights* in 1794. From 1803 to 1833 there were thirty-three editions and reprints; from 1835 to 1851 the catalogue lists fifteen entries. Certainly this great of number of entries indicates the popularity of this classic in America, as noted in David McKay's publication of Lane's edition. John D. Yohannan in *A Treasury of Asian Literature* (New York: John Day Company, 1956), 56, also notes that the *Arabian Nights* was a popular reading in America and Britain from the eighteenth century. Magazines featured many stories based on the classic. Another work of John Yohannan (1977, 107–11), cites two popular American works based on the *Arabian Nights*: Maria Brooks *Zophiel or the Bride of Seven,* and "Tales of Hafez" in the first edition of the *New York Magazine or Literary Repository* (1790). Also cited is a popular tale which adapted Persian poetry for an American audience, entitled *Gulzar: or the Rose Bower, A Tale of Persia.* The popularity of the *Arabian Nights* stimulated periodical literature which led to popular adaptations of Persian poetry.

3. Julian Hawthorne, *Hawthorne Reading* (Cleveland, OH: The Folcroft Press, 1902), 113.

4. M. D. Conway, "Transcendentalists of Concord," *Eclectic Magazine* 63, no. 2 (October 1864), 231–248.

5. G. W. Cooke, ed., *Letters: George William Curtis to John S. Dwight* (New York: Harper & Brothers, 1893), 17.

6. G. B. Kirby, *Years of Experience: An Autobiographical Narrative* (New York: AMS Press, 1971), 151.

7. E. Zolla, "Naturphilosophie and Transcendentalism Revisited," *Sophia Perennis* 3:2 (1977): 65–99. This work connects German philosophy, English Romanticism, and American Transcendental literature to Sufism.

8. John D. Yohannan, *Persian Poetry in England and America: A 200-Year History* (Delmar, NY: Caravan Books, 1977), 48.

9. A. Christy, *The Orient in American Transcendentalism* (New York: Octagon Books, 1932), 321.

10. Louisa S. Costello, ed. and trans., *The Rose Garden of Persia* (London: Longman, Brown, Green, & Longmans, 1845).

11. E. B. Cowell, "The Rose Garden of Persia," *Westminster Review* (July 1847), 145–63.

12. Christy, *The Orient in American Transcendentalism,* 42.

13. Yohannan, *Persian Poetry*, 117.

14. Theodore Parker, *Catalogue of Books* (Concord, MA: Concord Public Library, undated).

15. Robert N. Hudspeth, ed., *The Letters of Margaret Fuller* (Ithaca, NY: Cornell University Press, 1965), vol. II, 121–122.

16. Christy, *The Orient in American Transcendentalism*, 145.

17. Samuel Longfellow, ed., *Life of Henry Wadsworth Longfellow* (Cambridge, MA: Houghton Mifflin Co., 1896), vol. II, 158.

18. Ibid., 213.

19. Maria M. Tatar, *Spellbound: Studies on Mesmerism and Literature* (Princeton, NJ: Princeton University Press, 1978), 226.

20. M. J. Elder, *Nathaniel Hawthorne: Transcendental Symbolist* (Cleveland: Ohio University Press, 1969), 64.

21. R. J. Jacobson, *Hawthorne's Conception of the Creative Process* (Boston: Harvard University Press, 1965), 35.

22. Ralph Waldo Emerson, *Essays of Emerson* (New York: Random House, 1944), 537.

23. Henry David Thoreau, *Journal of Henry D. Thoreau*, ed. Bradford Torrey and Francis H. Allen (Boston: Houghton Mifflin, 1949), vol. IV, 48.

24. Ibid.

25. Emerson, *Essays of Emerson*, 306.

26. Margaret Fuller, "Leila," *Dial* (April 1841), 462.

27. Ibid.

28. Ibid., 463.

29. Ibid., 466–7.

30. Ibid., 463.

31. Cooke, *Letters: George William Curtis to John S. Dwight*, 40.

32. George William Curtis, *The Howadji in Syria* (New York: Harper and Brothers), 85.

33. Nathaniel Hawthorne, "Letter to George William Curtis," *Lenox* (29 April 1851).

34. Curtis, *The Howadji in Syria*, 323.

35. Edward W. Sa'id, *Orientalism* (New York: Vintage Books, 1979), 168.

36. I would like to acknowledge the assistance of Mrs. Marcia Moss, curator of the Concord Free Public Library, Concord, Massachusetts.

11

Omarian Poets of America[1]

Mehdi Aminrazavi

In the highways of Worcester I hear thee,
And down by the Southern seas,
In the glorious prairies of Texas
Thy music is flung to the breeze.

—*Twenty Years of Omar Khayyam Club of America 1921*

Omar Khayyam's *Quatrains (Ruba'iyyat)* are among the most often read and popular literature in America. The immense popularity of Omar has left an indelible mark on both the popular cultural and the literary circles interested in "Eastern philosophy." Though, technically, America never saw Omar Khayyam as an Islamic mystic, or "Sufi," he was understood by Western readers to possess that magic wisdom which comes from the East. Thus, Omar Khayyam is shrouded in an esoteric and mystical aura. His work is understood in a manner similar to the way modern America understands the message of Rumi, or is enchanted by Hafiz's narratives of love, wine, women, and *carpe diem*.

While some saw the *Ruba'iyyat* as the liberating wisdom upon which the West waited, others saw it as the "cult of Omar," a pagan impurity which the "other" inflicted on the very fabric of Christian morality in America. Omar was received in America's North as a champion of free thinking, a renaissance man whose *Ruba'iyyat* reflected perfectly the post-bellum spirit of the time, while in the South he was seen as the anti-Christ.

Omar Khayyam's great journey to America began in October of 1869, when Charles Eliott Norton published a review of FitzGerald's translation of the *Ruba'iyyat* in the *North American Review*. Norton gave it a glowing review and included with his article seventy-four of FitzGerald's translations of the *Ruba'iyyat*. These translations began the process of popularizing the *Ruba'iyyat*

221

among certain literary circles in New England. W. J. Black argues that America was uniquely prepared for the Khayyamian message since, as he said, the "lofty idealism that precipitated the Civil War had given way to a sordid materialism." America seems to have been ready to hear Khayyam saying,

> Ah, take the cash, and let the credit go
> Nor heed the rumble of a distant Drum!

The rise of materialism and the unraveling of the horrors of the Civil War had brought a sense of nihilism, hedonism, and moral decay. Khayyam's perceived message for *carpe diem* must have been quite timely:

> Ah, my Beloved, fill the Cup that clears
> To-Day of past requests and future Fears
> To-morrow?—Why, To-morrow I may be
> Myself with Yesterday's Sev'n Thousand Years[2]

The memory of hundreds of thousands of young men who had died in the war was haunting America. Khayyam's quatrains must have sounded very timely to the wounded American society as it dealt with death, emptiness, and horror. His advice to turn our attention to beauty, amidst the transient nature of life and death, is a form of existential therapy.

> And Those who husbanded the Golden grain,
> And Those who flung it to the winds like Rain,
> Alike to no such aureate Earth are Turn'd
> As, buried once, Men want dug up again.[3]

The secularization of American society, the disappearance of religious certainty, and what Black calls the resentful "struggle against a scientific hypothesis advanced by Darwin,"[4] found a voice in Khayyam. A nation founded by Puritans slipped into doubt.

> The Moving Finger writes; and, having writ,
> Moves on: nor all your Piety nor Wit
> Shall lure it back to cancel half a Line,
> Nor all your Tears wash out a Word of it.

The Omar Khayyam Club of America

While America was ready for the message of Omar Khayyam, at least as it was portrayed in the Victorian romanticism of Edward FitzGerald's skillful rendition, it took the systematic efforts of an organized club to introduce him more widely. The uniquely prepared American climate, the beauty of FitzGerald's Victorian English translation, and Khayyam's pessimism and sarcasm with regard to matters of faith were all catalysts in the birth of the Omar Khayyam Club of America.

The first session of the Club was held on the ninety-first birthday of Edward FitzGerald at the Young Hotel in Boston, Saturday, March 31, 1900. The meeting, which was called "the Festival of Saint Edward," consisted of a number of exclusive intellectuals, each of whom related to an aspect of Khayyam's thought. The nine original founders of the Club were Nathan H. Dole; Eben F. Thompson; Arthur Foote, who was a musician; Arthur Macy, a poet; Alfred C. Potter of Harvard Library; Sylvester Baxter and Ross Turner, both of whom were men of letters; William E. Story, a mathematician; and Colonel Thomas Wentworth Higginson, a man of letters.

The mission of the Club was agreed upon by the officers as "An association of men, mostly professional, who believe in good fellowship and who are interested in the Orient in one way or another; and more particularly in that 'King of the Wise,' the astronomer, philosopher, and poet, Omar Khayyam."[5]

Following the election of the officers,[6] the Club members met several times, including a major session in 1901, but the real work of the Club took place on the side. Members and their friends began to collect new versions of the *Ruba'iyyat* of Khayyam and amateur translations of them began to appear. Members composed poems following the style of the *Ruba'iyyat*. Notable among these members are Stephan C. Houghton, whose philosophical poem, "In the Path of the Persians," gained some recognition, and Charles Hardy Meigs, who composed a work of miniatures capturing the spirit of the *Ruba'iyyat*.

By 1919, the Omar Khayyam Club of America was responsible for introducing and translating the *Ruba'iyyat* as well as some of Khayyam's other works. Charles Burrage, the President of the Club, describes the achievements of the Club as follows: "The Club has as it were, stood over his [FitzGerald's] monumental translation of the whole of Omar Khayyam's quatrains—a formidable volume, very much more extended, of course, than FitzGerald's very free version and very different."[7]

The Omarian Poets of New England

With the Club having established itself as the center for literary figures concerned with Omar Khayyam, its members and affiliates began to create a literary school, calling themselves "Omarians." Omarians said this of Khayyam and themselves: "Omar Khayyam, Persian philosopher and poet, established a cult immortally cherished by the choice souls of successive generations. Omarians are generally gentle, always genial, and when opportunity offers, joyfully congenial."[8]

The Omarian literary movement influenced a number of both notable and less well-known figures who made an attempt to compose *Ruba'iyyat* of their own, spawning a new literary genre. Omarians saw themselves as the champions of free thinking and the guardians of secularism, sharing in Omar Khayyam's spirit of rebellion against puritanical morality. Nathan Haskell Dole, a member of the Club, wrote a long poem praising Omar for rejecting the prohibition against drinking in Islam. This must have resonated deeply with Americans who were also experiencing Prohibition initiated by Carry Nation and other Christian moralists. Dole writes:

To Omar Khayyam

(Written for the Omar Khayyam Club of America
Under the Stress of Prohibition)

The Prophet interdicted ruby Wine—
Which, made by God Himself, must be divine—
You stood on God's side, Omar, good for you!
And sang the Praise of Persia's fruitful Vine.
Men trample down the purple Grapes, whose Juice
Flows in a fragrant Stream from out the sluice;
Then God comes down and breathes upon the Vat,
And lo! the red Wine meant for joyous Use.
God's Spirit permeates the ruby Bowl
As in the Body lives the glowing Soul;
It thrills, it fills, it kills the ghastly Ills
That over hapless Men in Billows roll.
When Gloom or Disappointment settles down
And Stormy Skies disturb with horrid Frown,
One brimming Cup will put the Clouds to Flight
And all one's Sorrows in Oblivion drown.
One brimming Cup will make the sad Heart gay,
Will burn the Winter's Cold to warmth of May,
Will change a bitter Foe to faithful Friend,
Will make the recreant Muse the Will obey!
So, Omar, Haunter of the festive Shrine,
And Watcher of the Stars which nightly shine,
What think you of this sober Western World,
That joins Mohammed in forbidding Wine?
Do you look down with Pity in your Eyes
To see the cheering Draught you wont to prize

Made contraband by stern fanatic Laws
Which turn the Truths of God to Devil's Lies!
Good Wine, we know, is promised us in Heaven,
And tho the Loaf of Bread may have no leaven,
We will join you there and share your jocund Fare,
Where'er you are—in Number one or Seven!
Ah well! We've had full many a joyous Feast,
With you as our high Pattern and High Priest;
With Moderation which we all observe—
We of the West and you, Star of the East.
And though we have to hold an empty Glass,
'Tis filled with finest Spirit:—let it pass.
We drink your Health—Imagination reigns—
Down with the Dolts whose Ignorance is crass!
Mayhap our Burrage, with his Skill empirical
Will reperform the cana-marriage Miracle,
And (by a magic Word) change cold Water
To red red Wine to make our Praises lyrical!
Hail to you, Omar, friendliest of the Sages,
Your message cheers us, ringing through the Ages:—
Our Eben Francis has translated it
In golden Verses crowning creamy Pages.[9]

An unknown poet of the Omarian literary tradition read the following poem in one of the meetings of the Club:

On his high throne a cardinal sat,
Cogitating on this and on that;
"Omarkh," quoth he,
"Has nothing on me
For I have my own Rubyhat[10]
Not FitzGerald nor Thompson," he said
"Nor Dole, Whinfield nor Roe are ahead;
As surely as they
I am truly O.K.
For my Rubyhat is much red!"[11]

With the rise of the New England School of Transcendentalism, interest in Eastern philosophy was growing exponentially. As is evident by the meetings of the Club, Worcester seems to have become one of the centers of interest in a revival of Khayyam's wisdom.

A member of the Club from the Worcester Omarian Literary Circle, Henry Harman Chamberlin, being inspired by Khayyam's emphasis on temporality and death, composed a poem called "The Price." Mourning the death of love amidst what he calls "The Brotherhood of Man," especially at the time of war, Chamberlin read the following poem at the March 31, 1917 meeting of the Omar Khayyam Club of America:

The Price

Not only mourn the brave who died at morn,
Who struck their blow and perished in their pride,
But mourn those other lives who also died,
Vain hopes of generations yet unborn.
Nor mourn the stricken children bayonet torn,
Shell driven o'er the blazing countryside;
But mourn Man's twilight and his eventide,
And Brotherhood betrayed, and Faith forsworn.
Yea, chiefly mourn the most heartrending cost.
Two thousand years' slow progress spent and lost,
This goodly oak cut down as by a sword.
Brother of Death, Sin's crowned and armèd birth,
How long shall this new Anarch reign on earth,
Unsmitten of Thy thunderbolt, O Lord?

The following year, Chamberlin, who was deeply touched by the horrors of World War I, composed a number of *Ruba'iyyat* entitled *Champagne Song of the Wine of Victory* which he read in 1918 at the annual dinner of the Omar Khayyam Club of America. He writes:

Champagne Song or The Wine of Victory[12]

Still wine hath an intimate fire
That gratefully tickles each vein;
But the springtime of youth and desire
Bubbles up in the wine of champagne.

Chorus:
Bubbles up in the glass of champagne, my boys,
Bubbles up in the sparkling champagne, my boys,
Bubbles high in the golden champagne, my boys,
The sparkling, golden champagne.

With shot and with shell and the terrors of Hell,
The Germans swept over the Aisne,
But the spirit of France broke their onward advance,
And dashed all their hopes in Champagne.

Chorus:
Then here's the poilus of Champagne, my boys,
Who scattered the Boche in Champagne, my boys,
From the Marne and the Aisne to Champagne, my boys,
When red grew the grapes of Champagne.

They gave up their lives for their children and wives,
But they shed not their lifeblood in vain,
For the world they made free over land, over sea,
By the battles they fought in Champagne.

Chorus:
Then here's the Poilus of Champagne, my boys,
Who laid down their lives in Champagne, my boys,
To the living and dead in Champagne, my boys,
Let's drink to them all in champagne.

For the loved ones that mourn, they no more may return,
A tear for each bumper we drain;
But we at the height of this festival night,
Let our hearts be as light as champagne.

Chorus:
Then here's to the merry champagne, my boys,
And here's to the gallant champagne, my boys,
And the glory of France in Champagne, my boys,
The glorious, victorious champagne.

By 1920 the extent of the horrors of World War I and the American Civil War had been fully disclosed. Both of these wars were somewhat of a family feud, which made them seem even more senseless than if it were a war against the "noble savages." In April 1920, Henry Chamberlin writes in an ode entitled "Supplication in the Time of War:"

We who have loitered in the paths of ease,
Waken us all, O Lord, to the World's need!

Even as men, of Thee who took no heed,
On some far isle, begirt with slumberous seas,
Long years we dreamed. For this, our sons must bleed,
Because we loitered in the paths of ease.

Fondly we dreamed of Earth's eternal peace.
To our dull ears, the whisperings of War
Came like a fierce old legend, faint and far.
We dreamed of wealth and comfort, to release
Our souls from Fate, and Valor's guiding star;
Because we loitered in the paths of ease.

We dreamed that Time would change and Strife would cease,
And fair, soft words beguile a tyrant's hate.
Thy thunderbolt awoke us, not too late
To fight for Freedom and Thy Word. For these
Our sires had fought and made our nation great;
But we have loitered in the paths of ease.

Kindle our souls, that zeal for Thee increase,
So, that, in words of flame, our souls may see
Thy truth and we may win Thy victory!
Oh! make us worthier of a nobler peace,
Whereby our children, brave and wise and free,
No more shall loiter in the paths of ease.

While Khayyam's emphasis on temporality and the finality of death was deeply influential, his praise of beauty was more appealing to some than his emphasis on temporality. George C. Stratton, a notable literary figure in Washington DC, composed the following *Ruba'iyyat* closely following Khayyam's style and content:

When, on that Summer day at Twin Oaks, you
   First brought th' immortal Omar to my view
I gave the deathless quatrains scarce a thought—
   Ah, 'twas but very little then I knew!

But as, from time to time, I read them o'er
Their beauty grew upon me more and more.
And now I hope that I may be enrolled
With the Elect who've entered in the Door.

'Tis pleasant, then, to place upon the Shelf
With all my Omars, prized above mere pelf,
This handsome Book of those who love the Poet;
Which shows so much also of your own Self.[13]

Another poet, Charles Haywood Stratton, whose relationship to the previous poet is unknown, is clearly from the same Omarian tradition. He composed a long poem on Omar Khayyam only five days after George C. Stratton (May 27, 1921) in response to the following verse as it appears in the volume entitled *Twenty Years of Omar Khayyam Club of America*.

Reserve your censure; do not criticize
This book; 'Twas only meant for friendly eyes.

Charles Haywood Stratton writes in his long poem entitled "To the Editor:"

To the Editor,

You ask the reader not to criticize
The Book you only meant for friendly eyes.
Ingrate, indeed, must be the one who'd brook
Aught but the kindliest words upon your Book!
But may not criticism be in friendly view?
And serve to call your inspiration forth again?
Wise Omar said it well for all to read—
'Tis Fellowship that lets our Life proceed.
Your happy Book now adds another link
To his strong chain of evidence, I think.
And since 'tis Friendship makes our life worth while,
The chronicle of Friendship's tear, or smile,
For future man to keep and read again,
Is worthy subject for your worthy pen.
'Tis plain you generous are, as well as wise,
And know the objects that all men most prize
Are those in which themselves with toil have wrought
The precious product of their own hard thought,
So you have kept a store of pages white,
'Whereon each one of us may paste, or write—
Mayhap of interest to himself alone—
The things that really make the Book his own,

So now, though I have dared to criticize
You see 'tis but the view of friendly eyes.

        Charles Heywood Stratton[14]
        Washington, DC, May 27, 1921.

George Roe, an Omarian poet, rejoices at the widespread reception of Omar Khayyam in America in his *Rubaiyyat*. His use of Hindu, Buddhist, and Persian concepts like Nirvana, Maya, and Khuda (God), reveals his identification with an inclusive spirit in the wisdom of Omar Khayyam. Roe remarks:

Friend, Omar, thy voice is still singing,
Altho' thou art with us no more,
Thy numbers in melody ringing
Aloud on our Western shore,

In the highways of Worcester I hear thee,
And down by the Southern seas,
In the glorious prairies of Texas
Thy music is flung to the breeze.

And here in the City of Boston,
Where Freedom her glory hath shed,
Where Knowledge and Wisdom are cherished,
We gather to honor the dead.

And tho' for a while we're divided,
We, too, shall return to the sod
Where all living things are united
To dwell in the bosom of God.

Where anger and enmity perish,
Where sorrow forever is o'er,
Where sickness and pain cannot follow
And grief can pursue us no more.

Where Khuda (God) in love doth enfold us
And taketh our souls to his breast,
Where blessed Nirvána doth hold us
At peace in the Kingdom of Rest.

And there shall our spirits awaken,
When all are absorbed in the Whole,

And the Maya of Self is forgotten
And Union with God is the Goal.

George Roe,
San Antonio, Texas

The list of Omarians who traveled to attend the meetings of the Club or composed poems or, in so many cases, prose in the spirit of Khayyamian thought is too extensive to be included here, but some further examples will help illustrate the breadth and depth of this tradition in America.

William B. Scofield of Worcester was an Omarian poet who wrote poetically of Abraham Lincoln, applying the Omarian poetic style to his praise of the virtues of the American President's "great heart." His poem, read at the meeting of April 15, 1919, is as follows:

Somehow I think that in the near Beyond
He sits and broods O'er all this human strife
And that new furrows line his kindly face,
Full sad enough from his own weary life
While the great heart, that throbbed for others' care
Still thrills in pity for us, even there.

At another meeting of the Omar Khayyam Club of America, Scofield composed and dedicated the following prose to Charles D. Burrage, the founder of the Club. The text, one of the three he read at the meeting, may well be an indication of his own pain. The piece addresses Khayyam's regret for seeing his friends vanish in the wheel of life and death. The poem, read on April 2, 1921, reads:

He is often happy whose one thought is for friends. He shall know full days of willing sacrifice; and yet his friends may turn from his sweet ministry and then how shall he, rejected, face the coming days?[15]

With the Omarian poets now far and wide, George Roe from San Antonio, Texas varied the style, composing some quatrains, but forming his own format often consisting of five and six stanzas like this one:

Sad, severed from the sea, a raindrop sighed,
And, smiling gently, thus the sea replied,
"*A part* of God are we, but we seem *apart*
When Alif, moving, doth our union hide.

Stephan Magister, another Omarian, composed a long poem consisting of several pages called "A Sage's Console." Each section varies in length, but, inspired by Omar Khayyam, he too mourns the social and political injustices of his time. He begins what amounts to be a critique of American society and asserts:

> Maintain thy stature in men's eyes. If driven,
> On Fortune's breakers hope not to be shriven.
> Crimes, vices, follies, these may be condoned;
> Misfortune only may not be forgiven.

Magister's poems are a true reflection of the nineteenth century American social malaise. The America of which he writes "lost his wealth, his health, his grip," and yet "we can despise him." His poems are a long litany of "injustice, misery and hate" which, for him, represent a place where there is "no golden rule or moral law" anymore, only profiteers for whom "his neighbor is the man his sphere of action reaches." His critique of America ends as it begins:

> MAINTAIN YOUR STATURE IN MEN'S EYES, and you will
>   be respected
> By all discriminating souls who recognize in merit
> More excellence than in the store men gather or inherit;
> And though the thoughtless rabble, Power's votaries, may slight you,
> A consciousness of rectitude will solace and require you.[16]

Between 1906 and 1921, the Omar Khayyam Club of America published eighteen works,[17] most of which dealt with the *Ruba'iyyat*. While it appears that the Club continued its work for a few more years, the death of its key members, contributors, and patrons brought about its eventual demise as it withered away to obscurity and oblivion. The other reason for the decline of the Club may have been partially due to the completion of its goal of introducing Omar Khayyam to Americans. In most American high schools and colleges, students were exposed to Omar Khayyam's *Ruba'iyyat*. By the 1930s, Khayyam and his *Ruba'iyyat* had become household names in America and had left an indelible mark upon the spiritual landscape of American Society.

Let us now turn our attention to the more notable American literary figures and examine the influence of Khayyam and his *Ruba'iyyat* on mainstream literary culture.

The Ruba'iyyat of Mark Twain

Mark Twain's sense of humor, sarcasm, and skepticism concerning free will and determinism fit well with Khayyam's style, and the great personal tragedies Mark

Twain suffered enabled him to find in Khayyam what FitzGerald had found earlier: a familiar voice of discontent and a refusal to give into the urge to make sense of it all. The Reverend Conway, in a lecture he once delivered, said:

> I remember once conversing on the subject with Mark Twain—a humorous man and a man of great power as well—and he startled me, as I had not associated him with such poetic ideas. By saying that he regarded one quatrain of Omar Khayyam's—the famous and the bold one beginning: 'O thou, who man of baser Earth did make'—as containing the most far-reaching and grand thought ever expressed in so short a space in so few words.[18]

Mark Twain himself, who was quite familiar with English poetry, often quoting the works of Tennyson, expressed his utmost reverence for the *Ruba'iyyat*. Quoting the following quatrain he said, "No poem had given me so much pleasure before," and in 1907 he added of the *Ruba'iyyat*, "it is the only poem I have ever carried about with me; it has not been from under my hand for 28 years."[19]

> Oh Thou, who Man of baser Earth didst make
> And ev'n with Paradise devise the snake
> For all the sun where with the Face of Man
> Is blacken'd–Man's forgiveness give-and take![20]

Allegedly Mark Twain composed one-hundred-twenty poems from which Arthur L. Scott chose sixty-five of the less "embarrassing ones" and published them in *On the Poetry of Mark Twain with Selections from His Verse*. Some of the salient features of his poems and their burlesque nature resemble Omar Khayyam's sarcasm when the latter mentions the cruelty of fate and destiny. Mark Twain became exposed to the Ruba'iyyat in FitzGerald's translation sometime around the 1870s through Reverend Joseph H. Twichell, who drew his attention to several Ruba'iyyat in the Hartford *Courant*. It is clear from a letter Mark Twain wrote a friend that he may have been thinking of writing his own version of the Ruba'iyyat. In a letter to his friend, William Dean Howells, on November 26, 1876, Mark Twain wrote, "It is no harm to put these words into wise Omar Khayyam's mouth, for he would have said them if he thought of it."[21]

Mark Twain's intense interest in the Ruba'iyyat is evidenced by his collection of various copies of them. On May 19, 1884, he acquired the Osgood edition; on April 10, 1899, he ordered a half-crown copy of the Ruba'iyyat from Chatto Windus of London; and in 1900 he ordered a copy from Philadelphia. In October of 1898, under the influence of FitzGerald's translation, and having suffered numerous personal tragedies, Mark Twain began to write the Ruba'iyyat of his own. Due to recent deaths in his family including his daughter, these

Ruba'iyyat inevitably grapple with age, disease, and the gradual decaying of the human body. He composed forty-five quatrains and integrated them with two of FitzGerald's stanzas forming a work entitled *AGE–A Rubáiyát*.[22]

Mark Twain's Ruba'iyyat is a burlesque version of FitzGerald's. A. Gribben in his work *Mark Twain's Rubáiyát*, asserts that, "Mark Twain mimicked the prosody of what is called the Omar Khayyam quatrain . . . and tried to duplicate these features."[23] "How then Is Old Age better than the threatened Hell?"[24] becomes a theme that Twain embraces both in a prose format such as in "The Five Boons of Life" and in the poetic form. Twain turns and twists Khayyam's poetry, attributing sarcastic remarks to him, seeming to claim that, "It is no harm to put these words into wise Omar Khayyam's mouth." An example of such incorrect attribution is when Twain writes that some people are "able to govern kingdoms and empires but few there be that can keep a hotel."[25]

By October of 1898, the devastating effect of Twain's daughter's death had subsided and a much-improved financial situation brought him some degree of peace and serenity, but the question of old age and decay remained an insoluble problem for him. At this juncture Mark Twain wrote *AGE–A Rubáiyát*, a work that walks a fine line between satire and serious reflection on the cruelty of life. A. Gribben suggests that Mark Twain "could not decide whether he wanted to write a winking, mocking satire on revered old age, or a savage assault on the universal injustices of man's transient existence and unwelcome fate."[26]

The editors of *Mark Twain's Rubáiyát*, A. Gribben and K. B. MacDonnell, have argued that the salient features in Twain's *AGE–A Rubáiyát* appear in the form of several recurring themes. The first theme is the temporality of life and pleasures therein. Twain offers advice concerning the acceptance of old age and how one comes to terms with it. Because he lived at the time when germs and bacterium were discovered, he became preoccupied with the concept, and this preoccupation with the germ-ridden body became a theme in his Ruba'iyyat. The effects of old age and disease are the next recurring theme; for Twain, the horror of old age replaces "The Honor of Old Age." He suggests the "honor" paradigm is, perhaps, an attempt to retain our dignity against the insult of old age, or a response to the alluring temptation to make sense of the humiliation inflicted on the aging by the merciless forces of nature.

Twain deals with death next; that which Gribben, the noted scholar of Mark Twain, calls "the deepest, the darkest pit in this chamber of horrors, adumbrating the gloomy line of thought."[27] The horror of death ironically becomes the liberating power of death, for it is death that ends it all. In December 1905, in an essay entitled "Old Age,"[28] Mark Twain visits this theme and writes of death, "Yes, it is disappointing . . . you say 'is this it?—this?'" Twain's quatrains also seem preoccupied with sex and hedonism. Referring to his past sexual experiences as "the long past orgies," Twain expresses his utter frustration at his inability to enjoy sex in old age. This may have been why in a letter to his friend Andrew Chatto, he refers to his Ruba'iyyat as "Omar's Old Age" and instructs him to "*burn* them at once." In this letter, Mark Twain states:

> Confound it, this seems to be the right time to privately publish my "Omar's Old Age," written two or three months ago, but I've written only about 50 quatrains and am not ready. Besides, I am playing a game—no, thinking of it. An American friend said, "Try a new thing. Make a rare book for collectors—limited edition: 500 copies at $50 a copy, or 30 copies at $1,000 a copy; if the latter, I will buy one copy and place 5 for you." Come—is it a wild and vicious scheme? Samples enclosed. Read them, then *burn* them at once; don't let any see them or hear about them. In writing me, don't use a title, but speak of the work as "ABC."
>
> Ys sincerely,
> SLC[29]

After Mark Twain's death, Albert Bigelow Paine came to possess many of his manuscripts, poems, and memorabilia. Paine decided not to include Mark Twain's *Ruba'iyyat* in the official biography of his life, *Mark Twain: A Biography*, published in 1912; thus few came to know of his *Ruba'iyyat*. Paine remarked of Twain's quatrains,

> Mark Twain was not a good versifier—the demands of rhyme and meter were too much for him, as a rule, though at times he seemed to overcome his difficulties. These quatrains offer a fair example both of his successes and his failures. Some of the stanzas are not for delicate readers. These, of course, were not intended for print.[30]

A. Gribben, who estimates the composition date of the *AGE–A Rubáiyát* to have been around the autumn of 1898, considers Mark Twain's *Ruba'iyyat* to be the work of his "brooding late phase" and adds that "the poem affords glimpses of the plunging depths of his emotional state that otherwise would never be documented . . . Mark Twain may have meant *AGE-A Rubáiyát* to constitute his angry *In Memoriam*."[31]

The poetic license which allowed Khayyam and FitzGerald to express man's deepest existential discontent against a fundamentally cruel and unjust world seems to also have provided Mark Twain with that same relief. This volume includes all of Mark Twain's *Ruba'iyyat* separately, but in what follows several examples of them are provided to indicate his deep emotional and intellectual investment in Omar Khayyam. The following two quatrains express his frustration and outrage with aging:

34

And those who husbanded their golden Youth,
And those who flung it to the Winds, forsooth
 Must all alike succumb to Age
And know the nip of his remorseless Tooth.

39

Next, Deafness comes, and men must Shout
Into a foolish Trumpet, leaving out
 The Gist of what they want to say—and still
O'er what they *have* said hangs a crippling Doubt.

And the following *Ruba'iyyat* indicate how Mark Twain played with FitzGerald's translations and made a burlesque version of them:

Mark Twain	FitzGerald
1.	**1.**
Sleep! For the Sun the scores another Day Against the Tale allotted You to stay, Reminding You, is Risen, and now Serves Notice—ah, ignore it while You may!	Wake! For the Sun, who scatter'd into flight Drives Night along with them from Heav'n, and strikes The Sultán's Turret with a Shaft of Light.
2.	**3.**
The chill Wind blew, and those who stood before The Tavern murmured, "Having drunk his Score, Why tarries He with empty Cup? Behold, The Wind of Youth once poured, is poured no more.	And, as the Cock crew, those who stood before The Tavern shouted—"Open then the Door! "You know how little while we have to stay, "And, once departed, may return no more.

3.

"Come, leave the Cup, and on the
   Winter's Snow
Your Summer Garment of Enjoyment
   throw:
Your Tide of life is ebbing fast, and it
Exhausted once, for You no more shall
   flow."

7.

Come, fill the Cup, and in the fire of
   Spring
Your Winter-garment of Repentence
   fling:
The Bird of Time has but a little way
To flutter—and the Bird is on the Wing

27.

There was the door whereof I had The
   Key,
The Landlord too, who double seemed
   to me—
   Some heated Talk there was—and
      then, ah then
But Rags and Fragments were we—
   Me and He.

32.

There was the Door to which I found no
   Key;
There was the Veil through which I might
   not see:
Some little talk of ME and THEE
There was—and then no more of THEE
   and ME

The Eliots

Almost all the notable literary members of T. S. Eliot's family took great interest in the *Ruba'iyyat* of Omar Khayyam. This interest began with T. S. Eliot's grandfather, William Greenleaf Eliot (1811–1887) and was passed to his cousin, Charles Eliot Norton, who introduced the *Ruba'iyyat* in the review article previously mentioned, and then to another cousin, Charles William Eliot, and finally to T. S. Eliot himself. William G. Eliot, after his retirement from the Unitarian ministry, became the chancellor of Washington University and a civic leader. His relationship with the *Ruba'iyyat* was somewhere between his admiration for a rational theology and his awareness of and concern with the rise of skepticism and moral decay in America. Omar Khayyam's work was a helpful and interesting compliment to his thinking. Despite the fact that William G. Eliot's moral stance on the *Ruba'iyyat* clearly fell in line with the spirit of Puritanism, he must have been keenly interested in them. In 1879, Rev. S. J. Barrow wrote an essay entitled *Omar Khayyam*, published in the *Unitarian Review*, wherein he sarcastically refers to William G. Eliot's interest, stating "A ministerial friend of ours had already read the *Ruba'iyyat* sixty times."[32]

Charles Eliot Norton, who was a pioneer in introducing Khayyam to the American audience, was a relative of T. S. Eliot and an Emeritus Professor at Harvard. It was he who wrote the review of the *Ruba'iyyat* in 1869 but he did not know FitzGerald was the translator since the latter, as was previously discussed, published his translation anonymously. In England in 1868, Norton met Burne-Jones, a literary figure who was ecstatic to have discovered the *Ruba'iyyat* and gave a copy of FitzGerald's translation to Norton who brought them back to America and later reviewed them.

Norton, who saw unity of thought in the *Ruba'iyyat,* not only viewed Khayyam as a materialist but described his style as "moral," "shrewd," "inquisitive and independent," and as showing "penetrating imagination," and "a manly independence."[33] Norton's review, as previously explored, sparked much interest in the *Ruba'iyyat* in America and even he was surprised by the reception, calling it "a little craze" for the book.[34]

The other cousin, Charles William Eliot, a president of Harvard University, was also known for his interest in the *Ruba'iyyat*. In 1890 he was asked to lead a committee of fifty people to investigate the activities of a group called the Demon's Association with whom Khayyam had been identified. His conclusion was that the affiliation was as he said, "half baked" and a reflection of a culture still deeply influenced by the Puritans.

The impact and influence of Omar Khayyam and his *Ruba'iyyat* on T. S. Eliot, a giant among American-British literary figures, was even more profound than it had been on Mark Twain. Khayyam's voice spoke to Eliot's modern mind and Khayyam's spirit of discontent was perhaps even more admired by Eliot than the explicit message of the *Ruba'iyyat*.

Eliot was the son of St. Louis's founding Unitarian minister who at the age of fourteen, read the *Ruba'iyyat*. The effect was so profound that Eliot described it as a metamorphosis that made him a poet instantly for the rest of his life:

> I can recall clearly enough the moment when, at the age of fourteen or so, I happened to pick up a copy of FitzGerald's *Omar* which was lying about, and the almost overwhelming introduction to a new world of feeling which this poem was the occasion of giving me. It was like a sudden conversion; the world appeared anew, painted with bright, delicious and painful colours. . . .[35]

V. M. D'Ambrosio, in her work *Eliot Possessed: T. S. Eliot and FitzGerald's RUBA'IYYAT,*[36] elaborates on the spirit of rebelliousness that is given voice in those quatrains of Khayyam that Eliot quotes and the Khayyamian air that colors some of Eliot's works. In "Animula," section II, Eliot remarks:

> The heavy burden of the growing soul
> Perplexes and offends more, day by day;
> Week by week, offends and perplexes more
> With the imperatives of 'is and seems'
> And may and may not, desire and control.

> The pain of living and the drug of dreams
> Curl up the small soul in the window seat
> Behind the Encyclopœdia Britannica.[37]

Unlike some of the Omarian poets, Eliot's relationship with Khayyam and his *Ruba'iyyat* was far too complex and profound to allow Eliot to merely imitate him and compose quatrains copying the style of the *Ruba'iyyat*. Eliot went on to incorporate the "message" into his poetry and other writings. Eliot, who refers to his encounter with the *Ruba'iyyat* as having been "absorbed," shows the crisis this absorption created in a character in "Animula," the youth of the story, who hides his feelings of love and absorption from his family because, like Omar Khayyam, he too respects reason. Eliot admired Khayyam and felt himself faced with the same choice between the sobriety of reason identified as self-control and the drunkenness of wine associated with "drug," a vehicle of freedom and forgetfulness from the world.

Whatever the source of Eliot's pain and anguish might have been, like Khayyam, he takes refuge in many things. For Khayyam it is love, the beloved, and wine, while for Eliot, the *Encyclopedia Britannica,* becomes a thing for one to throw oneself into, an endless project to take one's angst away. One can,

> Curl up the small soul in the window seat
> Behind the Encyclopœdia Britannica.

Omar Khayyam and T. S. Eliot shared a common spirit, that of dismay and discontent for authority and control. Eliot even defends Khayyam against critics like Charles Whibley who, in alarm at Omar's popularity, had belittled Omarianism by exclaiming that, "We had pictured to ourselves the honest citizen returning from his toil with a legful of masterpieces and discussing with his family circle, Stevensonianism, Omarianism, and other strange cults."[38] To the above Eliot responded, "Whibley . . . whether he was opposing the act of a government . . . or the Omar Khayyam Club, he modulated his thunders according to the tree, shrub, or weed to be blasted."[39]

Eliot not only uses themes and concepts that reverberate throughout the *Ruba'iyyat,* he also borrows structural elements from the works of Khayyam. The *Ruba'iyyat* and *The Waste Land* both begin with a tavern scene and proceed to offer an illustrated depiction of spring.[40]

Other American Literary Movements and Figures

In 1878, Thomas Bailey Aldrich, a prolific Orientalist and author of *The Sultan Goes to Ispahan,*[41] wrote a review of the *Ruba'iyyat*. He said, "The world is very old to Omar and sentient with the dust of dead generations."[42] Aldrich admired

Khayyam for the beauty of the form of the *Ruba'iyyat* and the simple yet profound message of the quatrains, which he says, "has laws which are not to be broken with impunity." Aldrich remarks that the theme is an "instrument on which one may strike the highest or the deepest note, but it must be a full note."[43]

Unlike Eliot and Norton, who felt they had to defend the moral, spiritual, and religious aspects of the *Ruba'iyyat,* Aldrich's attention is focused more on the technical aspects and the very form of quatrains. In fact, Aldrich claims that "unlike Hafiz, Firdawsi, and the rest," Khayyam has little to say about love; and Aldrich never seems to grasp what Khayyam means by "beloved." Was it God, a mistress, or a friend? Despite Aldrich's primary interest in the formalistic aspect of the *Ruba'iyyat* and his admitted semantic confusion, he was not completely unaware of the work's message, as the following suggests:

> Like those intaglios turned up from time to time in Roman earth. Omar Khayyam has shown us once more that a little thing may be perfect, and that perfection is not a little thing. But are these poems in any sense little things? Here and there the poignant thought in them cuts very deep. It is like a crevasse in an Alpine glacier, only a finger's breadth at the edge, but reaching to unfathomable depths.[44]

Among these other American men of letters, James Whitcomb Riley, also known as the "Hoosier poet," became interested in Khayyam and wrote a book entitled *The Ruba'iyyat of Doc Sifers*.[45] Riley, a writer of notable distinction, embraced Khayyam's spirit of rationalism, humanism, and agnosticism and, speaking through a fictitious doctor named Sifers, he composed quatrains, though he changed the form from Khayyam's *aaba* to *aabb*. The following demonstrates his engagement with and modification of Omar Khayyam's *Ruba'iyyat*:

> Ef you don't know DOC SIFERS I'll jes argy,
>   here and now,
> You've bin a mighty little while about here,
>   Anyhow!
> 'Cause Doc he's rid these roads and woods—
>   er *swum* 'em, now and then—
> And practiced in this neighborhood sence hain't
>   no tellin' when!

John Hay, another notable follower of Khayyam, came from the American mid-West. In December 1897, he gave a lecture at the Omar Khayyam Club of London entitled, "In Praise of Omar." As he reported on the popularity of Khayyam and the *Ruba'iyyat* in America, he mentioned hearing a miner in the Rocky Mountains reciting the following quatrain of Khayyam:

> 'Tis but a Tent where takes him one day's rest
> A Sultan to the realm of Death address
> The Sultan rises, and the dark Ferrash
> Strikes and prepares it for another Guest

Instances like the one Hay shared show the far reaching folk influence of Khayyam's work.

John Hay was not only a respected literary figure, but he was also U.S. Ambassador to England and Secretary of State under President McKinley. His interest in Persian literature and his political stature gave credence to the *Ruba'iyyat* for the public. Hay referred to Khayyam as "a man of extraordinary genius," and went on to say that Omar "had sung a song of incomparable beauty and power in an environment no longer worthy of him, in a language of narrow range, for many generations the song was virtually lost." Referring to FitzGerald as "the win brother" of Khayyam, Hay praised the translator for singing the "forgotten poem, with all its original melody and force."[46]

He had this to say about the *Ruba'iyyat*:

> The exquisite beauty, the faultless form, the singular grace of those amazingly stanzas, were not more wonderful than the depth and breadth of their profound philosophy, their knowledge of life, their dauntless courage, their serene facing of the ultimate problems of life and death.[47]

The other major figure who should be mentioned is Ezra Pound, the eminent literary genius and a close friend of T. S. Eliot, who had also developed a great admiration for Khayyam and his *Ruba'iyyat;* a reverence, which, unlike Eliot's, lasted until the end. Questioning whether he should leave London for a different place, in a letter to his friend, William Carlos Williams, Pound paired himself with Omar Khayyam, asking:

> Whether self-inflicted torture ever has the slightest
>   Element of dignity in it?
> Or whether I am Omar,
> Have I a country after all?[48]

Again in a letter from Paris to his former professor, Pound wrote, "I am perhaps didactic; so in a sense, or different sense are Homer, Dante, Villon, and Omar, and FitzGerald's translation of Omar is the only good poem of the Victorian era."[49]

To many critics, Pound's passionate interest in Omar Khayyam remains a mystery, one that James Miller reflected on, saying, "Omar Khayyam was one of the Pound's genuine weaknesses, a bizarre taste for one who shaped the modernity of modern poetry."[50] Ezra Pound's highest admiration for Khayyam, in addition to his extensive references to him in works like Canto 80, can best be seen in the fact that he named his own son "Omar Shakespeare Pound," and said of the name, "Just note the crescendo."

Finally, Ralph Waldo Emerson, a figure of great eminence, must be mentioned, although his encounter with Khayyam was brief. Emerson read FitzGerald's translation on his trip to Europe and Egypt. His biographer, Ralph Rusk, writes, "During the voyage, Emerson read and reread Omar Khayyam forgetting that he had condemned it six months before."[51] His interest in Khayyam may have been dampened by the fact that Emerson himself was an avid proponent of transcendentalism while Khayyam, at least on the surface, was very earthly.

With the spirit of materialism on the rise, and the puritanical morality in decline, Khayyam's Ruba'iyyat became an easy target for those who sought a scapegoat. Omar's popularity even created an "anti-Omarian movement," with its own literary genre. It included intellectuals and preachers, statesmen and others concerned with the disintegration of the moral fiber of the society. A thorough study of the anti-Omarian literature in America is beyond the scope of our work here but it provides a fascinating example of how a literary genre was formed bent on destroying the influence of Omar Khayyam, who was thought of by some as the foreign anti-Christ.[52]

Notes

1. Although this chapter is significantly modified and revised, it is based on a section of chapter eight of the author's *The Wine of Wisdom* (Oxford: ONEWORLD Press, 2005), 230–67.

2. Omar Khayyam, *The Ruba'iyyat of Omar Khayyam*, trans. Edward FitzGerald (New York: Walter J. Black, 1942), 128.

3. Ibid., 126.

4. Ibid., 12.

5. Charles Burrage, ed., *Some Doings of the Omar Khayyam Club of America* (Boston, 1922), 17.

6. For a complete list of the officers see Ibid., 12.

7. Ibid., 25.

8. Ibid., 22.

9. Ibid., 23.

10. The author writes *Ruba'iyyat* as "*Rubyhat*."

11. Ibid., 24.

12. Burrage, *Some Doings of the Omar Khayyam Club of America*, 30–31.

13. Ibid., 34.

14. Ibid., 33.

15. Ibid., 8.

16. Ibid., 14.

17. For a complete list of the publications of the Club, see Ibid., 38–40.

18. A. J. Arberry, *The Romance of the Ruba'iyyat*, trans. FitzGerald (London, 1959, 1st ed.), 34.

19. A. Gribben and K. B. MacDonnell, *Mark Twain's Ruba'iyyat* (Austin, TX: Jenkins Publishing Co., 1983), 10.

20. Khayyam, *The Ruba'iyyat of Omar Khayyam*, 150.

21. Ibid., 10.

22. Gribben and MacDonnell, *Mark Twain's Ruba'iyyat*, 14.

23. Mark Twain Papers at Berkeley, Notebook 40, TS, 47.

24. Gribben and MacDonnell, *Mark Twain's Ruba'iyyat*, 15.

25. This appears in the Appendix A of *A Tramp Abroad* (1880); see Ibid., 11.

26. A. Gribben and K. B. MacDonnell, *Mark Twain's Ruba'iyyat*, 17.

27. Ibid., 18.

28. John S. Tuckey, ed., *Mark Twain's Fables of Man* (Berkeley: University of California Press, 1971), 441–442.

29. The original is in the archives of Chatto and Windus, Ltd., London; see A. Gribben and K. B. MacDonnell, *Mark Twain's Ruba'iyyat*, 27. The initials SLC stand for Samuel Langhorne Clemens.

30. Ibid., 24.

31. Ibid.

32. S. J. Barrow, "Editions Note Book," *Unitarian Review and Religious Magazine*, no. 11 (1879), 384–86.

33. Charles E. Norton, "Nicolas's Quatrains de Kheyam" *North American Review*, no. 225 (1869), 565–66.

34. A. K. Terhune, *The Life of Edward FitzGerald* (New Haven, CT: Yale University Press, 1947), 213.

35. T. S. Eliot, *The Use of Poetry and the Use of Criticism: Studies in the Relation of Poetry to Criticism in England* (London: Faber and Faber Press, 1985), 33.

36. V. M. D'Amrrosio, *Eliot Possessed: T. S. Eliot and FitzGerald's RUBA'IYYAT* (New York: New York University Press, 1989).

37. Eliot, *The Use of Poetry and the Use of Criticism*, 33.

38. Charles Whibley, "Musings Without Method," *Blackwood's*, no. 170 (1903), 287.

39. T.S. Eliot, *Selected Essays* (London: Faber and Faber,1951), 499.

40. D'Amrrosio, *Eliot Possessed*, 183–88. In her "Table of Textual Comparison," D'Ambrosio clearly has shown some of these similarities.

41. Cited and discussed in Charles E. Samuels, *Thomas Bailey Aldrich* (New York: Twayne, 1965), 55–58.

42. Thomas Bailey Aldrich, "A Persian Poet," *Atlantic Monthly*, no. 41(1878), 421–26.

43. Ibid., 424.

44. Ibid., 424.

45. James Whitcomb Riley, *The Ruba'iyyat of Doc Sifers*, illustrated by C.M. Relyea (New York: Century Co., 1897).

46. John Hay, *In Praise of Omar*, an address before the Omar Khayyam Club (Portland, 1897), 5. And also in the *New York Times*, October 21, 1905.

47. Ibid., 3.

48. Ezra Pound, *Letters of Ezra Pound*, (London: Faber and Faber, 1951), 158–59.

49. Ibid., 180.

50. James Miller, *T. S. Eliot's Personal Waste Land: Exorcism of the Demons* (Pennsylvania: Penn State Press, 1977), 154.

51. Ralph Rusk, *Life of Ralph Waldo Emerson* (New York: Scribners, 1949), 478.

52. For more information on the anti-Omarian literature see E. Heron-Allan, *Ruba'iyyat of 'Umar Khayyam*, (London, 1908), xv; H.G. Keene, "Omar Khayyam" in Nathan Haskell Dole, *Ruba'iyyat of Omar Khayyam* (Boston: 1891), 2:423; Richard Le Gallienne "Fin de Siecle Cult of FitzGerald's *Ruba'iyyat* of Omar Khayyam" in *Review of National Literature*, 2 (1971), 74–75. *Ruba'iyyat of Omar Khayyam, translated into Christian*; Charles Potter, *A Bibliography of the Ruba'iyyat of Omar Khayyam*, #1066. Richard Le Gallienne, having called Khayyam "the thinker-drinker" in 1897, wrote *Omar Repentant* (New York: Mitchell Kennerly, 1908) and pronounced "The Wine! The Grape! Oh, call it Whiskey and be done with it!" *Quatrains of Christ*. See also Charles Potter, *A Bibliography of the Ruba'iyyat of Omar Khayyam*, # 942 (1908) and *Omar or Christ*. See Ibid., 668 (1914); A. H. Miller, "The Omar Cult," *Academy*, no. 59 (1900), 55; Bernard Holland, "The Popularity of Omar," *National Review*, XXXIII, (June, 1899), 643–52; C.D. Broad, "The Philosophy of Omar Khayyam and Its Relation to that of Schopenhauer," *Review*, no. CLXVI (November 1906), 544–56; "The Harm of Omar," *T. P's Weekly*, no. XVI (September 9, 1910), 340. See also G. K. Chesterton, *Heretics* (London, 1906); William Hastie, *Festival of Spring from the Divan of Jelaledin* (Glasgow: James MacLehose and Sons, 1903), xxxiii, quoted in John D. Yohannan, "Fin de Siecle Cult of FitzGerald's *Ruba'iyat of Omar Khayyam*" in *Review of National Literature*, 2 (1971), 85; Havelock Ellis, "Sexual Inversion," *Studies in the Psychology of Sex*, 2 vols. (New York: Random House, 1942), vol. 1, 50–51; Edwin Arlington Robinson, *Untriangulated Stars: Letters of Edwin Arlington Robinson to Harry de Forest Smith, 1890–1905*, ed. Denham Sutcliffe, (Cambridge, MA: Harvard University Press, 1947), xxii. See also Sylvanus Urban, *Gentleman's Magazine*, Old Series, no. CCLXXXIV (Jan–June, 1898), 413; Willfred Meynell, "The Cause of Omar's Popularity," *Academy*, no. LXVI (March 1904), 274; Edmund Gosse, *Critical Kit-Kats*, (London: William Heinemann 1895), 65–92.

12

"Bond Slave to FitzGerald's Omar"

Mark Twain and *The Ruba'iyyat*

Alan Gribben

The irreverent American realist author and humorist Samuel L. Clemens (1835–1910), better known by his nom de plume, "Mark Twain," might seem like an unlikely admirer of the Persian mathematician, astronomer, and poet Omar Khayyam, who wrote a series of brooding meditations on human existence before he died in the twelfth century. After all, Twain's rather conventional tastes in poetry had made him an enthusiast of Alfred Lord Tennyson's stately eloquence and Rudyard Kipling's emphatic rhythms, though he also surprised some friends by being tremendously intrigued with Robert Browning's subtle mysteries. An avid reader of all types of literature, however, Twain was bound to encounter the intense vogue for Omar Khayyam's verses that swept across Great Britain and America in the second half of the nineteenth century. The English poet and translator Edward FitzGerald was responsible for the massive wave of interest in *The Ruba'iyyat*, though the craze commenced a number of years after he published, in 1859, a freely rendered English version of Omar Khayyam's arresting quatrains. FitzGerald went on to issue four revised editions during his lifetime, the last appearing in 1879. Favorable reviews finally made an impact in the last decade of FitzGerald's career, and he was able to savor the growing reception of his work before he passed away in 1883.

From the moment that Mark Twain first laid eyes on a translation of *The Ruba'iyyat*'s quatrains, he became a rapt and proselytizing devotee of both their beauty and their message. Number 45 in FitzGerald's fourth edition was perhaps Twain's favorite quatrain:

> A Moment's Halt—a momentary taste
> Of BEING from the Well amidst the waste—

And Lo!—the phantom Caravan has reach'd
The NOTHING it set out from—Oh, make haste![1]

The possibility that certain verses throughout *The Ruba'iyyat* might involve symbolic Muslim allusions to the spiritual doctrines of mystic Sufism seemed to matter little to Twain; he reveled in the bluntness of the speaker's advocacy of sybaritic hedonism and chose not to ponder any intimations regarding the purification of one's soul. The habitually skeptical side of Twain's psyche especially responded to the fatalistic tone struck repeatedly, as in Stanza 8:

Whether at Naishapur or Babylon,
Whether the Cup with sweet or bitter run,
The Wine of Life keeps oozing drop by drop,
The Leaves of Life keep falling one by one.

Or, similarly, Stanza 17:

Think, in this battered Caravanserai [an inn for travelers]
Whose Portals are alternate Night and Day,
How Sultan after Sultan with his Pomp
Abode his destined Hour, and went his way.

Egalitarian sentiments like these about the leveling consequence of death thrilled FitzGerald's Victorian Age with their daringly cynical message, as did the *carpe diem* messages in parts such as Stanza 24:

Ah, make the most of what we yet may spend,
Before we too into the Dust descend;
Dust into Dust, and under Dust to lie,
Sans Wine, sans Song, sans Singer, and—sans End!

These admonitions were reinforced by warnings such as Stanza 71:

The Moving Finger writes; and, having writ,
Moves on: nor all your Piety nor Wit
Shall lure it back to cancel half a Line,
Nor all your Tears wash out a Word of it.

Twain's first recorded reference to *The Ruba'iyyat*, merely a mention of "wise old Omar Kheyam [sic]," occurred in a letter he wrote in 1876.[2] The previous year his good friend the Reverend Joseph H. Twichell, despite being Twain's mainstay of spiritual reassurance in sermons and private conversations, had nevertheless urged him to

Read (if you haven't) the extracts from Omar Khayyam, on the first page of this morning's [Hartford, Connecticut] *Courant*. I think we'll have to get the book. I never yet came across anything that uttered certain thoughts of mine so adequately. And it's only a translation. Read it, and we'll talk it over. . . . Surely this Omar was a great poet. Anyhow, he has given me an immense revelation this morning.[3]

More than anything else this Congregational clergyman's enthusiastic recommendation attests to the evocative and haunting beauty of the ancient poem, which overcame at first blush a Protestant minister's fixed scruples against anything resembling a bleak determinism.

Presumably Mark Twain took the Reverend Twichell's advice about immediately obtaining the book, but in any event it is certain that Twain owned a personal copy of *The Ruba'iyyat* at least by 1884, when he instructed his business manager to order FitzGerald's final edition.[4] Today there is evidence that he and his family eventually possessed (or referred to having read) no fewer than nine different copies of various editions of *The Ruba'iyyat*, indicating that it definitely became a literary touchstone for Twain. The poem so thoroughly engrossed the entire Clemens household that one of the Clemens daughters, Clara, even owned a playful spin-off, *The Ruba'iyyat of a Persian Kitten*,[5] and in 1908 Twain named two of his favorite cats "Omar."[6]

Moreover, Twain's extensive comments about the poem are uniformly praising. One friend, Moncure D. Conway, recalled Twain's citing Stanza 81—"the famous and the bold one beginning: 'O Thou, who man of baser earth did make'—as containing the most far-reaching and grand thought ever expressed in so short a space in so few words." Conway said he was "startled . . . , as I had not associated him with such poetic ideas."[7] The quatrain to which Twain had alluded concerns the respective responsibility of God and man: "Oh Thou, who Man of baser Earth didst make, / And ev'n with Paradise devise the Snake: / For all the Sun wherewith the Face of Man / Is blacken'd—Man's forgiveness give—and take!"[8]

To another correspondent Twain pledged in 1899, "I am bond slave to FitzGerald's Omar."[9] No other single poem received this degree of applause from Twain, who more often played the part of a caustic critic of authors he was reading. The rival translations that followed FitzGerald's masterful rendition, on the other hand, usually did not please Twain's taste. Of Elizabeth Alden Curtis's 1899 effort, *One Hundred Quatrains, from the Ruba'iyyat of Omar Khayyam*, Twain wrote indignantly: "It is the most detailed & minutely circumstantial plagiarism that has yet been perpetrated in any century," denouncing it as a "sacrilege" committed upon "a noble poem." Her translation was "as if a Tammany boss should wreck the Taj [Mahal] & then rebuild it after *his* notions of what it ought to be."[10] Eben Francis Thompson's effort, *The Quatrains of Omar Khayyam of Nishapur*, fared a little better in Twain's estimation, but his secretary reported that Twain objected to its not resembling FitzGerald's translation in all respects, causing him to note facetiously that "Omar had changed his principles."[11] Even reading this less satisfactory version, however, prompted Twain to remark that "the more a disciple gets of Omar the thirstier he becomes."[12]

The supreme and most sincere act of flattery on Twain's part consisted of his effort to construct an imitation of the poem. Since his earliest years as a writer he had manifested an irrepressible urge to affectionately burlesque any literary work he truly admired, whether it be Shakespeare's *Hamlet* or Thomas Malory's *Morte D'Arthur*. Half in earnest, half tongue-in-cheek, then, he began to jot down a series of imitative quatrains, first in his notebook and then on small separate sheets of paper. Probably he was sojourning in Vienna in 1898 when he started this composition. Twain's *AGE—A Rubáiyát* would laboriously follow the stanza and metrical style of FitzGerald's translation, but whereas FitzGerald's version of *The Ruba'iyyat* celebrates youth, Twain's forty-five quatrains contrastingly catalogue and bemoan the ailments and regrets that afflict elderly men. Germs, tooth decay, gum disease, coughing, pneumonia, foot bunions, "disputatious" heirs, alcoholism, red noses, morning aches, incontinence, senility, diminished blood circulation, deafness, sexual impotence, poor eyesight, flatulence, whitened hair, rheumatism—hardly any possible indignity of old age is omitted from his dismal list.

By the time Twain turned to this project, he himself had plenty of cause to express remorse and had become all too familiar with the aches of both body and soul. His beloved daughter Susy had died a few years earlier of spinal meningitis, his daughter Jean was a victim of severe epilepsy, his family's idyllic existence in Hartford, Connecticut, had been shattered by bankruptcy, his financial problems had become worldwide newspaper fodder, his older brother Orion had recently died, and his wife Olivia was weighed down with early symptoms of heart disease. Add to this the fact that Twain himself, now in his mid-sixties, was beginning to feel the effects of aging in an era when the medications available to alleviate gerontic discomforts were relatively few. It is a small wonder that the miseries accompanying aging should suggest themselves to him as a literary topic.

Twain's verses mock the conventional notion of old age as bringing honor and security in one's golden years. But as so often happened with Twain's writings, he had difficulty in deciding whether he was composing a serious lament or a comic spoof. The result is a far cry from the shimmering perfection of Omar Khayyam's adjurations; indeed, about the best that can be said is that Twain's imitation manages to maintain a resemblance to the original. Twain's *Ruba'iyyat* adaptation, like his numerous other poetic attempts, will never be included in any anthology of American poetry; quite clearly his genius lay elsewhere. Still, *AGE—A Rubáiyát* contains passages that exceed what most amateur versifiers could achieve. Here follow nine sample passages from the forty-five quatrains that survive from Twain's abortive poetic experiment.

5

In this subduing Draught of tender green
And kindly Absinth, with its wimpling Sheen
   Of dusky half-lights, let me drown
The haunting Pathos of the Might-Have-Been.

9

Whether one hide in some secluded Nook—
Whether at Liverpool or Sandy Hook—
   'Tis one. Old Age will search him out—and He—
He—He—when ready will know where to look.

11

Think—in this battered Caravanserai,
Whose Portals open stand all Night and Day,
   How Microbe after Microbe with his Pomp
Arrives unasked, and comes to stay.

19

O Voices of the Long Ago that were so dear!
Fall'n Silent, now, for many a Mould'ring Year,
   O whither are ye flown? Come back,
And break my Heart but bless my grieving ear.

20

Some happy Day my Voice will Silent fall,
And answer not when some that love it call:
   Be glad for Me when this you note—and think
I've found the Voices lost, beyond the Pall.

23

O Death, sole Precious Thing in This World's gift,
Behold us in this shabby Life adrift!
   Have Thou our Worship—unto Thee,
Best Friend of Man, our tired Hearts we lift.

34

And those who husbanded their golden Youth,
And those who flung it to the Winds, forsooth
    Must all alike succumb to Age
And know the nip of his remorseless Tooth.

37

The bleary Eyes and then the fumbling Hands
Come next in turn and mark the wasting Sands
    Of that poor Life, a Wreck forlorn,
Dismantled driving toward the Unknown Lands.

45

Rheumatic Gout!—a momentary Taste
Of being dip'd in Hell full to the Waist,—
    And lo, the mortal Misery has reached
The Limit of Endurance—O make Haste![13]

Twain published twenty of his less disturbing quatrains in a humorous sketch titled *My Boyhood Dreams* that appeared in the January 1900 issue of *McClure's Magazine*. These lines exhorted readers to enjoy the pleasures of youth, anticipate the inevitability of old age, and watch for the deplorable signs of decrepitude. The rest of Twain's verses stayed out of print until 1983.

In 1907, summing up what Omar Khayyam's *Ruba'iyyat* had meant to him since he first discovered its appeal in the late 1870s, Twain announced, unreservedly: "No poem had ever given me so much pleasure before, and none has given me so much pleasure since; it is the only poem I have ever carried about with me; it has not been from under my hand for twenty-eight years."[14] Taking into account the evidence that FitzGerald's rendition of Omar Khayyam's poem deeply appealed to Twain in both his halcyon years of family stability, growing fame, and increasing wealth during the 1880s and likewise during his periods of grief and despair in the 1890s and 1900s, the hold this literary work retained on Twain's imagination is truly astounding. Only the Christian Bible had any comparably long-term effect on this changeable and often irascible author.

Notes

1. *The Sufistic Quatrains of Omar Khayyam in Definitive Form, Including the Translations of Edward FitzGerald,* intro. Robert Arnot (New York: M. Walter Dunne, 1903), 75.

2. Henry Nash Smith and William M. Gibson, eds., *Mark Twain-Howells Letters* (Cambridge, MA: Harvard University Press, Belknap Press, 1960), 164. Letter from Clemens to William D. Howells, November 26, 1876.

3. Albert Bigelow Paine, *Mark Twain: A Biography*, 2 vols. (New York: Harper & Brothers, 1912), vol. 1, 615. Paine apparently misdated Twichell's postcard, because in a soon-to-be unpublished note Dwayne Eutsey establishes that the Hartford *Courant* only printed excerpts from *The Ruba'iyyat* on December 22, 1875 ("Twichell Wrote '*Ruba'iyyat* Note' Four Years Earlier Than Previously Thought").

4. Samuel C. Webster, ed., Clemens to Charles L. Webster, May 19, 1884, *Mark Twain, Business Man* (Boston: Little, Brown and Co., 1946), 254.

5. Oliver Herford, *The Ruba'iyyat of a Persian Kitten.*, illus. by the author (New York: Charles Scribner's Sons, 1904). See Alan Gribben, *Mark Twain's Library: A Reconstruction*, 2 vols. (Boston: G. K. Hall & Co., 1980), 310.

6. Clemens to Dorothy Sturgis Harding, October 27, 1908, ALS at Columbia University, photocopy in the Mark Twain Papers, University of California at Berkeley.

7. A. J Arberry. *The Romance of the Ruba'iyyat: Edward FitzGerald's First Edition Reprinted with Introduction and Notes* (London: George Allen & Unwin, 1959), 34.

8. *The Sufistic Quatrains of Omar Khayyam*, 94.

9. Gribben, *Mark Twain's Library*, 516. Clemens to "Dr. Sullivan," November 8, 1899.

10. Ibid., Clemens to Joseph H. Twichell, January 1, 1900. Letter from the Mark Twain Papers, University of California at Berkeley.

11. Ibid., 517. Letter from the Isabel V. Lyon Journals, TS 221, Mark Twain Papers, University of California at Berkeley.

12. Ibid., Clemens to James Logan, February 2, 1907. Letter from the Mark Twain Papers, University of California at Berkeley.

13. Mark Twain, *Mark Twain's Ruba'iyyat*, intro. Alan Gribben. Textual note by Kevin B. MacDonnell (Austin, TX: Jenkins Publishing Co., 1983), 42–52.

14. Gribben, *Mark Twain's Library*, 518. Autobiographical Dictation, October 7, 1907. Quoted from the Mark Twain Papers, University of California at Berkeley.

13

Mark Twain's *Ruba'iyyat*

AGE–A Rubáiyát[1]

Mark Twain

1

Sleep! for the Sun that scores another Day
Against the Tale allotted You to stay,
Reminding You, is Risen, and now
Serves Notice—ah, ignore it while You may!

2

The chill Wind blew, and those who stood before
The Tavern murmured, "Having drunk his Score,
Why tarries He with empty Cup?" Behold,
The Wine of Youth once poured, is poured no more.

3

"Come, leave the Cup, and on the Winter's Snow
Your Summer Garment of Enjoyment throw:
Your Tide of life is ebbing fast, and it
Exhausted once, for You no more shall flow."

4

While yet the Phantom of false Youth was mine,
I heard a Voice from out the Darkness whine

"O Youth, O whither gone?—return,
And bathe my Age in thy reviving Wine."

5

In this subduing Draught of tender green
And kindly Absinth, with its wimpling Sheen
Of dusky half-lights, let me down
The haunting Pathos of the Might-Have-Been.

6

For I was Gay beyond the storied Clam
That at High Tide disports, or Playful Lamb
That happy skips; and foolishly
Rebuff'd Reproach, and did not care a Rap.

7

For every nickled Joy, marred and brief,
We pay some day its Weight in golden Grief
Mined from our Hearts. Ah, murmur not—
From this one-sided Bargain dream of no Relief!

8

The Joy of Life, that streaming through their Veins
Tumultuous swept, falls slack—and wanes
The Glory in the Eye—and one by one
Life's Pleasures perish and make place for Pains.

9

Whether one hide in some secluded Nook—
Whether at Liverpool or Sandy Hook—
'Tis one. Old Age will search him out—and He—
He—He—when ready will know where to look.

10

From Cradle unto Grave I keep a House
Of Entertainment where may drowse

Bacilli and Kindred Germs—or feed—or breed
Their festering Species in a deep Carouse.

11

Think—in this battered Caravanserai,
Whose Portals open stand all Night and Day,
How Microbe after Microbe with his Pomp
Arrives unasked, and comes to stay.

12

Our ivory Teeth, confessing to the Lust
Of masticating, once, now own Disgust
Of clay-plug'd Cavities—full soon our Snags
Are emptied, and our Mouths are filled with Dust.

13

Our Gums forsake the Teeth and tender grow,
And fat, like over-ripened Figs—we know
The sign—the Riggs Disease is ours, and we
Must list this Sorrow, add another Woe;

14

Our Lungs begin to fail and soon we Cough,
And chilly Streaks play up our Backs, and off
Our fever'd Foreheads drips an icy Sweat—
We scoffed before, but now we may not scoff.

15

Some for the Bunions that afflict us prate
Of Plasters unsurpassable, and hate
To cut a Corn—ah cut, and let the Plaster go,
Nor murmur if the Solace come too late.

16

Some for the Honors of Old Age, and some
Long for its Respite from the Hum

  And Clash of sordid Strife—O Fools,
Their Past should teach them what's to Come.

17

  Lo, for the Honors, cold Neglect instead!
   For Respite, disputatious Heirs a Bed
   Of Thorns for them will furnish. Go,
Seek not Here for Peace—but Yonder—with the Dead.

18

  For whether Zal and Rustum heed this Sign,
   And even smitten thus, will not repine,
   Let Zal and Rustum shuffle as they may,
The Fine once levied they must cash the Fine.

19

  O Voices of the Long Ago that were so dear!
Fall'n Silent, now, for many a Mould'ring Year,
   O whither are ye flown? Come back,
And break my Heart but bless my grieving ear.

20

  Some happy Day my Voice will Silent fall,
  And answer not when some that love it call:
Be glad for Me when this you note—and think
  I've found the Voices lost, beyond the Pall.

21

  O sorry Spectacle of fallen Pride
Whom Men compassionate and Gods deride,
You valued Life! Go hide your humbled Head,
  And envy those who in the Cradle died.

22

  So let me grateful drain the Magic Bowl
That medicines hurt Minds and on the Soul

The Healing of its Peace doth lay—if then
Death claim me—Welcome be his Dole!

23

O Death, sole Precious Thing in This World's gift,
Behold us in this shabby Life adrift!
Have Thou our Worship—unto Thee,
Best Friend of Man, our tired Hearts we lift.

24

The Thoughtless—erring—Kings have Happy styled:
It is not true. They are beguiled
And swindled like the rest. There's only One
Whose Life is wholly blest—the Still-Born Child.

25

I sometimes think, indeed that too much Grog
Did all too frequently my Vision clog,
And make my Gait eccentric—and the while
My mental Pharos smothered in a Fog;

26

Along the Earth's Rotundity I reeled,
And swayed and swung my random Way afield
And reached my Home, which round me spun—
I watched this Sight with Wonder unconcealed.

27

There was the Door whereof I had the Key,
The Landlord too, who double seemed to me—
Some heated Talk there was—and then, ah then
But Rags and Fragments were we—Me and He.

28

Along the Earth's Rotundity I reeled
And swayed and swung my random way afield
And reached my Home, which round me spun
I watched it, ah with wonder unconcealed—

29

I sometimes think that never glows so red
A Nose as when, from Age's Sunset shed,
   Upon it fall belated Rays that tell
Of long past Orgies of a Prime that's fled.

30

Into this Bawdy House, and *Why*, well knowing,
But *Whence*, for Wisdom's sake not showing,
   And out of it, the Wine exalting me,
I knew not *Whither*, windy went, a-blowing.

31

Myself when young did eagerly frequent
Some shady Houses, and heard Argument
   About It, and about: by evermore
I liked It well, and often in I went.

32

And there the Seed of Prudence did I sow
And with mine own Purse tried to make it grow,
   And this was all the Harvest that I reap'd:
I ordered Water, but Champagne did flow.

33

And so, in time,—this being noticed long
Ere I had noticed it myself—a Wrong
   To my Good Name was done; and thus
I Sold my Reputation for a Song;

34

And those who husbanded their golden Youth,
And those who flung it to the Winds, forsooth
   Must all alike succumb to Age
And know the nip of his remorseless Tooth.

35

Each morn a thousand Mis'ries brings, rebel
And curse we as we may. Ah, well,
It still leaves those acquired before—how then
Is Old Age better than the threaten'd Hell?

36

Ah, now in Age a feeble stream we Piss,
And maunder feebly over That and This,
Thinking we Think—alas, we do but Dream—
And wonder why our Moonings go amiss.

37

The bleary Eyes and then the fumbling Hands
Come next in turn and mark the wasting Sands
Of that poor Life, a Wreck forlorn,
Dismantled driving toward the Unknown Lands.

38

The Legs Refusing further Duty, now
In lazy Bath Chair let the Old Man plow
Adroop and dozing up and down
The Sunny Side and warm his frosty Pow.

39

Next, Deafness comes, and men must Shout
Into a foolish Trumpet, leaving out
The Gist of what they want to say—and still
O'er what they *have* said hangs a crippling Doubt.

40

We talk of *It*, and in the faded Eye
By fitful Glimmers flashes Lechery:
Then Each his Face unto his Wall doth turn,
And some do moan, and some do softly sigh,

41

Rebuilding Vanished Days—with films from Spain
When Flowers hid betwixt the Crotch did fain
   Deflowering hold a happy thing to hap,
    And with it cut—ah, cut and come again!

42

Some, being Fools and young, for Old Age hope,
Holding Life a "Boon" if they must even grope
   Blind and poor and weak at 'tother End, —
    wer't e'en the End that terminates a Rope!

43

Our Sphincters growing lax in their dear Art,
Their Grip relinquishing in whole or part,
   We fall a Prey to Confidence Misplaced,
    And Fart in places where we should not Fart.

44

They say that He who dyed his Hair and wrought
To Keep his youth by Falsities, and brought
   Sham Calves and such—why, that Wild Ass!
    The Lizard dances on his grave—and ought.

45

   Rheumatic Gout!—a momentary Taste
Of being dip'd in Hell full to the Waist,—
   And lo, the mortal Misery has reached
    The Limit of Endurance—O make Haste!

The Late Empress

For many years she has wandered
Europe under the concealment of a minor title,
   as Halley's comet might wander the

skies under the concealment of a fictitious name.
Private hurt—not sane.
An Optimist is a person under 45.
A Pessimist is a sane person over it.
Newspaper is telephone which brings
daily the cries of the human race to your ear.
Life is 50 times the affliction it was 50 yrs ago—
in certain particulars. But it was always a burden.
We are all asses—the K on this throne and
We are all insane, but in different ways.
Jetzt ist die arme Kairserin in de Heimat.

[On another sheet:]

spiritualized
when made remote
for by some subtle law.
Lost? They have gained; all tragic human experiences
gain in pathos by the perspective of time. We realize
this when in Naples we must over the poor Pompeeian
mother, lost in the historic storm of volcanic ashes
18 centuries ago, who lies with her child gripped close
to her breast, trying to save it, and whose despair
and grief have been eternalized by the fiery envelop which
took her life but kept eternal her form and her features.

She moves us, she haunts us, she stays in our thoughts
for many days, we do not know why, for she is nothing
to us, she has been nothing to anyone for 18 centuries;
whereas of the like case to-day we should say "poor thing,
it is pitiful," and forget it in an hour.

stand musing

[The following draft of Twain's eighth quatrain appears
in pencil on the verso of the leaf containing Stanza 5:]

The joy of Life, that streaming thro' their Veins
Tumultuous swept, falls slack—and wanes
The glory in the eye; and one by one
Life's pleasures perish and make place for pains

Note

1. Mark Twain, *Mark Twain's Ruba'iyyat*, intro. Alan Gribben, textual note by Kevin B. MacDonnell (Austin, TX: Jenkins Publishing Co., 1983), 41–56. Reproduced courtesy of the University of California Press.

Glossary

Akhlaq-i Jalali: Written by Jalal al-Din al-Dawani (1426–1502 AD), this treatise deals primarily with ethics and politics and includes a description of the perfect ruler.

Al-Insan Al-Kamil: Arabic phrase meaning "Perfect Man," was first used by Abd al-Qadir al-Jilani. Often identified with Prophet Muhammad or Imam Ali, it has been used to refer to the prototype of a Sufi master.

Arabian Nights: Also known as *One Thousand and One Nights* and dated as early as the tenth century, the text is composed of stories and folk tales centered on the narrator Shahrzad. After its translation into various Western languages, it contributed to the exoticized image of the Orient in the West.

Averroes/Ibn Rushd (1126–1198 AD): A twelfth-century Andalusian polymath who attempted to interpret and integrate Aristotelian philosophy into the Islamic intellectual tradition in order to reconcile faith and religion. His works cover a wide array of topics but he is primarily known as "the interpreter" of Aristotle, and a bridge through whom Aristotelian philosophy was transmitted to Europe. Some scholars believe that his influential emphasis on rationalism contributed to the rise of the Renaissance in Europe.

Avicenna/Ibn Sina (980–1037 AD): A Persian philosopher, he was the grand master of Islamic philosophy who established the foundation of Peripatetic philosophy (*mashsha'i*). His work synthesizes philosophers such as Plato and Aristotle, while incorporating Neoplatonism and Islamic intellectual traditions. He wrote what is considered the most important medical textbook of the medieval period, *The Canon of Medicine*, and several monumental encyclopedic works on philosophy, metaphysics and logic.

Bhagavad Gita: Described by some as the "Hindu Bible," this sacred Hindu scripture thought to be composed between the fifth and second centuries BCE. The text contains the essential doctrines of Hinduism and discusses Hindu metaphysics, ethics and mysticism.

Brook Farm: An experimental utopian community established in 1841 to facilitate the works of Transcendentalist artists and writers in an environment of simplicity and equality. It was deemed unsuccessful and closed in 1847.

carpe diem: From the Latin *capere* ("to seize") and *die* ("day"). The term originated with the lyric poet Horace and refers to the idea of living in the moment. It was a common theme in Sufism that referred to Sufi metaphysics, but the Transcendentalists somewhat erroneously understood it thematically in the spirit of the Romanticism.

Code of Manu, The: An early and integral text of Hinduism, said to have been written between 200 BCE and 200 AD *The Code* is structured as a frame story of Bhrigu, Manu's disciple, telling his own students the teachings of Brahma that have been passed down to him through a sacred lineage. The code sets forth rules about the four social classes, judiciary proceedings, and a brief cosmography.

Corbin, Henry (1903–1978 AD): A French philosopher and theologian whose encounter with Suhrawardi's School of Illumination inspired him to study and introduce Islamic philosophers to the Western academic community.

Firdawsi (Ferdawsi) (935–1020 AD): A Persian poet whose monumental work, *Shah-Nameh* consists of several hundred thousand verses of poetry on Persian mythology. He has been compared to Homer and is considered to have been the father of Persian nationalism since his work preserved a sense of Persian identity during a period of increased Arabic influence.

Ghazal: A poetic form characterized by rhyming couplets, a refrain, and a consistent meter throughout. Using allegory and symbolism, the form of the *ghazal* is often associated with poems expressing the pain or loss of love.

Gulistan: Literally meaning "flower garden," this collection of poems and stories was written in the thirteenth century by the Persian poet Sa'di. Widely quoted as a source of wisdom, the book primarily contains didactic aphorisms and offers advice on a variety of quotidian subjects.

Hafiz (Hafez) (c. 1320–c. 1388 AD): Hafiz and his poetry are considered supreme in the realm of Persian literature. Elevated almost to the level of sacred scripture, his *ghazals* are characterized by a romantic sense of the spiritual, incorporating themes of devotion to the Beloved. His extensive use of such imagery as wine, women, and love-making are deeply rooted in Sufi metaphysics and metaphor; these topics were initially taken literally by the English Romantics and later by American Transcendentalists. One of the outstanding features of Hafiz's *ghazals* is Divine Love and Unity, a theme reflected in much of his poetry that was written in the last decade of his life.

Hermeticism: This school of thought emerged in Late Antiquity, utilizing a variety of Greek, Egyptian, and Near Eastern elements to create a philosophical and religious system. The movement owes much to the large body of Hermitico–Pythagorean literature, which greatly influenced Western esoteric traditions during the Renaissance and Reformation.

Jones, Sir William (1746–1794): An English philologist credited with creating the field of comparative linguistics as a result of his discovery of a proto-Indo–European language while attempting to trace the roots of Sanskrit. His translations of Indian and Oriental texts into English, including the poetry of Hafiz, became highly influential for later Romantic and Transcendentalist writers.

Neoplatonism: A philosophical school of thought founded by Plotinus that flourished in Greece primarily from the third to the seventh centuries. Plotinus, in his major work *Enneads,* provided a philosophical scheme to bring about a rapprochement between metaphysics, ontology, ethics and theology. For centuries, Muslim philosophers and theologians thought *Enneads* was the lost work of Aristotle on theology.

Occident: A term used to distinguish those parts of Western Europe with roots in the Roman Empire from the Asian countries and cultures of the "east." Most often used in a literary context juxtaposed with the term "Orient."

Omar Khayyam (1048–1129 AD): An Iranian poet and polymath most famous for his *Ruba'iyyat,* a collection of poems written in quatrains. His popularity as a poet often overshadows his prolific contributions to various fields of science, including algebra, astronomy, non-Euclidian geometry and calendar reform.

Orientalism: A generalized term referring to the use of images or aspects of "eastern" culture in the work of Western artists and writers, particularly those that associate the East with themes of exoticism and sensuality. Once a form of artistic inspiration, it has since become associated with the stereotyping of Eastern, particularly Islamic, cultures.

Perennialism: A philosophical-religious school of thought that posits the existence of a universal truth that lies at the heart of all the divinely revealed religions. This theory in the modern era is used extensively as a model to account for the sameness and diversity of world religions.

Plotinus (204/5–270 AD): The founder of Neoplatonism whose work *Enneads* was compiled by his student Porphyry. The collection of lectures and debates proved immensely influential to philosophers in the Jewish, Christian and

Muslim traditions throughout the medieval period. His theory of emanation, for instance, offered an alternative to the doctrine of creation *ex nihilo*.

Romanticism: A literary movement spanning the eighteenth and nineteenth centuries that emphasized knowledge of oneself as gained through experiencing nature. The movement also notably drew inspiration from a sense of perceived exoticism from eastern cultures and literature. In turn, the American Transcendentalists of the late nineteenth century drew heavily from Romantic themes.

Rumi (1207–1273 AD): Perhaps the most well-known Persian Sufi poet, he is often regarded as the "poet of love." Rumi's encyclopedic works of poetry provide a remarkable commentary on Sufi and gnostic doctrine in Islam. His poetry advocates tolerance, love, and the universal nature of truth at the heart of all religions.

Sa'di (1184–c. 1283 AD): A Persian poet whose poems show equal mastery of the spiritual and mundane aspects of life, as well as a supreme consciousness of the mutability of human experience. He masterfully utilized poetic forms ranging from the lyric to the ode, and was noted for the humor in his work.

Shah-Nameh: Literally meaning *The Book of Kings*, this monumental epic by Ferdawsi (Firdawsi) offers three hundred thousand verses of poetry that incorporate Persian mythology, cosmography, a mythography, and a historiography. Having spent over thirty years composing this work, Ferdawsi traces the history of Greater Persia from the creation of the world through the heroic age that culminated in Alexander the Great, concluding with the Arab conquest of Persia in the seventh century. The work proved pivotal to the revival of Persian as a spoken language and to the preservation of Zoroastrian legacy in Persia.

Shiraz: A city in the southwest of Iran, notable for its status as a creative hub for poets and writers including Sa'di and Hafiz.

***sirr*:** An inner mystery, usually of an esoteric nature.

Spring: A common symbol of poetic inspiration often identified as a metaphor for spiritual rejuvenation.

Sufism: A tradition that emphasizes the esoteric and mystical dimension of Islam. Sufism highlights asceticism, purification of self, and esoteric knowledge of God as means of achieving Divine Unity. Practitioners of Sufism or Islamic mysticism can be found throughout the Islamic world today.

Swedenborgianism: Also called the "New Church." The religious movement, created by Emanuel Swedenborg during the eighteenth century, became popular during the nineteenth century because of its associations with mysticism, the occult, and alchemy.

Tamerlane (1336–1405 AD): A military leader whose armies conquered much of Western and Central Asia during the fourteenth century, including Persia and the Ottoman Empire.

***Vedas*:** Literally the "Books of Knowledge" in Sanskrit, these works are considered to be the oldest of sacred texts, dating as far back as the middle of the second millennium BCE. The four main Vedic texts govern the priestly performance of rituals, hymns, and sacrifices. Their divine revelation is disputed among Indian philosophies, only some of whom accept the texts as spiritual authority.

***Wahdat al-Wujud*:** The doctrine of the "Unity of Being," often attributed to Ibn 'Arabi, provides the basis for Islamic gnostic perspective that proposes all things are God but God is not all things.

Wine: The use of wine in Sufi Literature is often symbolic, rather than literal gesture of partaking in a sense of divine ecstasy through intoxication. Thematically, wine appears in most Sufi poetry and prose.

***Zend Avesta*:** The sacred text of Zoroastrianism, written in the Avestan language at an unknown date and allegedly containing writings by Zoroaster himself. Though the initial date of composition was several millennia BCE, the text was expanded and altered well into the fourth century AD.

Zoroastrianism: A religion based on the teachings of the ancient Persian Prophet, Zoroaster (Zartusht), whose major tenets included good thoughts, deeds and words. Monotheistic and dualist interpretations of the Zoroastrian religion exist, but both emphasize spiritual and physical purity.

Selected Bibliography

'Amili, Baha' al-Din Muhammad *Kulliyat-i ash'ar va athar-i farsi Shaykh Baha'i*, ed. 'Ali Katibi. Tehran: Nashr-i Chakama, n.d., 348.
Aminrazavi, Mehdi. *The Wine of Wisdom: The Life, Poetry and Philosophy of Omar Khayyam*. London: ONEWORLD Press, 2005.
Abrams, M. H. *Natural Supernaturalism: Tradition and Revolution in Romantic Literature*. New York: Norton & Co, 1971.
Ahmad, M. J. *Persian Poetry and the English Reader from the Eighteenth to the Twentieth Century*. University of Newcastle, 1971.
Al-Da'mi, Muhammed, and Daniel Walton. *Arabian Mirrors and Western Soothsayers*. New York: Peter Lang, 2002.
Aldrich, Thomas Baily. "A Persian Poet," in *Atlantic Monthly*, no. 41(1878), 421–26.
Alger, William R. *Poetry of the Orient*. Boston: Roberts Bros., 1865.
———. *The Poetry of the East*. Boston: Whittemore, Niles, and Hall, 1856.
Allen, George. *Walt Whitman Handbook*. New York: New York University Press, 1962.
———. *A Reader's Guide to Walt Whitman*. New York: Farrar, Straus, & Giroux, 1970.
———. *Walt Whitman Handbook*. Chicago: Packard & Co., 1946.
Ansari, M. Abd'l-Haq "The Doctrine of One Actor: Junayd's View of *Tawhid*," in *The Muslim World*, (1983), 45.
Arberry, A. John. *Hafiz, Fifty Poems*. Cambridge: Cambridge University Press, 1970.
———. *The Romance of the Rubaiyat*. 1st ed., trans. FitzGerald. London: G. Allen & Unwin, 1959.
———. *Persian Poems*. London: Everyman's Library, 1954.
'Attar, Farid al-Din. *Divan*, ed. T. Tafadduli, 3rd ed., Tehran: Markaz-i Intisharat-i 'Ilmi va Farhangi 1362 A.Hs./1983.
———. *The Conference of the Birds*. New York: Oxford University Press, 1924.
Austin, Ralph. "The Sophianic Feminine in the Work of Ibn 'Arabi and Rumi," in *The Heritage of Sufism*, vol. 2: *The Legacy of Mediæval Persian Sufism*, ed. L. Lewisohn. Oxford: ONEWORLD, 1999.
Barrow, S. J. "Editions Note Book," in *Unitarian Review and Religious Magazine*, no. 11 (1879), 384–86.
Barth, Robert. "Theological Implications of Coleridge's Theory of Imagination," in *Coleridge's Theory of Imagination Today*, ed. Christine Gallant. New York: AMS Press, 1989.
Benton, Joel. *Emerson as a Poet*. New York; M. F. Mansfield & A. Wessels, 1833.
Bergman, Jay. "Neoplatonism and American Aesthetics," in *Neoplatonism and Western Aesthetics*, ed. Aphrodite Alexandrakis and Nicholas Moutakfakis. Albany, NY: SUNY, 2002.

Bey, Hakim. *Temporary Autonomous Zones*. New York: Autonomedia, 1998 edition.
Bisland, Elizabeth. *The Life and Letters of Lafcadio Hearn*. 2 vols., Boston: Houghton Mifflin, 1906.
Blackstone, Bernard. "Byron and Islam: the triple Eros," in *Journal of European Studies* 4 (1974), 325–363.
Blodgett, Harold, and Bradley, Sculley. eds., *Leaves of Grass*. Chicago: 1946.
Bly, Robert, and Leonard Lewisohn. *The Wine Made Before Adam*. New York: HarperCollins, 2008.
Booth, Stephen. *Shakespeare's Sonnets: Edited with an Analytic Commentary*. New Haven, CT: Yale University Press, 2000.
Bralove, Jacquelyn. "The Mirror in Sufi Poetry," in *Sufi*, 20 (1993), 29–32.
Brinton, Crane. "Romanticism," in *Encyclopedia of Philosophy*, ed. Donald Borchert, 2nd ed,, 488. Farmington, MI: Thomson/Gale, 2006.
Broad, Charlie. "The Philosophy of Omar Khayyam and Its Relation to that of Schopenhauer," in *Review*, no. CLXVI (November 1906), 544–556.
Browne, Edward G. *A Literary History of Persia*. Cambridge, UK: Routledge, 1928.
Buell, Lawrence. *Emerson*. Cambridge, MA and London: Belknap Press, 2004.
Burckhardt, Titus. *Mirror of the Intellect*, trans. William Stoddart. United Kingdom: Quenta Essentia, 1987.
Bürgel, J. Christopher. *The Feather of Simurgh: the "Licit" Magic of the Arts in Medieval Islam*. New York: NYU Press, 1988.
Burrage, Charles, ed. *Some Doings of the Omar Khayyam Club of America*. Boston, 1922.
Butler, Mariyn. "Romanticism in England," in *Romanticism in National Context*, ed. Roy Porter, Mikulás. Cambridge, MA: Cambridge University Press, 1988.
Cameron, Kenneth W. *Ralph Waldo Emerson's Reading*. New York: Haskell House, 1941.
———. *The Transcendentalists and Minerva*. Hartford, CT: Transcendental Books, 1958.
———. *Emerson's Early Reading List 1819–1824*. New York: New York Public Library, 1951.
Carpenter, Frederic I. *Emerson and Asia*. Cambridge, MA: Harvard University Press, 1930.
———. *Emerson Handbook*. New York: Hendricks House, 1953.
Channing, William E. *Thoreau the Poet-Naturalist*. Boston: Goodspeed, 1902.
Chari, V. Krishna. *Whitman in the Light of Vedantic Mysticism: an Interpretation*. Lincoln, NE: University of Nebraska Press, 1964.
Chase, Richard. *Walt Whitman Reconsidered*. New York: William Sloane Associates, 1955. Reprinted in C. Feidelson, Jr., and Paul Brodtkorb, Jr., eds., *Interpretations of American Literature*, New York: Oxford University Press, 1959.
Cheetham, Tom. *The World Turned Inside Out: Henry Corbin and Islamic Mysticism*. Woodstock, CT: Spring Journal Books 2003, ch. 4.
Chesterton, G. Keith. *Heretics*. London, 1906.
Chittick, C. William. "The World of Imagination and Poetic Imagery according to Ibn 'Arabi," in *Temenos*, X (1989), 98–119.
Chodzko, Aleksander. *Specimen of the Popular Poetry of Persia*. London, 1842.
Christy, Arthur. "Emerson's Debt to the Orient," in *The Monist*, 38 (Jan. 1928), 44.
———. "Orientalism in New England: Whittier," in *American Literature*, I (January 1930).
———. *The Orient in American Transcendentalism: A Study of Emerson, Thoreau, and Alcott*. New York: Columbia University Press, 1932.

———. *The Asian Legacy and American Life.* New York: The John Day Co., 1945.
Clarke, James Freeman, and L. Clarke. *Exotics: An attempt to Domesticate Them.* Boston: Houghton Mifflin, 1875, 1876.
Coleridge, Samuel Taylor. *The Poetical Works of Samuel Taylor Coleridge,* ed. Ernest Hartley Coleridge, London: Oxford University Press, 1912.
———. *Biographia Literaria: or Biographical Sketches of My Literary Life and Opinions,* ed. George Watson. London: Everyman, 1975.
Conway, M. Daniel. "Transcendentalists of Concord," in *Eclectic Magazine* 63, no. 2 (October 1864), 231–248.
———. "Walt Whitman," In *Fortnightly Review,* VI (Oct. 15, 1866).
———. *Sacred Anthology (Oriental): a Book of Ethical Scripture.* 5th ed. New York: Henry Holt, 1877.
Corbin, Henry. *Creative Imagination in the Sufism of Ibn 'Arabi.* Princeton, NJ: Princeton University Press, 1969.
———. *Avicenna and the Visionary Recital.* Trans. Willard R. Trask. Dallas: University of Dallas, 1980.
———. "Traditional Knowledge and Spiritual Renaissance," trans. Kathleen Raine, *Temenos Academy Review,* I, (1998), 37–38.
Costello, Louisa S., ed. and trans., *The Rose Garden of Persia.* London: Longman, Brown, Green, & Longmans, 1845.
———. "The Rose Garden of Persia," in *Westminster Review* (July 1847), 145–63.
Cowell, E. Byles. "Hafiz, the Persian Poet," in *Fraser's Magazine,* L, 288 ff (September 1854).
Curtis, George William. *Letters: George William Curtis to John S. Dwight,* ed. G. W. Cooke. New York: Harper & Brothers, 1893.
———. *The Howadji in Syria.* New York: Harper and Brothers, 1856.
D'Amrrosio, V. Marie. *Eliot Possessed: T. S. Eliot and FitzGerald's RUBAIYAT.* New York: New York University Press, 1989.
De Sacy, Silvestre. *Exposé de la Religion des Druzes.* Paris: L'Imprimerie Royale, 1838.
Deveney, John Patrick. *Paschal Beverly Randolph: A Nineteenth-Century Black American Spiritualist, Rosicrucian, and Sex Magician.* Albany, NY: SUNY Press, 1997.
Divan-i Hakim Abu'l-Majdud ibn Adam Sana'i Ghaznavi, ed. Mudarris Razavi. Tehran: Sana'i Press, 1362 A.Hsh./1983.
Duperron, Anquetil. *Zendavesta, Ouvrage de Zorostre.* Paris: Tilliard, 1771.
Elder, Marjorie. *Nathaniel Hawthorne: Transcendental Symbolist.* Cleveland: Ohio University Press, 1969.
Ellis, Havelock. "Sexual Inversion," in his *Studies in the Psychology of Sex.* 2 vols. New York: Random House, 1942.
Emerson, Edward Waldo. *Emerson in Concord.* Cambridge, MA: The Riverside Press, 1889.
Emerson, Ralph Waldo. *The Poems.* Boston: Munroe, 1847.
———. "Persian Poetry," in *The Atlantic Monthly,* vol. 1 (April 1858), 724–34.
———. "Preface" to *The Gulistan Or Rose Garden by Musle-Huddeen Saadi of Shiraz,* trans. Francis Gladwin. Boston, 1865.
———. *The Complete Prose Works of Ralph Waldo Emerson, With a Critical Introduction.* London: Ward, Lock, and Bowden, 1889.
———. *The Complete Works of Ralph Waldo Emerson,* ed. E. W. Emerson, Boston: Houghton Mifflin & Co., 1903–1912.

———. *The Journals of Ralph Waldo Emerson with Annotations*. ed. E. W. Emerson and W. E. Forbes, 10 vols. Boston: Riverside Press, 1909–1914.

———. *Uncollected Lectures*, ed. Clarence Gohdes. New York: William E. Rudge, 1932.

———. *The Letters of Ralph Waldo Emerson*, 6 vols., ed. Ralph L. Rusk. New York: Columbia University Press, 1939.

———. *The Collected Works of Ralph Waldo Emerson*, ed. Robert E. Spiller, et al. Cambridge, MA: Harvard University Press, 1971.

———. *Ralph Waldo Emerson: Essays and Lectures*, ed. Joel Porte. New York: Library of America, 1983.

Farzan, Massud. "Whitman and Sufism: Towards a 'Persian Lesson,'" in *American Literature* (January 1976), 572–582.

Finkelstein, Dorothee M. *Melville's Orienda*. New Haven, CT: Yale University Press, 1961.

Firdausi. *Shah Nameh*, trans. James Atkinson. London: Oriental Translation Fund, 1832.

FitzGerald, Edward. *Rubaiyat of Omar Khayyam and the Soloman and Absal of Jami*. (London, n.d.).

Fuller, Margaret. "Leila," in *The Dial* (April 1841), 462.

Fuller, Margaret. *The Letters of Margaret Fuller*, ed. Robert N. Hudspeth. Ithaca, NY: Cornell University Press, 1965.

Gohdes, Clarence. *The Periodicals of American Transcendentalism*. Durham, NC: Duke University Press, 1931.

Gomez, Michael. *Black Crescent: The Experience and Legacy of African American Muslims in the Americas*. Cambridge, MA: Cambridge University Press, 2005.

Gosse, Edmund. *Critical Kit-Kats*. London: William Heinemann, 1895.

Gribben, Alan, and Kevin MacDonnell. *Mark Twain's Rubaiyat*. Austin, TX: Jenkins Publishing Co., 1983.

———. *Mark Twain's Library: A Reconstruction*, 2 vols. Boston: G. K. Hall & Co., 1980.

Gulshan-i raz in *Majmu'a-yi athar-i Shaykh Mahmud Shabistari*, ed. H. Muwahid. Tehran: Kitabkhanayi Tahuri, 1986.

Hafiz, *Diwan*, ed. P. N. Khanlari. Tehran: Khawarazmi Press, 1359 A.Hsh./1980.

Hafiz-namah: sharh-i alfaz, i'lam, mafahim-i kilidi va abyat-i dushvar-i Hafiz. Tehran: Intisharat-i Surush 1372 A.Hsh./1993.

Hanegraaf, Wouter J. "Romanticism and the Esoteric Connection," in *Gnosis and Hermeticism from Antiquity to Modern Times*, ed. Roelof van den Broek and Wouter J. Hanegraaf. Albany, NY: SUNY Press, 1998.

Haravi, 'Ali Husayn. *Sharh-i ghazalha-yi Hafiz*. Tehran: Nashr-i Nu, 1367 A.Hsh./1988.

Harris, Thomas Lake. *The Millennial Age: Twelve Discourses on the Spiritual and Social Aspects of the Times*. New York: New Church, 1860.

Harrison, John Smith. *The Teachers of Emerson*. New York: Sturgis & Walton Co., 1910.

Hastie, William. *Festival of Spring*, from the Divan of Jelaledin. Glasgow: James MacLehose and Sons, 1903.

Hawthorne, Julian. *Hawthorne Reading*. Cleveland: The Folcroft Press, 1902.

Hawthorne, Nathaniel. "Letter to George William Curtis," in *Lenox* (29 April 1851).

Hay, John. *In Praise of Omar*. Lecture at the Omar Khayyam Club. Portland, OR, 1897.

Hearn, Lafcadio. *Essays in European and Oriental Literature*. New York: Dodd, Mead and Co., 1923.

Herford, Oliver. *The Rubaiyat of a Persian Kitten*, illustrated by the author. New York: Charles Scribner's Sons, 1904.

Heron-Allan, E. *Rubaiyat of 'Umar Khayyam*. London: 1908.

Hodgson, Marshall G. S. *The Venture of Islam*. Chicago: University of Chicago Press, 1974.

Holland, Bernard. "The Popularity of Omar," in *National Review*, XXXIII (June, 1899).

Holloway, Emory, ed. *Uncollected Poetry and Prose of Walt Whitman*. New York: P. Smith, 1921.

Holmes, Richard. *Shelley: the Pursuit*. London: Flamingo, 1995.

Huda, Qamar'ul. "Reflections on Muslim Ascetics and Mystics: Sufi Theories of Annihilation and Subsistence," in *JUSUR: The UCLA Journal of Middle Eastern Studies*, 12 (1996), 17–35.

Human, Mahmud. *Hafiz cha miguyid*. Teheran: 1938 (in Persian).

Husayn Ilahi-Qumsha'i, *Dar qalamru-yi zarrin: 365 ruz ba adabiyat-i inglisi*. Tehran: Sukhan 1386/2007.

Ibn Arabi, *Fusus al-hikam* 'Affifi, Abu'l-'Ala, ed. 2 vols., Cairo: 1365/1946.

'Iraqi, Fakhruddin. *Divine Flashes*, trans. William Chittick and Peter Wilson. London: SPCK, 1982.

Jackson, Carl T. "The Orient in Post-Bellum American Thought," in *American Quarterly* 22 (Spring 1970).

Jahanpour, Farhang. "Western Encounters with Persian Sufi Literature," in *The Heritage of Sufism: Late Classical Persianate Sufism: the Safavid and Mughal Period*, ed. L. Lewisohn and D. Morgan. Oxford: ONEWORLD, 1999.

———. "Oriental Influences on the Work of Ralph Waldo Emerson." England: University of Hull, June 1965.

Javadi, Hasan. "Persian Literary Influence on English Literature," in *Indo-Iranica*, XXVI/1 (1973), 22.

Johnson, Samuel. *Oriental Religions and Their Relations to Universal Religions*. Boston: Houghton Mifflin, 1885.

Kader, A. H. Abdel. *The Life, Personality and Writings of al-Junayd*. London: E. J. W. Gibb Memorial Series, NS, 1962.

Keeler, Annebel. *Sufi Hermeneutics: The Qur'an Commentary of Rashid al-Din Maybudi*. Oxford: OUP, 2006.

Keene, H. George. "Omar Khayyam," in Nathan Haskell Dole, *Rubaiyat of Omar Khayyam*. Boston: 1891.

Khayyam, Omar. *The Rubaiyat of Omar Khayyam*, trans. Edward FitzGerald. New York: Walter J. Black, 1942.

———. *The Sufistic Quatrains of Omar Khayyam in Definitive Form, Including the Translations of Edward FitzGerald*. Introduction by Robert Arnot. New York: M. Walter Dunne, 1903.

Kinniburgh, Annie. *The Sufi Doctrine of Love as Political Prophecy: Islamic Mysticism in Percy Shelley's* Queen Mab *and Walt Whitman's "Song of Myself."* MA Thesis, University of Virginia, 2012.

Koyré, Alexandre. *Mystiques, Spirituels, Alchimistes due XVIème siècle allemande*. Paris: Librarie Armand Colin, 1955.

Le Gallienne, Richard. "Fin de Siecle Cult of FitzGerald's *Ruba'iyat* of Omar Khayyam," in *Review of National Literature*, 2 (1971).

———. *Omar Repentant*. New York: Mitchell Kennerley, 1908.
Lewisohn, Leonard. "Sufism and the School of Isfahan: *Tasawwuf* and *'Irfan* in Late Safavid Iran" 'Abd al-Razzaq Lahiji and Fayz-i Kashani on the Relation of *Tasawwuf, hikmat* and *'Irfan*," in L. Lewisohn and D. Morgan, eds., *The Heritage of Sufism*, vol. III: *Late Classical Persianate Sufism: The Safavid and Mughal Period*. Oxford: ONEWORLD, 1999.
———. *Beyond Faith and Infidelity: the Sufi Poetry and Teachings of Mahmud Shabistari*. London: Curzon Press, 1995.
Lipsey, Roger. "Notes on the Philosophy of Persian Art," in *Coomaraswamy: Selected Papers, Traditional Art and Symbolism*, vol. I, 261–62. Princeton, NJ: Princeton University Press, 1977.
Loloi, Parvin. "Tennyson, Fitzgerald, and Cowell: A Private Relationship with Public Consequences," in *Private and Public Voices in Victorian Poetry*, ed. Sabine Coelsch-Foisner, Holger Klein. Tübingen: Stauffenburg Verlag, 2000.
———. *Hafiz, Master of Persian Poetry: A Critical Bibliography; English Translations since the Eighteenth Century*. London: I. B. Tauris, 2004.
Longfellow, H. Wadsworth. *The Complete Poetical Works of Henry Wadsworth Longfellow*, ed. Horace E. Scudder. Boston: Houghton Mifflin, 1893.
———. *The Leap of Roushan Beg*. Facsimile of the original manuscript, ed. Arthur Christy. New York: William Rudge, 1931.
Life of Henry Wadsworth Longfellow, ed. Samuel Longfellow. Cambridge: Houghton Mifflin Co., 1896.
Lopez-Baralt, Luce. *Islam in Spanish Literature: from the Middle Ages to the Present*. Trans. Andrew Hurley. Leiden: Brill, 1992.
Lowell, James Russell. *Letters of James Russell Lowell*, ed. Charles E. Norton. New York: Harper, 1894.
Lyde, Rev. Samuel. *The Anseyreeh and Ismaeleh: A Visit to the Secret Sects of Northern Syria*. London: Hurst & Blackett, 1853.
Mansfield, Luther S. "The Emersonian Idiom and The Romantic Period in American Literature," in *Romanticism and the American Renaissance*, ed. Kenneth Walter Cameron. Hartford: 1977.
Marvin, Frederick R. *Poems and Translations*. Boston: Sherman, French & Co., 1914.
———. *The Companionship of Books*. New York: Putnam's Sons, 1906.
Melville, Herman. *The Confidence Man*. New York: Grove Press, 1949.
———. *The Letters of Herman Melville*, ed. Merrell R. Davis and William H. Gilman. New Haven, CT: Yale University Press, 1960.
———. *The Works of Herman Melville*, standard ed. New York: Russell and Russell, 1963.
Menocal, Maria Rosa. *Shards of Love: Exile and the Origins of the Lyric*. Durham, NC: Duke University Press, 1994.
Meynell, Willfred. "The Cause of Omar's Popularity." *Academy*, no. LXVI (March 1904), 274.
Miller, A. Henry. "The Omar Cult," in *Academy*, no. 59 (1900), 55.
Miller, James, Karl Shapiro, and Bernice Slote. *Start With the Sun: Studies in Cosmic Poetry*. Lincoln, NE: University of Nebraska Press, 1960.
Miller, James. *T. S. Eliot's Personal Waste Land: Exorcism of the Demons*. University Park, PA: Penn State Press, 1977.

Mills, Charles D. B. *Pebbles, Pearls and Gems of the Orient*. Boston: G. H. Ellis, 1882.
Mitchell, David. "Nature as Theophany," in *Temenos: A Journal Devoted to the Arts of the Imagination*, VII (1986), 95–114.
Musle-Huddeen Shaik Sady of Sheeraz. *The Gulistan or Rose-Garden*. Trans. Frances Gladwin. London: Kingsbury, Parbury & Allen, 1822.
Nasr, Seyyed Hossein. "Principial Knowledge and the Multiplicity of Sacred Forms," in *Knowledge and the Sacred*. Albany, NY: SUNY, 1989, 280–308.
———. *The Encounter of Man and Nature; The Spiritual Crisis of Modern Man*. London: George Allen and Unwin, 1968.
Nicholson, Rynold. *Rumi, Poet and Mystic*. London: G. Allen and Unwin, 1950.
Nizami, Khaliq Ahmad. *Akbar and Religion*. Dehli: Idarah-yi Adabiyat-i-Dehli, 1989.
Norton, Charles E. "Nicolas's Quatrains de Kheyam," in *North American Review*, no. 225 (1869), 565–566.
Notopoulos, James A. *The Platonism of Shelley: A Study of Platonism and the Poetic Mind*. Durham, NC: Duke University Press, 1949.
Nurbakhsh, Javad. *Spiritual Poverty in Sufism*, trans. Leonard Lewisohn. London: KNP, 1984.
———. *Sufi Symbolism: The Nurbakhsh Encyclopedia of Sufi Terminology*, trans. various authors. London and New York: KNP, 1984–2004.
Oliphant, Laurence. *Masollam: A Problem of the Period*. Leipzig: Tauchnitz, 1886.
———. *The Land of Gilead*. New York: Appleton, 1881.
Oliver, Bronson. "Emerson's 'Days,'" in *New England Quarterly* 19 (December 1946): 518–524.
Peters, F. Edwards. "The Origins of Islamic Platonism: the School Tradition," in *Islamic Philosophical Theology*, ed. Parviz Morewedge. Albany, NY: SUNY, 1979.
Potter, Charles. *A Bibliography of the Rubaiyat of Omar Khayyam*. # 942 (1908).
Pound, E. *Letters of Ezra Pound*. London: Faber and Faber, 1951.
Puli, Ali. *Centrum Naturae Concentratum*, trans. Edward Brice. London: J. Harris, 1696.
Purgstall, Joseph Von Hammer. *Der Divan von Mohammed Schemseddin Hafis*. Stutgart and Tubingen: 1812, 2 vols. Also *Geschichte der Schonen Redekunste Persien, mit einer Blutenlese aus Zweihundert Persischen Dichtern*. Wien, 1818.
Qamber, Akhtar. "The Mirror Symbol in the Teachings and Writings of Some Sufi Masters," in *Temenos*, XI (1990),163–179.
Qazvini, M. Muhammed, and Qasim Ghani. *Divan of Hafiz*. Teheran, 1941 (referred to as QG).
Raine, Kathleen. *Blake and Tradition*. Bollingen Series XXXV/11. Princeton, NJ: Princeton University Press, 1968.
———. "Traditional Symbolism in 'Kubla Khan,'" in *Defending Ancient Springs*. Suffolk: Golgonooza Press, 1985.
———. "The Human Face of God," in *Testimony to the Invisible: Essays on Swedenborg*, ed. James Lawrence, 75. West Chester, PA: Chrysalis Books, 1995.
Randolph, P. Beverly. *Eulis!*. Toledo: Randolph Publishing, 1874.
———. *The Ansairetic Mystery*. Toledo, OH: Liberal Printing House, 1873.
Rehder, Robert. "Persian Poets and Modern Critics," in *Edebiyat*, II/1 (1977), 98–99.
Riley, James Whitcomb. *The Ruba'iyyat of Doc Sifers*, illustrated by C. M. Relya. New York: Century Co, 1897.
Rumi, *The Mathnawí of Jalálu'ddín Rúmí*, trans. and ed. R. A. Nicholson. London: E. J. W. Gibb Memorial Trust 1924–40; reprint Gibb Memorial Series N.S. 1971, vol. 8, 245.

Russell, James. "Emerson and the Persians." Lecture Series: Near East in the Mind of America, 2002.
Rutherford, Samuel, "Liberty of Conscience," in *Religious Pluralism in the West,* ed. David Mullan. Oxford: Blackwell, 1998.
Saadi, Musle-Huddeen Sheik. *The Gulistan or Rose Garden*, trans. Francis Gladwin, with Preface by R. W. Emerson. Boston: Ticknor and Fields, 1865.
Saʻdi, *The Gulistan or Flower Garden*, trans. James Ross from the Persian Text of Gentius, with an Essay on Saʻdi. London, Richardson, 1823.
———. *The Gulistan: Rose Garden of Saadi,* trans. Francis Gladwin. Boston: Ticknor and Fields, 1865.
———. *Kuliyat,* ed. Mazahir Musaffa. Tehran: 1340/1961.
———. *Bustan,* ed. Gholam-Hossein Yusofi. Tehran: 1369/1990.
Saʻid, Edward. *Covering Islam: How the Media and the Experts Determine How We See the Rest of the World.* New York: Pantheon, 1981.
———. *Orientalism.* New York: Routledge, 1978.
Samuels, Charles E. *Thomas Baily Aldrich.* New York: 1965.
Sanborn, F. Benjamin. *Henry D. Thoreau.* Boston: Houghton Mifflin, 1895.
Schimmel, Annemarie. *A Two-Coloured Brocade: the Imagery of Persian Poetry.* Chapel Hill: University of North Carolina Press, 1992.
———. "The Genius of Shiraz: Saʻdi and Hafiz," in *Persian Literature* (1988): 214–225.
———. *The Mystical Dimensions of Islam.* Chapel-Hill: University of North Carolina Press, 1975.
Schroeder, Eric. "Verse Translation and Hafiz," in *Journal of Near Eastern Studies,* VII/4 (1948), 216.
Schuon, Frithof. *The Transcendental Unity of Religions.* London: Theosophical Publishing House, 1984.
Seabrook, William. *Adventures in Arabia.* New York: D. Appleton, 1928.
Sedgwick, Mark. *Against the Modern World.* Oxford: Oxford University Press, 2004.
Shams of Tabriz, "*guyand ishq chist bagu tarka ikhtiyar har ko ze ikhtiyar narast ikhtiyar nist.*" Trans. Reynold A. Nicholson, in *Divani Shams,* Tabriz. Cambridge: Routledge, 1952.
Sharafuddin, Mohammed. *Islam and Romantic Orientalism.* London: I. B. Tauris 1994.
Shea, David, and Anthony Troyer. *The Dabistan, or School of Manners.* Paris: Oriental Translation Fund, 1843.
Shelley, Percy Bysshe. *Shelley on Love: Selected Writings.* Ed. Richard Holmes. London: Flamingo, 1996.
Smith, Henry Nash, and William M. Gibson, ed. Clemens to William D. Howells, November 26, 1876, *Mark Twain-Howells Letters.* Cambridge, MA: Harvard University Press, Belknap Press, 1960.
Smith, Paul. "Hafiz of Shiraz: Hafiz's influence on Western Poetry," <www.hafizofshiraz.com>.
Sreekrishna Sarma. "A Short Study of the Oriental Influences upon Henry David Thoreau with Special Reference to his *Walden*," in *Jahrbuch für Amerikastudian.* Heidelberg, 1956.
Swainson, W. Perkes. *Thomas Lake Harris and His Occult Teaching.* London: William Rider & Son, 1922.

Tennyson, Alfred. *The Poems of Tennyson*. Ed. Christopher Ricks. London: Longmans, 1969.
Terhune, Alfred. *The Life of Edward FitzGerald*. New Haven, CT: Yale University Press, 1947.
Thoreau, Henry David. *Journal*, ed. Bradford Torrey and Francis H. Allen. Boston: Houghton Mifflin, 1906, VIII, 135 (Jan. 23, 1856).
———. *Writings of Henry David Thoreau*, ed. Bradford Torrey. Boston: Houghton Mifflin, 1906.
Tuckey, John S., ed. *Mark Twain's Fables of Man*. Berkeley: University of California Press, 1971.
Twain, Mark. *Mark Twain Papers at Berkeley*, Notebook 40, TS, 47.
———. *Mark Twain's Rubaiyat*. Introduction by Alan Gribben with textual note by Kevin B. MacDonnell. Austin, TX: Jenkins Publishing Co., 1983.
Urban, Sylvanus. *Gentleman's Magazine*. Old Series, no. CCLXXXIV (Jan–June, 1898), 413.
Walbridge, John. *The Wisdom of the Mystic East: Suhrawardi and Platonic Orientalism*. Albany, NY: SUNY, 2001.
Wansbrough, John. *Qoranic Studies*. Oxford: Oxford University Press, 1977.
Webster, Samuel C., ed. Clemens to Charles L. Webster, May 19, 1884, *Mark Twain, Business Man*. Boston: Little, Brown and Co., 1946.
Wellek, René. "The Concept of 'Romanticism' in Literary History," in *Comparative Literature*, I/1 (1949), 1–23, 147–172.
Whibley, Charles. "Musings Without Method." *Blackwood's*, no. 170 (1903), 287.
Whitman, Walt. *Leaves of Grass*. New York: Modern Library, 1980 (following the arrangement of the edition of 1891–92).
Whittier, John G. *The Complete Poetical Works*. Ed. Horace E. Scudder. Boston: Houghton Mifflin, 1894.
Williamson, George. "Emerson the Oriental," in *University of California Chronicle*, vol. XXX (1928), 281.
Wilson, Peter Lamborn. *Scandal: Essays in Islamic Heresy*. New York: Autonomedia, 1988.
Yohannan, John. *The Persian Poet Hafiz in England and America*. MA Thesis, Columbia University, 1939.
———. "Emerson's Translations of Persian Poetry from German Sources," in *American Literature*, vol. 14, no. 4, (Jan. 1943), 407–420.
———. "The Influence of Persian Poetry upon Emerson's Work," in *American Literature* 20 (March 1943).
———. "The Influence of Persian Poetry Upon Emerson's Work," in *American Literature*, vol, 15, no. 1, (1944), 25–41.
———. *A Treasury of Asian Literature*. New York: John Day Company, 1956.
———. "Fin de Siecle Cult of FitzGerald's *Ruba'iyat* of Omar Khayyam," in *Review of National Literature*, 2 (1971).
———. "Persian Poetry in England and America: A Two Hundred Year History," in *Persian Studies Series* no. 4. Delmar: New York, 1977.
———. "The Poet Sa'di: A Persian Humanist," in *Persian Studies Series*, no. 11, New York: 1987.
———. "Persian Literature in Translation," in *Persian Literature*, ed. Ehsan Yarshater. Bibliotheca Persica: New York, 1988.

Jami, "Yusuf va Zulaykha," in *Mathnawi-yi Haft awrang,* ed. A'la khan Afdahrad and Husayn A. Tarbiyat. Tehran: Nashr-i Mirath-i Maktub 1378 A.Hsh./1999, vol. 2, 34–36.

Zolla, E. "Naturphilosophie and Transcendentalism Revisited," In *Sophia Perennis* 3:2 (1977): 65–99.

Contributors

Mahnaz Ahmad is an independent scholar specializing in Comparative Literature and Middle Eastern Studies. Based in Washington DC, she holds degrees from the Universities of Cambridge, Sussex, and Punjab. She has taught at the University of the Punjab, King Saud University (Riyadh), and lectured at the Smithsonian Institution in Washington, DC.

Mehdi Aminrazavi received his early education in his native country of Iran and completed his graduate degrees from the University of Washington in Seattle and Temple University. He specializes in Islamic philosophy and theology, a topic upon which he has published numerous books and articles, including *Philosophy, Religion and the Question of Intolerance* (with D. Ambuel), *Suhrawardi and the School of Illumination, An Anthology of Philosophy in Persia*, 5 vols. co-edited with S. H. Nasr, and *The Wine of Wisdom: The Life, Poetry and Philosophy of Omar Khayyam*. At the University of Mary Washington, he is currently a Professor in the Philosophy and Religious Studies Departments, and co-director of the Leidecker Center for Asian Studies.

Phillip N. Edmondson received his doctoral degree from the George Washington University where he also taught in the English Department. The author of many articles, his literary interests include Asian influences on American literature.

Mansur Ekhtiyar received his doctoral degree in English literature. After teaching at several Western universities, he returned to Iran, where he became a distinguished Professor of English Literature at Tehran University. He specializes in addressing major American literary figures, and has been credited with introducing nineteenth-century American literature to a Persian-speaking audience.

Massud Farzan is a native of Iran. He received his PhD from the University of Michigan, and has continued to develop his reputation as a contemporary Sufi poet, scholar, short-story writer, critic, and translator. In addition to his popular work *The Tale of the Reed Pipe: Teachings of the Sufis*, he has written extensively on Persian literature. He is currently a Professor Emeritus of English at the Metropolitan College of Boston University.

Alan Gribben received his doctoral degree from the University of California at Berkeley. Gribben is a noted expert on the life and works of Mark Twain, and he co-founded and served as president of the Mark Twain Circle of America. He serves on the editorial board of American Literary Realism, and is both a Professor and the department chair of English and Philosophy at Auburn University at Montgomery, where he has been recognized as a Distinguished Research Professor.

Farhang Jahanpour received his doctoral degree in Oriental studies from the University of Cambridge and was formerly Dean of the Faculty of Languages at the University of Isfahan. He has taught at the universities of Cambridge and Oxford and has also taught online courses for Oxford, Yale and Stanford. His written works include editing *Nuzhat Nama-ye 'Ala'i*, and a Persian translation of Arnold Toynbee's *Civilization on Trial*. He is an Associate Fellow at the Faculty of Oriental Studies and tutor in Middle Eastern Studies at the Department of Continuing Education at the University of Oxford.

Leonard Lewisohn is Senior Lecturer in Persian at the University of Exeter. A renowned translator of Persian Sufi poetic and prose texts, he is the author of numerous works among which we can name *Beyond Faith and Infidelity*, editor of three volumes on *The Heritage of Sufis*, co-translator with Robert Bly of *The Angels Knocking on the Tavern Door: Thirty Poems of Hafiz*, editor of *Hafiz and the Religion of Love in Classical Persian Poetry*. He is the founder and editor of the *Mawlana Rumi Review*, an annual journal devoted to Jalal al-Din Rumi (d. 1273).

Parvin Loloi attended the Melli University in Tehran and the University of Wales (Swansea), where she received her doctoral degree and wrote her dissertation on the English translations of Hafiz and their influence on English poetry. She is an independent scholar; among her publications we can mention *Studies in English and Comparative Literature*; *Hafiz, Master of Persian Poetry: A Critical Bibliography*; and "Tennyson, Fitzgerald and Conwell: A Private Relation with Public Consequences" in *Private and Public Voices in Victorian Poetry*.

Jacob Needleman is an Emeritus Professor of Philosophy at San Francisco State University. He was educated in philosophy at Harvard, Yale and the University of Freiburg, Germany, and has taught in numerous national and international Universities. He has also been a Research Associate at the Rockefeller Institute for Medical Research, a Research Fellow at Union Theological Seminary, a Professor of Medical Ethics at the University of California Medical School and a visiting Professor of Religious Studies at the Sorbonne, Paris. Jacob Needleman was also General Editor of the Penguin Metaphysical Library and the General Editor of the Element Books series.

Among his numerous works we can mention *The New Religions*; *The Wisdom of Love*; *Money and the Meaning of Life*; *A Sense of the Cosmos*; *Lost Christianity*; *The Heart of Philosophy*; *The Way of the Physician*; *Time and the Soul*; *Sorcerers*; *The American Soul*; *Why Can't We Be Good?*; *The Essential Marcus Aurelius*; and his most recent book *What Is God?*

Marwan M. Obeidat is Professor of American Literature at the United Arab Emirates University. He has published numerous articles and books, including *American Literature and Orientalism*. He is currently a member of the Editorial Board of American Studies International and the Organization of American Historians; international co-editor for *The Journal of American History*, and also for *Connections: American History and Culture in an International Perspective*.

Arthur Versluis received his doctoral degree from Michigan State University, where he currently is a Professor in the College of Arts & Letters. Among his publications are *Magic and Mysticism: An Introduction to Western Esotericism*; *The Esoteric Origins of the American Renaissance*; *Wisdom's Book: The Sophia Anthology*; *Wisdom's Children: A Christian Esoteric Tradition*; and *American Transcendentalism and Asian Religions*. He is the founding editor of *Esoterica*, and co-editor of *Journal for the Study of Radicalism*. He is also the founding president of the Association for the Study of Esotericism.

John David Yohannan was a pioneer in introducing Persian Sufi literature to American literary circles. Born in 1910 in Dilman, Iran, he came to America in 1919. He received his doctoral degree from New York University where he studied Persian poetry's reception in England. Having taught at a number of major universities, he became a Professor of English and Comparative Literature at the City College of New York and CUNY Graduate Center, where he co-founded the Comparative Literature Program. His books include *Treasury of Asian Literature*, and *Persian Poetry in England and America: A Two Hundred Year History*.

Index

Abstract of the Persian Theology of Zoroaster, An, 118
Abu'l-Qasim al-Junayd, 28–29
Abu Talib al-Makki, 34–35
Academie des Inscriptions: (Zoroaster), 57–58
Addison, Joseph, 91
Adonais (Shelley), 30–31, 34, 35
Adventures in Arabia (Seabrook), 186
AGE–A Rubáiyát (Twain): complete version of, 253–262; selected examples of, 236–237; writing of, 233–234, 248. See also *Ruba'iyyat* of Mark Twain; Twain, Mark
Ahasuerus, the Wandering Jew, 25
"Akbar's Dream" (Tennyson), 39–40
Akhlaq-i Jalali (Davani), 58
Alcott, Amos Bronson, 9, 75, 109, 196, 215
Al-Da'mi, Muhammed, 175–176
Aldrich, Thomas Bailey, 239–240
Alger, William Rounesville: and Emerson influence, 196–197; on Emerson's *Bacchus*, 63–64; and Hafiz, 204; and Omar Khayyam, 107; and *Poetry of the East* (*Poetry of the Orient*), 9, 118, 196
"All Religions are One" (tract) (Blake), 40
Alphonso of Castille (Emerson), 62
American Civil War, 2–3, 222
American Monthly Magazine, 4, 214

American Museum or Universal Magazine, 4
American Transcendentalists and Sufism, 191–210; overview, 9, 191–192; and Alcott, 196; and Alger, 196–197; and Conway, 9, 197–198; and Emerson's domination of Persian literature, 191–192, 198; and Hearn, 208–210; and Johnson (Unitarian clergyman), 198; and Longfellow, 199–201; and Lowell, 201–203; and Whitman, 194–195; and Whittier, 195–196. See also Melville, Herman; Thoreau, Henry David; *specific names of writers*
Anagogic correspondences between Sufi and Romantic poetry, 22–38; overview, 22; Annihilation, Mystical death, *Fana,'* 28–38; carpe diem, 22–23; *Mundus imaginalis*, 25–28; *Nunc Aeternum*, 23–25; Platonic poetics and, 40–42
Anagogic criticism, 19–21
"Animula," section II (Eliot), 238–239
Ansairetic Mystery, The (Randolph), 184
Ansariyeh (Middle Eastern sect), 181–182
Anti-Omarian movement, 242
Arabian Mirrors and Western Soothsayers (Al-Da'mi), 175–176
Arabian Nights: popularity of, 213; and Thoreau, 192

283

Arcana of Christianity (Harris), 177
Archetypal criticism, 17–19
Aristophanes, 33, 96
Arnold, Sir Edwin, 209
Arte of English Poesie, The (Puttenham, tr.), 1
"Asia" (Emerson), 55, 56–57
Asiatic Miscellany (journal), 3, 118
Asiatic Researches (journal), 3
Asiatic Society of Bengal, 3
Atkinson, J. A., Esq. (translator), 214
Atkinson, James (translator), 118, 214
Attar, Farid al-Din, 64
Avicenna, 107–108

Bacchus (Emerson): Alger on, 63–64; compared to Emerson translation of *Saqi-Nameh* by Hafiz, 136–141; and Hafiz's influence, 8, 62, 135; text of, 134–136; wine as metaphor for spiritual intoxication, 140–141
Bangs, Edward, 64
Barrow, S. J., 237
Baxter, Sylvester, 223
Bayazid-i Bastami, 169–170
Bed of Roses. See *Gulistan* (Sa'di)
Benton, Joel, 117, 145
Billy Budd (Melville), 205
Bin Laden, Osama, 5
Black Crescent (Gomez), 182
Blake, William: "All Religions are One" (tract), 40; and *carpe diem*, 23; on existence as thought, 27; *Four Zoas*, 20; Hafiz and, 6, 19; *Milton*, 24; and Platonism, 16
Blavatsky, H. P., 185
Blithedale Romance, The (Hawthorne), 217
Blumen aus Morgenländischen Dichtern Gesammelt (Herder), 91
Body of the World (Sufi doctrine), 37, 62

Book of Kings, The. See *Shah Namah*
"Books" (Emerson), 94
Breath of God with Man, The (Harris), 177
Bring Me Wine (Hafiz), 63
Brockhaus, F. A., 96
Burrage, Charles, 223, 231
Bush, George W. administration, 176
Byron, George Gordon, 34, 39–40, 69, 201

Cameron, Kenneth W., 56
Carlyle, Thomas, 175–176
Carpe diem (seize the day): anagogic perspective of, 22–23; grand theme in classical English literature, 18; origin of, 2; and Victorian audience, 246
Chadzko, Aleksander. See Chodzko, Aleksander
Chamberlin, Henry Harman, 4, 227
Champagne Song of the Wine of Victory (Chamberlin), 226–227
Channing, William E., 192
Chardin, Sir John, 1–2
Chenu, M. D., 20
Chodzko, Aleksander, 118, 199
Cholmondeley, Thomas, 192
Christy, Arthur E., 56, 93, 196
Clarel (Melville), 205–206
Clemens, Clara (daughter), 247
Clemens, Jean (daughter), 248
Clemens, Samuel Langhorne. See Train, Mark
Clemens, Susy (daughter), 248
Coleridge, Samuel Taylor, 16, 21, 26, 27, 104
Comparative Persian-English poetics, 17–22
Compensation (Emerson), 59
Concord, Mass. See Persians of Concord

Conduct of Life, The (Emerson), 79–80, 81
Confidence Man, The (Melville), 204
Conway, Moncure Daniel, 9, 194, 197–198, 233, 247
Coomaraswamy, Ananda, 21
Corson, Kate. *See* Randolph, Kate Corson
Costello, Louisa S., 214
Crashaw, Richard, 28
"Curse of Kehama, The" (Southy), 56
Curtis, Elizabeth Alden, 247
Curtis, George William, 9, 213, 215, 217

Dabistan, The, or School of Manners (Troyer), 118–119
D'Ambrosio, V. M., 238
Davani, Jalal al-Din, 58
Days (Emerson), 65, 67, 131–132
Dehlavi, Amir Khusraw-yi, 60
Demon's Association, 238
Der Persianischer Rosenthal, 91
Deveney, John Patrick, 183
Dial, The (magazine): Emerson as founding member of, 109–110; "Saadi" published in, 8, 59–60, 94, 99, 123
Divan (Hafiz): and comparative studies, 17; and Emerson, 58, 64, 70; and English audiences, 1; and Hammer-Purgstall, 4, 118; and I-Thou relationship, 165; and Jones, 3; and transcendence of time, 23; unconventionality of, 155–156
Divine Flashes (Lama'at) of Fakhr al-Din 'Iraqi, 33, 34
Divine Scintillations (Lawayih) (Jami), 33
Dole, Nathan Haskell, 4, 223, 224
Donne, John, 28, 31
"Drum Taps" (Whitman), 163

Druze (Middle Eastern sect), 180, 181–182, 185, 186–187
Duisberg, J. V., 91
Duperron, Anquetil, 118

Elements of Theology (Proclus), 24
Eliade, Mircea, 21
Eliot, Charles William (cousin), 237, 238
Eliot, T. S.: family interest in the *Ruba'iyyat*, 163, 237–238; impact of *Ruba'iyyat* on, 238–239; Khayyam's influence on, 10; and Pound, 241
Eliot, William Greenleaf (grandfather), 237
Eliot Possessed (D'Ambrosio), 238
Eliots, the, 237–239
Emerson (Hafiz echoed in verse of), 131–145; analysis of similarities, 132, 134–135, 140–141, 142, 145; and comparison with Hafiz poem in *Persian Poetry*, 142; and *Days*, 131–132; and *Fragmentary Bachhus*, 141–142; and *Ghaselle: From the Persian of Hafiz II*, 132–133; and "Give All to Love," 143–144; and "From Hafiz," 66, 67, 130, 144; and "Hermione," 143; and "To J. W.," 132–133; and *May Day*, 134; and *Mithridates*, 62, 144; and *Monadnoc*, 144; and *Saqi-Nameh*, 134–136; uniqueness attributable to Persian influence, 131. See also *Bacchus*; Emerson, Ralph Waldo (works of); Emerson on Hafiz and Sa'di; Emerson's writings on Persian literature; Hafiz
Emerson, Edward (son), 63, 117, 132
Emerson, Lidian (wife), 55
Emerson, Mary Moody (aunt), 75
Emerson, Ralph Waldo, and Whitman, 155

Emerson, Ralph Waldo (chronology of Persian mysticism interest), 55–70; overview, 6–7; and *Arabian Nights*, 56; and *Asia*, 57; and college, 55; and Dehlavi, 60; and doctrine of "Beautiful Necessity," 59; and Firdawsi, 65; and Gernado, 57; and Hafiz, 59–61, 62–64, 66–67, 69–70; and Hindu philosophy, 58, 69; mysticism studied (1858–64), 69; and Neoplatonism, 58, 60, 69; and *The Orientalist*, 65; as Orientalist in 1845, 58; and Platonism, 61; and Plotinus, 57; and "The Poet," 21–22; and Proclus, 60; and Rumi, 59, 61, 68–69, 118, 128; and Sa'di, 60, 61, 69; and *Shah Namah*, 64, 65; and Shakespeare, 61; and solitude concept, 66; and Southy, 56; and Sufism, 5; and Thoreau, 60; title of "Master," 6; and Wilk, 56; and wine as theme, 62–63; and Zoroastrianism, 57–58, 61–62. *See also under* Hammer-Purgstall von, Joseph; *Journals* (Emerson)

Emerson, Ralph Waldo (Muslim Orient and), 75–88; early interest in, 6–7, 76, 118; and fatalism, 80; and Hafiz, 82–83; on Hindu mythologies, 75; and involvement with outer form of Muslim Orient, 79–80; and Muhammad, 85–86; and Muslim East as congenial, 87; and Nature, 83; and Plato, 77; and pro-Western stance, 77–79, 87–88; and quality of freedom of Persian poets, 82; and Sa'di, 82–83, 84; and simplifications of Islam, 85; on spread of Islam, 86–87; Sufi masters as ideal poets, 80, 83–85, 87–88; on transformation of Islam, 87. *See also* Emerson, Ralph Waldo (works of)

Emerson, Ralph Waldo (Sa'di and), 91–113; overview, 6–7; ambiguity in attitude toward Sa'di, 95–96; comparison discontinuity of themes in Persian poetry, 98–99; comparison of Hafiz and Sa'di by Emerson, 97–98; concurrent study of Platonism, Neoplatonism, and Orientalism, 108; and Dante in *Divine Comedy*, 110–111; on dictionaries and autobiography, 96; and "divine essence" as key to Nature study, 109; and "flawed" reading of Platonism, 108–109; on "genius of Saadi," 99; immersion into study of Sa'di, 95; *Journal* entry on affinity with Sa'di, 112; and "Nature," 111; and Neoplatonism, 106–107, 108; overview, 91–92; and "The Poet," 94, 112; and "P" on nature in *The Dial*, 109–110; Qur'an compared with Plato by, 109; Sa'di and Hafiz widely read in nineteenth-century America, 93; Sa'di as poet of Nature, 111; and Sa'di on nature, 110; and Sa'di popularity in America, 113; Sa'di preferred to Hafiz, 112–113; and Sa'di revered by Transcendentalists, 111; similarities between Emerson and Sa'di, 95; and Trismegistus, 108. *See also* Sa'di

Emerson, Ralph Waldo (works of): *Alphonso of Castille*, 62; "Asia," 55, 56–57; "Books," 94; "Brahma," 61, 201; *Compensation*, 59; *Conduct of Life, The*, 79–80, 81; *Days*, 65, 67, 131–132; *Fate*, 59, 79, 80–81; *Fragmentary Bachhus*, 141–142;

Fragment on the Poet (on Sa'idi), 111; *Fragments on the Poet and the Poetic Gift*, 119, 123–125; *Ghaselle: From the Persian of Hafiz II* (translation), 133–134; "Give All to Love," 143–144; "From Hafiz" (translation), 30, 66, 67, 144; "Hermione," 143; *Illusion*, 61, 81; *Intellect*, 144; "To J. W.," 132; *Merlin*, 62; *From Omar Khayyam* (translation), 66; *Orientalist* notebook, 127–128; *Of Passionate Abandonment* (translation), 129–130; *Plato*, 61, 78, 109; *Preface to Gulistan*, 80, 82, 95, 97, 105, 119, 123; *Shakespeare*, 82; *Social Aims*, 85; *Song of Nature*, 65; *Spiritual Law*, 59; *Superlative*, 66. See also *Bacchus*; Emerson's writings on Persian literature; *Journals* (Emerson); *Persian Poetry*; 'Saadi"

Emerson and the Persians (Russell), 155

Emerson as a Poet (Cabot), 66

Emerson in Concord (E. Emerson), 63

Emerson on Hafiz and Sa'di, 117–149; overview, 7, 117; Emerson's encounter with Persian literature, 117–119; Emerson's translations from Hafiz, 128–131. See also Emerson (Hafiz echoed in verse of); Emerson, Ralph Waldo (works of); Emerson's translations from Hafiz; Emerson's writings on Persian literature; Sa'di

Emerson's writings on Persian literature, 119–128; *Fragments on the Poet and the Poetic Gift*, 123–125; the *Journals* (on Hafiz), 126–127; *Orientalist* notebook, 127–128; *Persian Poetry*, 119–123; *The Poet* (poem), 125–126; *Preface to Gulistan*, 80, 82, 95, 97, 105, 119, 123. See also Emerson, Ralph Waldo (works of)

English Romanics, and Platonism, 15–16

English Romanics and Persian Sufi poets, 15–52; overview, 5–6; anagogic correspondences between Sufi and Romantic poetry, 22–38; comparative Persian-English poetics, 17–22; Platonic poets and anagogic criticism, 40–42; Platonism in Romantic and Sufi poetry, 15–17; unity of religions, 38–40

Epipsychidion (Shelley), 24, 32–33

Experience (Emerson), 62

Fables of Pilpay, and Thoreau, 192

Faerie Queen, The (Spenser), 21–22, 31

Far, Peter Lamborn Wilson, 35, 188

Farzan, Massud, 17

Fatalism, doctrine of, 80

Fate (Emerson), 59, 79, 80–81

Ficino, Marsilio, 16, 31, 37

Firdawsi, 1, 118, 194

Fitzgerald, Edward (aka FitzGerald): and America, 198–199; and birth of Omar Khayyam Club of America, 222–223; and Eliot, 238–239; and Emerson, 199, 242; Emerson's English translations preceded those of, 128; and Norton review, 237–238; and Pound, 241; quotations from translations of, 18; reception of in America, 245; *Ruba'iyyat* translation of 1859, 10; *Ruba'iyyat* translation of 1868, 4, 202–203, 209, 221–222; and Tennyson, 39. See also *AGE-A Rubáiyát* (Twain)

"Five Boons of Life" (Twain), 234

"Flaming Heart upon the Book and Picture of the Seraphical Saint Teresa, The" (Crashaw), 28
Foote, Arthur, 223
Four Zoas (Blake), 20
Fragmentary Bachhus (Emerson), 141–142
Fragment on the Poet (on Sa'idi) (Emerson), 111
Fragments on the Poet and the Poetic Gift (Emerson), 119, 123–125
"Friend, Omar, thy voice is still singing" (Roe), 230–231
Friendship (Hafiz), 66
"From Hafiz" (Emerson, tr.), 66, 67, 130, 144
From Omar Khayyam (Emerson, tr.), 66
Frothingham, Octavius Brook, 68
Frye, Northrop, 17, 19–20, 22
Fuller, Margaret: and autobiographical *Leila*, 216–217; as Eastern-like mystic, 214; and Emerson, 58, 215, 217; and Persian influence, 213; as Transcendentalist writer, 9
Fusus al-hikam by Ibn 'Arabi, 33

Garden of Mystery (Shabistari), 23, 29
Gentius, Georgius (Gentz), 1, 91
German Romanticism, 215
Gernado, Marie Josef de, 57
Ghaselle: From the Persian of Hafiz II (Emerson, tr.), 133–134
"Give All to Love" (Emerson), 143–144
Gladwin, Francis, 65, 69, 92, 119
Goethe, as Representative Men, 113
Golden Child, The (Harris), 177–178
Gomez, Michael, 182–183
Gribben, A., 233, 235
Guénon, René, 188
Gulistan, The (Sa'di): availability in Latin, 1, 91; and Emerson, 7, 60, 67, 68, 69, 94, 95; and Hearn, 209; and Jones, 92; and Longfellow, 199, 200; and Melville, 203, 205; review of, 92–93; and Thoreau, 192; and Whitman, 8. See also *Preface to Gulistan*
Gulshan-i raz (Shabistari), 1
Gurdjieff, 176

Hafiz: and anti-orthodoxy, 157; and Blake, 6, 19; compared to Sa'di, 97–98; Emerson on, 119–121; love central to worldview of, 158–159; and Melville, 203–205; and mysticism, 156–157; and nostalgia of, 158; popularity of, 4; "Preeternal" role of Beauty and, 36, 37; and Shelley, 37; and state of "not-Being," 161; as Sufi master, 1; and symbolism of wine, 156–157; and Tennyson, 39–40; unconventionality of, 155–156; universal love and, 153; as widely read in nineteenth century, 93. See also Emerson (Hafiz echoed in verse of)
Hammer-Purgstall von, Joseph: and Emerson, 4, 6, 58, 65, 95, 214–215; and Emerson tribute to, 119; on Sa'di, 92; translations from Persian poetry, 4, 118
"Haroun Al Raschid" (Longfellow), 200
Harris, Thomas Lake: overview, 8–9; *Arcana of Christianity*, 177; *Breath of God with Man*, 177; and Brocton community, 179–180; controversial life of, 177; and doctrine of counterparts, 178; and Fountain Grove community, 178; *Golden Child*, 177–178; *Millennial Age*, 177; and Oliphant, 179–180; and Oliphant as disciple, 177, 178, 179,

180–181; philosophy of, 177–178; and questions on link to Sufism, 185–186, 188
Harvard College Library, 215
Hawthorne, Julian (son), 213
Hawthorne, Nathaniel: *Arabian Nights* as inspiration for, 213; and *Blithedale Romance*, 217; and Concord, 9–10; and Curtis's *Nile Notes*, 217; and German Romanticism, 215
Hawthorne, Sophia (wife), 217
Hay, John, 240–241
Hearn, Lafcadio: Asian literature esteemed by, 209; and concept of syncretic world faith, 209; exotic background of, 208–209; and *Ruba'iyyat* lecture, 209–210; and *Stray Leaves from Strange Literatures*, 209
"Hearts of Gold" (Melville), 208
"He is often happy whose one thought is for friends." (Scofield), 231
Hellas (Shelley), 25, 27
Herder, Johann, 91
"Hermione" (Emerson), 143
Higginson, Thomas Wentworth, 223
Histoire Comparée des systèmes de philosophie (Gernado), 57
Historical Sketches of the South of India (Wilk), 56
History of the Persian Language (Jones), 92
Holy Sonnet XIV (Donne), 28
"Honor of Old Age" Twain, 234
Horace, 2
Houghton, Stephan C., 223
Howadji in Syria, The (Curtis), 217
"Hymn to Narayena" (Jones, tr.), 55–56

Illusion (Emerson), 61, 81
Influence of Persian Poetry on Emerson's Work in American Literature, The (Yohannan), 64
"In Praise of Omar" (Hay), 240
Intellect (essay) (Emerson), 144
"In the Path of the Persians" (Houghton), 223
Irving, Washington, 175–176

Jami: and *Divine Scintillations* (*Lawayih*), 33; and Emerson, 7, 118, 128; and *Joseph and Zulayka* (*Yusuf va Zulaykha*) (Jami), 35; Sa'di compared to, 105; as Sufi master, 1
Jean, 36
Johnson, Samuel (Unitarian clergyman), 198
Jones, Sir William: and Emerson, 92, 118; "father of English Orientalism," 93; first reliable translations of Sufi poetry by, 214; and Hafiz, 5; and Melville, 203; on Sa'di, 203; significance of, 3; and Thoreau, 192; translations of, 92. See also Jones, Sir William (works of)
Jones, Sir William (works of): *History of the Persian Language*, 92; "Hymn to Narayena" (tr.), 55–56; *Persian Grammar*, 92; "Persian Song, A" (Hafiz) (tr.), 3; *Rain Drop The* (Sa'di) (tr.), 92; *Scented Mud* (Sa'di) (tr.), 92; *Works*, 3, 92, 118. See also Jones, Sir William
Joseph and Zulayka (*Yusuf va Zulaykha*) (Jami), 35
Journals (Emerson), Persian thought in, 55–57, 59, 61, 62, 70, 126–127

Karim, Abud'l, 65
"Keramos" (Longfellow), 200–201

Khayyam, Omar: and Alger, 197; American reception of, 221; and America's materialism, 2–3, 222; and Conway, 9, 197; and Emerson, 66–67, 128–129, 132; and English audiences, 1; and FitzGerald's translations, 4, 221–222; impact on American audience, 10, 198; and Longfellow, 200–201; and Lowell, 202–203; and Melville, 205, 206–207, 208; and Omarian literary movement, 224–226; pessimism of, 223, 233; popularity of, 4, 221–222; and Stratton, 228–229; and Thoreau, 18. *See also* Eliots, the; Mark Twain and *The Ruba'iyyat*; Omarian poets of America; Omar Khayyam Club of America; *Ruba'iyyat* (aka *Rub'iyyat*) (Khayyam)

Knickerbocker, 4, 214

Konversations-Lexikon (Brockhaus), 96–97

Kubla Khan (Coleridge), 104

Kurroglou, 199

Laili and Majnun (Nazami), 214

Land of Gilead, The (Oliphant), 181–182

"Leap of Roushan Beg, The" (Longfellow), 199–200

Leaves of Grass (Whitman): affinity to Persian poetry, 164; city of love projected in, 157; praise for, 163; publication of, 8; and Sufi connection passed over, 164; and Sufi-inspired poetry, 167–168; Thoreau on, 163–164, 194

Leila (Fuller), 216–217

L'Empire des Roses. *See Gulistan* (Sa'di)

"Lilacs" (Whitman), 163

Literary "Masters": Harris, Oliphant, and Randolph, 175–188; overview, 9, 175–176. *See also* Harris, Thomas Lake; Oliphant, Lawrence; Randolph, Paschal Beverly

Loloi, Parvin, 17

Longfellow, Henry Wadsworth: cue on Persian literature from Emerson, 199; and "Haroun Al Raschid" (text), 200; and "Keramos," 200–201; and "Leap of Roushan Beg" from Chodzko, 199–200; and "Spanish Jew's Tale," 200; and Sufi poets in library of, 214, 215

Lopez-Baralt, Luce, 17

Lowell, James Russell: and Byronic affinity with East, 69, 201; as Emerson disciple, 9, 191; and Firdawsi, 201–202; and poems written in Oriental manner, 202; and Rumi's parable, 202; tribute to *Ruba'iyyat* by, 202–203; and "Youssouf" (Yusuf), 202

MacDonnell, K. B., 234

Macrobius, 36

Macy, Arthur, 223

Magia Sexualis (Randolph) (Naglowska, tr.), 185

Magister, Stephan, 232

Man the Reformer (Emerson), 86–87

Mardi (Melville), 203

Mark Twain: A Biography (Paine), 234

Mark Twain and *The Ruba'iyyat*. *See* Train, Mark

Mark Twain Project, 11

Mark Twain's Rubáiyát (Gribben and MacDonnell, eds.), 234

Martin, Frederick R., 199

Marvell, Andrew, 19

Masollam (Oliphant), 180–181, 186

Mathnavi (Rumi), 1, 30, 33, 34. 169
May Day (Emerson), 134
May Day and Other Poems (Emerson), 65
Meigs, Charles Hardy, 223
Melville, Herman: and Emerson, 9, 191, 203, 207, 208; and Hafiz, 203; on Hafiz's wine, 204–205; and Holy Land journey, 205; and Omar Khayyam, 206–207; and Persian Sufism, 175; and Sa'di, 204, 205; and Sa'di's *Gulistan*, 203, 205; and superficiality of Oriental interest, 204. *See also* Melville, Herman (works of)
Melville, Herman (works of): *Billy Budd*, 205; *Clarel*, 205–206; *Confidence Man*, 204; "Hearts of Gold," 208; *Mardi*, 203; *Miscellaneous Poems*, 207–208; "New Rosicrucians," 207; *Pierre*, 204; *Under the Rose*, 206–207; "Rose Farmer," 207. *See also* Melville, Herman
Memoirs of Khojeh Abdulkureem, The (Abdulkurreem), 65
Menocal, Maria Rosa, 17
Merlin (Emerson), 62
Millennial Age, The (Harris), 177
Miller, Samuel, 58
Mills, Charles D. B., 198
Milton (Blake), 24, 29–30
Miscellaneous Poems (Melville), 207–208
Mithridates (Emerson), 62, 144
Mohl, Jules, 209
Monadnoc (Emerson), 144
More, Henry, 40
Mundus Imaginalis, 25–28
My Boyhood Dreams (Twain), 250
"Mystic Trumpete, The" (Whitman), 157

Naglowska, Maria, 185
Natural Religion (Emerson), 79
Natural Supernaturalism (Abrams), 41
"Nature" (essay) (Emerson), 94, 111
"Nature" (poem) (Emerson), 111
Nature, Man, and Society in the 12th Century (Chenu), 20
Neoplatonism: as common language for Romantics and Sufis, 6, 7, 15; and Emerson, 57–60, 69, 106–108; and Hafiz, 154; and mutual philosophical heritage, 16–17; Symbolist Mentality of Christian, 20–21
Newman, John Henry Cardinal, 175–176
"New Rosicrucians, The" (Melville), 207
New York Magazine or Literary Repository, 4
Nile Notes (Curtis), 217
Norton, Charles Eliot (T. S. Eliot's cousin), review of the *Ruba'iyyat* by, 199, 237–238
Notopoulos, James, 16
Nott, John, 4
Nunc Aeternum, 23–25

"Ode Translated from the Persian of Hafez" (Nott, tr.), 4
Of Passionate Abandonment (Emerson, tr.), 129–130
"Old Age" Twain, 234
Olearius, Adam, 91
Oliphant, Alice le Strange (wife), 179–181
Oliphant, Anthony (father), 179
Oliphant, Lawrence, 179–182; and Ansariyeh sect, 181–182; and Druze sect, 9, 181–182, 185, 186; and Harris, 179–180; and *Land of Gilead*, 181–182; and *Masollam*,

Oliphant, Lawrence *(continued)* 180–181, 186; and questions on link to Sufism, 185, 186, 187–188; and *Scientific Religion*, 180; and *Sympneumata*, 180; syncretic philosophy of, 180; travels of, 9, 179

Oliphant, Mary (mother), 179

Omarianism, 239

Omarian poets of America, 221–242; overview, 10, 221–222; The Eliots, 237–239; Omarian poets of New England, 223–232; Omar Khayyam Club of America, 222–223; Ruba'iyyat of Mark Twain, 232–237. *See also* Aldrich, Thomas Bailey; Eliot, T. S.; Hay, John; Pound, Ezra; Riley, James Whitcomb; *entries beginning with* Emerson

Omar Khayyam (Barrow), 237

Omar Khayyam Club of America: beginning of, 4, 10, 222–223; decline of, 232; Hay's lecture at, 240–241; poems written for, 224, 226, 229; and Scofield prose dedicated to Burrage, 231

"One Hour to Madness and Joy" (Whitman), 156

One Hundred Quatrains, from the Ruba'iyyat of Omar Khayyam (Curtis), 247

On the Poetry of Mark Twain with Selections from His Verse (Scott, ed.), 233

Oracles of Zoroaster, the Founder of the Persian Magi, 118

Orientalia, 192–193

Orientalist notebook (Emerson), 127–128

Oriental Translation Fund, 4, 214

Orient in American Transcendentalism, The (Christy), 196

Orient in Post-Bellum American Thought, The (Johnson), 198

Ouseley, Sir William, 4

Paine, Albert Bigelow, 235

Pantheism, 155, 194–195, 202

Paschal Beverly Randolph (Deveney), 183

"Passage to India" (Whitman), 194

Perennialism, 3

Persian Grammar (Jones), 92

Persian Lesson, A (Whitman): as coda for *Leaves of Grass*, 171; and mysticism of, 8, 160, 170–171; originally *A Sufi Lesson*, 164; and pantheism, 195; publication of, 170, 171

Persian Poetry (essay) (Emerson): and admiration for Orient, 78; allusions to wine in, 62; and fatalism, 80; on Hafiz, 81, 119–121, 122–123; publication of, 68; Sa'di bypassed in, 94–95

Persians of Concord, 213–218; overview, 9–10, 213; Concord as mecca of Transcendentalism, 214; and Curtis, 217; and Emerson's English translations of Sufi poets, 215; and Emerson's "Saadi," 215, 216; and German Romanticism, 215; and Harvard College Library, 215; and Hawthorne, 213, 215, 217; and impact on New England writing of nineteenth century, 215, 217–218; and Longfellow, 215; Sufi translations read by Concordians, 214; and Thoreau's identification with Sa'di, 215–216. *See also* Curtis, George William; Emerson,

Ralph Waldo; *entries beginning with* Emerson; Fuller, Margaret; Hawthorne, Nathaniel; Thoreau, Henry David
"Persian Song, A" (Hafiz) (Jones, tr.), 3
"Philosophy of Persian Art, The": (Coomaraswamy), 21
Phoenix, The, 118
Pierre (Melville), 204
Plato (Emerson), 61, 78, 109
Platonism: and Emerson, 61; Emerson's "flawed" reading of, 108–109; in Romantic and Sufi poetry, 15–17; and Shelley, 16, 24–25, 32–34
Platonism of Shelley, The (Notopoulos), 16
Plotinus, 16, 57, 110
"Poet, The" (essay) (Emerson), 21–22, 94, 112
Poet, The (poem) (Emerson), 125–126
Poetry and Imagination (Emerson), 62
Poetry of the East, The (Alger) (later *Poetry of the Orient*), 9, 118, 196
Potter, Alfred C., 223
Pound, Ezra, 241–242
Pound, Omar Shakespeare (son), 242
Power (Emerson), 80, 81
Preface to Gulistan (Emerson), 80, 82, 95, 97, 105, 119, 123. See also *Gulistan, The* (Sa'di)
"Price, The" (Chamberlin), 226
Proclus, 60
Prometheus Unbound (Shelley), 22
Prophet and a Pilgrim, A (Schneider), 183
Puttenham, George, 1

Quatrains of Omar Khayyam of Nishapur (Thompson), 247

Rain Drop The (Sa'di) (Jones, tr.), 92
Randolph, Kate Corson (second wife), 184, 185
Randolph, Mary Jane (first wife), 183
Randolph, Osiris Budh (son), 184
Randolph, Paschal Beverly, 182–188; admissions of as "mystic," 187; and animal magnetism, 184; *Ansairetic Mystery*, 184; background of, 182–183; death of, 185; and *Eulis*, 186; and Harris, 183; and *Magia Sexualis*, 185; as novelist of occult, 184; and questions on link to Sufism, 185–186, 187–188; and sexual philosophy, 187; and Sufism, 182–183; and the Theosophical Society, 184–185; and travels of, 9, 183–184
Recital of the Occidental Exile, The (al-Ghurbat al-gharbiyyah) (Suhrawardi), 107
Representative Men (Occidental biographical lectures) (Emerson), 77, 108, 113
Riley, James Whitcomb, 240
Roe, George, 230–231
Romantic Movement, emergence of, 93–94
Rosarium (Gentius, tr.), 1, 91
"Rose Farmer, The" (Melville), 207
Rose Garden of Persia, The (Costello), 214
Ross, James, 92, 118
Royal Asiatic Society of Great Britain and Ireland, 4
Ruba'iyyat (Khayyam): and Emerson, 128, 198–199; and English audiences, 1, 198–199; and Hearn, 209–210; impact on American audience, 10; and Longfellow, 200–201; Lowell's tribute to,

Ruba'iyyat (Khayyam) *(continued)* 202–203; and Melville, 205, 206, 208. *See also* Omar Khayyam Club of America

Ruba'iyyat of Doc Sifers, The (Riley), 240

Ruba'iyyat of Mark Twain, 232–237; Conway on Twain and Khayyam, 233; examples from, 236–237; omission of from Paine biography, 235; and request of Twain to burn, 235; themes of old age and death, 234–235; Twain's reverence for the *Ruba'iyyat*, 233; Twain's writing of burlesque *Ruba'iyyat*, 233–234; work of "brooding late phase," 235–236. See also *AGE–A Rubáiyát* (Twain)

Ruba'iyyat of Omar Khayyam, The (FitzGerald, tr.), 4

Rumi, Jalal al-Din: and death of the "I," 170; and Emerson, 59, 61, 68–69, 118, 128; and Hearn, 209; and *Mathnawi* (aka *Mathnavi*), 1, 30, 33, 34, 169; and Neoplatonic doctrine, 33; parable demonstrating Sufi pantheism, 202; and self-annihilation, 30; as Sufi master, 1; translations as best sellers, 11; and Universal mind, 27. *See also under* Whitman and Sufism

Rusk, Ralph, 242

Russell, James, 155, 157

Ryer, André du, 91

"Saadi" (poem) (Emerson): admiration for the FitzGerald *Ruba'iyyat* expressed by, 59–60; analysis of, 104–106; autobiographical nature of, 7, 215; influence of *The Saki Song*, 64; on Nature, 111; on Persian poetry, 119; publication of, 99; read by Whitman, 8; and self-reliance in Sa'di, 82–83; text of, 99–104

Sacred Anthology (Oriental) (Conway), 197

"Sad, severed from the sea, a raindrop s"di: and *Bustan*, 21; bypassed in Emerson's "Persian Poetry," 94–95; compared to Hafiz, 97–98; and Emerson, 7, 82; Emerson's discovery of, 7, 94; as Emerson's ideal poet, 94; and fatalism, 80; Herder on, 91–92; as insignificant, 92–93; popularity of, 4; as Sufi master, 1; widely read in nineteenth century, 93. *See also* Emerson, Ralph Waldo (Sa'di and); Emerson on Hafiz and Sa'di

Safavid Dynasty, 2

"Sage's Console" (Magister), 232

Sa'id, Edward, 176, 217

Saki Song. See *Saqi-Namah*

"Salut Au Monde!" (Whitman), 155, 157–158

Sana'i (Sufi poet), 42

Saqi-Nameḥ (Emerson's translation of Hafiz), 64, 134–136, 140–141

Scandal: Essays in Islamic Heresy (Wilson), 187

Scented Mud, The (Sa'di) (Jones, tr.), 92

Schneider, Hebert, 183

Schuon, Frithjof, 188

Scientific Religion (Oliphant), 180

Scofield, William B., 231

Scott, Arthur L., 233

Seabrook, William, 186–187

Self-annihilation, shared concept of, 28–30

Shabistari, Mahmud, 1, 26

Shah Nameh (Firdawsi), 1, 64, 65, 118, 198, 201–202, 209, 214

Shakespeare (Emerson), 82
Shakespeare, William, Sufi doctrine espoused by, 31–32, 36, 61, 82, 203
Shapiro, Karl, 163
Shaykh Baha'i (Sufi poet), 38
Shea, David, 118
Shelley, Percy Bysshe: and existence as thought, 27; and Hafiz, 37; and Persian Sufi influence, 6, 16, 35–36; Platonism of, 24–25, 32–34. See also *Symposium*
Shirin Maghribi, Muhammad, 29
Social Aims (Emerson), 85
"Somehow I think that in the near Beyond" (Scofield), 231
"Song of Myself" (Whitman), 164–167; and ethnic scriptures, 194; and Hafiz from *Divan*, 165; and lover-soul-deity, 165; mystical insight in, 153; and Rumi, 166, 168; and sexual imagery, 165; and similarity to Hafiz, 153–154, 159–160; and Sufi-inspired poetry, 167
Song of Nature (Emerson), 65
Song of Songs, The (Whitman), 194
"Song of the Open Road, The" (Whitman), 161, 163
Sonnet 53 (Shakespeare), 31–32
Southy, Robert, 56
"Spanish Jew's Tale, The" (Longfellow), 200
Specimen of the Popular Poetry of Persia (Chodzko), 118
Specimens of Ancient Persian Poetry (Chadzko), 64, 65
Spenser, Edmund, 21–22, 31, 32, 37, 201
Spiritual Law (Emerson), 59
"Star of Bethlehem, The" (Whittier), 195
Start With the Sun (Shapiro), 163
Story, William E., 223

Strangford, Lord Viscount, 164
Stratton, Charles Haywood, 229–230
Stratton, George C., 228–229
Stray Leaves from Strange Literatures (Hearn), 209
Sufi Lesson, A. See *Persian Lesson, A*
Sufism: Americn literary scene and, 1–3; doctrines of, 154; German influence and, 4; and Sufi orders in Black Africa, 182–183; twentieth-century version of, 4–5
Suhrawardi, 107–108
Sultan Goes to Ispahan, The (Aldrich), 239
Superlative (Emerson), 66
"Supplication in the Time of War" (Chamberlin), 227–228
Sympneumata (Oliphant), 180
Symposium (Shelley, tr.), 16, 21, 24–25, 31, 37. See also Shelley, Percy Bysshe

Tagore, Rabindranath, 3
"Tale of Hafez," 4
Tales of a Wayside Inn (Longfellow), 200
Taylor, Thomas, 16
Tennyson, Alfred, 39–40, 207, 233, 245
Thompson, Eben Francis, 223, 247
Thoreau, Henry David: and *Carpe Diem*, 18; Emerson disciple, 9, 16, 60, 75, 113, 191; and "Ethical Scriptures," 8, 192; and nature, 109, 112, 192; and Sa'di, 164, 193–194, 215–216; and Sufi poets, 164; superficial interest in Persian literature, 192–194; and *Walden*, 164, 193; and *A Week On the Concord and Merrimac Rivers*, 192; on Whitman's *Leaves of Grass*, 163–164, 194; as a Yogi, 192

Thousand and One Nights, The. See
   Arabian Nights
"To J. W." (Emerson), 132
"To Omar Khayyam" (Dole),
   224–225
"To the Editor" (C. H. Stratton),
   229–230
To the Maiden in the East (Thoreau),
   192
Transcendentalism, American: and
   Concord, 214; and Conway, 197–
   198; ebbing of, 203; and Emerson,
   242; and Islamic mysticism, 10–11;
   and Johnson, 198; and Melville's
   satire, 204; and Neoplatonism,
   113; and New England School of,
   225; and Persian poetry, 198; and
   Romanticism, 10; and Sufi poetry,
   3
Transcendentalists and Minerva, The
   (Cameron), 65
"Transcendent Unity of Being" (Sufi
   doctrine), 154
Travels of Sir John Chardin, The, 1–2
Trismegistus, Hermes, 108
Troyer, Anthony, 118–119
Turner, Ross, 223
Twain, Mark: overview, 10; copies of
   Ruba'iyyat owned by, 247; examples
   of burlesque verses by, 249–250;
   favorite *Ruba'iyyat* verses of,
   245–246; first mention of Khayyam
   by, 10, 246–247; and indignities of
   growing old, 248; Khayyam's style
   and, 232–233; life-long interest in
   the *Ruba'iyyat*, 10, 247–248, 250;
   poetic efforts not praiseworthy,
   248; and Tennyson, 233, 245;
   and writing of *AGE–A Rubáiyát*,
   248. See also *AGE-A Rubáiyát*;
   Rubá'iyát of Mark Twain
Twichell, Joseph H., 233, 246–247

Under the Rose (Melville), 206–207
Unity of religions, 38–40
"Universal or Perfect Man" (Sufi
   doctrine), 154
Users, 36

Vali, Seyyd Ni'matullah, 67
Vedder, Elihu, 206
Voltaire, 91

Walden (Thoreau), 164, 193
Waste Land, The (Eliot), 239
*Week On the Concord and Merrimac
   Rivers, A* (Thoreau), 192
Westminster Review, 214
"When, on that Summer day at Twin
   Oaks," (G. C. Stratton), 228–229
Whibley, Charles, 239
Whitman, Walt (works of): "Drum
   Taps," 163; "Lilacs," 163; "Mystic
   Trumpete," 157; "One Hour to
   Madness and Joy," 156; "Passage to
   India," 194; "Salut Au Monde!,"
   155, 157–158; *Song of Songs*, 194;
   "Song of the Open Road," 161,
   163. See also *Leaves of Grass*;
   Persian Lesson, A; "Song of
   Myself"
Whitman and an All-Inclusive America
   (Russell), 157
Whitman and Hafiz. *See under*
   Whitman and Sufism
Whitman and Sufism, 153–172;
   overview, 7–8; and access to Persian
   poetry, 194; and body and soul as
   "intimate lovers," 159–160; and
   comparative studies, 163–164; and
   Emerson as conduit, 155, 156; and
   "Graybeard Sufi," 160; and Hafiz's
   mysticism, 156–157; and paradoxes
   of self-identification, 169; and
   A Persian Lesson (text), 170–172;

and reevaluation of Whitman, 163; Rumi and the conscious "I," 167–169; Rumi celebrates death of the "I," 170; and state of "being or not-being," 161; and Sufism doctrines, 154; and vocative "you" of Sufis, 168; Whitman and the divine, 160; Whitman compared to Sufis, 169; and Whitman echoes Hafiz, 153–155, 157–158, 161; and Whitman on codified religion, 157; and Whitman's meeting ground for all religions, 163–164. *See also* Hafiz; Leaves of Grass; *Persian Lesson, A*; Rumi, Jalal al-Din; "Song of Myself"; Whitman, Walt (works of)

Whittier, John Greenleaf, and superficiality of Persian thought, 195–196
Wilk, Mark, 56
Wilson, Peter Lamborn, 187, 188
Works (Jones), 3, 92, 118

Yohannan, J. D., 64, 95
"Youssouf" (Yusuf) (Lowell), 202

Zadig (Voltaire), 91
Zend-Avesta, 118
Zendavesta, Ouvrage de Zorostre (Duperron), 118
Zoroaster, 59
Zoroastrianism, 198
Zoroastrian scripture, 118